European University Studies
Europäische Hochschulschriften
Publications Universitaires Européennes

Series XXII
Sociology

Reihe XXII Série XXII
Soziologie
Sociologie

Vol./Bd. 403

PETER LANG
Frankfurt am Main · Berlin · Bern · Bruxelles · New York · Oxford · Wien

Katrin Golsch

The Impact of Labour Market Insecurity on the Work and Family Life of Men and Women

A Comparison of Germany, Great Britain, and Spain

PETER LANG
Europäischer Verlag der Wissenschaften

Bibliographic Information published by Die Deutsche Bibliothek
Die Deutsche Bibliothek lists this publication in the Deutsche Nationalbibliografie; detailed bibliographic data is available in the internet at <http://dnb.ddb.de>.

Zugl.: Bielefeld, Univ., Diss., 2004

D 361
ISSN 0721-3379
ISBN 3-631-54016-7
US-ISBN 0-8204-7732-X

www.peterlang.de

Contents

Figures

Tables

Text boxes

Preface

Once upon a time there was a student at the Faculty of Sociology at Bielefeld University who finished her diploma enthusiastically and was curious to see what life as a real sociologist would be. On the very next day she started as a researcher in the Globalife project, financed by the Volkswagen Foundation and directed by Hans-Peter Blossfeld. At that time she had never thought about globalisation and its impact on individual life courses. It began a hard, but fruitful time of literature review, seemingly endless discussions, and tiring pilot studies. And slowly but surely all project members discovered one by one that they were somehow affected by globalisation.

It is now four years that I started to reflect for the first time upon globalisation. If someone was to ask me how globalisation impacts me, I would simply pass on this manuscript, the result of my studies within the Globalife project and later on as a lecturer at the Faculty of Sociology at Bielefeld University. It is not only that I will always associate this study with the term globalisation – and it is not easy to escape from it in daily life. Rather, in one way or another one may also identify certain parallels between my personal life course and the ones analysed in this study. Beyond a doubt, PhD students always lack life course security, and the various aspects of insecurity during the last four years obviously led me to defer self-binding life course decisions. Luckily for me, I have had many companions that helped me in endless ways and I am glad to have made this venture with their support.

First and foremost I would like to thank Hans-Peter Blossfeld and Hans-Jürgen Andreß, my supervisors. They encouraged me to make this great adventure and advised me during the past four years in countless ways. I am particularly thankful for their thoughtful reading of a draft version of this manuscript and their steady motivation to participate in conferences and workshops. Special thanks to Hans-Peter Blossfeld who gave me the great opportunity to study abroad for a couple of months while being a researcher in the Globalife project. Special appreciation also goes to Hans-Jürgen Andreß. I knew that I could rush into his office any time to discuss issues of methodology and this was of great help.

Furthermore, I am grateful to my colleagues at the Globalife project. I am particularly indebted to Carles Simó with whom I have closely co-operated for over two years. I thank him for his great friendship and for his fruitful comments on draft versions. I also greatly benefited from Erik Klijzing, a grand advisor during all highs and lows, who kindly edited previous working papers and provided me with excellent literature. And, last but not least, I am grateful to Melinda Mills and Ingeborg McIntyre, two further friends at Globalife.

During the last four years this manuscript travelled a lot. Early 2001 I spent a three months study visit at the Institute for Social and Economic Research (ISER), University of Essex (UK), financially supported by a Marie Curie Fellowship of the EU. It was during this study visit that I developed principal ideas and pursued some first analyses, laying the foundation for this manuscript. I am grateful to have had the chance to work with Marco Francesconi who served as a grand mentor to familiarise with BHPS data and discrete-time methods. I would also like to express gratitude to Alison Booth and Stephen Jenkins who co-ordinated my study visit and Kate Tucker who kept us fellows always warm.

Later in 2001, I spent another three months at the Centre D'Estudis Demogràfics (CED), Barcelona (Spain), again funded by an EU Marie Curie Fellowship. The analyses on Spain have been undertaken during this study visit and I would like to thank the Centre D'Estudis Demogràfics for providing the ECHP data. I am particularly indebted to Anna Cabré, Maria José González López, Hermínia Pujol, Joaquim Recaño and Montserrat Solsona who gave guidance and useful suggestions and therewith helped me to get to the bottom of the Spanish case. Though I was not able to speak Spanish or Catalan they made me feel comfortable at the centre.

Some of the chapters in this book have greatly benefited from the work I did for various conferences and workshops. I presented earlier analyses of Chapters Eight and Nine on various Globalife workshops on *"Globalization and the transition from youth to adulthood"*, in Bielefeld, Germany, March 2001; on *"Globalization and Job Mobility over the Life Course of Men: the Role of Country-Specific Institutions"*, in March 2002 in Bielefeld; and on *"Globalization and the Work-Family Linkage: How does Globalization affect Women's Relationship to the Labour Force"*, in Bamberg, Germany, in March 2003. Moreover, principal ideas and preliminary results were presented on the 10th workshop of the European research network on transitions in youth (Florence, Italy, September 2002), the RC28 meeting on *"Expanding markets, welfare state retrenchment and their impact on social stratification"* (April 2001 in Mannheim, Germany), as well as in the CED seminar (Barcelona, Spain, December 2001). Selected parts of the analyses presented in Chapter Eight were published in Work, Employment and Society (Golsch, 2003). Previous versions of the analysis on Great Britain in Chapters Seven and Eight will appear in the first Globalife volume edited by Blossfeld *et al.* (forthcoming) (Francesconi and Golsch, forthcoming). Preceding analyses of Chapter Nine can be found in Golsch (2002).

Apart from these study visits and conferences, I also took this manuscript to various other places: La Stuppa, Lago Maggiore (Italy), La Tiniana, Greve (Italy), Haus Möwe, Zingst (Germany), and Wangerooge (Germany). It was during these times of rest and composure that I developed fundamental ideas and gained new energies to progress. After all, it was in Tuscany when I discovered that I should not only analyse life course transitions with survey data, but also make an important partnership decision.

Particular thanks to Alan and Róisín Burrell who polished my English in the theoretical part and Michael White and Peter Varnes who helped to established this contact. Likewise, I am indebted to Elizabeth deRerenzy, a former fellow student, who volunteered to refine my English in the empirical part of this thesis.

Last but not least, I am very much grateful to my family. Alexander always transmitted endless enthusiasm, patiently listened when I reported on my daily progress and regress, accepted my tendency to travel around Europe, adapted to my 'Twenty Four Seven' rhythm, and commuted with me between my office, our house, and my parent's home during the final stages. I am likewise thankful to Anke, Michael, and Marianne, who always assured contact to the real outside world and kindly called attention to my slightly sociologically biased viewpoint. The persons that I am most grateful to, however, are my parents. I know that they were a bit sceptical about sociology. Still, they have always been a source of strength in moments of need and helped me and Alexander in countless ways. I would like to thank them for their unquestionable confidence and it is with the greatest of pleasure that I dedicate this thesis to them.

Bielefeld, November 2003 *Katrin Golsch*

Foreword

Profound and in fact accelerating social and economic transformations have taken place in the last two decades in modern societies. These changes are often referred to as globalisation, which involves (1) the declining importance of national borders for all kinds of economic transactions, (2) the rising worldwide interconnectedness through the information and communication technology revolution, (3) the tougher tax competition between countries and the deregulation, privatisation, and liberalisation of domestic industries and markets, and (4) the rising importance of, and exposure to, a world market with less predictable disruptions. Paradoxically, in a period of OECD growth slowdown since the mid 1970s, globalisation seems to elevate both, prosperity and individual uncertainty. The promises of globalisation, such as lower prices, more choices, greater freedom, and higher living standards through improved productivity seem to come with painful disruptions such as salary cuts, lost jobs, layoffs, bankruptcies, vanished companies, and shattered communities. In this volume, Katrin Golsch does not aim to address the entire range of questions that are implied in the relationship between globalisation and work. Rather she concentrates on the more specific task of describing and analysing the changes of labour market insecurity on the work and family life of younger and mid-career men and women in Germany, Great Britain, and Spain.

This volume is a big step forward in the new effort to study empirically the impact of globalisation in modern societies. Using a life course approach, unique longitudinal data such as the *German Socio-Economic Panel* (GSOEP), the *British Household Panel Survey* (BHPS), and the *European Community Household Panel* (ECHP) as well as advanced methods of data analysis, it shows that employment and welfare regime constellations in the three countries filter the market forces of globalisation in different ways. The book is a rich source of information on nation-specific institutions in Germany, Britain, and Spain; and it demonstrates how the same macro trends impact the employment and family system in the three countries in different ways. The volume also exemplifies an exciting new analytical approach to cross-societal analysis. It uses a multilevel analysis which brings together changes at the macro level with country-specific institutions (at the meso level), and shows how the choices of individual actors are affected by these filtered effects of globalisation.

All in all, the book yields important new evidence on the impact of globalisation on life courses in the three countries under study. It shows that youth are increasingly vulnerable to uncertainty across all three countries. Youth, who have less labour market experience and who are not yet shielded by internal labour markets, are more greatly exposed to the forces of globalisation, which makes them to some extent the losers of globalisation. The amount of uncertainty youth holds in their employment relationship and degree of temporal uncertainty also has real consequences for family formation and fertility. The impact of having a fixed-term contract strongly reduced men's entry into first union and having a first baby. So, to some extent, declining nuptiality and fertility might be explained by globalisation forces. Golsch also shows that there are important differences in the vulnerability to globalisation in terms of education and gender. In general, the more educated and in particular the male insiders are much more shielded from globalisation.

The volume shows that rigorous multilevel comparative research and theoretically central questions offer important new evidence on the impact of globalisation in modern societies. The findings of this volume are certain to be widely debated in the field of social inequality and stratification; and they will doubtless be the starting point for more subsequent empirical analyses of globalisation effects on social inequality. We are proud and honoured to be the dissertation supervisors of this important work.

Hans-Peter Blossfeld
Otto-Friedrich University of Bamberg
Hans-Jürgen Andreß
University of Cologne

1 Introduction

1.1 Impetus and background

Since the Second World War modern societies have experienced multifaceted changes in various domains of individual, social, political, and economic life. Many of these transformations have had large scale consequences for the work and family life of men, women, and particularly among youth. More precisely, aspects of change embrace educational expansion and democratisation, more insecurity of education-to-work transitions and subsequent labour market careers, and diversification of living arrangements and family formation processes (for a discussion of these and related factors, see Coleman and Husén, 1985).

In all OECD countries a democratisation of the educational system and an extensive educational expansion especially in higher education can be observed. In particular, women increasingly extend their educational enrolment, are more career-oriented, and appear better equipped for job competition than ever before (Blossfeld, 1985, 1988, 1995). Simultaneously, the relevance of high educational credentials has strengthened over time and appears by now to be of vital importance for successful labour market entry (e.g., Blossfeld, 2002). In turn, those who do not manage to accomplish high educational certificates face a particular difficult situation during education-to-work transition and their subsequent labour market career. A parallel trend has been the progressing shift to services, creating an abundance of new job positions especially for women (Klijzing, forthcoming). With regard to the professional life, unemployment has become a continuous and serious problem of contemporary labour markets. Likewise, inactivity and non-standard work, such as temporary, part-time, and marginal employment, have gained ground. In particular, labour market entry patterns of first-employment seekers appear increasingly turbulent during the 1990s (see for instance, Bernardi, 2000; Gallie *et al.*, 1998; Taylor, 2000). Lastly, over the last decades, industrialised societies have also seen profound changes in family formation and organisation processes (Blossfeld, 1995; Blossfeld and Drobnič, 2001; Blossfeld and Hakim, 1997a; Corijn and Klijzing, 2001; Mills, 2000). Birth rates have declined greatly; childlessness and births out of wedlock are on the rise. A multitude of living arrangements has been exemplified showing growing proportions of solos, single-parent households, and non-marital cohabitation. At the same time, many Western societies have recently observed trends of declining marriage and higher divorce rates. Even though these changes have begun at different points in time and are developing at varying rates, the nature of family formation processes is changing across birth cohorts in terms of timing and sequencing in many Western European countries (Corijn and Klijzing, 2001). At the same time, a relatively modest and lopsided transformation of the gender division of labour can be observed in most modern societies (Blossfeld and Drobnič, 2001). While women were traditionally non-employed homemakers, this dated model appears more and more substituted by dual-earner families, in which women and mothers contribute to the household income through their own labour income either on a part-time or full-time basis. Nonetheless, women keep on carrying the brunt of responsibility in domestic work and childrearing. Related to all the above trends, Coleman and Husén (1985: 9) describe a new division of labour between the three main institutions of modern welfare societies:

> *"The conventional triangle, the economy, the family, and the State, where the economy produces, the family consumes, and the State redistributes, is not adequate any longer. The traditional meanings have changed. The economy educates as well as produces, the family produces (with most women in the labour force), and the State is drawn into the production system as a major provider of services."*

To summarise, various transformations in work and family life can be identified. While speed and pervasion of these economic and demographic developments differ, they appear mostly unidirectional and universal so that it can be safely claimed that modern societies experience a general change and confront a similar political call for action (Corijn and Klijzing, 2001; Kuijsten, 1996). One may argue that youth are particularly affected by these various aspects of change. On their way to adulthood individuals pass through various status and role changes. They have to decide about whether to continue education, which educational and occupational track to follow, whether and when to form a couple and have a child (Blossfeld and Nuthmann, 1988; Corijn and Klijzing, 2001). While these various interrelated transitions used to be rather straightforward and uniform, in recent times the integration into work, social, political, and economical life appears less standard and more step-wise. Some commentators thus identify the emergence of "*a period during which neither work nor family is settled, a kind of moratorium before assuming the responsibilities of adulthood*" (Coleman and Husén, 1985: 11).

Within the entire transition process to adulthood the education-to-work transition denotes an important step towards economic independence. This is because gainful employment shapes individual's life-styles and is the key source of socio-economic independence in modern societies (Kohli, 1985). Hence the timing of entry into the labour market and beyond, the start of a fairly stable, well-paid work career will determine an adult worker's status, and thus ensure their socio-economic standing. In respect thereof, educational enrolment, unemployment, and men's inactivity, on the one hand, and family formation, on the other, seem mutually exclusive. Rather career, and therefore economic certainty, largely remains prerequisites for transitions that involve long-term commitments. This is to say that the timing of the transition to a stable work career should appear as an important determinant of entry into marriage and parenthood (see also Oppenheimer, 1988). In contemporary societies, however, individuals are presumably less certain about whether and when to find a job and enter a stable career, as well as the level of remuneration. Consequently, the future socio-economic status is largely unpredictable and insecurity may be attached to (i) education-to-work transition, and, (ii) the nature of adult worker roles, which in turn may lead to less certainty about the future life course. Due to the profound educational expansion and the increasing need for further education and training, there is no longer a clear dividing rule between educational and occupational trajectories. Further, education-to-work transitions appear less straightforward and work careers less stable to the extent that they involve periods of unemployment, temporary employment, and inactivity. All in all, labour market integration can no more be seen as a single transition, but rather a multifaceted process. But why is this the case?

Recently, various scholars have commented on the numerous socio-economic changes in contemporary societies which become visible in the expansion of labour, capital, service, and product markets, and resemble an acceleration of social, economic, and political change, plus increased volatility of markets. It is mainly in this context that the fuzzy term *globalisation* is employed, even though there is little agreement on the concept itself (see for instance, Alasuutari, 2000; Goldthorpe, 2001a; Held *et al.*, 1999; Hirst and Thompson, 1996). Related key concepts are for instance political, economical, and cultural globalisation, 'network', 'risk', 'runaway', and 'world society' (Beck, 1986, 1999; Castells, 1996; Giddens, 2000; Stichweh, 2000, 2001). Without going into the variety of definitions and conceptualisations that have been proposed, one may grasp the recent popularity of the globalisation concept by counting the number of publications in the field of sociology and economy, its actuality in daily news, or purely the frequency of 'anti-globalisation' demonstrations all over the world. Globalisation is a highly debated, controversial concept. Yet, the present-day discussion reveals that recent restructuring processes seem to bother individuals and, hence, – in line with the Berger and Luckmann theorem (Berger and Luckman, 1980) – should also have a real effect on their daily lives.

There is a comparatively wide-shared view that some transformations on a global scale reshape national societies. First, a globalisation of production and worldwide demand has been identified. For sure, trade and investment have always been in action on both, a national and world-wide level. Yet, over the last decades, companies aim to increase their efficiency through multinational production and marketing strategies. Production and supply of goods and services have been globalised due to a growing extent of diversification of production; moving production to low-wage, low-production-cost countries, but selling goods in high-income countries. Another aspect of change that has been intimately related to the globalisation process is the deregulation of global capital markets, the resulting global circulation of money, and the instability of financial markets; including both, global consumption and investment. Simultaneously, with the globalisation of markets, progressing technological advancement allows for efficient labour-saving production techniques, international information interchange, and transport. While this burst of new and cheap technologies, all of which have tremendously increased in scope and efficiency, corroborates economic growth, it also imposes new operating requirements and demands on employees, which necessitate a highly skilled workforce. Furthermore, new information technologies facilitate the immediate information exchange around the world and dissociated from time and space. This increasing interconnection becomes also visible in the creation of multiple governmental and non-governmental organisations. Lastly, the intensification of competition on an international scale is clearly linked to the above processes and has thus been identified as an associated element of the globalisation process.

Though the globalisation concept has been excessively debated, its consequences on individual life courses remain a largely untouched research topic and therefore blurry. More specifically, is there evidence to suggest that these macro-level trends are somehow related to the above described economic and demographic developments? In line with Blossfeld (2002) and Mills and Blossfeld (forthcoming) the term *globalisation* is in the following used to refer to the complex interactions between the higher interdependence of regional and national economies around the world, the intensification of global competition, the spread of global networks, the greater volatility in the labour, capital, and product markets, plus the pronounced uncertainty in individual, family, social, and political life. It has been argued that this globalisation process is inherently unstable; it would segment the individual labour market careers and leads individuals to experience different types of uncertainty, which in turn may affect people's life chances, including some of the salient transitions in work and family life (e.g., Blossfeld, 2002; Mills and Blossfeld, forthcoming). This is not to say that there has been a kind of 'Golden Age' of secure and predictable employment careers in the past. Rather, the starting point is the argument that *today* is very different from the past. The above sketched profound transformations in the global economy, and intensification of competition on an international scale, are commonly assumed to lead to a transformation of the world of work with particular consequences for employment stability (see for instance Heery and Salmon, 2000; Ladipo and Wilkinson, 2002). Over the decades the fast and intense spread of technological innovations, increasing global competition, and volatility in product and capital markets along with intense labour shifts due to growing female labour force participation and educational expansion have deeply impacted national labour markets. However, the enhanced deregulation and flexibility of labour markets is a new reaction to these trends (see for instance Esping-Andersen and Regini, 2000; Leisink, 1999). This strengthened firms possibilities to adjust less costly, but more swiftly to the changing competitive demands. That is, governments opened the way for employers to pass on economic risks to employees by means of various atypical employment relationships; individual's continued gainful employment, income, as well as training and promotion aspects appear thus less predictable.

For sure some readers will be pessimistic about such an argument. There certainly remains heterogeneity between modern societies, and one may therefore raise the question of scope and validity of globalisation pressures. However, it is expected that globalisation does by no means lead to homogeneity across countries. Rather, despite common challenges, there remains room for various nation-specific arrangements in education, labour market, and welfare state provision to accentuate or moderate these processes; global, national, and local forces collude (Blossfeld, 2002; Blossfeld *et al.*, forthcoming; Esping-Andersen, 1999; Mayer, 1997). Due to these country-specific institutions and path dependence it is argued that a new heterogeneity will appear: Old, historically grown institutional arrangements impose certain rigidities and will rather mix up with new adaptation strategies.

The starting point for the following discourse is the argument that individual life courses are embedded in society at large (Mayer, 1986, 1997). A within-country as well as cross-country modelling of various single life transitions has been well established (see for instance, Blossfeld, 1995; Corijn and Klijzing, 2001; Mills, 2000). This study goes beyond earlier work in several respects. At issue here is the question in how far new structural constraints due to the recent restructuring process of European labour markets have an effect on life course decision-making. To this end, the impact of labour market insecurity on individual life courses will be gauged in three selected countries, namely Germany, Great Britain, and Spain during the 1990s.[1] In particular, what makes this study distinct is the comparative approach to country-specific labour market flexibility.

---

[1] The spotlight in this study is on Great Britain. In various descriptive sections, however, the perspective is broadened to the United Kingdom (Great Britain – England, Wales, and Scotland – and Northern Ireland). This will be indicated at the relevant points in the text. Since the main research focus is on the 1990s the discussion centres on unified Germany. Even though the reunification of the German Democratic Republic (GDR) and the Federal Republic of Germany (FRG) in 1990 led to a sudden transfer of West German institutional and legislative arrangements to the former Eastern part, this transformation process has expanded well into the 1990s and may even be seen as still ongoing. A special note on the living conditions in East Germany is therefore in several sections necessary.

1.2 Why compare Germany, Great Britain and Spain?

Over the last decades, comparative research has proliferated,[2] and one may ask: why is there a growing interest in international comparative research? Here several explanations come to mind (see also Gauthier, 2000). Cross-national research provides an insight into similarities and dissimilarities across countries and the extent to which individual life chances converge or diverge. Longitudinal data, and cross-national data in particular, permit a dynamic analysis of individual life courses and respective changes across history, lifetimes, birth cohorts, and countries. International comparative research may thus be seen as a tool to address major research questions as outlined by Mayer and Schoepflin (1989: 188):

> *"How are life courses in advanced societies shaped and regulated? How are the age-graded transitions between life-domains socially organized? How do life courses differ in contemporary societies from those in earlier societies? Which forces are shaping the allocation of life-time between life domains such as education, family activities, and employment?"*

From another point of view, cross-national comparisons are highly relevant for social policy. Policy makers search for the best practice solution and have therefore a vested interest to learn about practices and their efficiency in other countries. Compared to previous decades, national borders increasingly lose their importance, and so the exchange of labour, capital, goods, and also ideas across national borders quickens; transnational institutions and organisations act on a global level. Countries do no more operate in isolation and policy-makers increasingly exchange views at the European level. In this respect, an international perspective is highly valuable, not only as a benchmark for a comparison in efficiency of policies, but also as an example for future actions that policy makers may want to make. Hence, there is also an increasing need for a thorough research program to 'map' European countries.

Yet, while within-country differences have been extensively described and explained, cross-country comparisons incorporating a large group of countries remain rather exceptional and are mostly confined to specific life course transitions (e.g., Blossfeld, 1995; Blossfeld and Hakim, 1997a; Shavit and Müller, 1998). While in the first place many contributions aimed to solely identify and describe diverseness in demographic behaviour, the research focus has recently shifted to the explanation of cross-country differences (e.g., Mayer,

---

[2] The roots of comparative sociological research date back to the pioneer work of Durkheim, Marx, Weber, and de Tocqueville (see Smelser, 1976). Interested readers in theoretical and methodological developments as well as the current stage of comparative research, its limitations, and basic assumptions are referred to Armer and Marsh (1982), Mayer (1997), and Gauthier (2000).

1997). In such respects, international comparative research gains significant importance. In Kohn's words (1989: 77):

> *"[...] cross-national research is valuable, even indispensable, for establishing the generality of findings and the validity of interpretations derived from single-nation studies. In no other way can we be certain that what we believe to be social-structural regularities are not merely particularities, the product of some limited set of historical or cultural or political circumstances. [...] cross-national research is equally valuable, perhaps even more valuable, for forcing us to revise our interpretations to take account of cross-national differences and inconsistencies that could never be uncovered in single-nation research. [...] cross-national research provides an especially useful method for generating, testing, and further developing sociological theory."*

Once researchers decide on a cross-national comparative research program, they face a substantial methodological problem: How to select countries for comparison? And, how many countries have to be studied (see also Landman, 2000)?[3] Undoubtedly, the selection of countries appears arbitrary as long as we lack a substantive theoretical argument for our choice (see also Kohn, 1989). Researchers have often clustered countries according to regions, religious affiliation, or welfare state regimes, and selected some as representatives. Yet, a careful note on this strategy has to be made. Since even within these clusters significant differences may be on hand, the selection of countries may determine findings and conclusions; scholars are therefore advised to be prudent before conveying a certain result to other countries. Rather, the validity of a classification system has to be previously scrutinised. For the same reason, pooling data across countries may ease the presentation and discussion of results but will most likely mask such within-cluster differences. In turn, a focus on a limited number of countries enables researchers to pursue a systematic and in-depth analysis of hypotheses about social processes that is firmly embedded in a larger understanding of country-specific contexts.

Which of these research strategies did I use to start with in this study? A principle goal is to outline how to gauge labour market insecurity and exemplify its impact in three selected countries, namely Germany, Great Britain, and Spain. This choice is elaborate and theory-driven since all these countries entered on disparate and rather fast-paced flexible paths that are deeply rooted in their country-specific institutional context, which in turn may impose different

---

[3] Over the last decades, these questions have taken centre stage in the discussion on comparative methods in the social sciences. Interested readers may have a look at Ragin (1987, 1989) and Goldthorpe (1997) for a debate over what has been called case-oriented versus variable-oriented approaches. Intensive, case-oriented work generally scrutinises many casual and outcome variables in a constricted number of countries ('small N analysis'). In contrast, an extensive, variable-oriented study focuses on a restricted number of variables across a large number of countries ('large N analysis').

types, levels, and consequences of insecurity. From a European perspective, Great Britain and Spain stand out as two countries that have experienced increased levels of flexible change in the labour market over the 1980s (Deakin and Reed, 2000; Toharia and Malo, 2000). Due to the increased levels of labour market flexibility in the 1990s compared to previous decades, these two countries provide an interesting case study of the transformations in employment relationships. However, the flexible path that has been entered upon and its impact on labour market careers differ greatly. British deregulation measures have had strong repercussions on both employees in non-standard employment relationships and permanent full-time employees. In contrast, strong employment protection of Spaniards already employed has persisted. Rather, the fast and intense shift from one of the most rigid employment protection system to a highly flexible labour market was peculiar in that it deepened the so-called insider-outsider divide in Spain. While the British flexible path may thus be circumscribed as a guiding principle, in Spain flexibility is basically introduced at the margin (Regini, 2000b; Toharia and Malo, 2000). Though all three countries face a comparable global environment, Germany represents yet another unique example. Here policies adhere to comparatively high degrees of protection and welfare; flexibility has been utilised as a controlled experiment only (Regini, 2000b).

The empirical scope of this work is regionally limited. Yet, an effort will be made to widen the perspective to other settings by referring to other relevant country-specific analyses. It is against this backdrop that this study explicitly intends to motivate further investigations on other countries.

1.3 Overview on research questions

This study aims to give a comprehensive insight into the interplay of, on the one hand, macro-level changes that impact on national labour markets and, thus, determine individual work careers, and, on the other hand, various related life course transitions. More precisely, the focus is on the mutual interdependence of work and family life over a lifetime. To this end, lifetime is analytically broken down into various interrelated transitions, namely, school-to-work transition, labour market entry and subsequent career, partnership formation, and parenthood. The goal is to understand circumstances under which labour market insecurity is likely to interfere with life course decision-making.

First it is asked, is there evidence to suggest that labour market insecurity has an impeding impact on *transitions to adulthood*? Several related research questions are behind it: To what extent are young labour market entrants unsatisfied with their job security? Are some more likely than others to enter directly the labour market and find a stable position? If so, why? At issue is the extent to which the diffusion of various forms of flexible employment introduces insecurity in individual job careers at least for a short period in their life course, i.e., increases individual's risk of job or income loss, making work careers less predictable. Likewise, facing great difficulties in settling in the labour market, individuals may perceive their job as comparatively insecure. Once we have gained a deeper understanding of the various aspects of labour market insecurity, the discussion will shift to its impact on partnership formation and parenthood. More precisely, is job precariousness and perceived job insecurity systematically related to men's and women's early living arrangements and partnership formation? And, how does job precariousness and perceived job insecurity affect young people's decision to become parents?

This is not saying that labour market insecurity is assumed to operate quasi detached from contextual settings and individual characteristics. Rather, the above research question will be further elaborated in several respects and it is asked: is it possible to identify certain *risk profiles* coupled to country of residence, gender, career maturity, and individual resources?

First, individuals rely on a certain opportunity structure, including macro and micro factors, all of which are shaped by nation-specific institutional arrangements in education, labour market, and welfare. This study thus inquires into *country-specific adaptation strategies* and considers whether the impact of labour market insecurity is consistent across the three selected countries. In particular, to what extent do certain country-specific arrangements shelter individuals?

The second question explores *gender-specific adaptation strategies.* It has to be stressed that transition patterns tend to be gender-specific. This is partly due to provisions of welfare through State, family, and market that shape women's life courses in a particular manner (Orloff, 1993, 1996). This is to say that some life course transitions, particularly childbirth, modify the female life course much more than the male, including career interruption if not withdrawal and therewith substantial losses in remuneration and promotion prospects. Therefore, gainful employment to ensure economic security within a household remains largely within the male domain. But how does labour market flexibility affect men's and women's work and family careers? While flexibility and deregulation is assumed to introduce insecurity in male work careers, its impact on women appears more ambiguous: it may ease the combination of work and family career, thus creating family-friendly work arrangements; it may increase women's labour market attachment due to increasingly precarious job profiles of men, which in turn may necessitate a double income; others may want to give up gainful employment and opt for a family career if they perceive that their job has no future; lastly, some may not seek to gain a permanent place in the labour market, but concentrate on their family career. These various adaptation strategies have to be dynamically unfolded over individuals' life courses.

The third research question further explores the effect of *career maturity*. Is job insecurity equally spread over men's and women's entire labour market career, or is it confined only to early labour market positions? From the employer's point of view, non-standard employment relationships are first and foremost efficient in order to screen the work potential of new employees and lower the possible costs of job-mismatch. In turn, labour force experience and seniority should function as an important buffer against labour market insecurity: a changeover to another company implies substantial costs for the company and employers are therefore presumably more likely to offer permanent posts, higher levels of remuneration or premiums as incentives to stay with the same employer. One may therefore ask, whether and to what extent stable, life-long employment relationships have been eroded for all employees alike? More specifically, is there evidence to suggest that workers with specific characteristics face a higher risk of unemployment, or is the risk of becoming unemployed equally spread? Will people who lose their jobs manage to re-enter the labour market more easily? And finally, do workers equally face chances of upward mobility or downward occupational mobility?

And this brings us to a final question: Are there inequalities related to *individual resources*? Both educational attainment and occupational class may determine different degrees of insecurity: Are those highly qualified and working in high occupational classes more protected? Or, are recent deregulation and flexible measures mainly confined to those poorly skilled and in low occupational classes? In such respects, deregulation and flexible measures accentuate social inequality and labour market exclusion if flexible work arrangements imply high risks of job or income loss. On the other hand, however, atypical work may increase chances of gainful employment and, in particular, may function as a main route back to the labour market after periods of unemployment or economic inactivity. Thus, to fully gauge the implications of labour market restructuring processes the role of what one may call individual resources is crucial.

In many respects these various research questions are mutually interdependent. For instance, gender-specific adaptation strategies may simultaneously turn out to be country-specific; career maturity may play an important role in one country, in another country its impact may be negligible due to distinct institutional entrenchment and path-dependence. For that reason, to evaluate the repercussions of labour market insecurity on individual life courses it is not sufficient to study one country or one single life course transition. Rather, the above sketched research questions necessitate a dynamic, cross-country research program on multiple, interdependent life course transitions.

1.4 Comparative methods and areas of analysis

To evaluate the goodness and explanatory power of a comparative research program one needs to think about the possibilities and limitations of international sociological country comparisons. A well-conducted research strategy should enable us to shed light on similarities and cross-country differences. In particular, as to the latter finding, a theoretical approach should permit an answer to the question of which of the many possible peculiarities of country-specific institutional packages is the driving force that explains its distinctiveness. A crucial aspect to this is the appropriateness and genuineness of country descriptions. To understand the complex interplay of the various country-specific factors that shape individual life courses, international comparisons have to refer to institutional and historical developments. Furthermore, the equivalence of terms, observations, measurement, and explanations used for the analysis of these various contextual settings may be challenged:

> *"How do we know we are studying 'the same phenomena' in different contexts; how do we know that our observations and conclusions do not actually refer to 'quite different things', which we unjustifiably include into the same conceptual categories? Or if they seem to be different, are they really different with respect to the same (qualitatively or quantitatively understood) variable, or is our conclusion about the difference between them scientifically meaningless?"* (Nowak 1976: 105).

This imposes further requirements for the theoretical framework (Nowak, 1989): processes, concepts, and transitions included, along with their exact meaning in each country, have to be explicitly defined and contextual variables have to be integrated to permit an empirical investigation of the hypotheses and to evaluate the validity of indicators for each country-specific context. The following theoretical chapters thus aim to thoroughly discuss salient trends and characteristics of the three nation-specific contexts under study and this discourse is included in a larger theoretical framework that interrelates labour market pressures, country-specific institutions, and individual's work and family life. Furthermore, the selection of harmonised data sources is crucial. In fact, various aggregate indicators, harmonised individual-level survey data as well as a series of identical individual-level surveys conducted in different countries are available for comparative sociological research (Gauthier, 2000). Various data sources permit aggregate-level, individual-level, as well as multilevel research strategies. In this work both aggregate indicators and individual-level data are used. Aggregate-level data will be used for country-rankings to give an important insight into within-country characteristics and changes across birth cohorts and historical time. From these pictures typologies concerning demographic behaviour and employment regimes will be deduced. In the empirical part, however, this study will exclusively concentrate on individual-level data, and, more precisely, it is embarked on two research strategies. First, whenever it is surmised that a single model applies to all countries (and data permits), data will be pooled for all three countries and general models estimated. Yet, in some cases such an assumption does not correspond to the theoretical framework of this study; in other cases a comparative perspective in research is not possible due to data limitations; and, sometimes this modelling is also not wanted since it would conceal country specifics. Second, separate models will therefore be estimated for each country. Depending on the theoretical considerations, these are either parallel (using the same set of variables) or separate analyses. Table 1.1 at the end of this chapter gives an overview on the various data sources used for any single area of analysis.

1.5 Outline of study

To address the above outlined research questions, this study is organised into two principal parts. Part One, comprised of Chapters Two to Five, develops the theoretical framework for understanding how labour market insecurity and life course decisions appear interrelated via the concept of life course security. More precisely, *Chapter Two* identifies the life course decisions under study, describes country-specific trends in life course decisions, and introduces life course security as the key concept to grasping individual life course decision-making. It seeks to identify recent changes in economic and social structure, cultural changes, and technological innovations, which not only open up more options for rational decision-makers, but also interpolate new sources of insecurity in individual life courses. The remainder of this study focuses on one aspect of change, namely labour market insecurity. Accordingly, *Chapter Three* identifies key labour market trends and discusses labour market deregulation and flexibility pressures. The core part of Chapter Three defines job security and establishes how growing labour market insecurity might be considered a specific dilemma for young decision-makers. From this, Chapter Three raises major research questions and derives a so-called insecurity hypothesis. Yet, an idea that runs implicitly and explicitly through the various sections of this study is that individual resources determine individual degrees of insecurity. Furthermore, according to one central assumption within the comparative framework of this study, country-specific institutional filters play a crucial role and may accentuate or moderate these processes. Hence, *Chapter Four* puts this study into context by contrasting employment relations and flexibility routes, educational systems, welfare state regimes, and gender divisions of labour in Germany, Great Britain, and Spain. Finally, *Chapter Five* relates all key concepts of this study and puts forward five so-called risk profile hypotheses on the mediating impact of institutional filters and individual characteristics.

Part Two, which consists of Chapters Six to Nine, provides the empirical evidence. *Chapter Six* presents the data and statistical methods to be used in the analysis. This is followed by three chapters which discuss the major findings of the analysis. *Chapter Seven* deals with labour market insecurity and its impact on labour market entry and early career in the three countries under study. More specifically, this chapter inquires into transitions into employment, perceived job security, and employment relationships along with longitudinal employment profiles in early labour market careers. *Chapter Eight* moves beyond description of labour market integration and focuses on labour market insecurity and its repercussions on partnership and parenthood decisions in Germany, Great Britain, and Spain. *Chapter Nine* finally provides a detailed analysis of the consequences of labour market insecurity on the work and family life of adult workers.

Lastly, *Chapter Ten* synthesises the main results and conclusions of this study, summarises the implications of this research, and looks forward to challenges that the field will face in the foreseeable future. A discussion of who is likely to lose in increasingly insecure labour markets completes the study.

Table 1.1 Data sources and areas of analysis

Data sources			Areas of analysis: Labour market insecurity and its impact on labour market entry and early career			partnership and parenthood decisions			work and family life of adult workers			
Aggregate data	Country	Individual-level data	Transitions into employment	Perceived job security and employment	Longitudinal employment profiles in	1st marriage / cohabitation	Cohabitation to marriage	1st parenthood	Work and unemployment	Work and family	Work and occupational mobility	Work and job satisfaction
Demographic Indicators: FFS Country Reports	Germany	German Socio-Economic Panel (GSOEP), 1984-2001				■	■	■				
UK Office for National Statistics Council of Europe, 1996 Iacovou, 2001	Germany	European Community Household Panel (ECHP), 1994-1997	■	■	■							
Economic Indicators: ILO, 2001-2002	Great Britain	British Household Panel Survey (BHPS), 1991-2000				■	■	■	■	■	■	■
FFS Country Reports Schömann et al., 1998 Eurostat, various years OECD, 2001	Great Britain	European Community Household Panel (ECHP), 1994-1997	■	■	■							
Muffels and Fourage, 2000 Clark, 1998	Spain	European Community Household Panel (ECHP), 1994-1997	■	■	■	■		■				

2 Life course decisions and the concept of life course security

The main purpose of this chapter is to discuss the determinants of individual life course decisions. More precisely, the underlying proposition which will be further elaborated throughout this study is that *life course security* functions as the major tool to bridge labour market insecurity on the one hand and life course decisions on the other. Section 2.1 identifies the three life course decisions under study, which are employment, partnership, and parenthood decisions. It raises two central questions: First, how can we best describe transition patterns in the three selected countries under study? And second, what are the main determinants of life course decision-making? In order to answer these important questions, the remainder of this chapter is divided into three central parts. In Section 2.2, country specific trends in life course transitions will be compared. Starting from the body of literature on life course analysis, the core of this chapter will then introduce life course security as a key concept to understand individual life course decision-making (Section 2.3). Section 2.4 reviews key explanatory approaches that examine economic and social changes, cultural changes, and technological innovations and their impact on life course decisions-making. The final section identifies the main dilemmas arising from increasing labour market insecurity and summarises the principal conclusions.

2.1 Life course decisions under study

During their entire life course individuals make various life course decisions and experience many status and role changes. In these terms, the life span from youth to adulthood is particularly intense: individual decision-making processes encompass decisions about when to leave the parental home, which educational or occupational qualification track to follow, or whether and when to partner and parent. The transition to adulthood may thus be seen as a step by step process in which individuals take on responsibilities in various life domains and participate increasingly in adult activities (Blossfeld and Nuthmann, 1988; Corijn and Klijzing, 2001; Hogan and Astone, 1986; Irwin, 1995).[4] Family and work career

---

[4] In the following, when talking about transitions to adulthood it is thus neither referred to a certain age range, for instance fixed by the age when individuals take on citizenship rights, nor to the emotional and psychological development of individuals. This approach provides only an ideal type picture because there are much more diverse paths to adulthood. Some

related decisions are mutually interdependent and imply long-term, if not life-long commitments. Hence, decisions made on the way from youth to adulthood are "life-shaping" (Hobcraft and Kiernan, 1995: 2). At the same time, such life course decisions are engrained in gender-specific role models and country-specific institutions that may substantially ease the integration of work and family life. Hence, their implications differ pronouncedly for men and women.

Based on these considerations, this study analyses three interrelated transitions that are particularly meaningful for the work and family life of men and women, namely, (i) *entry into the labour market and subsequent career*, (ii) *partnership formation*, and, (iii) *birth of the first child*. Within the transition process from youth to adulthood, entry into the labour market gains particular importance. In modern societies that are organised around the employment system (Kohli, 1985), leaving the educational system and entering a stable job ensures a certain degree of economic security; educational enrolment commonly expands the period of economic dependence. Thus, the latter transition marks an important step towards independence, a basis that is often seen as a prerequisite for partnership formation and parenthood (see for instance Blossfeld and Nuthmann, 1988). At the same time, decisions to form a union and have a child shape adult work life, particularly among women. Two important questions may be posed at this point.

The first question is this: how can we best describe transition patterns in the three selected countries under study? More precisely, what country-specific characteristics are on hand? What are the main identifiable changes across birth cohorts and historical time? And, in a more general sense, where do Germany, Great Britain, and Spain rank from a European perspective? Empirical evidence from various studies points to changes in timing, sequencing, and prevalence of transitions to adulthood as well as profound changes in work and family identities among couples (see for instance Corijn and Klijzing, 2001; Blossfeld and Drobnič, 2001). A postponement of various transitions such as leaving home, finishing educational qualification, and entering the labour market can be observed. Also, marriage and childbearing are occurring increasingly later in people's lives (Hullen, 2001 for Germany; Ermisch and Francesconi, 2000a and 2000b for Great Britain; Baizán, 2001; Billari *et al.*, 2002; Delgado and Martín, 1998; Castro Martín, 1992 for Spain). At the same time, transitions to adulthood appear less standard (Corijn and Klijzing, 2001): The heretofore widely spread standard sequence, or what has been called the normative model – that is, first leave the educational system, then enter the labour market, then marry and finally have a baby – is becoming more outdated for recent cohorts or simply

transitions appear to be repeatable; some are not necessarily exclusive and might therefore overlap. Individuals may break off certain engagements and, apart from a considerable delay of transitions in the life course, even forgo one or the other transition. For a discussion on psychological variables see Goossens (2001).

incompatible with their living situation. Furthermore, a growing dissociation between marriage and childbearing can be observed. First union formation is a decision-making process in which individuals make decisions about the timing, but also the kind of partnership (marriage or cohabitation). In most Western European countries the numbers of living in a non-marital cohabitation have significantly increased (Kiernan, 1999, 2001). Hence, formerly characterised by a high degree of chronologisation and age standardisation (Kohli, 1985), some commentators identify a shift from a 'standard transition' to a 'choice transition' from youth to adulthood (Liefbroer and de Jong Gierveld, 1995). These various trends lead to more variation in trajectories and make transitions to adulthood less predictable. On that account, these trends also impose heretofore unknown challenges to social actors, question the future functioning of the welfare state and hence may become a significant burden to politicians. At the same time, however, differences in transition patterns seem to prevail from a European perspective (Corijn and Klijzing, 2001; Kuijsten, 1996). The next section is therefore devoted to an illustration of these trends and locates the three countries under study in a broader European context.

Once the importance of country-specific variations is stressed the second question that arises is: what are the determinants of the speed of the transition to adulthood? And, how can we explain changes in the nature of this transition? There are several major contributions to the study of the transition to adulthood: cross-national comparative studies that present a description of the similarities and dissimilarities in timing, kind, and determinants of the transition to adulthood in various countries (Blossfeld *et al.*, forthcoming; Corijn and Klijzing, 2001); cross-country comparisons that investigate specific life course transitions (see for instance Blossfeld, 1995; Mills 2000; Shavit and Müller, 1998); as well as a huge number of country-specific studies that contribute to our knowledge of various determinants of the diverse paths to adulthood (see for instance Blossfeld and Huinink, 1991; Blossfeld *et al.,* 1999; Liefbroer, 2000; Manting, 1994; Oppenheimer *et al.*, 1997). These studies evaluate the age-relatedness and destandardisation, the impact of educational enrolment and educational attainment, the repercussion of non-employment, the impact of value change, and the effect of religion on the transition to adulthood. Sections 2.3 will develop a comprehensive theoretical framework for this study and Section 2.4 recapitulates what we already know about the main driving forces of recent changes in life course decision-making.

2.2 Comparing country-specific trends in life course transitions

The goal of this section is to address recent trends along with similarities and dissimilarities as regards *employment decisions* (2.2.1), *partnership decisions*

(2.2.2), and *parenthood decisions* (2.2.3) in the three countries under study. To this end, data from country reports of the Fertility and Family Surveys (FFS), the Council of Europe (2001), as well as three recent publications by Iacovou (2001) and the OECD (1998, 2001) have been used.[5] To broaden this description, results from major comparative and country-specific studies will slip into the discussion. Various other European countries are included in the argument to provide the necessary background to map the three countries under study. Most presented figures follow a particular design in order to highlight cross-country differences in transition patterns. To this end, countries are grouped into four regional clusters, that is, Scandinavian (Sweden, Norway, Finland, Denmark), Central European (Germany, Netherlands, France, Belgium), Southern European countries (Italy, Spain, Portugal, Greece) and the UK and Ireland.[6] These countries differ considerably with respect to their structural and political history, social structure, family policy, influence of religion, and the organisation of the educational system, thus constituting an interesting sample of industrialised societies.[7]

2.2.1 Employment decisions

There is ample evidence to suggest that education-to-work transitions are becoming more complex and increasingly deferred. In this respect, educational enrolment has been portrayed as a 'transitional role', which is largely mediating the transition to adulthood (Marini, 1985). Over the last decades, a profound upgrading process of individual skills can be observed, leading to a prolongation of educational enrolment. High educational and occupational qualification increasingly appear as significant prerequisites to enter the labour market and

---

5 The 'Fertility and Family Survey' project, 1992-99, was funded by the United Nations Population Fund, and was implemented by the Population Activities Unit of the United Nations Economic Commission for Europe. In total twenty-four different countries participated in the FFS project. More information can be obtained from the following website: http://www.unece.org/ead/pau/ffs/ffs_h.htm [20.01.03]. The demographic year book published by the Council of Europe is also available in electronic form at: http://www.coe.int/t/e/social_cohesion/population/demographic_year_book/ [24.01.03].

6 This is not to say that all selected countries fit entirely into these country clusters. As will become evident in the following sections, to every classification there are also exceptions or at least significant differences in pace and pervasion of changes in demographic behaviour. For instance, in several respects Ireland may well fit into the Southern European cluster.

7 Eastern European countries are not taken into account. Due to the major political and economical transformations in recent times, these countries have experienced substantial changes in living standards, all of which require a special discussion. Interested readers may have a look at Kowalska and Wróblewska (2001), Róbert and Bukodi (forthcoming), Holzer and Kowalska (1997), Katus *et al.* (2000).

compete with others on expanding global markets of knowledge-based and increasingly service-oriented economies (Blossfeld, 2002). The trend of educational expansion appears particularly pervasive for women and reflects their growing desire to invest in human capital and participate in the labour market, as well as their improved labour market chances and promotion prospects (Blossfeld, 1985, 1988, 1995). Therefore, this section starts out with a survey of the *process of educational expansion.*

Figure 2.1 Percent of women with medium or higher level qualifications by country, 1950-2000

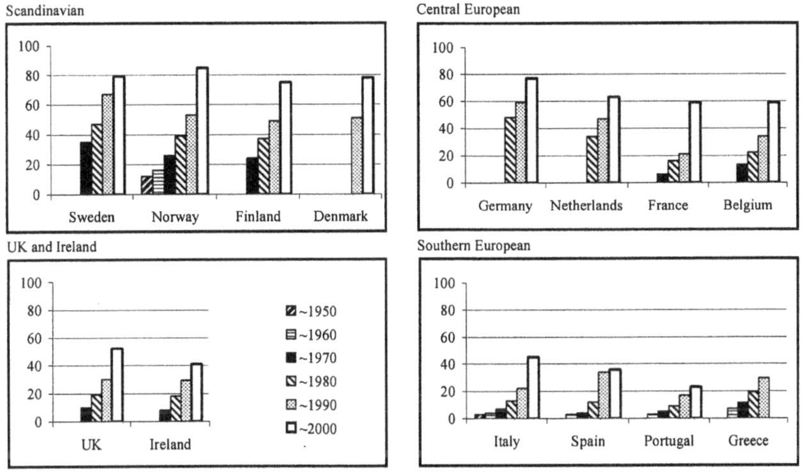

Note: Definitions of educational levels may vary between countries so that the figure can only show the extent of educational expansion at a glance.

Source: FFS Standard Country Report, Table 1f, except for Ireland and the UK (ILO, 2001-2001, gross enrolment ratios in tertiary education).

Figure 2.1 shows the percentage of women with medium or higher level qualifications in selected European countries between 1950 and 2000. Almost all European countries have experienced a steady and tremendous educational expansion, particularly the Scandinavian and Central European countries (Klijzing, forthcoming). In the former countries, by the end of the last century around 80 percent of women achieve a medium or higher level of education. This compares to approximately 60 percent in the Central European countries. Germany stands out as a country with a high percentage of women with medium or higher qualifications.[8] By the year 2000, percentages are comparable to the

[8] Disparate trends can be observed in the former western and eastern parts of Germany.

Scandinavian countries, though the educational expansion took place more rapidly in Norway, Finland, and Denmark. These large proportions of highly skilled women contrast to a less pervasive educational expansion in Spain and the Southern European countries in general. The UK seems to take a rather intermediate position. Formerly characterised as a 'low participation system', participation rates in higher education have steadily increased in the UK (see also Steinmann, 1998/99).

At present women have extended their involvement in higher education to such a degree that a catching-up process of women can be observed. In such respects, women appear increasingly better equipped to compete on labour markets and eager to employ their skills. As a consequence, the tremendous increase in women's enrolment in higher education is mirrored in increasing female labour force participation rates in most European countries (see Chapter Three).

After the above description of the tremendous educational expansion, a *delay in labour market entry* across birth cohorts is not surprising (Hullen, 2001; Taylor, 2000; Baizán, 2001). Yet, age at labour market entry is also less straightforwardly defined. In general, the first labour market entry sets in motion a process towards economic independence. In recent times, however, career-entry processes have become less straightforward and might include short-term and part-time employment, job experimentation, periods of non-employment, further education and training, or gainful employment while enrolled in educational programs (Bernardi, 2000; Gallie *et al.*, 1998; OECD, 1996a, 1996b, 1998; Taylor, 2000). This is to say that education-to-work transitions can no longer be grasped as a single step. Rather, labour market integration appears a more complex process in which individuals gradually increase in their career maturity (Oppenheimer *et al.*, 1997).

Figure 2.2 on the next page contrasts the employment probabilities of new school leavers aged 16 to 29 years one year after leaving education in various European countries. The presented employment probabilities can be seen as an indicator for the smoothness of education-to-work transitions. Two important findings should be stressed. First, towards the mid-1990s labour market integration seems particularly smooth in Germany – a result that has been

---

While in the FRG the proportion of youngsters with higher secondary education increased significantly and steadily, and, consequently, the time of educational enrolment in higher education expanded, in the GDR efforts in the field of educational policy towards educational expansion were confined to the first two decades following its constitution. From the 1970s onwards, educational policy was largely determined by economic needs and directed towards an early selection on educational paths, limiting access to universities and further training for the benefit of vocational training. Hence, the former GDR stands out as the only European country to curb educational expansion by national means (see for instance, Huinink *et al.*, 1995a).

attributed to the German apprenticeship system (Blossfeld and Stockmann, 1998/1999; Shavit and Müller, 1998). Quite the contrary, employment probabilities are much lower in Spain: less than 40 percent of new school leavers manage to enter gainful employment within one year after leaving education. This compares to 68 percent in the UK. Second, in most European countries labour market integration has become more turbulent. Between 1989 and 1996 the employment probabilities of school graduates declined by 8% and 7% points in the UK and Spain respectively. Interestingly, the reverse trend can be observed in Germany (and Ireland). Here employment prospects of school leavers seem to have improved over the early 1990s.

Figure 2.2 Employment probabilities of new school leavers aged 16-29 years one year after leaving education by country, 1989-1996

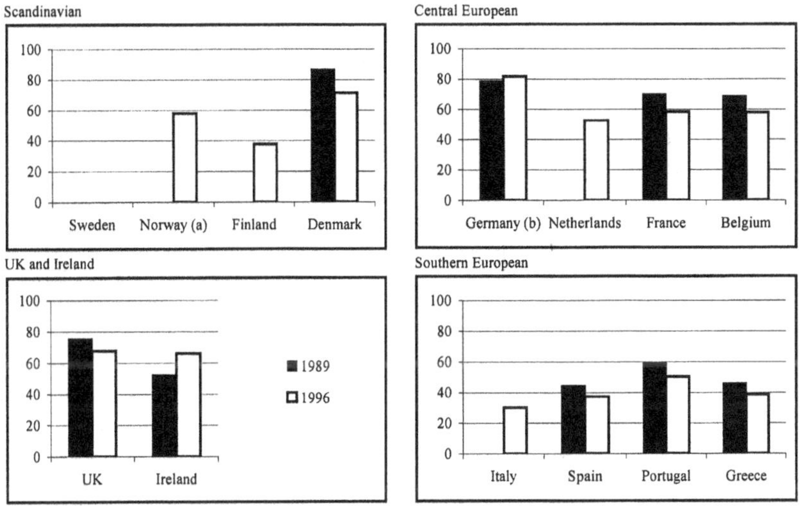

Note: (a) data refer to 1994. (b) Data refer to 1990 and 1995; the data for 1990 refer to western Germany, while the data for 1995 refer to the whole of Germany. No data available for Sweden.

Source: OECD (1998).

As the OECD (1998) demonstrated recently, employment probabilities vary for men and women. While in most European countries labour market integration appears more difficult for women, employment probabilities seem higher for women in the UK. This is in particular sharp contrast to Spain and the Southern European countries in general, where chances to enter gainful employment are considerably lower for women. However, over the 1990s employment prospects seem to have worsened much more for men. In the UK and Spain chances to enter gainful employment declined by 9% points for men. This corresponds to a decline by 7% and 2% points for women in the former two countries. Quite the contrary, in Germany male employment prospects have not deteriorated and employment probabilities of women have even significantly increased by 7% points (OECD, 1998).

Figure 2.3 Employment rate of all mothers with a child under six by country, 1989-1999

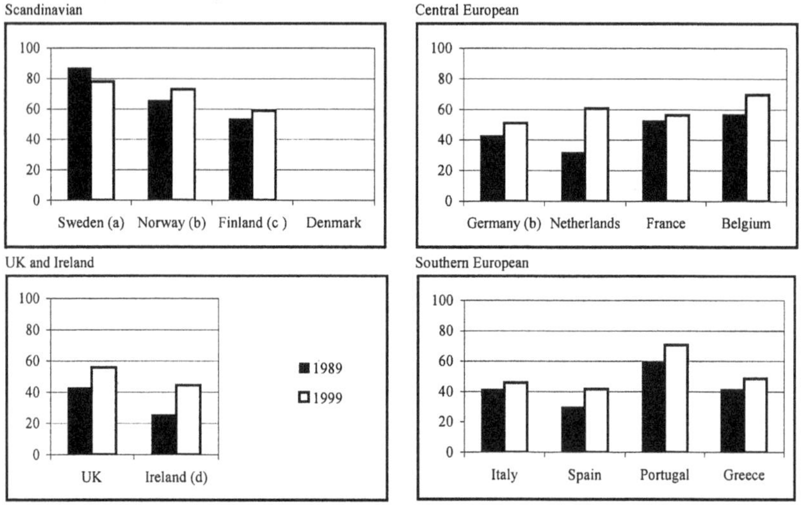

Note: The information is restricted to families with no-one over 60. Multi-family households were excluded. (a) mothers aged 25-54, 1990 and 2000. (b) 1991. (c) 1995 and 1998. (d) 1997. No data available for Denmark.

Source: OECD (2001).

However, education, work, partnership, and parenthood can not be grasped as single, but rather as parallel, highly interdependent areas (Rindfuss, 1991). In other words, employment decisions may frame family life while partnership and parenthood decisions may determine employment decisions. Recently, various commentators identify substantive changes in gender roles, all of which are mainly traced back to the fact that women and mothers increasingly participate in the labour market. Indeed, most modern societies pass through a gradual trend from male breadwinner towards dual earner societies (Blossfeld and Drobnič, 2001).[9] Nonetheless, unsalaried domestic work, and childrearing in particular,

---

9 According to the male breadwinner model, the man provides the solid economic basis through his labour force participation, while the woman takes major responsibility in

remain largely women's tasks. So one may ask: how do women balance work and family life (see also Bielby and Bielby, 1989; Hakim, 1991)?

Figure 2.3 shows *employment rates of mothers* with a child under six in selected European countries. Though labour force participation rates of mothers with young children have increased in most countries, by the late 1990s quite some between-country variation can be observed (OECD, 2001; Blossfeld and Drobnič, 2001). In 1999, employment rates seem highest in Sweden and Norway (78 and 73 percent) and lowest in Spain (42 percent). In Germany and the UK employment rates of mothers with a child under six appear also considerably lower than in the Scandinavian countries, the Netherlands, and Belgium.

Figure 2.4 Trends in employment patterns in couple families with a child under six in Germany, the UK, and Spain, 1989-1999

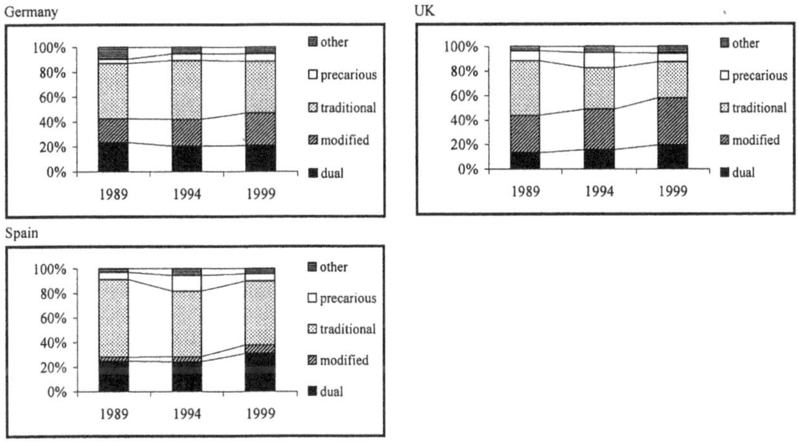

Note: Dual – proportion with man full-time, woman full-time; modified – proportion with man full-time, woman part-time; traditional – proportion with man full-time, woman not working; precarious – proportion with neither man nor woman working; other – all other employment patterns.

Source: OECD (2001).

Figure 2.4 differentiates five *employment patterns in couple families* with a child under six. More specifically, dual earner couples are separated from couples with a modified or traditional division of work, couples in financially insecure situations (both not working) and couples with other employment patterns. As to

---

domestic work and child-rearing. In dual earner couples both spouses contribute to the household income through their full-time work. The so-called modified model describes a gender division of labour in which the woman substitutes the household income through part-time employment, while the man remains the main breadwinner.

dual earner couples, Figure 2.4 reveals that while the respective proportion remains fairly stable in Germany, there is a clear rise in dual earner couples in the UK and Spain. Accordingly, the modified model seems to have spread in all three countries while the traditional model has lost quite some of its importance. In all three countries there is also a clear increase in the proportion of precarious employment patterns in couples with young children, particularly in the mid-1990s. This growing insecurity appears especially evident in the UK and Spain. All in all, the traditional model is far more widespread in Spain with small and only slightly growing proportions of couples with modified employment patterns. In turn, the modified model is of comparatively higher significance in the UK, but also Germany. Surprisingly, however, compared to their British counterparts there appear more dual earner couples with young children in Spain.

To conclude, the observed diversity in women's employment strategies is certainly related to differences in gender roles, the availability of family-friendly and flexible work arrangements, as well as family-friendly policies in terms of childcare provision and statutory regulation of leave for care of sick children, maternity and parental leave (OECD, 2001; Blossfeld, 1995; Blossfeld and Hakim, 1997b; Blossfeld and Drobnič, 2001).

2.2.2 Partnership decisions

The next question that arises at this point is: when do youngsters partner and what type of union do they form? The following discourse centres on three main aspects of present partnership formation processes: (i) the *decoupling process of parental home leaving and first partnering*, (ii) the *rise of consensual unions,* and, (iii) the *postponement of first marriage*.

Leaving the parental home plays a crucial role in the transition process from youth to adulthood. This is because nest-leaving involves the decision to set up one's own household, and thus, implies new responsibilities and a loosening of social bounds to parents. Over the last three decades, the process of leaving the parental home has changed significantly and quite diverse pathways can be observed. Nest-leaving may be induced to take up studies. In other cases, it may follow educational and occupational qualification with the intent to found one's own household either as a single or in a flat-sharing community. Parental home leaving may also be equivalent to first union formation.

Figure 2.5 shows the percentage of individuals leaving parental home by destination and country. Apparently, in the Central European, the Scandinavian, and the Anglo-Saxon countries a high proportion of parental home leavers sets up their own household as singles (Iacovou, 2001). In Germany[10] and the UK

---

[10] In the former GDR, youngsters left significantly earlier the parental home and the timing of

almost 40 percent leave parental home as solos. Conversely, these proportions are comparatively low in Spain, and Southern Europe in general, where nest-leaving appears predominately associated to partnership formation. For more than 80 percent of young Spanish women leaving parental home is equivalent to union formation. In all three countries under study, leaving for educational reasons plays a minor role, particularly in Spain.[11] The picture for men is slightly different. Compared to women, men are generally more likely to leave parental home as solos (Iacovou, 2001). Only in Germany (and Belgium and Portugal, respectively) women seem to equally (or even slightly more) often leave as singles.

Figure 2.5 Women's destinations on leaving home by country

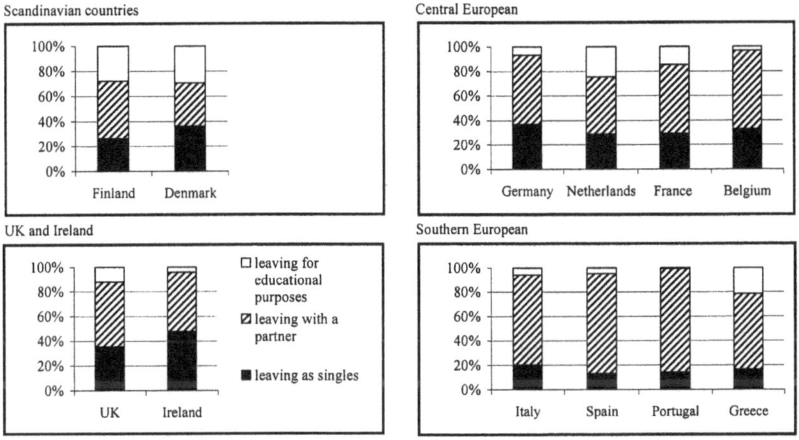

Note: All figures refer to 18 to 35 year olds living with their parents at time t and leaving parental home the following year (1994-1997).
Source: Iacovou (2001).

There is evidence to suggest that the kind of living arrangement entered after nest-leaving changes significantly (Billari et al., 2002; Ermisch and Francesconi,

---

this transition appears relatively constant over time. Some commentators have linked this to a lack of housing. As regards the allotting of flats, the government gave preferential treatment to young families and lone mothers. This in turn functioned as a great incentive for partners to marry and for young marrieds to have a child. These transitions occurred earlier in the life course, not uncommonly before finishing educational qualification (see for instance Hullen, 2001).

[11] However, in most Spanish surveys students who share apartments while studying are considered as living in the parental home since they are economically dependent on their parents.

2000a). More young adults leave the parental home for educational or job related reasons and, hence, the proportion of single person households and living communities is on the rise. In other countries, like Spain, individuals tend to postpone parental home leaving mainly due to housing shortages or worse economic prospects (see for instance Jurado Guerrero, 1999; Miret-Gamundi, 1997). These trends fuelled a progressive de-coupling process of marriage and parental home leaving which it is dealt with next.

Figure 2.6 Median ages of women at leaving home and first partnering in Germany and Spain by birth cohort

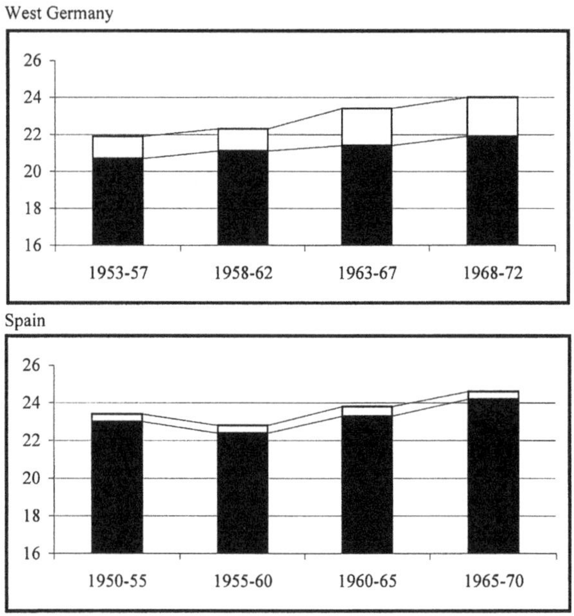

Note: The black bar represents the median age at parental home leaving; the white one refers to age at first partnering. Under-estimates for youngest birth cohort in Germany.
Source: FFS Standard Country Reports, Tables 6e and 8a.

Figure 2.6 presents an exemplary picture of median ages of women at leaving home and first partnering in Germany and Spain (for a broader comparison see Klijzing, forthcoming).[12] In Germany, both the median age of nest-leaving and

[12] The median age refers to the age at which 50 percent of the population have already left the parental home and partnered.

first union formation have increased over birth cohorts. In all four birth cohorts partnering occurs significantly later[13], but the interval between leaving home and partnership formation expands. Quite the opposite, the age distance is conspicuously small and remains fairly constant in Spain. Yet, the younger births cohorts postpone parental home leaving, and hence, first partnering. As compared to their German counterparts, young Spaniards stick significantly longer to the parental home. Similar studies for Great Britain show that while in Spain young adults tend to prolong the time before leaving the parental home and marry 'directly' (Baizán, 2001; Simó *et al.*, 2001), in Great Britain the proportion of women and men leaving the parental home to live with a partner has declined significantly. Men and women are increasingly more likely to live independently for a certain period before entering a partnership (Ermisch and Francesconi, 2000a).

But why do the Southern European countries appear significantly different? In Spain, there is a strong link between parental home-leaving, first union formation, and entry into first parenthood (Baizán, 2001; Holdsworth, 2000; Holdsworth and Irazoqui Solda, 2002). Spaniards tend to stay in the parental home until they have established a solid economic basis and intend to form a first union. This holds also true for other Southern European countries (Bernardi and Nazio, 2001; Billari *et al.*, 2002). Nest-leaving, founding one's own household, and entry into first union are in the majority of cases simultaneous transitions that are generally made at much later ages than finishing educational and occupational qualification and entering the labour market. The strong linkage between home-leaving and first union formation is probably because of the Spanish housing market. With almost 80 percent home-owners, Spain is one of the European countries with the lowest rate of rented dwellings (Holdsworth and Irazoqui Solda 2002). As Iacovou (2001) shows, the proportion of owner-occupiers among parental home leavers is outstandingly high in Southern Europe.[14] Therefore, founding one's own household is in most of the cases equivalent to becoming a home-owner, thus implying a long-term economic commitment.

As already indicated above, in most European countries a delay of first union formation and an increase in consensual unions as the mode of first live-in partnership can be discerned (Haskey and Kiernan, 1989; Kiernan, 1999; Ermisch and Francesconi, 2000a and 2000b; Nazio and Blossfeld, 2003).[15]

---

[13] In general, individuals partnered earlier in the former GDR than the FRG. Nest-leaving and partnership formation often happened together. In contrast, in the FRG transitions appear less age-related and more diverse (see for instance Hullen, 2001).

[14] For instance, among women around 70 percent leave as owner-occupiers in Spain. This relates to 16 percent in Germany (Iacovou, 2001).

[15] Cohabitation is by no means a novel living arrangement. Some types, particularly 'post-

Nevertheless, there remains a great deal of diversity in the incidence of consensual unions among European countries.

Figure 2.7 Cumulative percentage of women who had entered a consensual union as their first partnership by age 23 by birth cohort and country

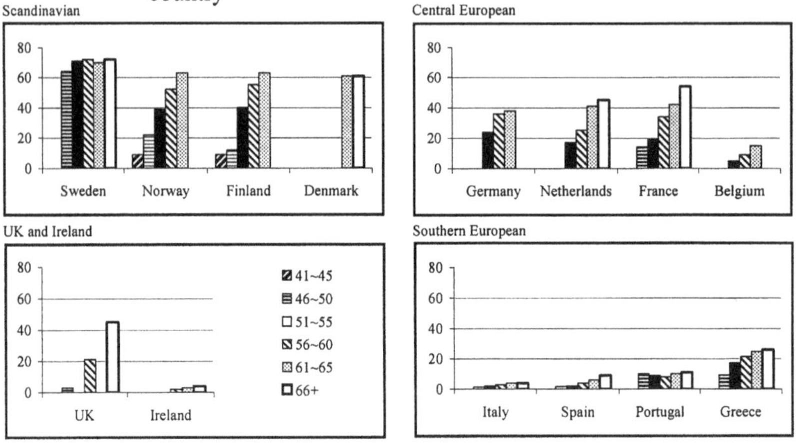

Source: FFS Standard Country Report, Table 8c, except for Ireland (Kiernan, 2002) and UK (Ermisch and Francesconi, 2000b).

Figure 2.7 presents cumulative percentages of women who have entered a consensual union up to age 23. Non-marital cohabitation is particularly widespread in the Scandinavian countries. Cohabitation is also on the rise in Germany. In Great Britain cohabitation is the most common type of first partnership chosen. About three-quarters of first partnerships are cohabitations even though these are rarely long-term (Ermisch and Francesconi, 2000a, 2000b). Cohabitation odds continue to increase among more recent cohorts, with these young people delaying first partnership altogether (Haskey and Kiernan, 1989; Kiernan, 1999; Ermisch and Francesconi, 2000a and 2000b). Quite the opposite, the respective proportions remain low in the Southern European countries, but also Ireland and Belgium. In these countries first union formation is still in most of the cases equivalent to entry into marriage, with only modest and slowly increasing rates of non-marital cohabitation (Baizán, 2001; Delgado

marital' cohabitation, are fairly familiar. What has been called the Golden Age of Marriage – a period characterised by marriage as the universal mode of partnership and young ages at first marriage – came to an end with the first small scale, later more and more pervasively partnership transition towards 'pre-marital' cohabitation and cohabitation as a socially acceptable alternative living arrangement (Kiernan, 2001).

and Castro Martín, 1998; Nazio and Blossfeld, 2003). This may be coupled with a strong family oriented ideology, religiosity, and a shortage of affordable housing in one or the other of these countries.

Next one may ask, does the observed increase in the incidence of cohabitation resemble a growing tendency to live with a partner for a certain probationary period before individuals either dissolve or transform cohabitation into marriage? Or, does this trend reflect a spreading social acceptability of cohabitation as an alternative to marriage, and hence, a growing propensity to forgo marriage? Recent findings indicate that in Sweden marriage and cohabitation are largely alike and transformation rates into marriage are below par (Kiernan, 2001). Quite the opposite, cohabitation is rather short-term and functions as a prelude to marriage in most other European countries. But when do cohabitants decide to marry? Blossfeld *et al.* (1999) investigates the interrelationship between, on the one hand, pregnancy and childbirth, and, on the other hand, the transition rate into marriage for couples living in non-marital unions. The results point to an intimately time-dependent process in which transformation rates are low as long as women are not pregnant. Once a woman is pregnant cohabitants tend to convert their non-marital union into marriage. Yet, this increased propensity is restricted to a certain time period around the time of childbirth.

A postponement of parental home leaving and partnering, along with a growing propensity to cohabit, lead to a significant decrease in the proportion of direct marriages (Kiernan, 2001). Some evidence points also to a shrinking propensity to marry at all (Miret-Gamundi, 1997; Kiernan, 2001). Figure 2.8 on the next page reveals an increase in the mean age at first marriage that can be observed in all European countries under consideration. However, with respect to timing and intensity there are striking differences between countries. In Scandinavia, from 1970 onwards women marry at increasingly higher ages. A similar trend can be noted for the Central European, UK and Ireland, and Southern European countries. Yet its beginnings were delayed, that is in the mid-seventies in Central Europe and at the beginning of the 1980s in Southern Europe, the UK, and Ireland.

Current partnership formation processes are not only characterised by a postponement of first union formation and increasing non-marital cohabitation. Several studies highlight that also partnership dissolution has grown greatly. This is partly due to the nature of cohabitations that are generally regarded as less binding and can be easily resolved, partly due to the increasing instability of marital unions.[16] Over the last decades, in most selected European countries the

[16] Empirical contributions show that consensual unions are most frail (Kiernan, 2001), while marriages but also converted consensual unions have a much lower risk to dissolve.

divorce rate has significantly increased. Again, the Southern European countries represent an exception to this trend. For example, though since the enactment of the divorce law in 1981 Spain has experienced an increase in separation and divorce, its incidence is still comparatively low from a European perspective (Simó *et al.*, 1999; Solsona *et al.*, 2000).

Figure 2.8 Female mean age at first marriage by country, 1960-2000

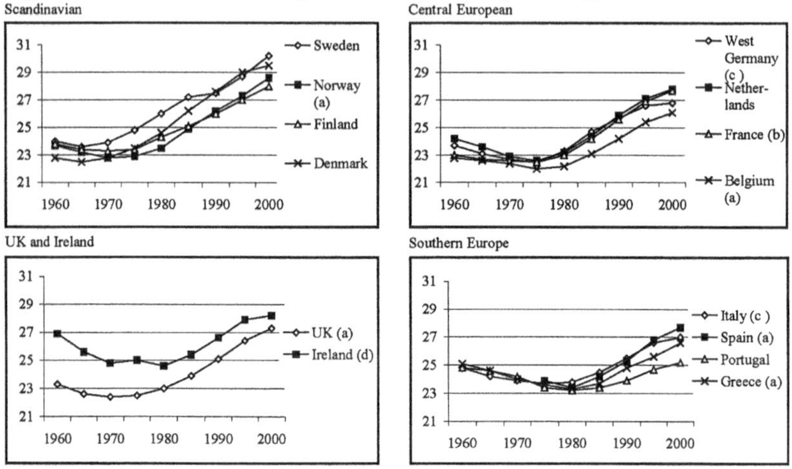

Note: (a) 2000 refers to 1999; (b) 2000 refers to 1998; (c) 2000 refers to 1997; (d) 2000 refers to 1996.

Source: Council of Europe (2001).

2.2.3 Parenthood decisions

Parenthood decisions are decisions about whether and when to have a child and the number of children. In contemporary European countries fertility is clearly determined by postponement, ageing, less intensity, and growing childlessness. As can be seen from Figure 2.9 on the following page, a *significant decline of the total fertility rate*[17] can be observed in all countries under consideration. This

---

Nonetheless, as for the latter pre-marital cohabitation leads to a higher risk of marital break-up.

[17] "*The* total fertility rate, *total fertility or period total fertility rates is a summary index of period fertility which refers to a particular year or period and is computed by the summation of the series of age-specific fertility rates. The term cohort fertility refers to the reproductive performance of particular birth or union cohorts. While completed fertility, lifetime fertility and total cohort fertility rate the cumulative fertility until the date when all members of the cohort have reached the end of the reproductive period*" (International

decrease is particularly evident in Southern Europe. Formerly characterised as countries with high fertility rates and parity orders, the Southern European countries became the 'lowest low-fertility countries'. Quite the opposite, in the Scandinavian countries fertility rates tend to increase since the mid 1980s and the decline seems to level off in the Central European countries (see also Frejka and Calot, 2001). Yet, the period total fertility rate gives only a cross-sectional picture and does not yield information on whether women perpetuate lower fertility levels than previous cohorts or simply postpone transitions to first motherhood. The discussion shifts therefore to a parallel trend which is the increasing age of mothers at childbearing.

Figure 2.9 Total fertility rate by country, 1960-2000

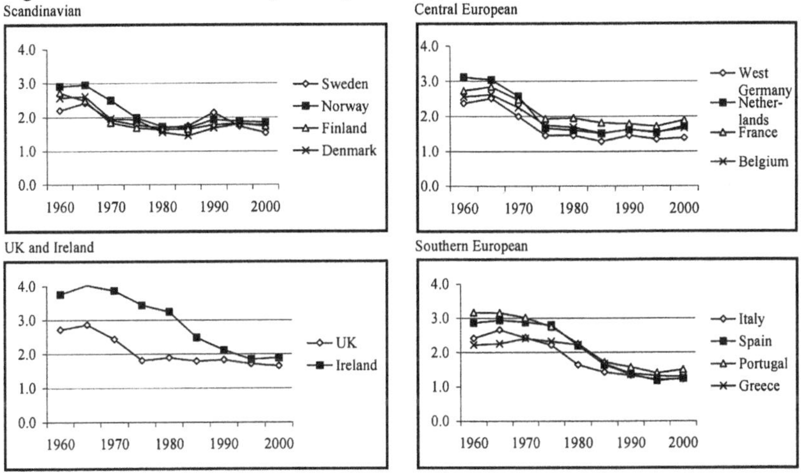

Source: Council of Europe (2001).

As can be seen from Figure 2.10 on the next page, in all European countries *women increasingly postpone the decision to have their first child.*[18] Frejka and

---

Union for the Scientific Study of Population (1982) Multilingual Demographic Dictionary, English section, Liège, Ordina editions).

[18] Between 1950 and 1975, a parallel trend in fertility can be observed in the GDR and FRG. In the mid 1960s fertility rates started to decline, but this trend only continued in West Germany, while it reversed in the former East where family formation and entry into first parenthood were significantly earlier and the timing of these transitions remained virtually unchanged (Pohl, 1995; Hullen, 2001). Since the reunification fertility rates declined rapidly in the GDR and, by now, are much lower than in West Germany. In Britain, teenage fertility rates are amongst the highest in Europe but have decreased dramatically between 1970 and 1976 and, since then, fluctuate around 28 and 33 per 1000 births (Kiernan, 1997).

Calot (2001) give a more comprehensive picture on levels and trends of cohort fertility, postponement, childlessness, and parity progression ratios. As described in more detail in their study, women increasingly postpone the decision to have a child but seem to recuperate at later ages. However, they do not accomplish same fertility levels as older birth cohorts. Hence there is a *growing tendency towards childlessness and one-child-families.* All in all, Frejka and Calot's findings leave no doubt that fertility levels dwindle across birth cohorts and the authors expect this trend to continue or to be precise to remain significantly below replacement-level in most low-fertility countries for another decade.

Figure 2.10 Mean age of mother at first live birth by country, 1960-2000

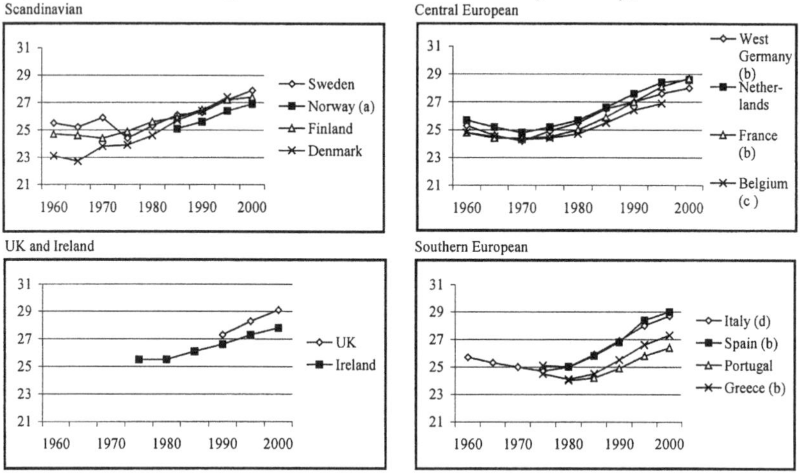

Note: (a) 1985 refers to 1986; (b) 2000 refers to 1999; (c) 1995 refers to 1993; (d) 2000 refers to 1997.
Source: Council of Europe (2001).

Lastly, individuals increasingly decide to have *children out-of-wedlock.* As one would expect, Figure 2.11 on the following page shows that non-marital childbearing tends to be high in countries where cohabitation is fairly wide-spread and the other way around. The increasing proportion of out-of-wedlock births has been associated to three important changes: an increase in the rate of childbearing among unmarried women, a decline in the rate of childbearing among married women along with a decline in the proportion of married women. More specifically, though the vast majority of first births are still within marriage, there has been a dramatic rise in the percentage of out-of-wedlock births that occur within cohabiting partnerships in almost all European countries

(Kiernan, 2001; for Great Britain see Ermisch and Francesconi, 2000a, 2000b). In contrast, childbirth outside of a partnership remains exceptional.

Figure 2.11 Extra-marital births as a percentage of all live births by country, 1960-2000

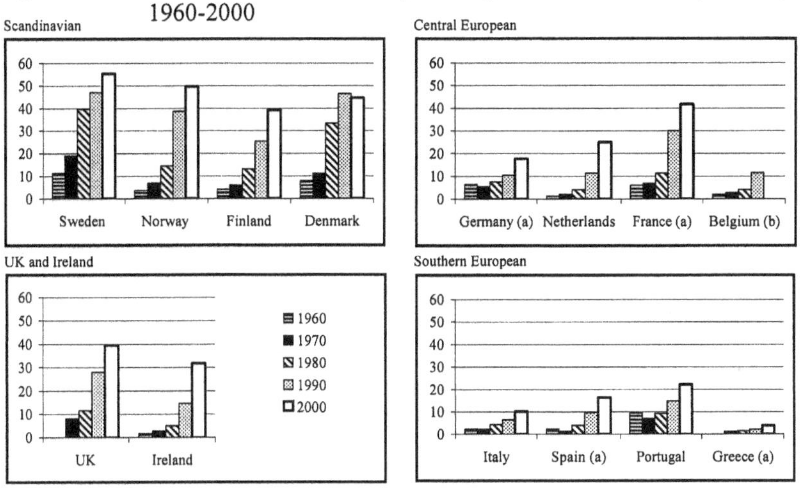

Note: (a) West Germany, 2000 refers to 1999; (b) 1995 refers to 1994.
Source: Council of Europe (2001), own calculations.

2.3 The concept of life course security

The above identified trends in transitions point to a diversification of living arrangements and a fading institutionalisation of individual life courses. Key words to describe the observed trends are prolongation, diverseness, less standardisation, and more individualisation. The discussion now moves beyond this mere description to the identification of the driving forces of life course decision-making and, more precisely, the importance of life course security.

Individuals make various life course decisions all of which determine their work and family life. The outstanding feature of the transition to adulthood is various rapid role and status changes towards adult worker, spouse, and parenting (Marini, 1985). Three long-term if not life-long commitments are in the spotlight of this work: (i) labour market entry and subsequent career, as the main determinant of growing economic independence from the family of origin and the key source of economic security in modern societies; (ii) marriage, seen as a partnership with the object of joint production and consumption that has to be long lasting to fully profit from these advantages; and, (iii) having the first child, as an irreversible, long-term joint project that constraints behaviour of both partners, particularly of women. Over the entire life course, transitions are repeatable, non exclusive, and optional. Previous decisions determine current and future decisions. Individuals face different options that are constantly under consideration and it is up to them whether or not to make such transitions. If so, individuals have to decide about the timing.

The above discourse is implicitly embedded in a rational actor perspective. From this theoretical perspective, individuals can be seen as decision-makers acting within the boundaries of country-specific institutions, welfare regimes, and society at large, and trying to optimise the decision process itself and the output they can obtain from it. In other words, actors will always choose a course of action that satisfies their preferences best, given their current opportunity structures, resources, and goals (Blossfeld, 2002; Blossfeld and Prein, 1998). Following Elster (1989: 4), decision-makers can be characterised as trying to achieve three optimisations: *"finding the best action, for given beliefs and desires; forming the best-grounded belief, for given evidence; and collecting the right amount of evidence, for given desires and prior beliefs"*. In these terms, employment, partnership, and parenthood decisions are well thought through and well-balanced regarding past experiences, current circumstances, and future expectations. The pivotal question that arises at this point is whether and when rational actors make such life course decisions. What are the perceived prerequisites that have to be met prior to the decision to make life-shaping commitments? A key concept in this respect is *readiness*. A main argument of this study is that individuals make life course decisions when they feel ready to make long-term commitments. Readiness in turn is first and foremost determined by life course security.

According to the fundamental idea of this study, individuals make life-shaping decisions when they can rely on some measure of medium- or even long-term *life course security*. Life course security in turn is tantamount to relative certainty about one's future life course. From a life course perspective, the decision to embark upon a certain educational or occupational route, to form a union, or have a child is framed by individuals' general perceptions about the broad social and economic future developments, but also their past, current, and future individual life course perspectives (see also Liefbroer, 1999; Van Peer, 2002). In other words, life course security is linked to the stability and predictability of employment, partnership, and parenthood career, and hence, to the degree to which individual actors can rely on State, family, and market.

The conceptualisation of life course security derives from the main lines of the life course approach (see among others Blossfeld and Huinink, 2001; Kohli, 1985; Mayer, 1987; Willekens, 1999). More precisely, the following main presumptions form the basis. Education, work, partnership, and parenthood are mutually interdependent paths. Related to this, personal experiences, previous events in individual work and family life, current material, social, and cultural resources along with future prospects in the employment, partnership, and parenthood domain govern individual life-shaping decisions (Mayer, 1986; Blossfeld and Huinink, 2001). At the same time, individual life courses are embedded in society at large. More precisely, the individual employment, partnership, and parenthood career is interrelated with the life course of significant others. Thus, life course decisions and life events of significant others and the partner in particular may modify individual decision-making processes. Above that, various social institutions shape individual lives and introduce structural constraints on their life course. As Mayer (1986: 166) puts it, institutional careers (e.g. within the educational system) are *"specific sequences of roles with an autonomous time scheduling according to an institutionalized logic"*. Furthermore, through interventions and regulations the *"state legalizes, defines and standardizes most parts of entry and exit: Into and out of employment, into and out of marital status, into and out of sickness and disability, into and out of formal education"* (Mayer, 1986: 167). State and market also determine the opportunity structure of rational actors and may channel social risks to specific groups while opening life chances for others. With this it is especially referred to a country's employment relations system and flexibility route, which frame individual employment relationships and thus their employment careers (Blossfeld, 2002; Mills and Blossfeld, forthcoming; Mayer, 1997). Related to this, welfare states protect and promote to varying degrees the welfare of the population (Esping-Andersen, 1999). In particular, as for individual employment careers the State may launch employment-sustaining labour market policies and welfare-sustaining employment policies which ensure a considerable degree of social security.

To conclude, life course security to make long-term, self-binding commitments appears related to specific contexts, namely the labour market context, the gender-related context, the welfare state context, and the partnership context. The key assumption developed here is that rational actors are more prone to postpone life course decisions if they are uncertain about their future prospects in these domains. So one may pose the question: What are significant sources of insecurity in these contextual settings?

To take on new responsibilities, and to make self-binding decisions in particular, a solid economic basis and a certain degree of stability in the labour market are essential. However, there is quite some debate that suggests that male-oriented and female-oriented explanations have to be developed (see Section 2.4). Men in insecure employment relationships may perceive themselves as less ready to form a union or become a father. For women constraints are possibly due to lacking part-time positions that could ease the combination of work and family career. Whether or not these constraints play a crucial role depends on the gender-related context. In rather traditional family and work identities, the man acts as the sole income provider. A less straightforward labour market entry and an unstable work career will make it difficult to solidify the economic household basis. In contrast, women's gainful employment may help to establish such a basis, but it is probably highly incompatible with the wish to have a child. The latter is interrelated with the labour market context, but also the welfare state context that may offer substantial support to gainfully employed mothers (e.g., through childcare facilities) and lower social risks through employment-sustaining and welfare-sustaining policies. Life course security is also determined by the type and durability of a union. It is important to keep in mind that sources of insecurity in these four contextual settings may vary greatly between countries.

Turning again to the conceptual framework on the determinants of life course decisions, it is vital to stress that readiness is a more complex theoretical concept as discussed above. A related concept that determines readiness is *developmental* (Goosens, 2001) and *socio-economic background factors*. The latter is meant to grasp parental home and early life course effects: parents' educational level, socio-economic status, and income as well as growing-up in non-intact families after parental separation and divorce are significantly related to a child's employment, partnership, and parenthood decisions.[19] Lastly, *values, norms, and beliefs* shape individual views on employment, marriage, and birth, and hence, impact their life course decision-making.

Undoubtedly, feeling 'not ready' to make life course decisions is hard to pin down. But this does not mean that it can not be empirically grasped. The relationship between structural changes on the macro-level and individual-level decision-making processes can be systematically studied since rational actors respond to an objective and measurable reality that is determined by historically grown and country-specific institutional arrangements (Blossfeld, 2000; Blossfeld and Müller, 1996; Blossfeld and Prein, 1998). The labour market context, the gender-related context, the welfare state context, and the partnership

---

[19] A rationale for the impact of socio-economic background factors may be that parents with a higher socio-economic status are in a better position to support children during extended educational and occupational qualification periods, and thus, offer better career opportunities. Parents of higher social classes are also more prone to convey career orientations, values and beliefs. Yet, parents' social class does not only determine a child's access to the higher educational system. A mediated effect is the impact on social networks and contact opportunities with future spouses, a result of several studies on homogamy (see for instance Blossfeld and Timm, 1997). Interested readers in parental home and early life course effects may have a look at Blossfeld and Huinink, 1989; Blossfeld and Jaenichen, 1990; Berrington, 2001; Cherlin *et al.*, 1995; Ermisch and Di Salvo, 1997; Ermisch, 1999; Ermisch and Francesconi, 2000a, 2001a, 2001b; Kiernan, 1992, 1997, 2001; Kiernan and Diamond, 1983; Kiernan and Eldridge, 1987; Kiernan and Hobcraft, 1997; McLanahan and Bumpass, 1988; Thornton, 1991.

context are mutually interdependent. They determine life course security, and hence, shape individual life course decisions apart from personal values and beliefs as well as developmental and socio-economic background factors. These various ideas are diagrammed in Figure 2.12.

Figure 2.12 The determinants of life course decisions

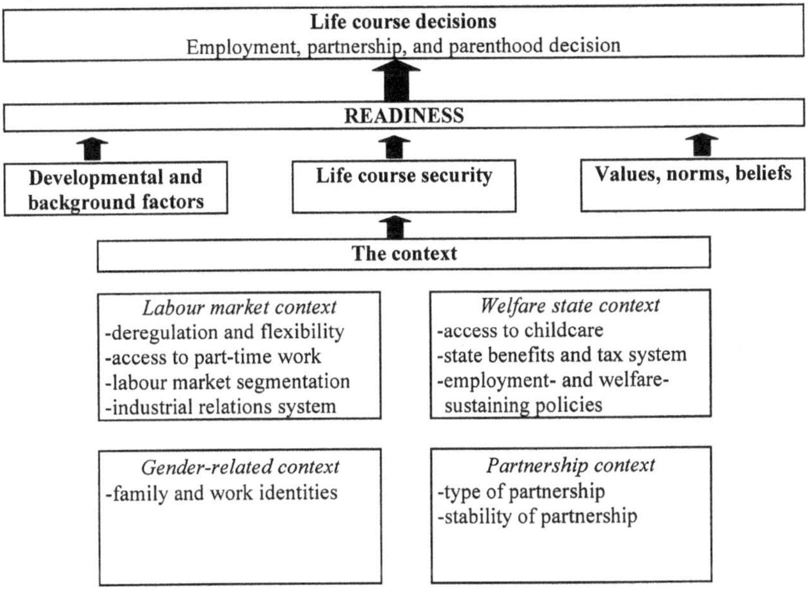

Readiness is by no means a new concept, albeit some commentators may associate different meanings with it (see for instance Erikson, 1950; Hobcraft, 2002; Hobcraft and Kiernan, 1995; Mills, 2000: 52-53; Oppenheimer, 1988). As regards the above described determinants of life course security, these have certainly influenced decisions in the past about whether and when to enter a job, partner, or have a child. However, what has changed over time are the contextual settings that determine life course security, and thus, readiness. More precisely, as will be amplified throughout this study, significant *changes in the economic and social structure* interpolate new sources of insecurity in individual life courses. Deregulation and flexibility of contemporary labour markets introduce insecurity in individual labour market careers as becomes visible in high unemployment, temporary employment, and inactivity. This is to say that education-to-work transitions and adult worker roles appear less certain for the rational actor. Related to this is the increasing need for further education and learning in today's learning societies which goes hand-in-hand with less certainty for the individual whether this will pay off in the future. Another aspect of change that is clearly linked to life course security is the substantial retrenchment of welfare states over the last decades, which has lowered the degree of social security individuals can rely on. All in all, these economic and social changes result in a decline of life course security. A further aspect that is associated to this is the growing instability of partnerships.

From another point of view one may argue that changes in life course decision-making are linked to profound *cultural changes*. A decline in normative control, increasing individualisation, and feminism has opened new options for individual actors (Liefbroer, 1999). Apart from changing views on marriage and birth, progressing educational expansion and growing female labour force participation give increasingly more power to women to choose a work career. Related to this economic development, the progressing trend towards dual-earner couples changes fundamentally the gender-related context in most European countries. The outlined contextual changes occur in tandem with various *technological innovations* in the field of producing and rearing children that give considerable freedom of choice with respect to parenthood decisions. Furthermore, with the dissemination of new communication technologies and mass media, rational actors continuously and speedily learn about new values, norms, and beliefs. There are ample empirical studies to these determinants of life course decisions. The following section reviews this literature and outlines what we already know about the driving forces of recent changes in life course decision-making.

2.4 Theoretical approaches and previous research

Over the last decades various scholars developed theoretical approaches in the field of economy, demography, and sociology to explain changes in the nature, speed, and sequence of transitions to adulthood.[20] Some focus on single transitions only, others attempt to develop a more comprehensive theoretical approach. The aim of the following discussion is neither to present an all-embracing list of contributions and empirical facts, nor to thoroughly debate about every single approach. The following sections discuss major hypotheses and review key findings regarding the main driving forces of the trends in life course transitions in a rather integrated manner. For this purpose it is distinguished between (i) *changes in economic and social structure* (Section 2.3.1), (ii) *cultural changes* (Section 2.3.2), and, (iii) *technological innovations* (Section 2.3.3) (see also Liefbroer, 1999; Van de Kaa, 1994).

---

[20] For a review see for instance Oppenheim Mason (1997), Hotz *et al.* (1997), Weiss (1997), Namboodiri and Wei (1998).

2.4.1 Changes in economic and social structure

Already in the early post-war period, the functional importance of differentiated sex roles as a requisite for marital stability and societal cohesion has been stressed by Parsons (1949). Later, Becker takes up again this argument. According to the so-called New Home Economics, individual's gains from family formation shrink the more women invest in their education and work career (Becker, 1973, 1981). Ideally, in a traditional family system the husband functions as a provider of household income through his continuous market work, while the wife carries the brunt of responsibilities in domestic work and childrearing. Such a gender division of labour creates a mutual interdependence between husband and wife and, so the argument of the economic theory, is most beneficial for both partners. In reverse, women's career investments increase their earning power which in turn makes them less dependent on a husband's income and cause substantial opportunity costs of children due to a high incompatibility of work and family career. Combined with a rising demand for gender equality, a traditional specialisation appears less attractive; the gains from marriage and parenthood decrease. Following the main lines of this approach, women's investments in human capital accumulation, rising earnings, and growing career orientation become thus the main determinants of family formation and may even enfeeble the family as a social institution. Yet, a discussion on the various driving forces of changes in costs and preferences is not provided in this theory and, as will be shown below, evidences from recent studies are by no means always in line with theory.

Previous studies provide ample evidence for a significantly lower propensity to partner, and to enter into marriage in particular, when being enrolled in education (Blossfeld, 1995; Blossfeld and Huinink, 1989, 1991; Blossfeld and Jaenichen, 1990; Hoem, 1986; MacDonald and Rindfuss, 1981). Such an incompatibility has also been shown for entry into first motherhood (Blossfeld, 1995; Blossfeld and Huinink, 1989, 1991; Blossfeld and Jaenichen, 1990). Due to substantial opportunity costs, basically in terms of time and income constraints, marriage and childbearing appear a competing activity to educational enrolment and are generally postponed until the end of studies. These opportunity costs appear utmost for highly educated and women in general. In other respects Becker's hypothesis has been challenged. Oppenheimer (1994; see also Oppenheimer and Lew 1995, Oppenheimer *et al.*, 1997) scrutinises whether women's educational enrolment and gainful employment leads to a delay of marriage rather than non-marriage. She argues that

> *"economic factors, school enrolment, service in the military, getting established in a career, and so on, may all signify the necessity or desirability of delaying marriage, without affecting the desirability of marriage per se"* (Oppenheimer, 1994: 304).

In another study, Blossfeld and Huinink disentangle the separate effects of educational enrolment and educational attainment and stress that

> *"[...] The delaying effect of education on the timing of first marriage is [..] a result of the fact that, across cohorts, educational expansion has increased the time of educational participation and has delayed the transition from youth to adulthood [...] Prolonged participation in the educational system leads to a delay in women's transition to adulthood and thereby to a delay in their having a first child"* (1991: 163 f.).

Once having left the educational system, most women seem to catch up with their less educated counterparts, most likely due to age norms and health reasons. In other words, extended educational enrolment and growing female labour force participation intensify a deferment but not a foregoing of marriage (Oppenheimer, 1994; Blossfeld, 1995). Nonetheless, empirical support for the New Home Economics hypothesis has been found for the career effect on the timing of entry into first motherhood. Women with high resources seem more likely to postpone or may even forgo this decision. This has been related to the strong interrelation between, first, the provision of child-care facilities, second, the availability of part-time positions, and, third, work and family identities among couples (Blossfeld and Drobnič, 2001). Liefbroer and Corijn (1999) emphasise the prevailing incompatibility of labour force participation and family formation for women that is attributable to constraints on the cultural level (i.e., ideologies, values, and norms according to which women should not invest in both careers) and the structural level (i.e., actual barriers to combine both activities).

So, what is suggested by the empirical results for men? Are there also some male-oriented explanations, linking work careers and recent changes in life course decision-making? Ever since Malthus' Population Theory (Malthus, 1890), the hypothesis that the timing of partnership formation is determined by men's economic status has been elaborated. It was and largely remains men's responsibility to provide an economic basis for a partner and children. Educational attainment as well as career and income prospects of men have been shown as significant determinants of partnership formation (Blossfeld and Huinink, 1989, 1991). Various contributions point out that economic developments affect adversely young adults' chances to set up a solid economic basis. For instance, there is evidence that individuals marry earlier the more prosperous their present-day economic situation is. This has been related to more economic and social security, and hence, better chances to stand on one's own legs at early ages and come up with expectations to confront new long-term commitments (Blossfeld and Huinink, 1989, 1991; Oppenheimer, 1988). The same relation has been shown for transitions to first parenthood even though this effect appears largely mediated by marriage (Blossfeld and Huinink, 1989, 1991). Furthermore, due to high youth unemployment rates youngsters are likely to face poor economic prospects at the beginning of their labour market career which will lower individual's chances to become economically independent (Raffe, 1987; Ashton *et al.*, 1990). Less stable and more progressive labour market integration of young adults and declining male earnings during early labour market careers have been associated with the increasing postponement of parental home leaving and recent changes in family formation processes (Oppenheimer, 1994; Jurado Guerrero, 1999). For instance, as Jurado Guerrero (1999) shows for Spain, a stable market income is an important predictor of men's nest leaving. Yet, once having left the educational system, Spanish men confront lots of barriers for leaving home because of various difficulties in finding a job, particularly a permanent one. The combination of housing market and unstable labour market entry patterns lead to a postponement of parental home-leaving, and thus, to a delay of first union formation and entry into first parenthood (Baizán, 2001; Jurado Guerrero, 1999). In other studies, marriage formation has been related to gainful employment during the early labour market career and empirical evidence for a significant effect of the deterioration in young men's labour market position on life course decision-making has been provided (Oppenheimer *et al.*, 1997). The argument goes as follows: Low incomes at the beginning of the labour market career hamper young men's chances to set up an economic basis and difficulties in finding a stable job at career entry involve considerable uncertainty about future job prospects which may affect assortative bonding (see also Oppenheimer, 1988). Some empirical evidence points to a higher propensity to postpone marriage the longer such difficulties persist. In these terms and as compared to marriage, cohabitation may be perceived as a less binding partnership, and hence, as an adaptation strategy. Following Oppenheimer, in a context of considerable career instability and uncertainty a gender-specific specialisation can be seen as a high risk strategy since *"specialization involves a potentially serious loss of flexibility"* and *"[...] can make the family particularly vulnerable to the temporary or permanent loss of a unique individual who provides an essential function"* (Oppenheimer, 1994: 317f). Women's labour force participation may actually ease partnership formation. This is to say that (i) through their gainful employment women can contribute to an economic basis that men can possibly not (yet) solidify, and thus, spouses share risks within marriage; and, (ii) following the main lines of the homogamy approach, women may have a better access to the marriage market. Thus, *"[...] wives' employment in a modern low-mortality society can be viewed as a highly adaptive family strategy rather than as a threat to the family as a social institution"* (Oppenheimer, 1994: 321).

2.4.2 Cultural changes

Increased secularisation and individuation have been spotted as driving forces of recent changes in partnership and parenthood decisions in Western European countries since the 1960s. Observed transformations in timing, type, commonness, and durability of unions along with changes in level and pattern of fertility have been summarised under the heading 'Second demographic transition' (Van de Kaa, 1987, 1994; Lesthaeghe and Surkyn, 1988). Proponents of this approach have amplified Classic Demographic Transition Theory (Thompson, 1930; Notestein, 1953), stating that apart from economic modernisation a shift in values has taken place (Lestheaghe, 1983). Following the main lines of the Second Demographic Theory, the speedy and pervasive secularisation and individuation become palpable in individual's striving after individual autonomy and self-fulfilment as well as a decline in religiosity (Lesthaeghe and Surkyn, 1988). Furthermore, the emphasis of individual's equal opportunities and freedom of choice in behaviour strengthened over time (Van de Kaa, 1987). Advocates of this approach expect that all European countries run through this transformation process and expound that present variations in family formation are transient and simply represent different stages of the same process (Van de Kaa, 1987; Lesthaeghe and Surkyn, 1988). Due to persistent cross-country differences in demographic behaviour and significant peculiarities of country-specific institutional arrangements, all of which are assumed to frame transition processes, other scholars have questioned this convergence hypothesis and provided counterfactual evidences (see for instance Corijn and Klijzing, 2001; Kuijsten, 1996).

Prior research on transitions to adulthood has intensively focused on the growing corrosion of religious and political authority as well as the incremented meaning of individual freedom and their implications for partnership and parenthood decisions (e.g., Bumpass, 1990; Goldscheider and Waite, 1991). For instance, various scholars associate type and timing of union formation with religious affiliation and strength of religious commitment (Mills, 2000; Thornton *et al.*, 1992; Kiernan, 2001). In these studies religion has been shown to have a negative effect on individual's tendency to cohabit; higher levels of religiosity are significantly correlated with a higher propensity to marry. The latter holds especially true for Catholics, and this result has been ascribed to traditional family values and a taboo of premarital sexual relations.

Over the last decades, several commentators have also identified a decrease in normative control and a change in the meaning attributed to certain life course transitions. An instance of cultural change is the transformation of norms and attitudes towards non-marital cohabitation (Manting, 1994, 1996; Mills, 2000). Heretofore rated as a deviant, and thus, tabooed living arrangement, from the 1970s onwards cohabitation has matured and is by now a tolerable and more and more common mode of partnership. However, pace and extent of this evolution as well as the meaning of cohabitation are by no means uniform, but vary greatly between different nation-specific contexts (see Section 2.2.2).

Increasing individualisation and changes in perceptions and norms have also been related to parenthood decisions. Here it has been argued that individual's perceptions have changed and a new norm of family size appeared (Davis, 1963). Other scholars argue that with the disintegration of the household as a unit of reproduction, production, and consumption the demand for children changed. In former times various incentives for having children have been identified since children used to work for the household and offered a help for parents. In modern societies, however, the so-called intergenerational wealth flow within families reversed and became more unilateral (Caldwell, 1976, 1982).

2.4.3 Technological innovations

Over the last decades, numerous technological innovations have not only thoroughly restructured national economies and the demand side of labour markets. The influx of various technological innovations has also had far-reaching consequences on individual decision-making processes. Several researchers relate recent changes in parenthood decisions to technological innovations in the field of producing and rearing children, particularly to the increasing accessibility of effective contraceptive methods (Preston, 1986; Lewis and Kiernan, 1996; Lesthaeghe, 1983; Kohler, 1997; Thomson, 1997; Goldin and Katz, 2000). Medical innovations in the field of gynaecology and obstetrics lower health risks, but also open the way for induced abortion and artificial insemination. With the contraceptive revolution, a progressive destandardisation process got under way, step-wisely de-coupling marriage from sexual intercourse, partnering, and eventually parenting. Individuals have in their hands the decision about whether, when, and how often to parent; hence, transitions to parenthood appear more often planned and wished for.

A further aspect of technological change that has been associated with recent changes in life course decision-making is the speedy dissemination of communication technologies and mass media. According to the ideational theory, the timing of transitions to parenthood is linked to the diffusion of information and new social norms about birth control. Thus, the diffusion of new ideas and perceptions about fertility along with the processes through which diffusion comes about become important determinants of the fertility decline (Cleland and Wilson, 1987).

A more recent approach by Nazio and Blossfeld (2003) develops hypotheses on the diffusion process of cohabitation. Drawing from Rogers (1983), diffusion is grasped as an individual-level process by which the members of a society learn about new behavioural manners that they may take on or not. The propensity to adopt cohabitation as a new mode of live-in partnership is assumed to be determined by the extent of prior adoption of individuals from previous cohorts in a population (Strang, 1991). That is to say that the diffusion of cohabitation is a matter of knowledge-awareness and social acceptability. The influx and dissemination of new communication technologies is seen as a driving force of this self-reinforcing process. Through enhanced access to information, individuals continuously learn about new ideas, possible options, perceptions, conceptions, fashions, and new norms. Yet, the findings of this study by Nazio and Blossfeld suggest that the growing information exchange does not suffice to explain the diffusion of cohabitation. Following Strang (1991), new patterns of behaviour appear most appealing if individuals can observe the pros and cons of these in daily life of individuals like themselves. Thus, Nazio and Blossfeld (2003) surmise that cumulative peer group adoption is a salient driving force of the diffusion process, and presumably even more important than the proportion of prior adopters. Observed differences in the mode of dissemination, swiftness, and degree of adoption have been related to country-specific distinctness of normative contexts, prevailing gender roles, as well as the availability of affordable housing (Nazio and Blossfeld, 2003).

2.5 Conclusion

This chapter identified the three life course decisions under study, outlined changes in life course transitions, and introduced readiness and life course security as key concepts to grasp individual decision-making. A wide array of empirical evidence from various European countries has been presented that contributes to our knowledge of the various determinants of life course decision-making. As the previous sections made clear, we do have quite some understanding of how life course decisions are correlated with various individual characteristics and circumstances of the family of origin. There is also a growing body of research contributions on the impact of values, norms, and beliefs. Both cultural changes and technological innovations open new options for individual decision-makers. At the same time, however, various profound changes in the social and economic structure lower individual degrees of life course security. To summarise, recent contextual changes can be subsumed under the formula: *more options and less security.*

To analyse nature and speed of transitions to adulthood plenty of determinants have to be considered, none of which will fully suffice to model individual pathways. The aim of this study is not to develop a theoretical model that integrates all these factors into a single comprehensive framework. This work asks whether and to what extent present macro-level changes in labour markets impact individual decision-making processes. This chapter already hinted how growing labour market insecurity might be considered a specific dilemma for young adults. Two theoretical and empirical questions arise at this point:

First, *is labour market insecurity systematically related to difficulties in entering and settling in the labour market, and thus, leading to less life course security?* In other words, are recent birth cohorts less ready to make long-term commitments because of less certainty about their individual labour market careers? At present our knowledge of the relationship of labour market insecurity and its various forms of uncertainty with employment, partnership, and parenthood decisions is scant. In particular, we do not yet know whether or not labour market insecurity implies distinct outcomes for men and women. Above that, to fully grasp the effect of labour market insecurity on the individual life course, its potential disadvantageous effect on subsequent transitions in the labour market as well as on the interplay of family and work career have to be dynamically unfolded. Again, this remains a theoretical and empirical matter. Chapter Three is thus devoted to a discussion of recent trends in European labour markets, a conceptualisation of labour market insecurity and its causes, and a theoretical framework relating these structural macro-level changes to individual decision-making processes.

Second, *do certain country-specific institutional arrangements filter labour market insecurity?* With respect to the convergence hypothesis, the above discussion reveals that country-specific variations in the work and family life of men and women remain strong. Pace and extent with which changes in life course decision-making spread from one country to another appear determined by a variety of institutional, cultural, and environmental conditions. One may therefore also ask whether and to what extent changes accompanying the restructuring process of national labour markets can be modelled differently in the selected countries due to such path-dependencies. The approach of this study is clearly interactive: it concedes that individual pathways from youth to adulthood and later on are rooted in historically grown, pre-existing institutional arrangements in a society as well as the larger, global environment, impacting national labour markets. Chapter Four delves deeper into the role of institutional filters and provides a detailed outline of nation-specific arrangements in labour market, education, and welfare provision in the three selected countries under study.

3 Labour market insecurity

Since the mid-1970s, large-scale shifts towards a technology- and knowledge-based economy, increasing global competition, volatility in product and capital markets along with intense sectoral and labour shifts have led to unprecedented changes on the demand and supply side of labour markets. Key assumptions of previous economic policy were to an increasing degree outdated and labour markets appeared too rigid to absorb economic downturns and global pressures (Streeck, 1992). Hence, over the 1980s and 1990s governments introduced various deregulation and flexible measures in an attempt to make the previous rigid employment systems more flexible and thus more competitive and adaptable to rapidly changing market opportunities and demands.[21] In most European countries there has been a shift towards more part-time, temporary, and agency work (Schömann *et al.*, 1998) and the emergence of a new labour force stratum of so-called "flexi-workers" (Standing, 1997: 24).

The following discourse is firmly embedded in the interplay of the above specified structural changes on the macro-level. These may be subsumed under three main headings, (i) from national product, capital, and labour markets towards expanding global markets; (ii) from standard-employment relationships towards growing non-standard, flexible employment; and, (iii) from pre-career education towards life-long learning societies. This chapter describes and analyses these trends, develops rationales, and purposes to relate the identified structural changes on the macro-level to individual-level decision-making processes. The main aim is to inquire into patterns of insecurity and labour market exclusion.

The remainder of this chapter outlines the background against which this study is motivated and is structured as follows. The next section describes different types of employment regimes and is devoted to a description of labour market trends characterising most European countries. Section 3.2 discusses the

---

[21] This is not to say that degree, direction and pace of this trend was common to all European countries, nor that a change from a stable labour market in a kind of 'Golden Age' towards a highly flexible labour market today took place. As will become obvious in the following sections, country-specific adaptation strategies are to be expected. One may argue that employment was presumably also insecure in times of a more rigid employment regulation, since firms might have used other instruments to gain flexibility. New is, however, that employers have an increasingly free hand to actively frame employment relationships.

concept of employment flexibility and its causes, deals with the question of how employment flexibility impacts individual labour market outcomes, and defines job insecurity. The consequences of growing insecurity on individual labour market careers and life course decision-making are then speculated on (Section 3.3). The chapter concludes in Section 3.4 with a risk profile hypothesis.

3.1 Employment regimes and flexible labour

Over the last three decades, European labour markets have been deeply restructured, altering the composition of the labour force (see for instance Esping-Andersen and Regini, 2000; Schömann *et al.*, 1998; Standing, 1997). Yet, despite the common challenges accompanying the globalisation process, country differences persist and pace and degree of the restructuring process differ considerably. Likewise, common demands and pressures have had varying impacts on the labour force. It has been commonly acknowledged that the observed dissimilarities are rooted in country-specific arrangements in labour legislation, employment relations systems, as well as education and welfare provision (Esping-Andersen and Regini, 2000; Mills and Blossfeld, forthcoming; see Chapter Four). This section does not aim to identify these nation-specific rationales. It traces key labour market trends in Germany, Great Britain, and Spain, embeds this discussion in a more comprehensive picture on economic developments in a number of European labour markets, and poses the question where the three countries under study rank from a European perspective. To this end, the following sections provide ample evidence on major labour market trends in selected European labour markets in Scandinavian (Sweden, Finland, Denmark), Central European (Germany, The Netherlands, France, Belgium, Austria), and Southern European countries (Italy, Spain, Portugal, Greece) as well as the UK and Ireland. The debate is centred on those economic developments that are meaningful for individuals' work and family life, particularly on their way to adulthood. More precisely, using international comparative data from various sources the discussion focuses on five main topics, that is selected economic developments (Section 3.1.1), the growth of flexi-workers (Section 3.1.2), education-to-work transitions (Section 3.1.3), longitudinal employment profiles (Section 3.1.4), and job satisfaction (Section 3.1.5). On these grounds it is finally assessed whether and to what extent distinct employment regimes can be identified in Germany, Great Britain, and Spain (Section 3.1.6).

3.1.1 Economic developments

One of the key labour market trends observed in modern societies is the shift to service sector employment (see also Klijzing, forthcoming). Figure 3.1 shows the percentage of employed men and women working in the service sector between 1950 and 2000 in Germany, the UK, and Spain.

Figure 3.1 Percent of employed men and women working in the service sector in Germany, the UK, and Spain, 1950-2000

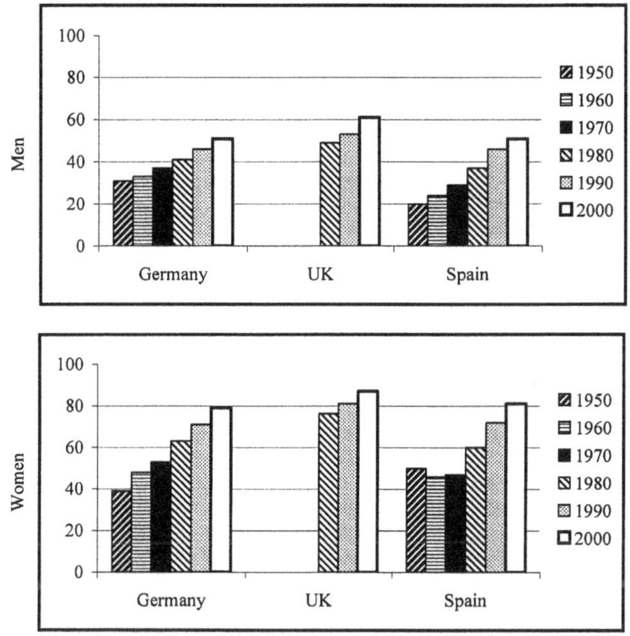

Source: Delgado and Castro Martín (1998); Hullen (forthcoming); ILO (2001-2002).

In all three countries a steady increase in service sector employment of men and women can be observed. By the year 2000, around 50 percent of men in Germany and Spain and 60 percent in the UK were employed in the service sector. The shift to services is even more obvious for women (see the bottom panel of Figure 3.1). Here the respective figures relate to around 80 percent. The same trend has been detected in other European countries, though swiftness and extent of the shift to service sector employment vary (Klijzing, forthcoming).

The described structural change is linked to a growth in new job opportunities in the service sector (Blossfeld, 1985). Since labour markets remain gender segregated and women enter the service sector more often than men, particularly women profit from this shift to services. The next figure highlights the increase in female labour force participation over the last two decades. With an almost 30% points increase between 1980 and 1997, women's labour market integration occurs most pervasively and rapidly in Spain. Nonetheless, female labour force participation is significantly higher in Germany and the UK. While over the 1980s, the female labour force participation rate is lower in Germany than in the UK, it becomes closer over the 1990s and appears equally high by the late 1990s. In 1999, the participation rate reaches around 75 percent in Great Britain and Germany as compared to less than 60 percent in Spain.

Figure 3.2 Female labour force participation in Germany, the UK, and Spain, 1980-1999

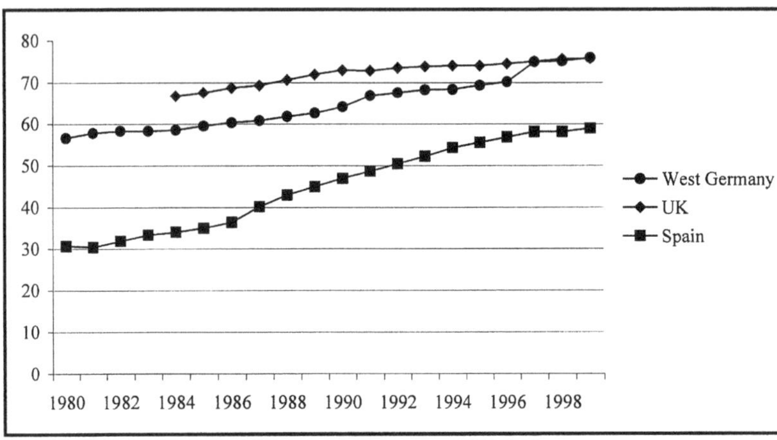

Note: Women 25-54 years old; including part-time and full-time positions.
Source: Key Indicators of the Labour Market (KILM 1), ILO, 2001-2002.

As will be discussed in more detail later on, increasing female labour force participation goes hand in hand with expanding part-time labour markets. Yet, the Spanish part-time labour market is still comparatively underdeveloped, which may be seen as one explanation for persistently lower participation rates. The comparatively high labour force participation rates in the UK and Germany are only surpassed in the Scandinavian and post-socialist countries (Klijzing, forthcoming). This has been related to a more extensive promotion of gender equality and high wage incentives for dual earner couples in Scandinavia as well as specific family and social policies in the former socialist countries that were targeted on high female labour force participation (Blossfeld and Drobnič, 2001).

Low youth unemployment may be seen as an indicator for the smoothness of education-to-work transitions. Figure 3.3 shows the respective developments in Germany, the UK and Spain between 1980 and 2000. In all three countries youth unemployment appears particularly high during the mid 1980s and early

1990s, thus clearly resembling the economic recessions at these times. Yet, youth unemployment is extraordinarily high in Spain. At all times the unemployment rate is significantly higher than in Germany and the UK, varying between 25 and 44 percent. Youth unemployment rates are also particularly high in other Southern European countries, even though these clearly remain under the Spanish ones (Klijzing, forthcoming). In contrast, youth unemployment is comparatively low in Germany and less clearly marked by economic downturns. In the UK, youth unemployment rates appear fairly similar to other market economies (Klijzing, forthcoming). As compared to Germany, during the more prosperous economic times at the beginning and the end of 1990s unemployment rates in the UK seem more similar to German ones.

Figure 3.3 Youth unemployment among the 15-24 years old in Germany, the UK, and Spain, 1980-2000

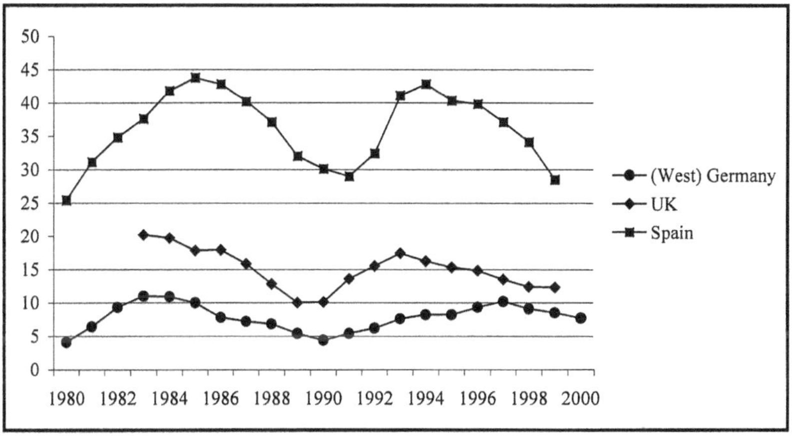

Note: 1980-1990 West Germany, 1991-2000 Unified Germany.
Source: Key Indicators of the Labour Market (KILM 9), ILO, 2001-2002.

A related issue is the question to what extent unemployment experience at labour market entry impacts subsequent labour market careers. Recent studies provide some evidence that unemployment has a severe penalty on subsequent job tenure (Arulampalam, 2000; Böheim and Taylor, 2000; Gregg and Wadsworth, 2000; Kurz *et al.*, 2002; Simó *et al.*, 2002a). When re-entering the labour market from unemployment individuals are not only more likely to be in temporary employment. They also seem more likely to re-enter unemployment speedily. Furthermore, job positions taken up after a spell out of work are often part-time and entry wages are substantially below the average for all workers. These findings underline that unemployment does lead to economic insecurity while being unemployed, but also seems to destabilise the subsequent job career. All in all, the described differences have been linked to the distinctness of national employment relations systems and institutional arrangements in education and welfare, all of which determine the smoothness of education-to-work transitions (Shavit and Müller, 1998; Regini, 1997; Mills and Blossfeld, forthcoming; see Chapter Four). However, even if labour market entries proceed smoothly, they may be risky. More precisely, job instability and youth unemployment may be high if there are a high proportion of insecure employment contracts among school leavers. In the following section, the attention shifts therefore to the nature of employment relationships.

3.1.2 The growth of flexi-workers

Over the last two decades a growth in the use of various forms of non-standard employment relationships can be observed in most European countries. By the late 1990s, the bulk of new jobs are fixed-term or part-time and there are a growing proportion of own-account workers (i.e., self-employed without employees). In the following, empirical evidence on the growth of these so-called flexi-workers is presented.

Figure 3.4 on the next page shows fixed-term employment as a percentage of total dependent employment in thirteen selected European countries in 2000. It reveals a substantial variation in the incidence of temporary employment. Spain is clearly outstanding with around 32 percent of all dependent employees being on a fixed-term post. This compares to 7 and 5 percent in the UK and Ireland respectively. The Southern European countries are by no means homogenous. While Spain and Portugal rank highest, a difference of almost 12% points is remarkably high. Greece and Italy score also fairly low and appear more similar to the Western European countries and Denmark. With around 13 percent of fixed-term employment, Germany marks the average of all OECD countries.

But is there evidence to suggest that fixed-term employment has significantly increased over time? Figure 3.5 shows fixed-term employment as a percentage of total dependent employment in Germany, the UK, and Spain between 1983 and 2000. In Spain fixed-term employment increases markedly up to 35 percent and it is not before 1995 that this trend levels off. Unlike Spain, fixed-term employment appears comparatively low in Germany and the UK. While in the UK the incidence of fixed-term employment remains fairly stable during the 1980s and early 1990s, in Germany fixed-term employment jumps from around 7 to almost 12 percent in 1997. Thereafter it continues to increase slightly.

Figure 3.4 Fixed-term employment as a percentage of total dependent employment by country, 2000

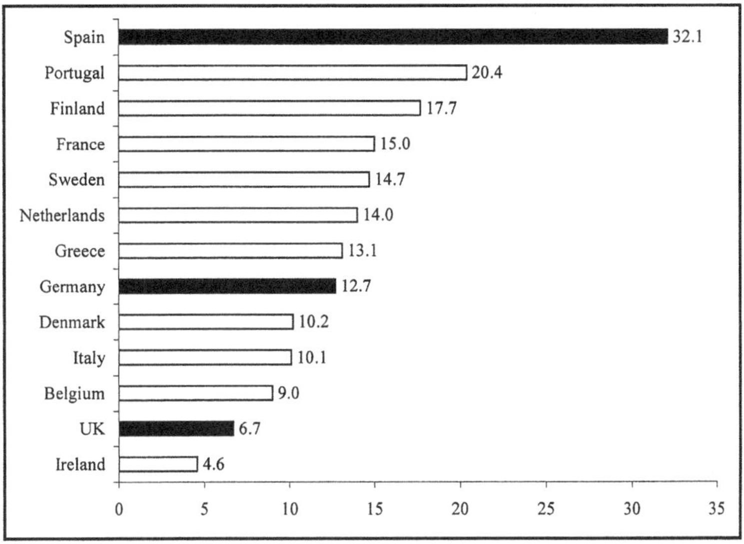

Source: Eurostat (2001).

Figure 3.5 Fixed-term employment as a percentage of total dependent employment in Germany, the UK, and Spain, 1983-2000

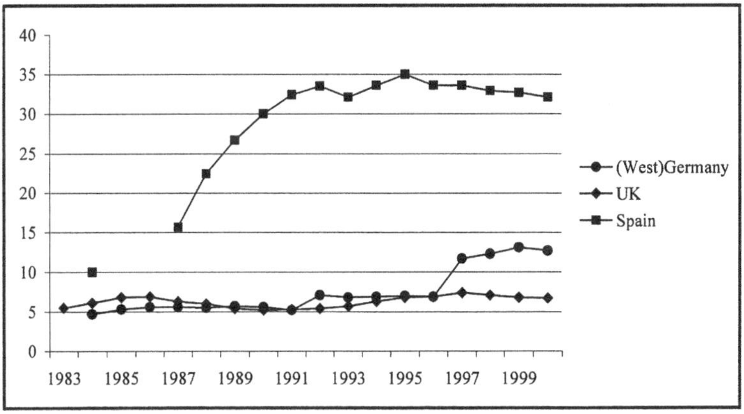

Note: 1983-1991 West Germany, 1992-2000 Unified Germany.

Source: Schömann *et al.* (1998) for the period 1983-1996, Eurostat (various years) for the period 1997-2000.

Figure 3.6 Relative importance of temporary employment by sector in Germany, the UK, and Spain, 1999

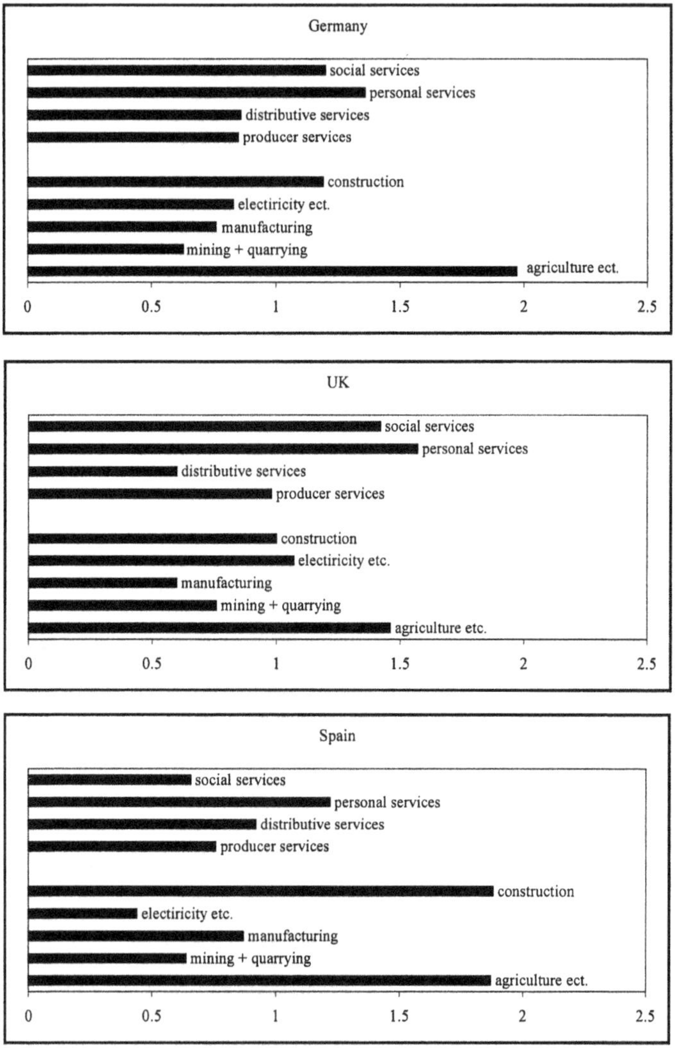

Note: Ratio of incidence of temporary employment in each sector to average incidence for all sectors. The data refer to wage and salary workers only.

Source: OECD (2001).

Yet, as Booth *et al.* (2002) found recently, it is necessary to distinguish among those being in temporary work. Temporary workers include fixed-term employees, but also employees on casual contracts and seasonal workers. Booth *et al.* report major differences in terms of earnings, occupational class, job tenure, promotion prospects, training, and entry into permanent work between workers with fixed-term contracts and workers in seasonal/casual jobs, with workers on fixed-term contracts being better off (see also Gallie *et al.*, 1998).

Figure 3.6 shows the relative importance of temporary employment by sector and lends support to the assumption that the incidence of temporary employment varies greatly between industrial sectors due to differing employers' strategies and labour demand. To illuminate sectoral differences employment is split up into a goods-producing sector (construction; electricity, gas and water supply; manufacturing; mining and quarrying; agriculture, hunting and forestry) and a service sector. Within the latter it is differentiated between social (e.g., health and education services), personal (domestic services; hotels, bars, restaurants; recreational services and entertainment), distributive (e.g., retail trade, wholesale trade; transport) and producer services (financial services; real estate; insurance and financial services) (OECD, 2000b; see also Browning and Singelmann, 1978). In all three countries temporary employment seems particularly important in agriculture, hunting and forestry and much less so in other goods-producing sectors. The construction sector in Spain depicts an exception, showing an outstandingly high incidence of temporary employment. As to the service sector, there is quite some heterogeneity. Temporary employment seems more widespread in the social (with the exception of Spain) and personal services, while its incidence is comparatively low in the distributive and producer services.

To summarise, even though European countries show considerable variation in the incidence of fixed-term employment, non-permanent work appears concentrated on specific sectors. Temporary employment is also highly confined to young labour market entrants and women (see for instance Gallie *et al.*, 1998; Schömann *et al.*, 1998). Changes in the incidence of temporary employment are associated to changes in employment legislation in the three countries under study. To the degree that deregulating measures have been launched and the usage of non-temporary contracts eased, the country-specific employment legislation may in one way or the other impose constraints on employers or give them a relatively free hand in shaping employment relationships. So, the differing levels of temporary employment as well as their repercussions on individual labour market careers have to be seen as being rooted in the country-specific employment relations system and employment protection legislation (see Chapter Four).

Figure 3.7 Part-time employment as a proportion of total employment by country, 2000

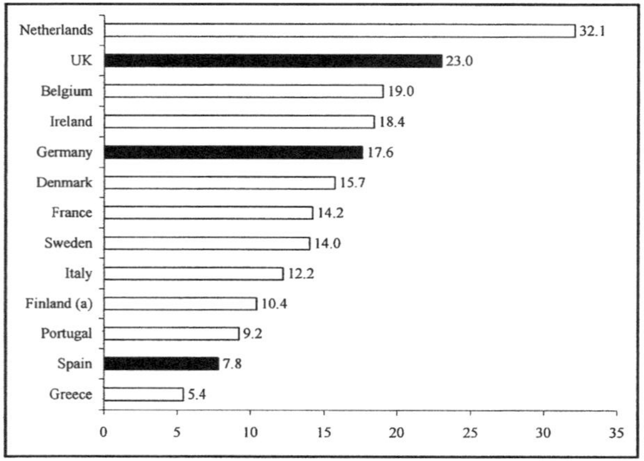

Note: Part-time employment refers to persons who usually work less than 30 hours per week in their main job. Data include only persons declaring usual hours. (a) Data are based on actual hours worked.

Source: OECD (2001).

Figure 3.8 Women's share in part-time employment by country, 2000

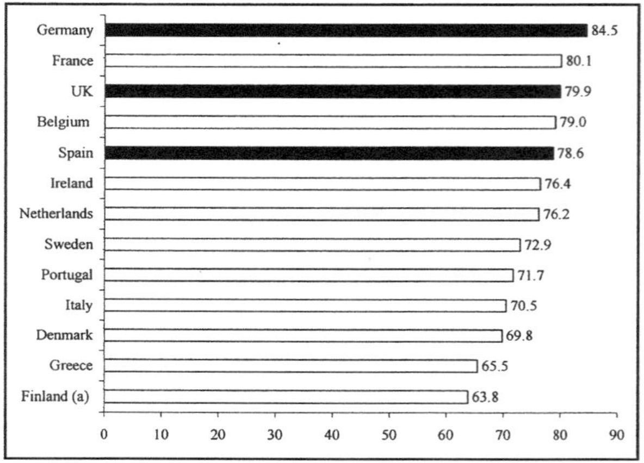

Note: Part-time employment refers to persons who usually work less than 30 hours per week in their main job. Data include only persons declaring usual hours. (a) Data are based on actual hours worked.

Source: OECD (2001).

There is also significant variation in the incidence of part-time employment. Figure 3.7 provides an illustration of part-time employment as a proportion of total employment for the same thirteen countries and again referring to the year 2000. Now the Netherlands has the upper band. The part-time labour market appears also comparatively well developed in the UK. In contrast, the Southern European countries cluster at the other end with a fairly low incidence of part-time employment. In Germany, the proportion of part-time employment is slightly above OECD average (OECD, 2001). In general, part-time employment is a female domain, particularly among married women and mothers (Burchell *et al.*, 1997; Blossfeld and Rohwer, 1997). However, countries show some variation in women's share in part-time employment. As can be seen from Figure 3.8, women's share is highest in Germany with about 85 percent. This compares to 80 and 79 percent in the UK and Spain, respectively.

Next, it is asked whether the three countries under study experience an equal trend towards increasing part-time employment (Figure 3.9). Between 1983 and 1999, in the UK the percentage of women working part-time is high and remains fairly stable. Quite the opposite, from the 1990s onwards part-time employment is on the rise in Germany and Spain. In general the increase in part-time work has to be seen in the context of labour shortages in the 1960s as well as the large-scale shift to services in the late 1970s and early 1980s (Burchell *et al.*, 1997; Bardasi and Gornick, 2000; Blossfeld, 1985, 1995). It has been an active state policy to pull women into part-time work. These women have often had only low educational and occupational skills and the positions offered were mainly low-paid occupations with little prospect of upward career.

Figure 3.9 Part-time employment among women as a percentage of their total employment in Germany, the UK, and Spain, 1983-1999

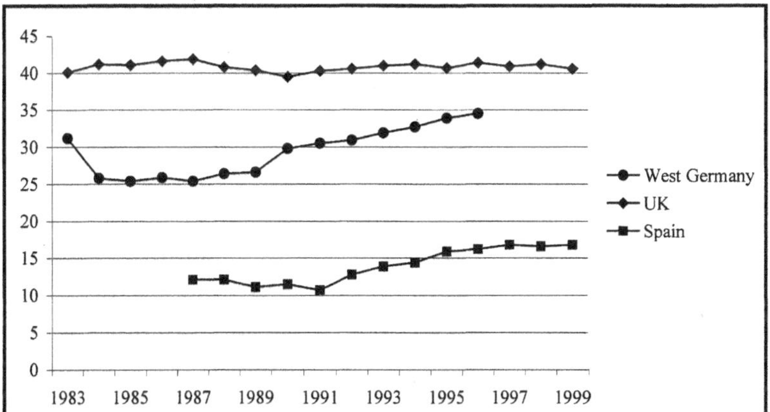

Source: Key Indicators of the Labour Market (KILM 5), ILO, 2001-2002.

Figure 3.10 Relative importance of part-time employment by sector in Germany, the UK, and Spain, 1999

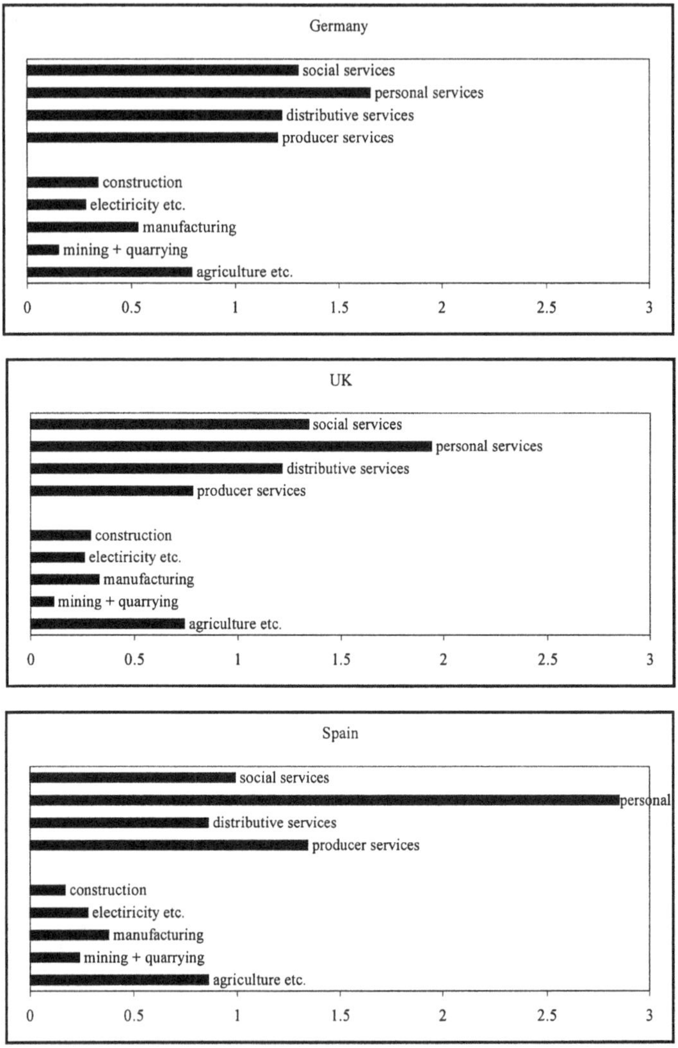

Note: Ratio of incidence of part-time employment in each sector to average incidence for all sectors. Part-time employment refers to usual weekly hours of work of less than 30.

Source: OECD (2001).

One may assume that also part-time employment is highly concentrated in specific industrial sectors. Figure 3.10 shows the relative importance of part-time employment by sector in Germany, the UK, and Spain. In all three countries part-time employment is outstandingly high in the service sector, particularly in the personal services. Interestingly, part-time employment is especially concentrated in personal services in Spain, where the overall part-time labour market remains comparatively under-developed. All in all, personal services offer numerous part-time job opportunities, especially for women. Simultaneously, due to increasing outsourcing and outservicing strategies, there is a growing demand for personal as well as social services. In the goods-producing sector the reverse is true; here there are only a few part-time positions.

Figure 3.11 Marginal part-time employment (working less than 11 hours a week) as a percentage of total employment in Germany, the UK and Spain, 1990-1996

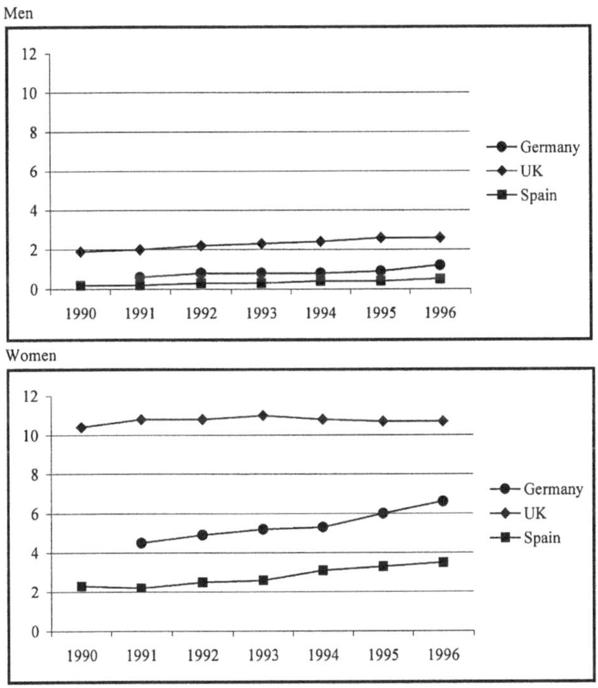

Source: Key Indicators of the Labour Market (KILM 6a), ILO 2001-2002.

Figure 3.11 provides some insight into marginal part-time employment in the three countries under study. With marginal part-time work it is referred to job positions with less than eleven hours a week. These positions are often particularly insecure since they jeopardise one's economic basis and often circumvent employment protection legislation. Three main conclusions can be drawn from Figure 3.11. First, marginal part-time employment is generally low. Second, this labour market is clearly gender segregated with women being more than twice as often on a marginal part-time post. Third, as already highlighted for part-time employment in general, marginal part-time work appears particularly predominant for women in the UK. Yet, it is on the rise in Germany and Spain all over the 1990s, even though this is less obvious among men.

Figure 3.12 Proportion of employers in self-employment by country, 1997

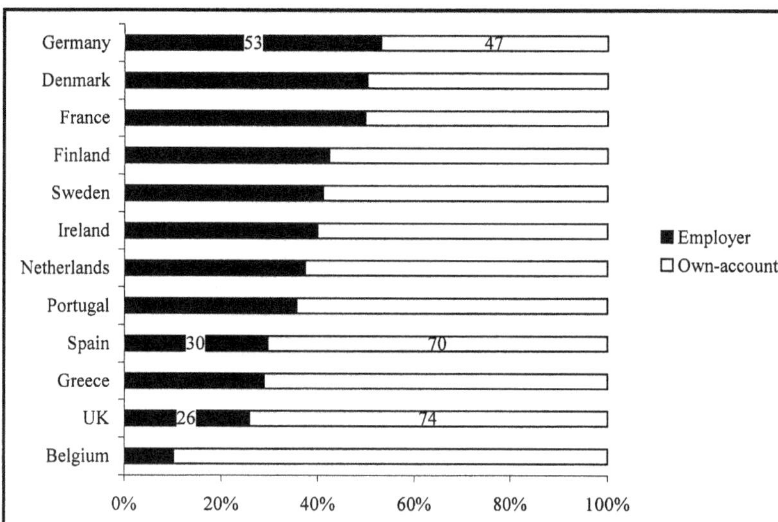

Note: Excluding agricultural sector and unpaid family workers. For some countries, all or part of owner-managers of incorporated businesses is excluded from self-employment.
Source: OECD (2000b).

Figure 3.12 shows the proportion of self-employed with employees (employers) and without employees (own-account workers). In all three countries self-employed are mainly men (OECD, 2000b). However, Figure 3.12 reveals marked differences in the proportion of own-account workers between the selected countries. With the exception of the Netherlands and Belgium, the Western European as well as the Northern European countries are characterised by a high percentage of employers. Nonetheless, since the early 1980s the proportion of own-account workers increases significantly in Germany and in 1997 the respective proportion corresponds to 47 percent (as compared to 39 percent in 1983; OECD, 2000b). Compared to this, the incidence of own-account workers seems considerably higher in the Southern European countries. In Spain approximately 70 percent of those self-employed are own-account workers. In the UK the proportion of own-account workers is even higher and increases markedly form around 62 up to 74 percent between 1983 and 1997 (OECD, 2000b). This has to be seen in connection with some policy measures that have been introduced by the government to ease the process of setting up one's own business (in particular for non-employed) and sub-contracting in public sector (Chapter Four).

To summarise, European labour markets show considerable variation with respect to incidence and pace of change in non-standard employment. Flexi-workers appear to be young, more often women, and employed in specific sectors. But to what extent do the observed trends impact education-to-work transitions?

3.1.3 Education-to-work transition

European countries differ with respect to the smoothness of education-to-work transitions (Blossfeld and Shavit, 1993; Shavit and Müller, 1998). Some countries stand out with markedly high proportions of direct education-to-work transitions, particularly into stable, full-time employment. In other countries transition patterns appear more turbulent, less often direct and into standard employment relationships. Youth unemployment, seen as an indicator for high economic insecurity during the transition to adulthood, has already been discussed. Here the question is raised to what extent entry jobs are temporary and part-time. Atypical work does not necessarily imply insecurity. Depending on the country-specific educational system, temporary or part-time employment may also be part of occupational training. Therefore Figure 3.13 shows the proportion of involuntary temporary (left panel) and part-time entry-level jobs (right panel) as compared to those entered for training reasons.

In Spain temporary entry-level jobs are predominantly involuntary positions. Around 70 percent of school leavers can not find a permanent job. This is in sharp contrast to Germany. As one would expect in a country with an apprenticeship-based training system, temporary contracts are mostly held for training reasons. In the UK proportions of temporary jobs among school leavers are low. This picture alters when studying part-time entry jobs. The part-time labour market is generally restricted in Spain, and hence, comparatively low proportions of part-time entry positions of either type can be observed. Compared to this, part-time employment plays a crucial role for school-leavers in Germany and the UK. However, the rationale behind this is quite different. In Germany part-time employment is clearly related to the dual-system that combines theoretical learning and practical job experience and generally leads to smooth transitions into full-time work (Blossfeld and Stockmann, 1998/1999; Shavit and Müller, 1998; Section 2.2.1). In contrast, there is evidence to suggest that the education-to-work transition is increasingly uncertain in Great Britain (Taylor, 2000): full-time employment as a first labour market destination declined from over 90 percent of men and women in the 1950s/60s to one third in the 1990s (see also Section 2.2.1). Once having entered the labour market, job mobility is comparatively high by European standards, which is a striking feature of the British labour market especially in the 1990s (Booth and Francesconi, 1999).

Figure 3.13 Entry-level jobs held by new school leavers aged 16-29 years one year after leaving education in Germany, the UK and Spain, 1996

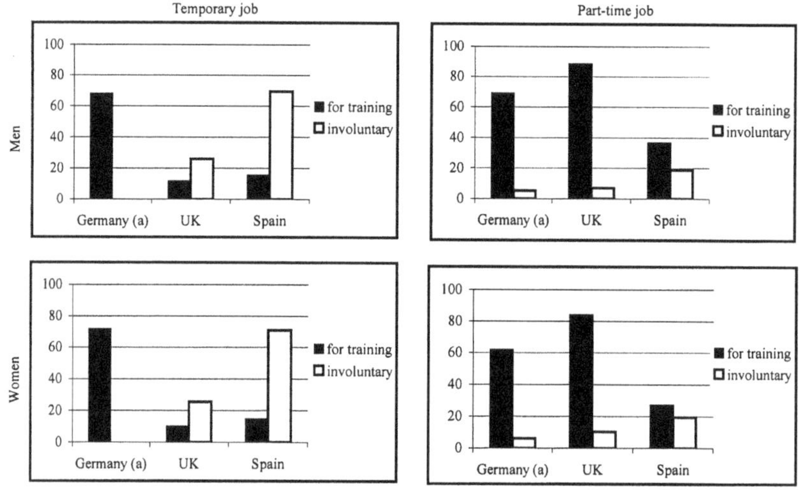

Note: Temporary jobs for training – contract covering a period of training (apprentices, trainees, research assistants, etc.); involuntary temporary job – the person could not find a permanent job; part-time for training – persons working part-time and undergoing school-based education or training; involuntary part-time job – the person could not find a full-time job. (a) Data refer to 1995. No data available for involuntary temporary jobs.

Source: OECD (1998).

3.1.4 Longitudinal employment profiles

The last sections gave an overview on key developments in European labour markets, but the presented figures show only a snapshot of one selected year or a series of annual labour force statistics. Such stock information tends to overestimate the stability of employment profiles since long duration states are systematically over-represented. In globalising labour markets, characterised by ever so fast changing market demands combined with an acceleration of pace and flow of work, these rather static pictures are more and more inappropriate to capture the restructuring process European countries pass through. To give a comprehensive and more adequate picture of insecurity and labour market exclusion, information on the inflows and outflows of labour is required. For instance, longitudinal employment profiles give us a better understanding of how long temporary employment can last, whether individuals enter an unemployment trap, and to what extent own-account work leads to a stable employment career.

Figure 3.14 Distribution of longitudinal employment patterns by country, 1993-1994

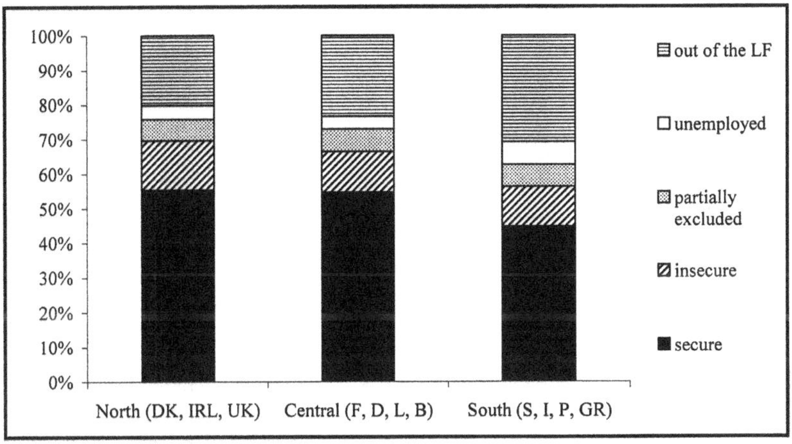

Note: Longitudinal employment patterns have been defined as a proportion of time spent in employment between 1993 and 1994: 100%-secure; 50-99%-insecure; 0-50%-partially excluded; 0%-fully excluded.

Source: Muffels and Fourage (2000), ECHP (1994-1995).

Figure 3.14 shows the distribution of longitudinal employment profiles as defined by Muffels and Fourage (2000). Based on the proportion of time spent in employment, secure employment profiles are contrasted to insecure profiles, partial, and full exclusion. Within the latter it is separated between economically inactive and unemployed. The idea behind this conceptualisation is that 'part year' employment denotes job instability (for a similar approach, see Oppenheimer *et al.*, 1997). To give a broad overview, Muffels and Fourage

(2000) group selected European countries into a Northern European, Central European, and Southern European cluster.

The Southern European cluster reveals a high proportion of fully excluded individuals, while the percentage of individuals in secure positions is comparatively low. This stands in sharp contrast to the other two clusters, where the proportion of secure employment seems higher and fewer individuals are fully excluded. While the share of secure employment profiles appears equally high in the Northern and Central European countries, the former show a higher percentage of insecure employment. In turn, the Central European countries exhibit considerably higher proportions of inactive. With respect to partial exclusion, no differences can be observed.

To conclude, the above figure illuminates that secure and insecure profiles as well as unemployment and inactivity can by no means be grasped time-independently. Rather, with around 55 percent of secure employment patterns in the Northern and Central European countries and 45 percent in the Southern European countries, respectively, substantial annual change in employment profiles can be observed.

3.1.5 Job satisfaction

Various job items determine individual's overall job satisfaction (for a discussion of concept and determinants of job satisfaction see Locke, 1976). For instance, individuals may evaluate their level of remuneration, job security, working hours and working time, as well as working conditions, training opportunities, and distance to job. One may intuitively argue that overall job satisfaction increases with better job protection, prospects, and conditions (e.g., hours worked and overtime) which are commensurate with individual's expectations. This concurs with the results of some recent empirical contributions (Hamermesh, 2001; Clark, 1997; Clark *et al.*, 1996; Kaiser, 2002).[22]

Yet, as shown above, in some countries a significant share of non-standard employment relations can be observed that largely impede individual's predictions of the above specified job characteristics. Moreover, due to swiftly changing opportunities and demands in globalising labour markets, individuals may perceive their future job prospects as less certain, independently of their current labour market situation. More specifically, job security may become a crucial item and appears of particular importance during the transition from

[22] Moreover, job satisfaction appears linked to age, education, industrial sector and occupation, managerial duties, workplace and size of firm, health, marital status, and gender. The results for gender, however, are less clear, with significantly higher degrees of satisfaction for women in Great Britain, insignificant or reversed effects in other European countries (Clark, 1997; Kaiser, 2002).

youth to adulthood, a life span where individuals make long-term, if not life-long commitments that require a stable economic basis. Also, individual's perception of past, present, and future job continuation may significantly shape work and family life of adult workers for instance in terms of job mobility, occupational career as well as career interruption and withdrawal.

Figure 3.15 Job values and quality – job security by age and country

Percentage saying that job security is very important

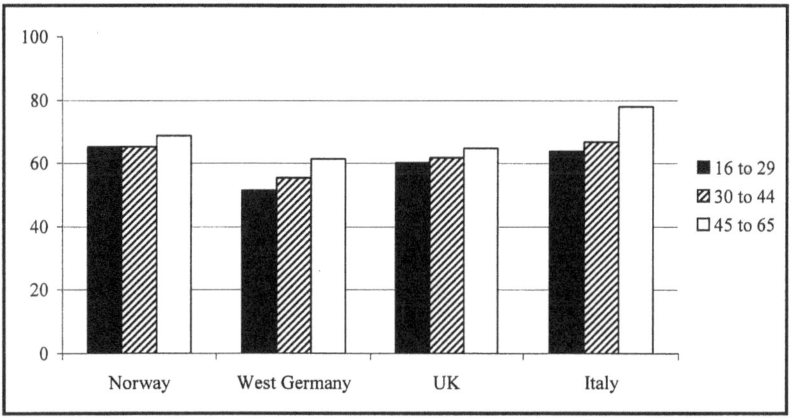

Percentage saying that their job is secure

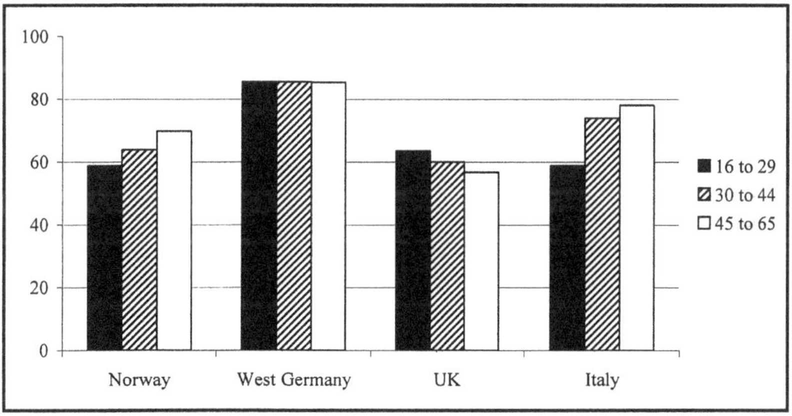

Source: Clark (1998).

Using the 1989 International Social Survey Program Data (ISSP), Clark (1998) provides data on job satisfaction in some selected OECD countries. The study reveals that job security is a highly valued aspect of work life. Figure 3.15 summarises the findings for West Germany and the UK[23] and contrasts these with two selected countries of the regional clusters heretofore used in this study. The upper panel refers to job values and represents the percentage of men and women who state that job security is important to workers; the lower panel shows the percentage of individuals saying that their actual job is secure.

Young attach less importance to job security. In contrast, those 30-44 years old, that is individuals who are most likely in their first years of family formation, state more often that security is a very important job value. Same is true for those approaching the end of their labour market career that is those who are less occupationally mobile and face comparatively low chances to re-enter the labour market after a possible job loss. Looking at the bottom panel of Figure 3.15, it becomes obvious that satisfaction with job security is generally high, particularly in Germany. Around 85 percent declare that their job is secure and this is the case for all three age groups. Quite the opposite, the proportion of individuals in secure jobs appears significantly lower in the UK. The percentage of secure jobs among young corresponds to 64 percent and declines for the two older age groups. Also, young seem to confront less job security in Italy and Norway, but the proportion of individuals on secure posts grows significantly with age.

A more recent study using data from the second round on work orientations in the ISSP reveals that, over the 1990s, overall job satisfaction seems to have declined in West Germany and polarised in Great Britain (Sousa-Poza and Sousa-Poza, 2000). Nonetheless, from a European perspective overall job satisfaction and satisfaction with job security, in particular, seems lowest in the Southern European countries and the UK (Kaiser, 2002).

3.1.6 Summary

The last sections gave an insight into multifaceted differences between the three countries under study and located these in a broader European context. Recent transformations of the world of work appear mostly unidirectional, but pace, degree, and ubiquity of the discussed labour market trends vary considerably. The question that arises at this point is whether distinct employment regimes can be defined. Table 3.1 summarises the main trends observed in the three countries under study.

Firstly, key labour market trends in these three countries have been described. Even though the swiftness of the shift to service sector employment varies, by the late 1990s the percentage of employed in the service sector appears equally high. What makes the three countries distinct is the trend towards female labour

---

[23] Notice that Spain was not included in the study by Clark (1998).

force participation and youth unemployment. As to the former, the role of women's rising labour force participation varies. In Germany and Great Britain, women, and particularly married with children, are mostly part-timers (and marginal workers) while men are the main breadwinners (see also Blossfeld and Drobnič, 2001). In contrast, in Spain the proportion of gainfully employed women remains low and part-time work is rare. Men function as the sole breadwinner (Section 2.2.1; see also Blossfeld and Drobnič, 2001).[24] The discussion of youth unemployment contained a first indication of different degrees of insecurity and the countries can be clearly ranked with outstandingly high youth unemployment in Spain.

Table 3.1 Key characteristics of employment regimes in Germany, the UK, and Spain

	Germany	UK	Spain
Key labour market trends			
Shift to services	High ++	High	High ++
Female labour force participation	(High) +	High	Low ++
Youth unemployment	Low	Intermediate	High
Growth of flexi-workers			
Temporary employment	Intermediate +	Low	High ++
Part-time employment	(High) +	High	Low +
Marginal part-time employment	(Low) +	High	Low +
Own-account workers	Low	High	High
Education-to-work transitions			
Involuntary precarious entry-level job	Low	(Intermediate)	High
Longitudinal employment profiles			
Insecurity	Low	Intermediate	Low
Exclusion	Intermediate	Intermediate	High
Satisfaction with job security	High	Low	Low

Secondly, in all three countries a growth of flexi-workers can be observed. However, the above discussion suggests that disparate flexibility paths have been entered upon. As compared to Germany, flexible work arrangements appear far more wide-spread in Great Britain and Spain. Yet, the latter two countries differ considerably in terms of temporary, part-time, and marginal

[24] The Scandinavian countries form a third cluster, where women traditionally supplement a husband's income. Though not considered here, it should be stressed that also the former socialist countries depict a distinct case where female labour force participation was generally high due to an active state policy to integrate women into paid work.

work. But, at the same time, Great Britain and Spain reveal almost equally high proportions of own-account work. *Thirdly*, as to involuntary precarious entry jobs, Germany and Spain appear as clearly opposed cases. The case of Great Britain is less clear. On the one hand, involuntary part-time and temporary jobs are much more seldom as compared to Spain. On the other hand, however, entry-level jobs seem to function less often as a direct bridge into stable full-time employment than in Germany. *Fourthly*, the discussion of longitudinal employment patterns makes clear that insecurity and labour market exclusion are not evenly distributed in Germany, Great Britain, and Spain. *Lastly*, the presented figures shed some light on differences as regards satisfaction with job security.

The above summary depicts distinct job situations in the three countries under consideration and thus leads to the conclusion that disparate employment regimes can be identified. In view of the various characteristics summarised in Table 3.1 a multitude of questions cross one's mind. One may ask: why do the labour market situations appear so different despite common global challenges? Or more precisely, why is there a fast-paced and pervasive move towards temporary jobs in Spain but not in Great Britain? Why does it seem that education-to-work transitions are smoother in Germany? How can we explain less secure employment profiles in Spain? Or, why does it appear that workers are more concerned about job security in Great Britain? One may even go a step further and ask, to what extent do flexible jobs introduce insecurity in individual job careers? These considerations bring us back to the recurring question of country-specific flexibility paths and the role of institutional filters. The discussion therefore now shifts from the description of labour market trends to the level of labour market regulation, flexibility, and insecurity.

3.2 Labour market flexibility and job insecurity

In contemporary countries, the growing need for flexibility and its impact on labour markets are highly debated issues. Employers have been increasingly asking for more labour market flexibility. Facing high unemployment rates and the pressure of companies, governments attempted to introduce flexibility in work regulations, enhancing the diffusion of various types of atypical work in European countries. But why is this the case?

On the one hand, firms are forced to adapt quickly and efficiently to rapidly changing market opportunities and demands in an age of globalisation. Recent times have been characterised by a large-scale shift towards a technology- and knowledge-based economy and the influx of new technologies since the late 1970s has resulted in a growing demand for multi-skilled labour (Blossfeld, 2002; Gallie *et al.*, 1998; Mills and Blossfeld, forthcoming; Regini, 1997). At the same time, with a growing internationalisation of information, technology, capital flows, and labour markets, national borders become less and less important and firms are increasingly confronted with global competition. This goes hand in hand with profound transformations of production processes towards more flexible specialisation, extensive restructuring of organisations, downsizing, subcontracting as well as commercialisation of the public sector (Castells, 1996; Soskice, 1999). Also, national labour markets have experienced a shift to services as the agricultural sector has declined tremendously and the production sector turned out to be more volatile and dependent on the overall economic cycle (see Section 3.1.1; Klijzing, forthcoming).

On the other hand, the tremendous educational expansion that European countries have experienced has led to changes on the supply side of labour markets (see Section 2.2.1; Klijzing, forthcoming). The educational expansion is leading to an extending involvement of both men and women in higher education, but also to growing female labour force participation rates, and hence, to a catching-up process of women (Blossfeld, 1995; Blossfeld and Drobnič, 2001; Blossfeld and Hakim, 1997a; Shavit and Müller, 1998).

Given these changes on the demand and supply side of national labour markets, one can also expect changes in the way job-seekers are recruited for open job positions. Employers make use of flexible kinds of work arrangements to screen the work potential of labour market entrants, but will also attempt to shed employees or force them into more insecure and poorly paid positions in case of adverse shocks. To put it into other words, increasing economic risks are being passed on to employees through a demand for greater flexibility and an acceleration of the pace and flow of work. This becomes visible in a growing fragmentation of employment profiles, a shift in bargaining power, and less powerful unions (Leisink, 1999). It is assumed that the school-to-work transition is becoming particularly uncertain in contemporary European countries. First, labour market entrants have accumulated little or no experience and established only weak ties to the labour market. So, young adults have less bargaining power as compared to experienced workers who have developed stronger ties. Second, educational certificates are more and more important while specific educational degrees can no longer be seen as ensuring a direct school-to-work transition into a well-paid and secure job position. With the rise in demand for multi-skilled and experienced labour, first-employment seekers are not only to a growing extent competing with those already employed, thus lowering their chances of getting a job. In today's learning societies, they are also confronted with the need for constantly upgrading their skills (Blossfeld, 2002; Regini, 1997).

Due to the above sketched volatility of labour, capital, and product markets, intensified global competition as well as recent demographic trends, European economies face common challenges threatening family, State, and market

(Regini, 2000b). Yet, despite these common challenges, nation-specific adaptation strategies differ. Two opposed ideal-typical responses have been identified: deregulation (i.e., measures to remove or weaken regulatory restrictions and, hence, foster free market play) and concertation (i.e., measures that aim to bolster up regulations based on a general consensus) (Regini, 2000b). From a European perspective, depending on the policy area under study measures of either type can be pinpointed and national adaptation strategies appear mostly a mixture of both responses. Despite the distinct ways to confront recent challenges, there is something that is common to most European countries – the attempt to achieve a higher degree of flexibility.

Yet, flexibility is a widely used and multi-dimensional term. Flexibility may have an impact on different areas of employment relationships, such as inter- and intra-firm mobility, assignment of tasks, adjustment of working-time and wages, as well as on different stages of labour market careers. In line with Atkinson (1984; see also Regini, 2000a; Standing, 1997), one can differentiate between four different types of labour market flexibility:

- *numerical flexibility:* adaptation of the number of employees to labour demands through short-term contracts and layoffs;
- *functional flexibility:* transferability between different job positions;
- *wage flexibility:* wage adjustments;
- *temporal flexibility:* adjustments in working time.

The crucial question that arises at this point is to what extent deregulation and concertation of national labour markets impact individual labour market careers. In general, a restrictive and rigid employment protection system ensures high security in terms of risks of job or income loss. Thus, individual labour market careers appear more predictable and a certain economic basis can be more easily established and solidified. Long-term co-operative employment relationships based on trust evolve, which provide employers and employees with substantial benefits. Provided that long-term employment relationships entail more work commitment, and hence, equip firms with certain prerequisites to master new challenges in times of increasing global competition and rapid technological innovation, employers face high incentives to invest in workers' skills (e.g., to increase workers' productivity) and make use of functional flexibility. For employees this implies better chances to receive work-related training and to climb internal career ladders. Likewise, job satisfaction may be comparatively higher. Enhanced flexibility of employment protection systems may question such a balanced system that is characterised by a largely symmetrical share of power between employers and employees. While restrictive employment protection legislation imposes drastic constraints on firms' options to adjust their workforce swiftly to rapidly changing market demands, deregulating measures open the way for new, soft options. To the extent that flexibility facilitates layoffs, wage adjustments or temporary employment, these measures are likely to lessen the degree of security employees can rely on.

Yet, a relaxation of employment protection legislation does not only impose costs on individual workers. A rigid system may also work as a significant barrier for those trying to (re-)enter the labour market, especially for young job seekers, unemployed or mothers. If they do not manage to enter a permanent post that is commensurate to their skills or fits with their childrearing responsibilities, they are likely to remain 'outsiders'. A rigid system may also impede job experimentation during early labour market careers. Quite the opposite, those already employed on permanent posts enjoy good career prospects and training opportunities and hence are protected 'insiders'. Long-term employment relationships for insiders are thus likely to go hand in hand with long unemployment/inactivity duration for outsiders, accentuating labour market inequality and social exclusion. If a restrictive employment protection system enhances such a closed system, it may also hinder individual job (between-firm) mobility. Restrictive employment protection laws also imply substantial costs for employers. For example, to avoid severance payments employers are presumably more hesitant to fire non-productive workers or a surplus of workers during economic downturns. Rather, employers may introduce wage or temporal flexibility to reduce their labour costs.

According to the main argument of this study, the various discussed flexibility types lead to a growing proportion of workers in various non-standard employment relationships. Yet, these types of labour market flexibility are not necessarily mutually exclusive, but may reinforce as well as cancel out one another (Regini, 2000a). Also, the flexibility types are not seen as equally leading to insecurity; rather, some may introduce insecurity in individual labour market careers, while others may play a crucial role in matching needs of employees. However, as elaborated later, and notwithstanding that non-standard employment relationships may have been accepted voluntarily, these employment relationships imply less certainty about individual job prospects, and thus, question future labour market career and economic household basis.

Recently, definition and measurement of insecurity along with empirical evidences for an increase in labour market insecurity has been debated by several scholars. For instance, Heery and Salmon (2000) propose a three-dimensional definition taking into account the property of jobs (risk of involuntary job loss and uncertainty about the level of remuneration), the property of the environment in which jobs exist (forfeit of job loss, degree of protective labour market regulation), and the subjective experience. In the following, job insecurity is conceptualised as being determined by the likelihood of job or income loss and its consequences. The former is dependent on the property of jobs as well as on personal characteristics. That is, certain job positions may be work-insecure in economic respects. As a consequence of wage flexibility, employees face a high probability that real wages fall. They experience more income insecurity and, consequently, greater difficulties in establishing a solid economic basis. Temporal flexibility may lead to substantial reductions in working hours. Notwithstanding that part-time work may be voluntary, and particularly so for women, it provides lower degrees of income security and most likely does not yield to high degrees of career maturity, nor does it necessarily serve as a stepping-stone to secure, reasonably paid employment. Employees may also be work-insecure due to numerical flexibility. As regards temporary work, these employment relationships entrap individuals in particularly insecure situations since there is less certainty about the continuation of an employment relationship and individual's risk of job loss appears high. At the same time, a weakening of employment protection makes it easier for firms to lay off workers and involuntary job loss often goes hand in hand with an increased risk of unemployment and reduced remuneration. Hence, those who expect their contract to expire soon, those on casual posts only, and those in certain industrial sectors with a high unemployment risk face more contractual insecurity. Apart from this, employees in non-standard employment relationships often lack entitlements to various benefits (e.g., sickness benefit, holiday entitlement and pay, as well as pension entitlement). Above that, certain personal characteristics have been shown to increase the likelihood to experience job or income loss (see for instance Nickell, 1999; Simó *et al.*, 2002a; Kurz *et al.*, 2002).

Figure 3.16 The sources of job security

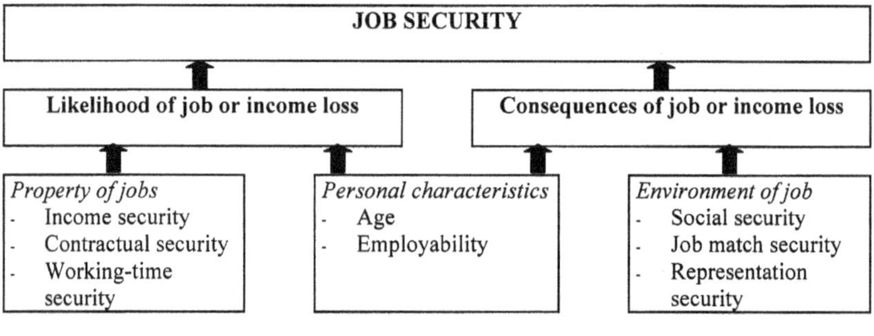

Insecurity is not only attached to the property of jobs, but also to the country-specific and historically grown environment in which jobs exist. First, consequences of job or income loss depend on social security, i.e. the degree of protective regulations that may lower the risk of job loss and absorb economic risks during times of non-employment. Second, insecurity may be substantially lower if employees can rely on representation security, i.e., strong unions and coverage by collective bargaining. Lastly, policies may facilitate labour market (re-)entries, and hence, represent job match security. Additionally, individuals with certain characteristics may perform better in a highly competitive labour market including better chances of re-employment (Alba-Ramírez, 1998; Böheim and Taylor, 2000; Kurz *et al.*, 2002). Figure 3.16 puts these various ideas into perspective.

Yet, the deregulation and flexibility process is likely to affect not only labour market careers, but also individual's psychological well-being, perceptions, and expectations about their labour market career and social life. Several recent empirical contributions provide an insight into individuals' perceptions of growing insecurity in a context of flexibility and intensifying international competition (Heery and Salmon, 2000; Burchell *et al.*, 2002; Gallie *et al.*, 1998). An increase in labour market deregulation and flexibility implies less predictability of level of remuneration, length of contract, number of working hours, and job contents. It may thus lead to lower degrees of job satisfaction and less satisfaction with job security, total pay, and promotion prospects, in particular. Apart from the determinants outlined above, individuals' perception of job security is also likely to be influenced by factors that are independent of the workplace and its environment. For example, those carrying major responsibilities for other family members may feel more insecure than those living on their own.

To summarise, this section interrelates macro-level changes to individual labour market outcomes and perceptions. However, how exactly actual and perceived job insecurity impact individual decision-making and who is particularly losing in such a context remains a theoretical matter which it is dealt with below.

3.3 Research questions, insecurity hypothesis, and operationalisation

In contemporary societies, various macroeconomic changes accompanying the globalisation process lead to increasing uncertainty of future developments and growing instability of social relations. On the one hand, the intense spread of information and communication technologies as well as transport facilities increasingly interlink societies, thereby reducing spatial uncertainties (Breen, 1997). These new technologies thus facilitate the exchange of information around the world and speed up the diffusion of ideas, new forms and patterns of living arrangements. Taken together, the outlined processes open new options and hence may affect individual life planning in several ways. On the other hand, the acceleration of pace and flow of capital, products, and labour on international markets as well as rapid technological advancement increase temporal uncertainties. Social and economic outcomes appear less predictable and individuals are increasingly forced to continuously adjust their individual behaviour to new constraints and demands. All in all, uncertainty in individual, family, social, and political life is more and more pronounced in recent times and implies three different aspects: rising uncertainty about the behavioural alternatives themselves, growing uncertainty about the probability of behavioural outcomes, and increasing uncertainty about the amount of information to be collected for a particular decision (Blossfeld, 2002; Mills and Blossfeld, forthcoming; see also Section 2.3).

From the individual-level perspective, growing temporal uncertainty may become visible in increased job insecurity, and thus, new risks and hurdles to solidify medium- to long-term life course security that is required for making long-term, self-binding decisions. This is because the manifold interactions between the increased volatility of markets, the higher interdependence of regional and national economies around the world as well as their complex interplay with national adaptation strategies are seen as leading to more employment insecurity. The widely discussed insecurity thesis proposes that: *"employment in the developed economies has become more insecure or unstable in the sense that both continued employment and the level of remuneration have become less predictable and contingent on factors which lie beyond the employee's control"* (Heery and Salmon, 2000: 2). Through contingent employment and remuneration, economic risks are being passed on to employees. Stable, standard employment relationships are expected to be increasingly substituted by insecure, non-standard employment relationships and spreading among all kinds of employees. That is, *"the incidence of both job instability and feelings of insecurity is changing and previously secure groups are now finding themselves in a precarious position"* (Heery and Salmon, 2000: 4). Since contemporary societies move towards learning societies, individuals are also forced to constantly upgrade their skills, even though there is less certainty about whether this will pay off in the future (Blossfeld, 2002).

Figure 3.17 The link between labour market deregulation and flexibility and life course decision-making

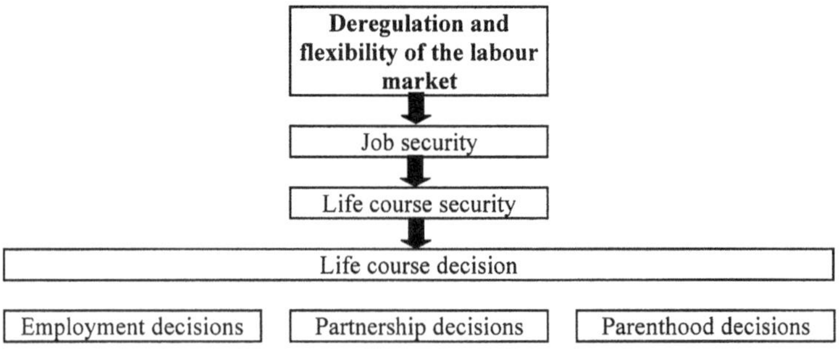

In summary, growing uncertainty on the macro-level triggers a restructuring process within societies, flooding individual life courses. With the emergence of labour market flexibility the nature of employment relationships changes, eroding job security and deeply altering individual career profiles and prospects. The main assumption of this work is that increasing insecurity has a direct impact on individual life course decision-making. Firstly, stable career expectations and a consolidated economic basis allow for life course decisions that involve long-term commitments. Conversely, insecurity should lead to a delay of partnership and parenthood decisions. Secondly, deregulation and flexibility may be seen as influencing factors of work and family life of adult jobholders, introducing insecurity in adult male careers and shaping work orientations of women. Hence, deregulation and flexibility are also assumed to shape individual employment decisions. Figure 3.17 puts the various theoretical concepts into perspective.

The first research question of this study asks to what extent young adults are confronted with job insecurity and whether there is empirical evidence for an impeding impact on transitions to adulthood. More specifically, four research questions will be addressed:

(1) To what extent are labour market entrants unsatisfied with their job security?

The outlined processes are likely to affect individual's perception of the broader political and economical environment, local labour market developments and, consequently, their labour market chances. In turn, enhanced uncertainty about future developments on a societal level and exacerbated insecurity in individual labour market careers may impact individuals' perceptions and expectations about their role as workers, partners, and parents. Yet, to what extent young labour market entrants are unsatisfied with their job security is a matter of empirical analysis. One may also ask: to what extent is there evidence to suggest that obviously insecure job positions carry increased dissatisfaction with job security? Those obviously in work-secure positions may actually feel insecure. The empirical part of this study will inquire into these research questions.

(2) Are some labour market entrants more likely than others to enter directly the labour market and find a stable position? If so, why?

A second research question deals with the investigation of whether young labour market entrants are likely to become holders of precarious jobs at least for a short period of their life. Labour market entry patterns and subsequent job profiles will be studied. Firstly, job insecurity may become obvious in an increased prevalence of non-standard work as well as unemployment and inactivity spells among new labour market entrants. At the same time, it becomes increasingly difficult for school leavers to come up with a job position in accordance with obtained certificates. Those who find a job are likely to be contracted on a time-limited basis only, poorly paid, and often without benefit entitlements. Facing these constraints, some may opt for an extended participation in the educational system rather than becoming unemployed (Offe, 1977). But who is particularly affected by these processes? Secondly, the education-to-work transition clearly determines individual's subsequent work career. The decision whether or not to stay on at school after compulsory education may be decisive in today's learning societies. Increased labour market deregulation and flexibility are likely to have an impact on entry-level jobs, but also on job tenure in general. There may be serious repercussions on future labour market careers if education-to-work transitions proceed through unemployment. Previous unemployment experience does not only seem to increase the risk of future unemployment. Also, entry jobs obtained after unemployment spells are often less well-paid and temporary (Gregg and Wadsworth, 2000). Even successful (direct) education-to-work transitions do not necessarily imply reasonable degrees of stability if entry jobs are temporary and part-time. Here the question arises whether job insecurity at early stages of the labour market career induces adverse labour market outcomes in terms of subsequent unemployment spells, temporary employment, and downward occupational mobility, independent of individual's human capital, gender, family background, and business cycle. So, to what extent does job insecurity increase the risk of social exclusion? For whom are temporary jobs dead-end roads, for whom temporary bridges to secure full-time employment?

(3) Is job precariousness and perceived job insecurity systematically related to men's and women's early living arrangements and partnership formation?

Facing increasing insecurity due to less stable entry patterns into the labour market, young adults may be less likely to make durable relationships, particularly during their early labour market career (Mills and Blossfeld, forthcoming). At the same time, the increasing need of education leads to prolonged educational careers and, combined with increasing labour market flexibility, it carries a certain amount of uncertainty for the rational actor about whether one can find a job that pays off. Once individuals leave the educational system they will therefore try to establish themselves in the labour market first, thereby getting hold off some measure of security. This work aims to contribute to the empirical question of whether individual's job insecurity, and hence uncertainty regarding his or her future labour market career, makes a postponement of partnership formation more likely. Moreover, individuals may opt for a less binding relationship, namely cohabitation (Mills, 2000; Sommer *et al.*, 2000), or be more hesitant to transform cohabitation into marriage. While various previous empirical contributions reveal the repercussions of non-employment on individual's propensity to marry (see for instance, Blossfeld and Huinink, 1991; Liefbroer, 1991) our knowledge of the impact of insecure job profiles remains scant. Whether and, if so, how exactly job insecurity affects first union formation will thus be analysed in the empirical part of this study. It thereby adds to our current understanding of union formation as such, and, more particularly, whether and when young people marry and convert their cohabitation into marriage.

(4) How does job precariousness and perceived job insecurity affect young people's decision to become parents?

Having a child can be increasingly regarded as a decision made by rational actors (Simó *et al.*, 2002b). A solid economic basis and a certain degree of stability in the labour market are regarded as a necessary prerequisite for making such a decision. As a consequence of less stable entry patterns into the labour market it becomes harder for individuals to meet these requirements, particularly at younger ages. But is there evidence to suggest that long-term commitments become less appealing, making a postponement of first childbirth more likely? Since marriage and parenthood still appear to be interconnected events, a postponement of the later transition may also be a mediated effect due to a shift to cohabitation as well as a deferment of first union formation as such. There has not been a detailed analysis of insecurity in young men's and women's labour market profiles and transitions to first parenthood. How exactly job insecurity affects the transition to first parenthood is therefore at this point an empirical matter that will be investigated in this study.

To conclude, a central question of this study is: To what extent are individuals confronted with job insecurity and thus less likely to be ready at all and less likely to be ready early to make life course decisions? The main argument developed here is that in a globalising economy individual labour market profiles are more insecure, and hence, less predictable. The insecurity hypothesis suggests:

> *With increasing job insecurity individuals lack the ability to envisage future developments and to plan ahead, thus implying less life course security. Both job precariousness and perceived job insecurity will therefore make a postponement of life course decisions more likely.*

To capture insecurity, the analysis is centred on actual and perceived job security. With respect to the former, the impact of different activity statuses, employment statuses, and employment relationships will be studied. First, individuals experience varying degrees of insecurity depending on their *activity status*. Men enrolled in education lack the income to solidify an economic basis to make self-binding decisions, while women in such a position face substantial opportunity costs and high hurdles to combine studies with family obligations. Unemployed men and women will presumably wait for re-employment to be in a more secure position. Thus, the propensity as well as the timing of partnership formation and first parenthood is expected to be chiefly attached to finishing educational and occupational qualification and entering the labour market. Yet, gainful employment does not necessarily imply high degrees of life course security. Some may not yet have reached a stable basis due to job insecurity. Thus, on a second analytical level, different *employment statuses* among the employed have to be taken into account and own-account workers, employers, apprentices, and employees are distinguished. Third, the *employment relationship* of employees is described through their employment contract and working hours. Full-time positions are separated from part-time and marginal part-time; within these it is further distinguished between permanent, fixed-term contracts, and casual jobs. It is expected that employees on temporary posts face insecurity in terms of job tenure. During times of high labour market flexibility, employers are more likely to lay off workers (or simply not prolong contracts for workers) on temporary contracts because this is less costly. This may lead to a higher risk of entry into unemployment. With increasing job insecurity part-time posts also gain importance and they do so in several respects. First, a second household income may be necessary if the male earner faces job insecurity. This makes the double household earner model more likely, pulling women into the labour market in general and, due to the double burden of child-rearing and domestic work, into part-time work in particular (Blossfeld and Hakim, 1997b). Second, in times of high labour market flexibility and in a context of little employment protection, not only temporary work but also part-time work may become to a rising extent an option for men to have at least a foot in the labour market while being unemployed otherwise. Men's part-time employment, however, does not open auspicious career opportunities, but may rather imply less career prospects as well as high degrees of insecurity due to lower remuneration, less fringe benefits, and a high concentration in low-skill positions (Oppenheimer *et al.*, 1997; Gallie *et al.*, 1998).

Apart from this objective definition of work-insecure positions, the self-reported degree of satisfaction with job security will be analysed. It is assumed that the individual perception of job security is strongly related to the growing insecurity of employment relationships and those who rate their job as comparatively insecure are probably much more likely to wait for better times and, consequently, more hesitant to make long-term commitments. One may argue that the subjective perception of insecurity plays a more significant role in individual decision processes than the actual employment relationship. At present, however, our knowledge of the relationship between perceived job security and transitions to adulthood is scant.

The above discussion is detached from contextual settings and individual characteristics. Yet, the various previous sections suggest that institutional filters and individual resources play a crucial role. Hence, a second research question within the comparative framework of this study explores their impact and the following section develops the idea of risk profiles.

3.4 Conclusion and the idea of risk profiles

This chapter had a twofold goal. It provided a description of recent labour market restructuring processes in Germany, Great Britain, and Spain, and related labour market insecurity, individual positions of insecurity, and life course decision-making. An idea that runs implicitly and explicitly through the various previous sections is that labour market deregulation and flexibility do not equally exert influence on individual labour market careers. Rather, despite growing common challenges, there remains *room for national systems* to either accentuate or moderate pressures of insecurity (Mills and Blossfeld, forthcoming; Regini, 2000b). Employment protection legislation and employment relations system, education systems, and welfare provision appear to be crucial contextual influences that have to be taken into account. Thus one may ask: to what extent are young labour market entrants in the respective countries sheltered from these processes? *Gender-specific adaptation strategies* are also expected. For men, future job prospects are probably less certain. Before partnering or having a baby they may wish to wait until they have achieved a more solid and secure career-cycle stage rather than run the risk of foregoing chances of upward mobility, further training opportunities, or job experimentation. Female oriented explanations are less straightforward. On the one hand, labour market deregulation and flexibility may increase the availability of flexible jobs, which in turn may facilitate women's labour market (re-)entry and combination of work and family career. It may thus modify their attitudes to work and their work and family identities (Blossfeld and Drobnič, 2001). On the other hand, increasing job insecurity may prevent them from either embarking on a job career or becoming mothers in the first place. Also, since women's career prospects and labour market attachment have grown, opportunity costs of an interruption of work career are substantially higher than in the past. From another view point, it is debatable whether insecurity extends well into adult worker careers. In other words, is there evidence to suggest that increasing *career maturity* filters insecurity? Lastly, the implications of job insecurity are likely to be very disparate depending on whether increases in insecurity are equally spread in a society, or inequality and labour market exclusion are highly confined to *employees with specific resources,* where those resources include educational attainment and occupational standing. All things considered, the above insecurity hypothesis is oversimplified and has to be further elaborated. A second research question of this study therefore inquires into individual risk profiles and the corresponding hypothesis states:

> *Individual degrees of job insecurity are substantially filtered by institutional arrangements in one's country of residence, gender, career maturity, and individual resources. These various filters are highly interdependent, determine life course security, and shape men's and women's work and family life. One may therefore identify diverse adaptation strategies depending on the context under study.*

The following chapter provides a discussion of institutional filters and elaborates the question to what extent these matter in the life course transitions under study.

4 The role of institutional filters

4.1 Comparing institutional context

As discussed in the previous chapter, profound transformations in the global economy and the intensification of competition on an international scale are assumed to lead to a transformation of the world of work. Deregulation and flexibility have been described as key concepts to adjust to very fast changing market opportunities and demands. Yet, countries differ with respect to the 'flexibility route' they have entered upon (Esping-Andersen and Regini, 2000). Requirements for labour market flexibility vary and its insertion strongly depends on a country's production system and industrial relations structures. Also, flexibility may be directed at different target groups and enhance as well as hamper individual labour market chances. So one may ask: to what extent do these structural changes on the macro-level shape individual-level decision-making processes (Blossfeld, 2002; Blossfeld and Müller, 1996; Blossfeld and Prein, 1998)? From a different angle, it is also important to stress that various nation-specific, historically grown arrangements in educational systems and welfare state provisions either accentuate or moderate these processes and that individual life courses are embedded in these country-specific institutional contexts (Blossfeld, 2002; Mayer, 1997; Mills and Blossfeld, forthcoming). A question that arises at this point is whether and to what extent country-specific institutions and structures mediate the outlined macro processes.

The following sections describe salient characteristics of the nation-specific institutional context and deal with four related theoretical questions. Why is there a growing requirement for labour market flexibility and in which area of employment relationships? Which flexibility path has a country entered upon? What is the target group and the impact of enhanced flexibility on labour market careers? And, what is the role of nation-specific institutions? In view of these theoretical questions, the discussion shifts to differences in employment relations systems and the German, British, and Spanish flexibility route will be described in more detail in the next section. It follows with an illustration of the intervening impact of educational systems and a brief description of respective systems in the selected three countries (Section 4.3). Section 4.4 is devoted to a discussion of different welfare regimes and gender divisions of work.

4.2 Employment relations and flexibility routes

Industrialised countries vary considerably with regard to their employment relations systems. Major differences manifest themselves in terms of types of work councils, collective bargaining systems, and union coverage as well as labour legislation, all of which patently frame the country-specific nature of industrial relations. This observed diversity translates into unequivocal differences as regards occupational structures and industries, collective bargaining and union coverage, type of employment relationships, and thus, job security (Soskice, 1991, 1999; Streeck, 1992). Various approaches have been proffered to capture these differences. For instance, several authors differentiate between 'open' and 'closed' employment relations (Sørensen, 1983). Others classify market economies as 'co-ordinated' or 'uncoordinated' (Soskice, 1999; see also Soskice, 1990); DiPrete *et al.* (1997) identify 'individualist' versus 'collectivist' regimes. What these approaches have in common is a distinction of employment relations systems where industrial relations are rather decentralised, free market forces prevail, and competition is largely unconstrained. These are contrasted to more centralised systems that offer a relatively high degree of labour market protection through regulation.

The United States, but also Great Britain are commonly described as open employment systems. Employees lack security due to generally weak labour unions, low coverage by collective bargaining, and a weak protective labour legislation. Confronted with ever so fast changing opportunities and demands in a growing global market, employees are less shielded against market risks than workers in countries with relatively closed employment relationships. As will be discussed in more detail later on, since individual's resources play a crucial role in matching processes (DiPrete *et al.*, 1997) and school-to-work transitions are less clear-cut (Blossfeld and Stockmann, 1998/1999; Shavit and Müller, 1998), young and poorly qualified individuals suffer most from increasing insecurity in these countries.

Quite the opposite, the Central and Nordic European countries as well as Spain and Italy are characterised by rather closed employment relationships and centralised collective bargaining (see for instance Regini, 2000b). Those already employed are fairly protected in an age of globalisation while increasing economic and social risks are basically passed on to the economically inactive, that is young job-seekers, unemployed, and mothers trying to re-enter the labour market after career interruptions. Strong occupationally segmented labour markets and restrictions in labour law impede individual mobility in these so-called collectivist regimes (DiPrete *et al.*, 1997). Yet, this cluster is characterised by a great deal of diversity. For example, as discussed in more depth later on, Spain stands out as an extreme example of an insider-outsider labour market.[25]

As illustrated in Chapter Three, in most European countries there has been a shift towards more insecure, atypical employment. However, since distinct types of employment relations systems frame nation-specific adjustments to common challenges in times of intensifying global competition and rapidly changing market opportunities and demands, deregulation measures vary considerably among European countries (Esping-Andersen and Regini, 2000). For instance, the degree to which firms enjoy freedom in shaping employment relationships, and thus, can introduce flexibility in employment relationships, is clearly restricted in some countries, relatively unconstrained in others. Taking into account these various ideas, Regini infers that

> *"[..] in some cases – such as Britain, Ireland, and Denmark, as well as to a lesser extent the Netherlands and Sweden – flexibility has acquired the role of a general principle on which the working of labor markets is based and of the guiding principle that informs all new legislation and social partners' strategies. There is a tendency in these countries to intervene with a few general rules that apply to all workers, leaving ample regulatory autonomy to the social partners. [...] In other cases – such as France, Germany, Spain, Norway, and Italy – although measures to deregulate the labor market have been introduced, they have been contradicted by others meant to reregulate it. Or, more important, they have been conceived as limited and partial exceptions to the general rules that apply to a labor market and are not called into question as such. That is to say, they are introduced as controlled experiments designed to inject flexibility into some or other segment of the labor market, but they are subject to monitoring and possible revocation and in no case intended for generalized extension" (Regini, 2000: 11-12).*

A similar divergence can be observed for collective bargaining systems. The degree of centralisation puts obstacles in employer's path to determine wage levels (Marsden, 1995). While over the 1980s, collective bargaining systems have been decentralised in European countries (Katz, 1993), a number of countries turned away from this general decentralisation trend over the 1990s. Currently, countries have been divided into two clusters, those with an ongoing decentralisation of the bargaining structure and those showing a decentralisation with more co-ordination (Regini, 2000). Table 4.1 contrasts European countries along the various discussed dimensions.

With respect to employment relations and level of flexibility, the three countries under study entered upon opposed routes with varying effects on

[25] Though this study does not focus on Eastern European countries it is noteworthy that with their sudden exposure to global competition and the breakdown of the socialist political system at the beginning of the 1990s, these countries rapidly moved from closed to open employment systems. While the socialist systems provided high job security to all employees alike, the more recent labour market entry cohorts suffer unknown degrees of job insecurity (see for instance, Róbert and Bukodi, forthcoming).

individual labour market careers. The following discussion describes their salient characteristics and centres on main developments over the 1980s and 1990s.

Table 4.1 Classification of responses to common global challenges by European economies

	Labour Market Regime (entry and exit)	Wage Bargaining (bargaining structure)
Types of response (traditional alternatives and actual trends)		
Rigidity/flexibility		
(a) Flexibility as controlled exception	I, D, F, E, N	
(b) Flexibility as general principle	GB, EI, NL, DK, (S)	
Centralisation/decentralisation		
(a) Decentralisation with more co-ordination		I, NL, N, EI
(b) Decentralisation without more co-ordination		GB, F, E, DK, (S), (D)

Note: D = Germany, DK = Denmark, E = Spain, EI = Ireland, F = France, GB = Great Britain, I = Italy, N = Norway, NL = the Netherlands, S = Sweden.
Source: Adopted from Regini (2000b).

4.2.1 Germany – Flexibility as a controlled experiment

The German economy has been described as flexibly co-ordinated (Soskice, 1991, 1999; Mayer, 1997). A significant importance is attached to long-term co-operative employment relationships based on trust. In this respect, it has been argued that the German vocational training system, widespread workers' councils within firms, and the extensive coverage by collective bargaining strongly determine the nature of employment relationships (Soskice, 1999; Soskice and Schettkat, 1993). As will be described in more detail in Section 4.3.1, employer organisations, work councils, and unions are agents in the German vocational training system that safeguards a clear-cut match of school, training, and work (Soskice, 1991; Soskice and Schettkat, 1993). Through their involvement in workers' councils, employees gain rights of codetermination, are much more committed to firm decisions (concerning hiring, firing, working hours, and other aspects of the work environment), and establish co-operative relations with the employer (Schettkat, 1995; Soskice and Schettkat, 1993). Unions are widespread and organised in industry-specific umbrella associations (such as VERDI, the world's largest union). In collective bargaining rounds basic labour agreements are laid down for regions and industries. This leads to a high degree of intersectoral distinctions and the bargaining system has thus been described as moderately centralised (Bispinck, 1997). Due to the unions great influences and collective bargaining, negotiations of wages are more than a matter of rules but have a clearly fixed tariff agreement (*Flächentarifverträge*). These agreements are mandatory for all employers associated with an employers' associations.[26] Hence, the German collective bargaining system gives only little leeway to introduce wage flexibility (Soskice, 1991). Also, the employment legislation is comparatively restrictive and provides reliable protection against dismissal for all workers on permanent full-time and part-time posts. Dismissals have to be objectively given according to the length of employment and seniority of the employees. Moreover, the involvement of workers' councils in dismissal decisions also poses strong restrictions on employers (Schettkat, 1995).

With the globalisation of markets and increasing unemployment, the highly regulated employment system appeared more and more outdated and a debate on its efficiency flared up, which intensified over the 1980s and continues until today. Employers called into question the efficiency of the classical German model of labour organisation. They argued that the German system was too rigid to allow for fast and efficient adjustments to new labour demands and asked for more wage and numerical flexibility in labour relations through a weakening of collective bargaining agreements and dismissal protection. As a reaction, the government introduced various deregulative measures, among which the so-called opening clauses (*Öffnungsklauseln*) in collective agreements and the Employment Promotion Act (*Beschäftigungsförderungsgesetz*) were the most important. At the same time, dismissal protection remained initially unmodified. Opening clauses were first introduced in 1993 after heavy conflicts between unions and employers in the metal industry in East Germany. They allow for tariff agreements for specific businesses with serious economic difficulties (*Härteklauseln*), hence more wage dispersion (Bispinck, 1997; Dombois, 1999; Fuchs and Schettkat, 2000). These cautious changes in sectoral regional tariff agreements brought about increasing disregard of current tariff in other sectors. In the bargaining rounds of 1994 employers managed to limit increases in pay rates and came to a temporary agreement to cut pay scales, particularly for supplementary payments (Bispinck, 1997). Since 1997, opening clauses have also been put into practice in the West German metal industry (Fuchs and Schettkat, 2000). The Employment Promotion Act was introduced in 1985. While fixed-term employment was previously highly regulated and bounded to specific conditions, the new legislation facilitated the usage of fixed-term

---

[26] The degree of organisation of employers is exceptionally high (more than 90 percent) (Fuchs and Schettkat, 2000). If demanded by unions or employers associations, collective agreements can also be broadened to those employers who are not members of employers' associations.

contracts, allowing employers to contract new employees on a fixed-term contract for up to eighteen months (Bielenski, 1997). First restricted to a five year period, the legislation has been extended, substituted by the Part-time and Fixed-term Contract Act, and revised over the 1990s. In 1996, the maximum length of fixed-term contracts has been prolonged up to two years. In these terms, flexibility shall be deemed the exception to labour law, extending employers' course of action in times of high unemployment and as such characterised by impermanence (Bielenski, 1997). A further enactment in 1985 guaranteed equal treatment of part-time (with the exception of those working less than 15 hours per week) and full-time employment in terms of labour legislation as a matter of principle. After all, in 1996 the government relaxed dismissal protection, exempting employees in small and medium-sized companies (Fuchs and Schettkat, 2000).

Talking about the German flexibility route, a special note on developments in the East German labour market after unification in 1990 is required. With the beginning of the Cold War, the Federal Republic of Germany (FRG) and the German Democratic Republic (GDR) entered on disparate paths and distinct institutional arrangements crystallised. These in turn brought about discrete political, economic, educational, and welfare systems. While the FRG set up a social market-economy and a liberal, pluralistic, and democratic state evolved, the GDR built up a socialist state based on a one-party-system and characterised by collectivism and a state-controlled employment system. Low productivity aimed at full employment and there was officially no unemployment (Sackmann, 2000). In contrast to the former FRG, sectoral shifts occurred only modestly in the GDR and service sector employment never became more significant as employment in the production sector (Geißler, 1996). Certain incentives as to dwellings and earnings were offered to pull workers into specific industrial sectors. Also, low incomes pressured partners and parents to be in gainful employment, and thus, women's employment was high (Huinink *et al.*, 1995a). After the fall of the Berlin wall, the sudden opening-up of the economy and the restructuring of the labour market led to a tremendous rise in unemployment rates, in particular for women, unskilled, and semiskilled workers, along with significant changes in employment careers as well as family life (Diewald *et al.*, 1995; Huinink *et al.*, 1995b). While tensions on the West German labour market eased during the early 1990s, unemployment rates in the Eastern part surpassed those in the Western part and remain approximately twice as high.[27]

---

[27] In October 2003 registered unemployment reached 8.0 percent in West Germany and 17.3 percent in East Germany (http://www.arbeitsamt.de/hst/services/statistik/kurzinformation/bundesgebiet_wo/index.html [18.11.2003]).

With the change of government in 1998, policy makers partly broke new ground in labour legislation. Of primary importance are the foundation of a so-called Alliance for Jobs (*Bündnis für Arbeit*); the enactment of a new early retirement legislation; the abolition of restrictions of dismissal protection in small enterprises; and the introduction of social security contributions for marginal part-time employees in 1999. Due to persistently high unemployment, stagnating economic growth, and growing insolvency proceedings particularly in small and medium-sized companies as well as excessive national debt, the Schröder government came under heavy attack in recent years. The so-called *Hartz* concept, as elaborated by a government-appointed committee, has been implemented recently, including the formation of personal service agencies, the promotion of self-employment (*Ich-AG* and *Familien-AG*), the introduction of so-called *Mini-Jobs* to encourage low-paid employment along with bridge money for those aged 55 and over on unemployment benefit.[28]

To summarise, empirical data shows that temporary employment according to the new law has been scarcely utilised (Bielenski, 1997). Over the 1990s, the prevalence of fixed-term contracts has only slightly increased. Scholars thus identify only a remote effect on employment (Bielenski, 1997; Hoffmann and Walwei, 1998). All in all, temporary employment is particularly high among young labour market entrants and functions in many cases as a stepping stone to permanent employment (Klammer and Tillmann, 2001). This provides an indication of companies' strategy to take on workers on fixed-term contracts for a probationary period (Bielenski, 1997). Temporary employment is more widespread in small and medium-sized companies, the public sector, low-skilled occupations, and East Germany (Klammer and Tillmann, 2001; Kurz and Steinhage, 2001). The latter has to be seen in connection with the various employment-creation measures (*Arbeitsbeschaffungsmaßnahmen*) aiming to re-integrate the unemployed in the labour market (Klammer and Tillmann, 2001; Hoffmann and Walwei, 1998).

4.2.2 Great Britain – Flexibility as the guiding principle

The British development throughout the 1980s can be best described by strong neo-liberalism and free market play (Mayer, 1997; Soskice, 1999). Deregulation has been seen as a remedy for inflexibility, and thus, as the solution for high unemployment rates. Conservative governments reformed employment law to restrict the protection against unlawful dismissal; reduced some benefits, tighten eligibility requirements, increased sanction possibilities and work incentives for unemployed people, introduced in-work-benefits for low-income households,

---

[28] More information can be obtained at: http://www.dgb.de/themen/hartz/index_html [18.11.2003].

and abolished Wage Councils (i.e., institutions that formerly negotiated minimum income thresholds) (Deakin and Reed, 2000; Dingeldey, 1998; Towers, 1994). This has led to a decreasing proportion of the working population that is protected by employment rights. Furthermore, the weakening of employment protection legislation and the reduction in unemployment benefits have lowered the degree of social security that employees can rely on during times of unemployment. The deregulation of the British employment protection system has fostered a so-called 'hire-and-fire' system that allows employers to adjust their workforce fast and efficiently to competitive demands. As a result, a highly deregulated labour market evolved in which employees are comparatively less secure, but where opportunities to (re-)enter the labour market are greater than in more regulated employment systems.

Employers in Great Britain have increasingly used temporary and part-time employment to achieve higher levels of labour market flexibility (Dex and McCullogh, 1995; Gallie *et al.*, 1998). In this respect two important implications should be noted. First, the part-time labour market is comprised of a highly heterogeneous set of jobs which are often work-insecure and mainly taken by women (Burchell *et al.*, 1997; Hakim, 1998). Second, since British deregulation measures have had strong repercussions on both employees in non-standard employment relationships and permanent full-time employees, employer's incentives to contract new employees on a time-limited basis are comparatively low from a European perspective. Although limitation for the conclusion of time-limited contracts is lacking, this has not led to a tremendous spread of short-term contracts in Great Britain as compared to other countries such as Spain (Booth *et al.*, 2002; Simó *et al.*, 2002a; Schömann *et al.*, 1998; Section 3.2, 4.2.3).

The described processes have been accentuated by the strong decline in trade unions and coverage by collective bargaining. Conservative governments have systematically eroded the power of unions by placing restrictions on the right to strike and releasing employers from any obligation to negotiate with unions on wages and working conditions (Booth and Francesconi, 2003; Deakin and Reed, 2000; Dingeldey, 1998; Gallie *et al.*, 1998; Heery and Abbott, 2000; Ladipo and Wilkinson, 2002; Machin, 2000). Consequently, security of employees in Great Britain has been declining throughout the 1980s and 1990s. Aside from these legal changes, alterations in the composition of the workforce are accentuating the decline in the level of trade union membership. This refers to (i) a growth in part-time workers, a relatively stable proportion of temporary workers, and an increase in own-account workers, all of whom are less likely to belong to a union; and, (ii) a decline in firm size. The increase in non-standard employment relationships is related to increasing female labour force participation, an expanding service sector that has above all created job opportunities for female part-timers, and the government's promotion of self-employment as a route back to the labour market for the unemployed. The decline in firm size has to be seen in connection with the radical commercialisation of the public sector that introduced more insecurity in employment relationships (Ladipo and Wilkinson, 2002; Morgan *et al.*, 2000). Formerly characterised by large companies, employment in the public sector is more and more confined to small firms where employers make increased use of sub-contracting and outsourcing strategies. The latter has contributed to the increase in own-account workers.

Since the change of government in 1997, the so-called *Third Way,* as pursued by the Labour Party under Tony Blair, has modified the picture (Deacon, 2000; Dingeldey, 1998). There continues to be a high degree of deregulation and flexibility in the labour market but, at the same time, active labour market policies also aim to increase rates of transition from welfare benefit receipt to work (Deacon, 2000). Re-employment and re-skilling are also goals. To combat unemployment, new programmes under the rubric of the *New Deal* were introduced to help older unemployed individuals, as well as young people, disabled persons, lone parents, and partners of the unemployed back into the labour market.[29] Incentives to work were increased, but national insurance unemployment benefits were restricted further, and sanctions for not working were strengthened. To some extent there is also a departure from previous policy, as can be seen in the introduction of a statutory *National Minimum Wage* in 1999. The transformation of the Family Credit benefit to Working Families Tax Credit was intended to raise the resources going to low income working families. Furthermore, with the adoption of the EU's Part-time Working Directive, benefits on-hand to part-timers have been put on a par with those available to full-timers. There is also some indication that employment protection and union recognition is to be strengthened (Deakin and Reed, 2000).

To summarise, increased deregulation and flexibility have led to a substantial job growth in Great Britain, while in most other European countries job growth came to a halt or was even reversed during the 1990s. Also, unemployment rates appear to be comparatively low. However, workers are relatively exposed to market forces. Flexibility is mainly employer-led, with third party intervention and welfare state support largely lacking. The labour market deregulation served to exacerbate insecurity and to increase inequality: there is a strong polarisation in 'work-rich' and 'work-poor' households (Gregg *et al.*, 1999a), long-term unemployment is concentrated on a minority of households and individuals with certain characteristics (Gregg and Wadsworth, 1996; Arulampalam, 2000), chances of upward mobility are rather limited (Dearden *et al.*, 1997), wage and

---

[29] The so-called *New Deal for Young People* was first introduced in 1998. It followed with a series of New Deals for further target groups: long-term unemployed, disabled persons, lone parents, partners, musicians and for the '50plus' (for an overview see for instance Cebulla, 2001).

income inequality have increased (Machin, 1999; Jenkins, 2000), and poverty rates have gone up (Dickens and Ellwood, 2001; Jenkins and Rigg, 2001).

4.2.3 Spain – Flexibility at the margin

Since the end of the dictatorship in 1975 the Spanish economy has undergone a complete transformation. The Francoist model was characterised by high trade barriers, restricted access to foreign markets that protected domestic firms against foreign competition, guaranteed lifetime jobs, as well as a suppression of unions. With the opening-up of the Spanish economy for international competition, industrial restructuring and modernisation, and the large-scale labour shifts due to the unprecedented educational expansion and increasing female labour force participation, Spain experienced a profound structural change and intensive economic crisis between 1975 and 1985 (Jimeno and Toharia, 1994; Tamames, 1995; Banco de España, 1994; Garrido Medina, 1992; De Miguel Castaño, 1993). The unemployment rate grew tremendously and unevenly and women and youth were particularly affected by this economic crisis (Jurado Guerrero, 1995). Since the economy as a whole was profoundly changing and employers were risk-adverse, companies argued that firing regulations were too restrictive and would work as a disincentive to give job-seekers open positions (Bilbao, 1999; Falguera i Baró, 1999; Aragón Medina and Cachón-Rodríguez, 1999; Prieto, 1999; Recio, 1994). As a reaction to the economic development during this period and the enhancing pressure of companies asking for more flexibility in work relations, from the early 1980s onwards the government put forward various labour policies in an attempt to make the rigid employment system more flexible (Cousins, 1994; Moran, 1991; Falguera i Baró, 1999). Temporary contracts were regulated through the *Pactos de la Moncloa* and later the Workers' Statute of 1980 (*Ley del Estatuto de los Trabajadores*). At first, temporary contracts for young people aged 16-26 (in 1980 the age limit was expanded to 28) searching for employment were implemented. These short-term contracts could last between sixteen months and two years and a 75 percent subsidy of employers' social security contributions was granted as an incentive for employers. This program ended in 1981, but, over the 1980s, new reforms were launched, expanding the possibilities to use short-term contracts. The key year of the succeeding labour market reforms was 1984. New types of temporary practical training and practice contracts (*contrato en prácticas, contrato de aprendizaje*) as well as a so-called 'employment promotion fixed-term contract' (*contrato de promoción de empleo*) were introduced (Toharia and Malo, 2000). With this reform the government enabled employers to evade the 'principle of causality' that was previously in force, and thus, firms gained a free hand in the recruitment of employees; short-term contracts could be arranged with any new employee. The trade unions, which at that point were still rather weak and just building up, accepted the reforms reluctantly (Burgess, 2000). What followed was a recovery period between 1985 and 1990 (Jimeno and Toharia, 1994), characterised by an unprecedented growth in aggregate employment. However, the price paid for this economic recovery was growing employment flexibility. The distribution of fixed-term contracts increased markedly during this period to more than 30 percent of all dependent employees, which is extraordinarily high compared to all other European countries (Schömann *et al.*, 1998; Section 3.2). In this respect, two important implications have to be kept in mind. *First,* the flexibility of employment relations was peculiar in that it had been directed at individuals outside the labour market trying to (re-)enter, while job security of those already employed under permanent full-time contracts persisted (Toharia and Malo, 2000). Due to prevailing strong legal obligations that protect permanent employees from dismissal, employers opted for short-term contracts to lower their labour costs and to more easily, cheaply, and quickly adjust to economic conditions. This has to be seen in connection with the main objectives of trade unions and employers that were clearly oriented towards a protection of workers and their workplaces, particularly male breadwinners. As a result, an insider-outsider labour market evolved (Lindbeck and Snower, 1987, 1989; Sørensen and Kalleberg, 1981) that was based on, first, a strong segmentation between permanent and fixed-term employment, and, second, a strong segmentation between employees and economically inactive/unemployed. Compared to 'insiders', those trying to enter the labour market for the first time are most likely to start their labour market career on a fixed-term contract (OECD, 1998). *Second,* not only is the proportion of school-leavers starting their labour market career in a temporary positions extraordinarily high, but also, while in other countries such as Germany temporary contracts among labour market entrants are mostly training contracts, young Spaniards are often forced to take work-insecure positions without any qualification content (OECD, 1998; Section 3.1.3). During the first years of their labour market career, only a few manage to become insiders, while the majority are moving between fixed-term jobs and unemployment spells.[30] Consequently, job turnover rates have increased substantially, job insecurity is highest among women and youth, and career entry processes are characterised by a lack of security (Bentolila and Dolado, 1994; Dolado *et al.*, 2002; see also Iannelli and Soro-Bonmatí, 2001).

In the 1990s, this employment protection system came under heavy debate and the government launched reforms in an attempt to revive permanent employment (Dolado *et al.*, 2002; Toharia and Malo, 2000). In 1992, the

---

[30] This is mainly due to temporal restrictions of fixed-term contracts within the same firm. After three years of temporary employment within the same firm fixed-term contracts have to be converted into permanent contracts.

minimum length of fixed-term positions was increased. In 1994, the 1984 law was abrogated to a great extent since a new regulation eliminated the fixed-term contract as a general case. Firing costs for permanent workers were also lowered. In 1997, new permanent contracts with lower dismissal costs were introduced and incentives for these types of contracts granted. Yet, despite these changes in employment legislation, the strong segmentation of the labour market persists. At the same time, the economic recession of the 1990s led to a sharp rise in unemployment, which stood above 20 percent during the mid-1990s. It is only recently that an economic recovery is taking place (ILO, 1999).

The described segmentation of the labour market has important implications for the dynamics of wage setting. During the 1980s, the Spanish bargaining system was strongly centralised (Toharia and Malo, 2000). Overall, collective bargaining adhered to uniform wage increases throughout the economy and it is only since the end of the 1980s that an increase in collectively bargained wage dispersion can be observed. However, the degree of centralisation of collective bargaining has been described as moderately decentralised since it is characterised by a low degree of co-ordination and a low level of synchronisation (Toharia and Malo, 2000). Furthermore, the effectiveness of collective bargaining agreements reached at the industry level can be questioned due to the high incidence of employment in small firms which have no union protection and often insufficient information on collective bargaining agreements. Above that, the strong insider-outsider division is likely to lead to a self-reinforcing process since permanent workers have a much stronger bargaining power and will exert more pressure on collective bargaining than temporary workers who enjoy less legal protection and would be dismissed first (Bentolila and Dolado, 1994). Therefore, the Spanish industrial relations system provides little security for new labour market entrants.

As a result of the deregulation measures, the Spanish labour market of the 1990s is characterised by: an extraordinarily high proportion of fixed-term contracts and a high concentration of this type of less stable employment among youth; high unemployment which is very often long-term; low rates of job mobility; low levels of part-time employment; and low female labour force participation (Schömann *et al.*, 1998; OECD, 1998, 2001; ILO, 1999). All in all, the relatively closed Spanish employment system hampers females and youths in the start of a stable job career (see also Blossfeld, 2002; Simó *et al.*, 2001).

4.2.4 Comparing the three flexibility routes

A central hypothesis of this work is that the nation-specific flexibility routes determine individual labour market entry and career processes. Contrasting countries with rather open or closed employment relationship systems shows that the following disparate repercussions have been pinpointed:

Table 4.2 Main characteristics of open and closed employment relationship systems

Open employment relationship systems	Closed employment relationship systems
- Widespread risky employment, low economic security for most jobs	- high concentration of risky job positions among specific groups seeking access to the labour market (youth, women, unemployed)
- individual's resources play a crucial role and determine labour market outcomes	- individual's resources are of minor importance in job-to-person matches
- labour market entry is comparatively easy	- labour market entry is problematic, particularly under conditions of high general unemployment
- short unemployment duration	- longer unemployment duration
- relatively high rate of job mobility	- low rate of job mobility

Source: Adopted from Mills and Blossfeld (forthcoming).

Some scholars surmise that the openness of labour markets gives shape to flexibility (Mills and Blossfeld, forthcoming). In closed systems flexibility is likely to show up as functional flexibility for labour market insiders while numerical flexibility is mostly confined to those trying to (re-)enter the labour market. By contrast, in highly deregulated labour markets with open employment relations numerical flexibility is far more widespread, wage and temporal flexibility intensively used.

As to the three countries under study, Great Britain stands out as the country that has long had a relatively high degree of flexibility and change in the labor market. Due to employers using flexibility as the guiding principle, firms are able to adjust more swiftly and less costly to competitive demands (Regini, 2000b); employment relationships are rather short-term and trust relations are of little account (Soskice, 1991; Marsden, 1995). Yet, while Great Britain appears to be highly competitive on global markets, it lacks social solidarity. The prevalent 'hire-and-fire' system imposes almost no restrictions on numerical flexibility through layoffs and the various deregulation measures have had strong repercussions on all employees alike. Also, the collective bargaining system has been intensively decentralised, opening the way to introduce wage flexibility in labour relations. By and large, the British laissez-faire style has led to comparatively low overall job security.

Quite the opposite, in Germany more weight has been put on social solidarity. Within the closed employment system employees are largely shielded against market risks. Atypical employment remains a controlled experiment and as such confined to employees with specific characteristics and young labour market entrants (Regini, 2000). At the same time, the restrictive employment protection system, a co-ordinated bargaining system, and strong unions hinder employers from inserting numerical and wage flexibility. Rather, employers are much more prone to make use of functional flexibility for permanent workers (Marsden, 1995). At present, however, in view of persistently high unemployment and serious drawbacks in terms of competitiveness on global markets, the German flexibility path has come under heavy attack.

Though also in Spain flexibility has been seen as a controlled experiment (Regini, 2000), labour market outcomes are different. Over the 1980s, in both countries, Germany and Spain, similar reforms have been launched with the intention to facilitate temporary employment. However, in Spain the fast and intense shift from one of the most rigid employment protection system to a highly flexible labour market was peculiar in that flexibility has been introduced at the margin (Toharia and Malo, 2000), thereby deepening the so-called insider-outsider divide. Temporary employment contracts increased speedily and pervasively and are thus widely spread and less often transformed into permanent employment. This contrasts to a rather modest increase in Germany, a comparatively low share of temporary employment, a high concentration among labour market entrants and workers with certain characteristics, and high chances of attaining a permanent post (Klammer and Tillmann, 2001; Kurz and Steinhage, 2001). But how come? There is no single explanation for these disparate labour market outcomes (OECD, 1999a). As shown above, in Spain young labour market entrants do less often profit from apprenticeship contracts but rather fixed-term contracts without training content. By contrast, the German apprenticeship system ensures more often high occupational qualification, a direct entry into the labour market, and a smooth transition into permanent employment. This relates to the strong emphasis on long-term co-operative employment relationships and mutual trust in the German economy (Soskice, 1991). In this context, fixed-term contracts may be seen as a screening device to identify the work potential of future permanent employees, but there is no such tradition of social partnership in Spain. At the same time, few restrictions on the usage of fixed-term contracts and substantially higher firing costs for permanent employees work as an incentive for employers to contract new employees on a temporary basis to adjust easily and more speedily to changing labour demands.

In view of these country-specific flexibility routes, one may next ask, to what extent do nation-specific arrangements in education and welfare filter insecurities?

4.3 Educational system and education-to-work transitions

Labour market entries are not only regulated by the State through active employment policy, but also through the educational system (Allmendinger, 1989; Allmendinger and Hinz, 1997; Shavit and Müller, 1998; Regini, 1997). Educational systems have a significant impact on the timing of labour market entries as well as the recruitment process itself; vocational training systems predefine the subsequent labour market career and shape individual's chances of occupational mobility and risks of labour market exclusion. Yet, educational systems differ greatly among European countries. There is little convergence in the type of education and education-to-work transitions comprise a series of transition events, whose nature, speed, and sequence typically vary (Shavit and Müller, 1998).

In recent times, school-to-work transitions appear less standardised, less straightforward, and increasingly insecure (Bernardi, 2000; Gallie *et al.*, 1998; Taylor, 2000). With a movement towards life-long learning societies, education is also less confined to pre-career phases (Blossfeld, 2002). With the increasing global competition deeply altering the demand side of labour markets, a shift towards skilled jobs, and hence, the growing importance of high educational attainment, it is also fundamental whether and to what extent national educational systems manage to adapt to the challenges of expanding global markets (see also Regini, 1997). The efficiency of educational systems in terms of labour market integration is therefore debated and various researchers identify comparative advantages and disadvantages of nation-specific systems (see for instance, Blossfeld and Stockmann, 1998/1999). In many European countries the political debate is to a great extent shaped by these processes. European governments introduced labour policies and measures in the field of education and labour market integration to increase participation rates in secondary education, assure high standards in vocational education, smooth education-to-work transitions, particularly into stable full-time employment, lower unemployment rates, and provide equal chances to all individuals (Ryan and Büchtemann, 1997: 310).

In the past a principal focus of research has been the investigation of nation-specific institutional arrangements in education and their impact on education-to-work transitions. Numerous research contributions explore variations in transition systems and the nature of education-to-work transitions, the relationship between education and transition outcomes, as well as inequalities in the latter two processes (see among others, Brauns *et al.*, 1999; Blossfeld and Shavit, 1993; Gangl, 2001; Heinz, 1999; Shavit and Müller, 1998).[31] This

[31] For example, drawing data from the European Union Labour Force Survey, national Labour Force Survey data, and school leaver's surveys, the CATEWE project (Comparative

research underpins that across European countries labour market entry patterns among youth are becoming more insecure as can be seen in the increased prevalence of unemployment, part-time work, and inactivity among new labour market entrants as compared to more experienced workers (Bernardi, 2000; Gallie *et al.*, 1998; Schömann *et al.*, 1998; Taylor, 2000). While the increase in employment instability appears particularly pronounced in Southern Europe, Northern European countries hold a more intermediate position, and labour-market entrants in Central European countries seem to experience lower degrees of insecurity (see for instance, Bernardi, 2000; Mills and Blossfeld, forthcoming; Kurz and Steinhage, 2001).

In view of these cross-country differences, various scholars put forward ideal-typical typologies of educational systems. According to Allmendinger's (1989) two-dimensional typology, the efficiency of an educational system may be expressed by the level of 'standardisation' (i.e., the degree to which the quality of education meets the same standards nation-wide) and the level of 'stratification' (i.e., the proportion of a cohort that attains the maximum number of school years in a specific educational system). Hannan *et al.* (1997) differentiate three dimensions of transition systems, namely standardisation, educational differentiation, and the strength of linkages between education and employment. Shavit and Müller (1998) discuss three main dimensions of national institutional variations: stratification, the scale of tertiary education, and occupational specificity. Referring to these typologies, a discussion got under way as to whether and to what extent European countries can be grouped into ideal-typical clusters or placed on a continuum of national variation. For instance, some scholars juxtapose countries with a rather institutionalised vocational education system embedded in occupationally segmented labour markets and countries with a relatively open employment relations system where individual resources play a crucial role in person-to-job matches (OECD,

---

Analysis of Transitions from Education to Work in Europe) aims to develop a more comprehensive conceptual framework of education-to-work transitions in different national contexts (For more details consult the homepage at: http://www.mzes.uni-mannheim.de/projekte/catewe/Homepage.html [26.09.2002]). The CHEERS project (Careers after Higher Education: a European Research Study) focuses on education-to-work transitions of graduates in Europe and provides findings on conditions and dynamics of labour market entry processes as well as employment and job prospects of graduate students in the 1990s (http://www.uni-kassel.de/wz1/cheers.htm [26.09.2002]). The TSER STT project (Schooling, Training and Transitions) analyses transitions from school to work and labour market flexibility (http://www.cordis.lu/improving/socio-economic/area2.htm [26.09.2002]). A European Network on Transitions in Youth has been founded to bring together researchers from various European countries and enhance a regular exchange on new findings as well as challenges on international comparative research (Raffe *et al.*, 1998).

1999b). Kerckhoff (2000) sets side by side so-called Type 1 societies with highly stratified and standardised educational system and Type 2 societies, characterised by less standardisation and stratification and a less clear-cut education-to-work transition. The CATEWE project proposes a distinction between three ideal-typical groups of countries. First, Germany, Austria, and Denmark are grouped into one cluster characterised by a strengthened system of vocational training at upper secondary level. In contrast, the educational systems in Ireland and the UK as well as Belgium and France are typified as providing more often general rather than vocational qualifications. The third proposed cluster comprises the Southern European countries, characterised by lower levels of overall educational attainment and less vocational specialisation. In the following the focus shifts to the educational systems in the three countries under study.

4.3.1 The educational system in Germany

The German system shows high institutional continuity since the end of the Second World War. The highly standardised and stratified educational system leads to a strong linkage between educational achievement and labour market outcomes; labour market entry is clearly structured and strongly dependent on achieved educational credentials (Blossfeld and Stockmann, 1998/1999; Shavit and Müller, 1998; Scherer, 2001). A main characteristic of the German system is the distinction between general and occupational education. With respect to the former, the school system offers three educational routes following primary school: lower secondary school (*Hauptschule),* middle school *(Realschule),* and upper secondary school (*Gymnasium* or *Fachoberschule*) (EURYDICE/ CEDEFOP, 1995). The smoothness of school-to-work transition has been put down to the German vocational training system, particularly the dual-system that combines theoretical learning and practical job experience at the work place (Müller *et al.*, 1998; Shackleton, 1995; Winkelmann, 1996). This dual system ensures standardised and nation-wide recognised certificates, provides general rather than firm-specific skills, and offers a good basis for further qualifications (technicians, master craftsman), and thus, to career ladders within firms. As compared to countries with different training systems, youth unemployment rates are rather low (OECD, 1998; Section 3.1). In particular, entry patterns of vocationally qualified leavers are more often smooth and immediate whereas the least qualified are more likely to show less stable and less direct entry patterns (Brauns *et al.*, 1999; Kurz and Steinhage, 2001). The same can be said for unemployment risks as well as chances to exit from unemployment (Brauns *et al.*, 1999; Klammer and Tillmann, 2001; Kurz *et al.*, 2002). Standardised vocational training is also an important factor as regards the emergence of an occupationally segmented labour market (Brauns *et al.*, 1999; Blossfeld and

Stockmann, 1998/1999; Scherer, 2001; Shackleton, 1995). Within the occupational labour market the transition to work is fairly structured and stable; chances of promotion and degree of job security are dependent on recognised occupational qualifications acquired rather than educational credentials obtained at school. However, the great value of certificates for occupational outcomes can also be viewed as a drawback of the system, making it rather rigid and leading to low levels of job mobility (Blossfeld and Stockman, 1998/1999; Brauns *et al.*, 1999).

The educational system in the GDR headed for a different direction. Education-to-work transitions took place earlier, which may be seen as a result of generally shorter educational enrolment (Hullen, 2001; EURYDICE/ CEDEFOP, 1995). Working life and studying were also more clearly tied through state control. Education policy and labour market policy were laid out to train individuals for specific occupations and pull them into specific sectors to balance manpower shortages. More specifically, the state restricted access to higher education. Individual abilities and political attitude were crucial items in this respect. This implies a restricted selection of educational and occupational paths depending on economic demand but, at the same time, less uncertainty and few economic risks at early career stages due to relative certainty about prospective employment career and extended policy measures to reconcile work and family life (Huinink *et al.*, 1995b). A main objective of education policy in the GDR has been to offer equal chances and employment prospects for men and women, but the efficiency of this system has been questioned. Career opportunities were rather limited for more recent cohorts and determined by social class, the economic and occupational composition highly segregated, incomes unequally distributed (Huinink *et al.*, 1995a; Sørensen and Trappe, 1995).

As shown in Section 2.2.1, there has been a tremendous educational expansion and an overall shift to higher education in both parts of Germany. Over the 1980s and 1990s, the proportion of pupils having obtained the university entrance ticket (*Abitur*) and the proportion of students increased significantly, while the percentage of unskilled decreased tremendously (Geißler, 1996). However, this educational expansion seems to have lowered the value of educational credentials (Schömann *et al.*, 1995). Nonetheless, in both East and West Germany educational attainment and vocational education remain of particular importance as to occupational status, wages, and career opportunities (Diewald *et al.*, 1995; Schömann *et al.*, 1995).

4.3.2 The educational system in Great Britain

The educational system in the UK is highly decentralised. Due to self-governing powers, definite education and training systems are available in England, Wales, Northern Ireland, and Scotland (EURYDICE/CEDEFOP, 1995). The British educational system has been described as rather loosely coupled to the labour market (Blossfeld and Stockmann, 1998/1999; Shavit and Müller, 1998; Steinmann, 1998/1999). Level of standardisation and stratification are low, strong market orientated on-the-job training prevails. After six years of primary school, pupils continue in either comprehensive schools (90 percent of all schools), grammar schools, secondary modern schools, or public schools (EURYDICE/CEDEFOP, 1995). These are mainly all-day schools. At the age of seven, eleven, fourteen, and sixteen nation-wide qualification tests have to be passed. Of particular relevance is the so-called *General Certificate of Secondary Education* (*GCSE*, before 1986 *CSE* and *GCE O-level*), which is usually obtained at the end of compulsory education at the age of sixteen. Pupils may continue in upper secondary education to either obtain *A-levels* (advanced levels) that are equivalent to the *Abitur* in Germany and serve as an entrance ticket to universities or receive work-based job-specific training, or participate in vocational courses (Steinmann, 1998/1999). Those continuing at the university normally obtain a *Bachelor of Arts* (BA) or *Bachelor of Science* (BSc) after a three year undergraduate course. Following these a one year postgraduate course gives them a *Master of Arts* (MA). The end of studies does not always coincide with the end of educational qualification since studies are often followed by firm-specific training, for instance on a part-time basis after labour market entry.

Over the 1980s, the action of *Industrial Training Broads* weakened the possibilities to co-ordinate and regulate occupational qualifications nation-wide. Occupational qualifications are still undertaken in occupational schools for certain fields but apprenticeships, uniform nationwide exam standards, and binding curricula are no longer very common. Consequently, there is only low transparency of qualifications and a comparatively strong importance is attached to certificates which are general and not occupation-specific. Occupational qualification is mainly on the job and oriented at business-specific requirements; training is frequently continued within the company (Kerckhoff, 1990).

During the past twenty years, the government has attempted to improve the output and the efficiency of vocational training, with programs such as *Youth Training*, *Modern Apprenticeships*, *National Traineeships*, and *Youth Credits* (for an overview see e.g. Steinmann, 1998/1999; Hillmert, 2001). Over the last three decades, Great Britain has moved away from early selection on educational routes to more comprehensive schools and experienced a tremendous educational expansion, particularly after 1988 when the *General Certificate of Secondary Education* was introduced (EURYDICE/CEDEFOP, 1995; Heath and Cheung, 1998; Steinmann, 1998/1999; McVicar and Rice, 2001). Since the 1997's elections, the Labour Party has revived the discussion and the so-called three priorities '*education, education, and education*' have become the theme of the debate.

4.3.3 The educational system in Spain

Since the late 1970s, Spain experienced an unprecedented educational expansion particularly among women, and thus, an increased postponement of labour market integration (Garrido Medina, 1992; Delgado, 1995; Simó *et al.*, 2001, Billari *et al.*, 2002). The Spanish educational system is partly regulated on a nation-wide level by the government, partly governed by the seventeen autonomous communities. At present, seven communities have even full powers (EURYDICE/CEDEFOP, 1995). It can be classified as a system with a high degree of standardisation and medium degree of stratification (Ianelli and Soro-Bonmatí, 2001; Simó *et al.,* 2001). Curricula, certificates, and examinations are well-defined and universally valid. Over the last two decades, three main reforms have been launched: the Basic Law regulating the Right to Education (*Ley Orgánica del Derecho a la Educación*, 1985), the Basic Law on University Reform (*Ley Orgánica de Reforma Universitaria*, 1983), and the Basic Law on the General Structure and Organisation of the Education System (*Ley Orgánica de Ordenación General del Sistema Educativo*, 1990) (EURYDICE/CEDEFOP, 1995). The latter has led to a gradual reformation of compulsory education over the 1990s and the following discussion concentrates on this new legislation.

The educational system is divided into (non-compulsory) pre-school education (*Educación Infantil*), primary education for 6-12 year-olds (*Educación Primaria*), followed by compulsory secondary education up to age sixteen (*Educación Secundaria Obligatoria*). Afterwards, pupils may continue for two more years to obtain the *Bachillerato* or take up intermediate and higher vocational training (*Formación Profesional*). Access to university is highly selective since an exam at the end of upper-secondary (*Selectividad*) determines chances to be accepted for a course of study. The subject area in upper-secondary education (sciences or humanities) predetermines the branch of study. The vocational training system is organised as a dual system that combines theoretical learning and job experience and offers a rather general content of teaching. Training is basically provided in schools and training centres governed by the National Employment Institute (*Instituto Nacional de Empleo*) and the Autonomous Communities (EURYDICE/CEDEFOP, 1995). Despite this organisation of vocational training, and in contrast to other countries with a dual system like Germany, school-to-work transitions are more much often indirect through unemployment (Section 3.1). Due to the stepwise implementation of the Basic Law on the General Structure and Organisation of the Education System that has been completed only quite recently, improvements in output and efficiency of the educational system may become visible slowly but surely.

4.3.4 The three educational systems in comparative perspective

The three nation-specific educational systems vary on several grounds. Table 4.3 contrasts key characteristics of each system.

Table 4.3 Typology of the three educational systems

	Germany	Great Britain	Spain
Level of standardisation	High	Low	High
Level of stratification	High	Low	Intermediate
Level of occupational specificity	High	Intermediate	Intermediate
School-work linkage	Strong	Weak	Weak

Germany and Great Britain built up opposite systems. As Allmendinger and Hinz (1997) point out, the German and the British general system are stratifying and therefore rather comparable. What makes the two systems distinct is the degree of institutionalisation and differentiation following general education. The German system offers a highly standardised occupational qualification in a dual system. Training is mainly regulated by corporative actors, functions as an integration tool, and thus, ensures high degrees of job match security. In contrast, the British system is rather uncoordinated; the match between qualifications and jobs is much less clear-cut. What matters in job-to-person matches is the accumulation of ascribed credits rather than specific occupational certificates. In contrast to Germany where employers can rely on nation-wide recognised certificates, the recruitment of new employees is a more complicated task in Great Britain, where the lack of reliable and comparable educational standards necessitates business-specific, on-the-job training. In the deregulated low-trust environment of Great Britain, employers fear the poaching of trained work force. On the contrary, mutual trust and co-operation between work councils, employer organisations and chambers of commerce and industry provide the basis for training in Germany (Marsden, 1995; Shackleton, 1995). At the same time, employees have strong incentives to invest in transferable rather than specific business skills because the flexible business climate prevents employers from guaranteeing lifetime or long-term employment (Soskice, 1991). As compared to Germany, young labour market entrants experience therefore less job match security in Great Britain.

In Spain job-seekers also face lower degrees of security vis-à-vis their German counterparts. However, the rationale behind this is quite different. Entry processes of young adults in Great Britain are stepwise and they often take place through informal channels (Heath and Cheung, 1998; Lindley, 1996; Scherer, 2001). Yet, not least due to the 'hire-and-fire' system, unemployment rates as well as temporary employment among youth are much lower than in Spain (ILO, 1999; Schömann *et al.*, 1998; Section 3.1). In contrast, even though the Spanish system can be classified as one with a high degree of standardisation and a medium degree of stratification, and despite the fact that Spain aimed to copy the German dual system, school-to-work transitions proceed more often through unemployment and temporary employment (Simó *et al.*, 2001; Section 3.1). This inefficiency of the apprenticeship system also becomes obvious in comparatively low proportions of labour market entrants with vocational qualification. By and large, this may be linked to the lagged and stepwise transformation of the educational system, particularly during the speedy economic growth period, and no tradition of social partnership (see also Regini, 1997).

4.4 Welfare state regimes and gender division of labour

Between 1940 and 1970, modern countries have developed diverse welfare states with the intent to guarantee society and individual welfare, particularly through ensuring a minimal standard of living in the event of unemployment, accidents, disability, pregnancy or retirement (Esping-Andersen, 1999). The various European welfare states have been rooted in national ideologies and entered upon different routes according to the question of how to protect and promote the welfare of the population. This applies to the provision of education, labour market structure, and, especially, to labour market and family policies.

Clustering countries with respect to their specific interplay of State, family, and market in welfare provision, Esping-Andersen proposes ideal-type clusters, namely the liberal, the conservative, and the social-democratic (Esping-Andersen, 1999). The US, and to a lesser extent Canada and Great Britain, belong to the liberal welfare states. Passive labour market policies predominate and there is only moderate support for those in need. The dominant theme is a more laissez-faire policy based on the belief that individuals carry the brunt of responsibility for their fate. Quite the opposite, in the social-democratic regimes (Norway, Denmark, and Sweden) where much more emphasis is put on active labour market and taxation policies. As compared to the liberal model, individuals are largely shielded against labour market risks; full employment, gender equality, and a fair income distribution are on the political agenda. Another key element of the social-democratic policy is the highly progressive income tax system that acts as a further incentive for women to contribute to the household income. The conservative welfare state is strongly transfer oriented and social policies are made in order to decommodify economically inactive individuals (Germany, the Netherlands). It promotes the traditional division of labour in the family, and hence, backs wives and mothers who take care of household and child-caring. In addition to these ideal-type clusters, some scholars have identified a family-oriented welfare state model (Italy, Greece, and Spain) (Jurado Guerrero, 1995; Reher, 1998; see also Ferarra, 1996). Quite similar to the liberal welfare model in terms of labour market policy and welfare state provision, its distinctness becomes obvious in the fact that it is up to family and kinship to shield individuals against economic and social risks.[32]

Over the 1980s and 1990s, a trend towards heightened competition among nation-states as well as progressing welfare state retrenchment can be observed. Challenges that welfare states have to confront include changes in family structure, occupational structure, and individual's life cycle, along with changes in economic conditions and demographic trends, all of which are assumed to jeopardise the future functioning of welfare states (Esping-Andersen, 1996). The responses of European welfare states differ due to dependencies of the route they are following (Mills and Blossfeld, forthcoming; Regini, 2000). For instance, cutbacks on welfare state expenditures are particularly severe in the liberal welfare states, where means-tested benefit systems reign.

In the following sections, the main focus will be on employment- and welfare-sustaining policies that are particularly meaningful for first-employment seekers, unemployed persons, and employed women in Germany, Great Britain, and Spain. Governmental support for labour market integration and the unemployment benefit system provide to varying degrees security, and thus, determine individual labour market careers. Scope and generosity of family allowances and services also vary (Gauthier, 1996; Sainsbury, 1999). Welfare states provide different incentives for gainful work, regulate labour markets through socio-political measures, and thus, frame job careers as well as work and family identities (Allmendinger and Hinz, 1997). Taking into account that women take major responsibility in child-rearing, the pivotal question is how couples divide work. As Gonález-López (2001) puts it, women's employment strategies can be threefold, that is women can opt for a linear pattern (i.e., continuous labour force participation), an interrupted pattern (quitting and returning), and a curtailed pattern (permanent withdrawal). Their employment strategies do not only depend on values, attitudes, and labour market chances, but also to a great extent on labour market structure and employment regulation, as well as on welfare state support (Pfau-Effinger, 1996). For instance, an extended part-time labour market offers women the opportunity to combine job career and motherhood more easily. Maternity leave regulations, availability of child-care facilities, and job security are also important determinants.

---

[32] Esping-Andersen's typology fails to capture the rapid transitions in former socialist countries entering the capitalist global economy. With the sudden opening of borders and the breakdown of the state-socialist regimes, the whole country-specific institutional system experienced unknown competitive challenges, introducing new insecurities and calling into question institutional arrangements.

4.4.1 The German welfare state

The German welfare system belongs to the so-called conservative cluster of welfare regimes, and as such, it is strongly transfer oriented. Social policy intends to decommodify economically inactive (Esping-Andersen, 1993, 1999; Kurz, 1998; Meyers *et al.,* 1999) and is oriented towards men's standard employment relationship while it provides strong incentives for women to carry the brunt of household and child-care responsibilities (Dombois, 1999; Hinrichs, 1996; Pfau-Effinger, 1996). The male breadwinner family, and, complementary, the female homemaker family are thus key concepts, even though these assumptions are increasingly incompatible with actual work and family life (Dombois, 1999; Hinrichs, 1996). While the parental leave legislation allows for an employment interruption of up to three years and family-oriented benefits are comparatively generous, the provision of child-care facilities, especially for small infants, is rather low. At the same time, there is an extended part-time labour market for women. With regard to women's employment choices, it is thus likely that being a mother decreases the probability of woman's full-time work, and increases the probability of part-time work and inactivity (Blossfeld and Rohwer, 1997). Mothers also face great difficulties in re-entering the labour market after a certain period of career disruption.

In the former GDR, women's labour force participation was the target of family politics and social policies eased the combination of employment career and family (Geißler, 1996; Huinink and Wagner, 1995; Sørensen and Trappe, 1995; Strohmeier and Kuijsten, 1997). Over the 1950s and 1960s, as many women as possible were pulled into gainful employment. This has also to be seen in connection with a growing migration flow to the former FRG, leading to manpower shortage, and thus, making women's labour market integration an imperative. Over the 1970s and 1980s, fertility anyhow declined and various policies were launched to extend the network of child-care facilities, raise financial aid and family allowances, create family-friendly labour conditions, and make maternity leave legislation more generous. As a result, the female employment rate in general, and full-time employment in particular, was considerably higher in East Germany (Sørensen and Trappe, 1995). This enabled women in the East to stand on their own feet and their occupational careers became more similar to men's, that is, gainful employment was more and more stable and qualified rather than discontinuous and low-skilled. Due to their autonomy and extended welfare state protection women faced limited risks as to the decision to marry and have a child (Huinink and Wagner, 1995; Sørensen and Trappe, 1995). Since the reunification, East German women are confronted by far more uncertainties and it is increasingly difficult to realise their labour market and childbearing wishes due to cut-backs in child-care facilities and oftentimes dim job prospects in a tight job market.

4.4.2 The British welfare state

Great Britain, as an example of the liberal welfare state (Esping-Andersen, 1999), is characterised by passive labour market policies and only moderate support for those in need. Welfare support for the unemployed and inactive has been cut by British governments over the decades and major changes in legal regulation, based on the '*principle of responsibility and reciprocity*', have been made by the Labour party since its election in 1997 (Deacon, 2000). The welfare state is increasingly organised around paid work, so gainful employment is of fundamental importance and is the route out of dependence on social assistance benefits. As can be seen in various attempts to make work 'pay' and the *New Deal* on *Welfare to Work*, recipients are expected to acquire further qualifications to improve their chances for re-entering the labour market speedily (Deacon, 2000). This in turn implies that welfare is understood as a temporary assistance. By and large, a shift from passive to more active labour market policies can be observed in recent years.

The welfare state as well as the labour market structure and employment regulation plays a crucial role in the gendered division of labour. State-provided child-care facilities, particularly for pre-school children, are rather limited, as are leave entitlements (Burchell *et al.*, 1997; Gornick and Meyers, 2003). More particularly, entitlements to reduced working hours, paternity leave (which only came into force in 2003) as well as publicly funded childcare are absent. Hence, childcare provision is mainly market-based, or through relatives or other informal exchange networks, and this private purchase of day care affects mothers' work life, particularly mothers in secondary jobs with low remuneration.

In recent years, policymakers have passed various new laws to make it easier to reconcile parenthood and employment. These have included the *Working Families Tax Credit* in 1999 that includes a *Childcare Tax Credit* that pays up to 70 percent of childcare costs; an increase in the *Child Benefit* and *Family Credit*; the New Deal for Lone Parents that introduces incentives for single parents and those with an unemployed partner to (re-)enter gainful employment; and an extension of maternity leave. Despite these changes, policies to help parents balance work and family life remain among the weakest in Europe (Gornick and Meyers, 2003; Stier *et al.*, 2001).

On the other hand, and contrary to Spain, Great Britain has a much expanded part-time labour market that enables mothers to stay in the labour market. The growth in women's gainful employment is connected to a growth in women's part-time work and a rising number of career interruptions, thereby spreading the modified model of gender division of labour (Buck and Gershuny, 1996; González-López, 1998).

4.4.3 The Spanish welfare state

Spain has been called a family-oriented welfare state (Jurado Guerrero, 1995; Reher, 1998). For while in the social-democratic regimes individuals can rely on an extensive welfare provision in child-care, family allowances, parental leave as well as residential homes, unemployment benefits or help for old people, it is mainly family and kinship networks that give support to their members (Baizán, 1998; Esping-Andersen, 1999). With this conspicuous absence of help from the Spanish welfare state, the period that individuals rely on family support is currently well extended into adulthood (Delgado and Castro Martín, 1998). By and large, welfare provisions are organised around gainful employment of male breadwinners. Since family support is mostly provided by women, who are confronted with a double burden to combine labour market career and family obligations, the female labour force participation rate is low by international standards (OECD, 2001; ILO, 1999; Blossfeld and Hakim, 1997a; Cousins, 1994; Section 3.1). Hence, the traditional model of work and family identity remains the male breadwinner model, while the modified model as well as the dual earner model are rarer (Blossfeld and Drobnič, 2001; González-López, 1998, 2001; OECD, 2001; Section 2.2.1). This is partly due to the fact that the part-time labour market is still rather under-developed, which renders the combination of employment and housework difficult for women. Due to the absence of social policies concerning maternity leave, family allowances, and an under-developed child-caring system, working women have to rely on informal networks for child-care. Furthermore, employed women are most often atypical workers that are rarely entitled to maternity rights. There are some signs that the traditional division of labour is slowly changing. Increasing enrolment in higher education, progressing female labour force participation, and the growing reluctance of women to quit their labour market career force couples to rethink their gender division of labour.

With respect to welfare-sustaining policies for first-employment seekers, welfare state support is largely lacking particularly for those who do not manage to make a direct school-to-work transition. As already described in Section 4.2.3, governments tried to combat high youth unemployment mainly through a systematic flexibility of work relations with far-reaching consequences for labour market entry patterns of youth. They are mostly outsiders moving between short employment spells and unemployment. Given this relatively weak state support and the increasing difficulties of youth to settle in the labour market, youth is lacking social security, and thus, to a great extent dependent on any help coming from their parents.

4.4.4 Comparing the conservative, liberal and family-oriented regimes

The above sections indicate that the three countries under study differ with respect to their national ideologies how to protect and promote the welfare of the population. A guiding principle of the German welfare state is the principle of subsidiary. Compared to Great Britain and Spain, the social security net is more extensive and generous, and thus, inactive are highly decommodified. Social policy and tax system support the male breadwinner family. While childcare facilities for infants are scarce, parental leave legislation is fairly generous. All in all, the state significantly lowers social and economic risks. In contrast, in Great Britain the principle of responsibility and reciprocity reigns. A laissez-faire policy, means-tested benefit systems, and work incentives are crucial aspects that imply a higher degree of recommodification. At the same time, due to a lack of affordable child-care facilities and less generous leave entitlements, welfare support for female homemakers is weak. The Spanish welfare state rests on the explicit assumption that families give support to their members. Hence, individual's work and family life involve a greater commitment to one's family of origin and the partner. By and large, because of lacking welfare support for women's work and family life the female homemaker family is implicitly backed.

4.5 Conclusion

This chapter described the role of institutional filters and highlighted that employment relations and flexibility paths, educational systems, and welfare state regimes vary considerably among European countries (Blossfeld, 2002; Esping-Andersen, 1999; Esping-Andersen and Regini, 2000; Regini, 1997, 2000b). There remains heterogeneity between the three countries under study in the way in which they are able to ameliorate global pressures, and thus, the repercussions of labour market insecurity on the work and family life of men and women will be country-specific. The idea that individual resources such as educational attainement or occupational standing determine individual degrees of insecurity also runs implicitly and explicitly through the various sections. Based on these differences, the next chapter proposes five research hypotheses, which specify the impact of institutional filters and individual characteristics on the work and family life of men and women.

5 Risk profile hypotheses – Institutional filters and individual characteristics

The previous chapters elaborated on life course decision-making, labour market insecurity, and life course security as the key concept linking the two. The *insecurity hypothesis* of this study suggests that with increasing labour market insecurity individuals lack the ability to envisage future developments and to plan ahead, thus implying less life course security, which in turn will make a deferment of life course decisions more likely. Yet, as outlined in the *risk profile hypothesis*, it is proposed that individual degrees of insecurity are substantially filtered by, firstly, nation-specific arrangements in labour market, education, and welfare state provision, and, secondly, gender, career maturity, and individual resources. Figure 5.1 summarises how all central concepts of this study relate to each other.

Figure 5.1 Explanatory framework

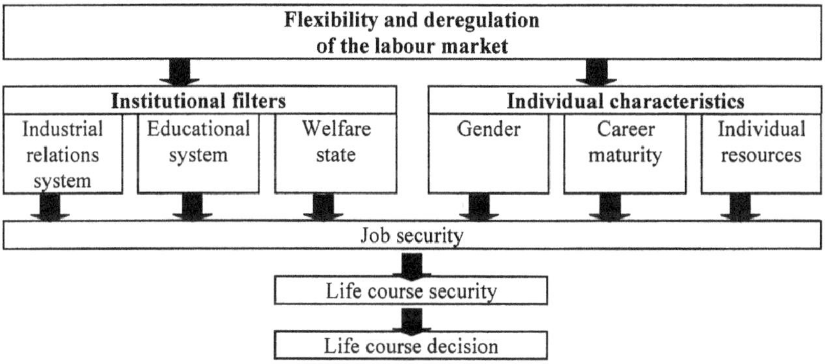

The goal of this chapter is to pinpoint how exactly institutional filters and individual characteristics intervene in the three countries under study. Based on the theoretical considerations on the impact of insecurity, institutional path-dependence, and gender specific role-models, five hypotheses are put forward.

5.1 Country-specific hypothesis – How insecure are precarious jobs?

As discussed in detail in Chapter Four, insecurity underlies the nature of employment relationships, but it also is embedded in the broader context of nation-specific institutional arrangements. The impact of enhanced flexibility on individuals' positions of insecurity varies considerably in Germany, Great Britain, and Spain. The fundamental question that arises at this point is therefore: How insecure are precarious jobs in the respective countries? Table 5.1 gives an overview on the varying degrees of job security in the three selected countries.

Table 5.1 Job security profiles in Germany, Great Britain, and Spain

	Germany	Great Britain	Spain
Property of job			
Contractual security	High	Low	Low
Income security	High	Low	High
Working-time security	High	Low	High
Environment of job			
Social security	High	Low	Low
Job match security	High	Intermediate	Low
Representation security	High	Low	Intermediate

In Germany, labour market flexibility can be understood as a controlled experiment in which flexible measures are selectively directed to specific individuals (Regini, 2000). Labour market outsiders trying to (re-)enter the labour force face increased degrees of insecurity. Yet, the strongly transfer-oriented German welfare system provides outsiders with comparatively high measures of social security. At the same time, the German educational system ensures smooth education-to-work transitions; unions remain strong and coverage by collective bargaining high. Consequently, individuals are largely shielded against new market risks. Notwithstanding, Germany represents a unique case in that the transformation into a service and knowledge society commenced earlier in the former FRG, while, up to reunification, individuals remained comparatively protected against insecurities in the former GDR. Nowadays, with the deep restructuring process of economy, education, and welfare system, and still adapting to the West German system, East Germans experience a significantly higher degree of insecurity. Compared to their West German counterparts, East Germans face many hurdles on their way to economic independence, making it presumably more difficult to make long-term commitments. Quite the opposite in Great Britain, where flexibility is a guiding principle of labour market policy and deregulation measures affect all employees alike. Overall there is not much employment protection regulation so that even employees in permanent job positions face insecurity. Still, employers will pre-select some employees for permanent job positions while there are substantial disincentives to give permanent posts to others. The 'hire-and-fire' system fosters high job mobility and rather short unemployment duration, so that the impact of a low degree of job security and social security may be offset by better chances to re-enter the labour market quickly. At the same time, weak welfare state support pressures individuals to overcome phases of non-employment as quickly as possible. All in all, one may expect that for a large group of temporary employees fixed-term contracts appear as stepping-stones to permanent work. In contrast, the Spanish labour market is characterised by a strong insider-outsider divide into, on the one hand, permanent full-time employees who can rely on high degrees of security, and, on the other hand, outsiders who face low degrees of social security and great difficulties in (re-)entering and settling in the labour market. There is a also large pool of job-insecure workers who face much lower degrees of security and the risk of falling back to the group of outsiders is comparatively higher than for permanent full-time employees. The type of employment contract counts most when it comes to the question of who is job-insecure in Spain and the crucial question is whether and when labour market entrants manage to take a permanent position. To summarise, the country-specific hypothesis suggests:

> *Job precariousness and perceived job insecurity is highest in Great Britain. Also, insecurity should be more equally spread than in Germany and Spain. In turn, insecurity is highly confined to labour market entrants in Spain. Since they face a high unemployment risk that goes hand-in-hand with a high risk of temporary employment, it is expected that Spaniards experience higher degrees of job insecurity and perceive their job as more insecure than their German counterparts. Lastly, one may expect a rather modest risk in terms of job insecurity in Germany.*

5.2 Transition-specific hypothesis – Different effects on distinct transitions?

Stable, foreseeable career prospects, and a certain economic basis function as important prerequisites to make long-term, if not life-long commitments such as partnership formation and entry into first parenthood (Oppenheimer, 1988). With respect to partnership formation, marriage is planned to be durable and involves long-term financial obligations. It is therefore expected that a couple's decision to marry is contingent on the current socio-economic status and the predictability of long-run socio-economic prospects. Thus, individuals who are confronted with job insecurity may either postpone partnership formation or opt for cohabitation, a living arrangement that is less self-binding as compared to marriage (in both respects, legally and normatively). In such respects, "*cohabiting gets young people out of high-cost search activities during a period of social immaturity but without incurring the penalties of either heterosexual isolation or promiscuity, and it often offers many of the benefits of marriage, including the pooling of resources and the economies of scale that living together provides*" (Oppenheimer, 1994: 308, 1988). Such an adaptation strategy may also become visible in lower transitions rates from cohabitation to marriage. Comparing partnership formation and entry into first parenthood, it is maintained that a solid economic basis and stable career prospects are even more important for the latter transition. Since the decision to have a child involves a strong commitment to a new dependent person and, in most of the cases, does lead to an interruption of women's labour force participation, if not withdrawal, men's stable employment career becomes a necessary prerequisite for this transition. To conclude, the transition-specific hypothesis reads as follows:

> *Job insecurity increases the propensity to remain single rather than partner, and to cohabit rather than marry. The effect of job insecurity is considerably higher for transitions into first parenthood.*

5.3 Gender-specific hypothesis – Different effects for men and women?

A large set of empirical findings points to gender-specific patterns in transitions from youth to adulthood as well as subsequent work and family life (see among others, Blossfeld, 1995; Blossfeld and Hakim, 1997; Blossfeld *et al.*, forthcoming; Corijn and Klijzing, 2001). This is partly due to provisions of welfare through State, family, and market that shape women's life courses in a particular manner (Orloff, 1993, 1996). The idea that male and female oriented explanations play a crucial role runs implicitly and explicitly through the previous chapters. Here it is argued that insecurity does not necessarily increase the likelihood to postpone long-term commitments. It may have different impacts on men and women, so gender-specific adaptation strategies can be expected (see also Oppenheimer, 1988). With increasing flexibility men are likely to see an increase in job insecurity that may discourage them to partner and become fathers. According to the traditional male bread-winner model still prevailing in Spain but also in Germany, and, to a lesser extent, in Great Britain, men are expected to consolidate a certain economic basis for the family while women carry the brunt of household tasks and child-rearing. This implies that man's secure full-time job is a requisite for making the transition to first partnership and first parenthood. Even though most European countries experience a shift towards dual earner societies, the consequences of job insecurity will remain the same for men since childrearing and domestic work are still largely a female domain. Yet, with the increasing insecurity of employment relationships in contemporary societies, men are likely to confront essential barriers to meet such preconditions. For women, consequences of increased job insecurity are more ambiguous. On the one hand, insecurity plays a less impeding and probably less distinct role in the transition processes under study. As compared to men, more flexibility offers job opportunities that ease women's (re-)entry into the labour market and the combination of family and work career, in particular. This is especially relevant in a country-specific context with largely lacking family policies. At the same time, women's gainful employment may enable a couple to marry even though the man is not yet on his own. As Oppenheimer (1994) argues, a less gender-specific division of labour may be seen as a flexible way to adapt to increasingly insecure male job careers, thereby lowering social risks. In turn, woman's insecure employment may not threaten the economic basis of a household if the man functions as the main breadwinner. On the other hand, some women may not look for a permanent place in the labour market if they opt for marriage and motherhood as their long-term family career, whereas others may be more work-oriented and embark on a work career (Hakim, 1991, 2000). Women who have already come to the decision to embark on a family career are expected to be more likely to marry and parent. With increasing female participation rates in higher education, which imply higher investments in human capital and stronger career orientations, women are presumably more likely to decide on a satisfying job career and defer childbearing wishes. At the same time, full-time and permanent posts offer more security in terms of maternity leave and re-entry after employment disruption. Conversely, being employed in a job position with little protection and career prospects, women may actually change their work orientation along with future plans and may be more likely to pursue a family career. These various considerations suggest that the employment status and job security of the partner may be very important when it comes to the decision to partner or have a child. Gender-specific adaptation strategies appear deeply rooted in nation-specific arrangements in welfare and prevailing gender roles. Hence, the gender-specific hypothesis appears interwoven with the country-specific hypothesis. In summary, a primary hypothesis is that

> *overall the effects of job insecurity are stronger for men than for women. Gender-specific adaptation strategies are always country-, and transition-specific. For men, insecurity should have the most adverse effect in Spain; the effect of men's job insecurity is rather intermediate in Germany, and comparatively weak in Great Britain. For women, job insecurity should be of utmost importance for transitions to first motherhood.*

5.4 Career maturity hypothesis – Equally spread risks over entire work career?

Labour market integration is seen as a step-wise process, characterised by periods of unemployment and non-employment, promotion, within- and between-firm occupational mobility. With progressing career advancement individuals gain career maturity, a crucial employee's benefit. This is because career advancement goes hand in hand with more commitment, loyalty, labour force experience, and profound occupation- and firm-specific knowledge. This implies rising benefits, but also costs for employers. As compared to less experienced and trained workers, layoffs and resignations are costly for the employer. In recent times employers seem also more reluctant to hire workers on a permanent full-time basis and will preferably offer temporary posts to new entrants in order to screen their work potential (recruitment strategy) and lower labour and non-labour costs in case of misfits or economic downturns (hire-and-fire strategy). In turn, incentives for permanent full-time contracts should be considerably higher for employees with high degrees of career maturity. Thus, adverse effects of flexibility and deregulation are supposed to be most pronounced at labour market entry, leading to a postponement of first entry into the primary labour market and a more uncertain education-to-work transition for more recent cohorts. It is thus proposed that

> *higher degrees of career maturity of adult workers significantly protect against insecurity. Since young labour market entrants lack career maturity they lose most in terms of job stability.*

However, this hypothesis has to be further elaborated. First, due to an acceleration of pace and flow of work in an age of globalisation, recent labour market entrants are increasingly likely to be 'job hoppers' and it is thus more difficult to make career advancements than in previous decades. Temporary entry-jobs will most likely heighten unemployment risks and, following the so-called scarring hypothesis, previous unemployment spells increase risks of future unemployment. In line with the above considerations, one may also expect that unemployed are more likely to be re-employed in a temporary post. Taken together job insecurity at labour market entry may lead to a 'low-pay no-pay cycle' and thus be seen as the onset of an unstable job career. In such respects individual resources may play a mediating role, an idea which is amplified in the following section. Second, one may expect gender-specific effects. Due to career interruptions and withdrawal, part-time and low-paid employment, it is more difficult for women with children to accumulate career maturity. However, flexibility may also help women to reconcile work and family life; others may not seek a permanent place in the labour market (Section 5.3). How exactly flexibility impacts women's work and family career is therefore an open research question. *Lastly*, it is surmised that the importance of career maturity depends on the nation-specific context. It is possibly more crucial in the German occupationally segmented labour market, where long-term relationships based on trust prevail and flexible employment mainly functions as a recruitment strategy rather than a hire-and-fire strategy. Career maturity also plays an important role in Spain, though the explanation for this is quite different: here it is basically the insider-outsider labour market that channels labour market risks towards outsiders and new labour market entrants. On the contrary, in the low-trust, hire-and-fire environment of Great Britain, career maturity may only have a modest impact. Due to increased levels of deregulation and flexibility and the least protective employment regulation system in Europe (Deakin and Reed, 2000) one may thus assume: If there is an overall decrease of job stability, Great Britain should be at the forefront from a European perspective.

5.5 Individual resources hypothesis – Educational attainment and occupational status as buffers?

While some researchers argue that an increase in employment instability would affect all employees alike (Beck, 1986, 1999), others expect that occupational class and educational differences function as a buffer against insecurity (Breen, 1997; Goldthorpe, 2001a). According to the latter argument one would therefore envisage differences in the probability to be in temporary employment, to enter into and exit from unemployment, or to experience upward rather than downward occupational mobility based on characteristics of persons and job positions. The crucial question becomes the following: Are there inequalities related to inter-individual differences in educational attainment and occupational status? With the shift towards skilled jobs and the growing importance of high educational credentials, insecurity will be particularly channelled towards those who are poorly equipped for the education-to-work transition, i.e. with no educational qualification. Young adults with low educational qualifications are presumably not only more likely to be in temporary posts in general, but seasonal/casual jobs in low-skilled occupations. Compared to this, school leavers with high educational qualifications are probably better off in terms of earnings and occupational class, as well as higher chances to enter permanent work more quickly. With respect to occupational class, the degree of insecurity faced by employees belonging to the service class is expected to differ from that faced by unskilled workers. More precisely, employers are more prone to offer permanent contracts, wage premiums, and higher remuneration to highly qualified workers, usually employed in positions with a lot of responsibility. Through this employers assure continual work commitment, motivation, and loyalty. Conversely, manual and low-qualified non-manual workers are readily recruited and monitored, their duties well-defined and constricted (see also Erikson and Goldthorpe, 1992). Differing degrees of insecurity are assumed to be reflected in higher unemployment risks, lower re-entry probabilities for the unemployed, and increased downward mobility risks among low-qualified employees. To conclude, it is maintained that

> *insecurity is filtered by educational qualification and occupational class. However, due to national differences in flexibility paths and institutional arrangements in education, individual resources may protect better from job insecurity in Germany, less so in Great Britain and Spain.*

5.6 Conclusion

This chapter proposed that country-specific institutional packages, career maturity, and individual resources have repercussions on the individual work and family life, albeit in different veins. The intention of the remainder of this book is to search for empirical evidence to either confirm or disconfirm the impact of labour market insecurity on the lifes of men and women.

6 Data, variables, and methods

Based on the theoretical framework elaborated in Chapters Two to Five, a series of important questions may be raised. For instance, how can one gauge labour market insecurity? How can one measure life-course decisions and which methods have to be applied to investigate the repercussions of labour market insecurity? One may also ask: how can one capture the role of individual resources? And, is it possible to define a yardstick which is meant to reflect international differences in the impact of labour market insecurity? This chapter seeks to answer these pivotal questions, all of which concern methodology and data comparability.

The discussion is divided into three main sections. A description of data sources and sample selection criteria is given first, followed by an outline of the transitions and variables of interest coupled with issues of data comparability in Section 6.2. Section 6.3 gives an account of the statistical methods employed in the analysis. It concludes with a summary and outlook in Section 6.4.

6.1 Data sources and sample selection criteria

The first question to pose is this: What data structure do we need to disentangle life course decisions, labour market insecurity, and the role of institutional filters and individual resources? And furthermore, what is highly valuable with respect to sampling and survey methodology and contents? In these terms, two major issues have to be considered: the need for a longitudinal design and the demand for data comparability.

Firstly, to address the research questions and hypotheses put forward in the theoretical part of this study, dynamic information on individual work and family life is essential. From a life course perspective, the previous life course determines current and future life course decisions. Individual life courses are embedded in society at large and the need for longitudinal data appears particularly evident in the process of globalisation and quickening social change. A longitudinal design allows a follow up of the same households and individuals over successive time intervals, and hence, the accumulation of individual and household information from a longitudinal perspective (Andreß, 1992; Blossfeld and Rohwer, 2001). More precisely, panel data permit the study of how individual decision-makers face change in their labour market career and socio-economic standing and how their employment, partnership, and parenthood decisions are linked with these changes dynamically over time. Longitudinal data is therefore an important tool for inquiring into individual life course decision-making.

Secondly, since this study aims to provide a deeper understanding of the role of institutional filters in mediating labour market insecurity, data comparability and accuracy is fundamental to juxtapose the three selected countries under study. To draw meaningful comparisons between the countries, the establishment of equivalent methodological approaches and measurement techniques used in the analysis is indispensable. Central measurement and estimation aspects to be kept in view are: (i) standardisation of methodology, design, and content; (ii) shared definitions of concepts and classifications, measures and variables along with survey population; and, (iii) standardisation of data structure, data processing, and statistical analysis. In this study data comparability proved to be more difficult to access than expected and issues of comparability of sampling and survey methods along with measures used will be recurring considerations in the chapters to follow.

So, what data sources can be used for the purpose of this study? The analysis to be presented here uses three different data sources, namely the German Socio-Economic Panel Study (GSOEP, 1984-2001), the British Household Panel Survey (BHPS, 1991-2000), and the European Community Household Panel (ECHP, 1994-1997). These data-sets provide ample information for a variety of issues surrounding individual's work and family life, and their employment, partnership, and parenthood decisions from a longitudinal perspective, in particular. Hence, the GSOEP, the BHPS, and the ECHP stand as major sources for life course analysis. The following paragraphs describe and contrast the sampling and survey methods of these three data sources in some detail. On the basis of this description, Section 6.1.4 provides reasons for the choice of these data sources and ends with an outline of the sample selection criteria for the analysis to follow.

6.1.1 The German Socio-economic Panel Study (GSOEP, 1984-2001)

The *German Socio-Economic Panel Study* (GSOEP) is carried out by the German Institute for Economic Research (DIW Berlin) and includes approximately 6,000 households and about 12,000 individuals in 1984 (Hanefeld, 1987; SOEP Group, 2001).[33] Since then the survey has been repeated

[33] The data were made available by the German Socio-Economic Panel Study (SOEP) at the German Institute for Economic Research (DIW), Berlin. The DIW does not bear any responsibility for the analyses or interpretations presented here. More information can be obtained at: http://www.diw.de/english/sop/index.html [15.04.03]. Interested readers may also have a look at the Desktop Companion which is available at: http://www.diw.de /english/sop/service/dtc/index.html [15.04.03].

annually and by the time of writing this study eighteen waves had been released. The initial GSOEP consisted of two samples: a sample of West German residents and a sample of foreigners living in West Germany (i.e., households with a Turkish, Greek, Yugoslavian, Spanish or Italian head of household). Further samples followed. In 1990, a new sample of East-Germans was added to the GSOEP. It was followed by two samples of immigrants to West Germany in 1994 and 1995; a so-called 'Refreshment sample' in 1998; and the 'Innovation sample' in 2000 (Haisken-DeNew and Frick, 2001). These different samples are multi-stage random samples. Foreigners, East Germans, and immigrants are over-sampled in order to gain large enough samples to permit independent analyses of these groups.

The GSOEP offers copious employment and household information obtained through individual and household questionnaires. Rich retrospective information on the occupational, family, and marital biography, social origin and first job as well as migration biography is also available. Data is collected for all household members aged 16 and over through pen-and-paper interviewing (except for computer assisted personal interview (CAPI) mode of data collection for some 50 percent of sample E). Children are also surveyed once they reach age 16. All sample members are to be interviewed once every year. In the case of household split-off, sample members are followed and persons in newly formed households of original sample members or those who move into original sample households are also surveyed. Great effort is made to maintain the panel. For example, there is an effort to keep interviewers consistent and respondents receive gifts related to the yearly topical module and a lottery ticket. Also, persons and households which could not be successfully surveyed in a given year are followed until there are two succeeding drop-outs or a final refusal. Response rates vary between the various sub-samples. About 91 percent of West German residents were re-interviewed for the second wave, while the corresponding response rate was somewhat lower in the sample of foreigners (88 percent). Ten years after the first sweep some 62 percent of the sample of West German residents and 60 percent of the sample of foreigners living in West Germany were still participating in the survey (Pannenberg, 2000).

6.1.2 The British Household Panel Survey (BHPS, 1991-2000)

The *British Household Panel Survey (BHPS)* began in September 1991 and since then it has been repeated annually. It is carried out by the Institute for Social and Economic Research (ISER) located at the University of Essex (Taylor, 1999).[34] The BHPS is based on a nationally representative sample of

---

[34] The data used in this study were made available through the ESRC Data Archive. The data were originally collected by the ESRC Research Centre on Micro-social Change (now

households which includes about 5.500 households containing approximately 10,000 individuals. In this original sample Northern Ireland, the North and West Highlands as well as persons in institutions are excluded. At later stages, supplementary samples were added to the BHPS. In 1997, a sub-sample of the United Kingdom European Community Household Panel (ECHP) and a low-income sample of the Great Britain panel were merged with the original BHPS data (see also Section 6.1.3). In 1999, two additional samples in Scotland and Wales were added to enlarge sample sizes in these two countries. At the time of writing this study ten panel waves were available.

In 1991, interviews were pursued with all members of the sample household aged 16 or over. From wave two onwards all these so-called original sample members are followed-up on each successive year and their children are also interviewed once they reach the age of 16. The BHPS is designed to keep track of original sample members if they split-off from the original sample household. The sample for each wave is thus not only composed of all adult original sample members and their descendants. If they leave their original household to form a new household, then all adult members of the new household enter the sample as temporary sample members. Hence, after the first wave new eligibility for sample inclusion can occur if an original sample member has a baby, an original sample member moves into a household with one or more new people, or one or more new people move in with an original sample member. Considerable effort has been put into panel maintenance in terms of gift vouchers, refusal conversion, and re-contact of households that refused to be surveyed in the previous year. About 88 percent and 90 percent of the original BHPS sample were re-interviewed for the second and third sweep, respectively. From the fourth wave onwards, response rates have been consistently higher than 95 percent (Taylor, 1999).

The BHPS is rich in information on household composition, individual employment history, education, income and payment, and a variety of other individual based information. The BHPS also provides retrospective information on employment history, family, and marital biography. Within each wave, individual-level and household-level data is collected via household, individual, and self-completion questionnaires, as well as a proxy schedule for those sample members that were absent or incapable of completing the interview. With respect to survey methods, the BHPS changed from pen-and-paper mode of data collection (PAPI) to computer assisted personal interviewing (CAPI) in 1999.

---

incorporated within the Institute for Social and Economic Research) at the University of Essex. Neither the original collectors of the data nor the Archive bear any responsibility for the analyses or interpretations presented here. For details on the BHPS questionnaire and survey methods consult the following web-site: http://iserwww.essex.ac.uk/ulsc/bhps/doc/ [18.11.03].

6.1.3 The European Community Household Panel (ECHP, 1994-1997)

The *European Community Household Panel (ECHP)* was designed as a harmonised longitudinal survey to collect information on employment, income, previous jobs, search for jobs, education, and satisfaction with various aspects of life and living conditions in the EU.[35] In 1994, a sample of approximately 60,500 nationally representative households and 130,000 adults aged 16 and over were surveyed in the then twelve Member States.[36] Since then, the ECHP follows up on the same households and its members in these Member States, and since 1995 and 1996 in Austria and Finland, respectively. The survey is based on a common questionnaire designed at Eurostat and ensures a high degree of data comparability through its common sampling methods, survey instruments, and contents. In 1997, however, Germany, Luxembourg, and the UK put an end to their ECHP survey. Since then the GSOEP and the BHPS are used to derive comparable data for the ECHP. The previous three panel waves have also been filled with this converted data, and hence, the German and the UK ECHP provide analysts with two data-sets covering the time period 1994-1996, namely the original ECHP and the converted data-set.

Through the application of the pen-and-paper mode of data collection (and self-completion questionnaires and proxy interviews in some exceptional cases), information is collected via household and individual questionnaires with all household members aged 16 and over. The following rules for subsequent waves require that all members of original sample households and new split households be traced. At the time of data-set preparation for this study, four waves were available due to a significant time lag between data collection and release. As in the GSOEP and the BHPS, considerable effort has been made to maintain the panel over consecutive waves. Yet, household and individual interview response rates vary greatly between the participating countries.[37]

---

[35] This study uses the ECHP "users' database" (UDB), a factual anonymised data-set which meets the objective anonymisation criteria. This data-set shows important drawbacks since some information has been confidentialised. As an illustration, all regional information has been deleted in Germany and it is therefore not possible to pursue separate analyses for East and West Germany. Other variables such as occupation codes are inaccurate measures since they have been recoded for confidentiality reasons. Eurostat does not bear any responsibility for the analyses or interpretations presented here. For more details on questionnaire and survey methods see European Commission Eurostat (1996) or consult the following web site: http://forum.europa.eu.int/irc/dsis/echpanel/info/data/information.html [15.04.03]. See Doc.Pan.108/99 for a report on data quality which is available at: http://forum.europa.eu.int/irc/dsis/echpanel/info/data/information.html [15.04.03].

[36] These were Germany, Denmark, The Netherlands, Belgium, Luxembourg, France, United Kingdom, Ireland, Italy, Greece, Spain, and Portugal.

[37] More information can be found in Doc.PAN 92/97 and Doc.Pan 108/99 (http://forum.europa.eu.int/irc/dsis/echpanel/info/data/information.html [15.04.03]).

6.1.4 Data comparability and conclusion

The data sources described above follow a longitudinal design and provide rich information on individual work and family life. Hence, for the purpose of this study these panel surveys meet the first requirement previously identified. The pivotal question is therefore, whether and to what extent these data sources also fulfil the demand for data comparability.

At first glance the ECHP appears to be a salient data source to meet the need for a longitudinal design and the demand for data comparability. However, for the purposes of this study, two important shortcomings have to be noted. First, as aforementioned, in 1997 Germany and the UK stopped their ECHP survey and filled the gap with converted data from the GSOEP and the BHPS. This integration of national panel data is likely to lower the degree of comparability, and hence, introduces additional complexity to the analysis of ECHP data. More precisely, due to differences in contents and methodology of the GSOEP and the BHPS, some pivotal information is not available or has been measured with varying precision for Germany and Great Britain. An illustration of this is that individual perception of job security has been measured with other response-scales in the GSOEP and the BHPS and these two national panel surveys also differ considerably from the ECHP with respect to measurement of employment and unemployment (see Section 6.2). Second, due to its relatively recent start in 1994 and a considerable time lag between data collection and release, the ECHP is still a comparatively young panel survey. If one was to use the more standardised data from the original German and UK ECHP sample, this would confine the observation period to 1994-96. Moreover, no retrospective information on the employment, family, and marital biography has been collected. Analyses based on the ECHP are therefore restricted to a short observation period, impeding the identification of changes in individual labour market career and socio-economic standing and their linkage with employment, partnership, and parenthood decisions over time. In light of these flaws, it is clear that the rich ECHP data source can not be fully exhausted for the purpose of this study.

Unlike the ECHP, the GSOEP and the BHPS were not designed as harmonised surveys, but both surveys have followed similar sampling and survey methods and provide data throughout the 1990s. Regarding data comparability, some shortcomings can be pinpointed. Some explanatory variables are measured with varying precision and crucial information may be lacking or may be confined to specific sub-groups. Over the intervening years, questionnaire and survey methods have also been subject to amendments in both surveys. As will become evident in the next section, such modifications and amendments increase the intricacy of processing, harmonising and analysing panel data.

Table 6.1 Synopsis of sampling and survey methods for panel surveys

	Germany		Great Britain		Spain
Panel survey	German Socio-Economic Panel Study (GSOEP)	German European Community Household Panel (ECHP)	British Household Panel Survey (BHPS)	UK European Community Household Panel (ECHP)	Spanish European Community Household Panel (ECHP)
Research Institute	DIW Berlin (German Institute for Economic Research)	Eurostat (EU statistical office)	Institute for Social and Economic Research (ISER), University of Essex.	Eurostat (EU statistical office)	Eurostat (EU statistical office)
Fieldwork	Feb – Oct 1984, eleven panel waves, repeated annually	May – July / Sept – Jan 1994, three panel waves, repeated annually	Sept – Dec 1991, ten panel waves, repeated annually	July – October 1994, three panel waves, repeated annually	Oct – Dec 1994, four panel waves, repeated annually
Sample size	Sub samples: A – "West German" residents, started in 1984, n=4528 hh C – "East-Germans" started in 1990, n=2179 hh	5,523 hh	Original sample: 5,500 hh	5,779 hh	7,206 hh
Interview technique	Face-to-face individual interviews (PAPI) with all hh members aged 16 and over (except for the refreshment sample: 50% CAPI), no proxy interviews	In principal personal face-to-face interviews, proxy interviewing	Face-to-face individual interviews (PAPI) with all hh members aged 16 and over, proxy interviews. Since wave 9 computer assisted personal interviewing (CAPI)	Principally personal face-to-face interviews, no proxy interviews	Principally personal face-to-face interviews, proxy interviewing
Response rates	Sub sample A – wave 1-2: 91%, wave 1-11: 62% Sub sample C – wave 1-2: 94%, wave 1-5: 80%	Wave 1-2: 94% of eligible persons	Wave 1-2: 88% of eligible adults, Wave: 2-3: 90%; since then response rates have been consistently higher than 95%	Wave 1-2: 78% of eligible persons	Wave 1-2: 91% of eligible persons

Which of these data sources did I use to address the various research questions of this study? As to the country-specific analyses to follow in Chapters Seven to Nine, the GSOEP, the BHPS, and the Spanish ECHP are used. By using the GSOEP and the BHPS, the analyses on Germany and Great Britain cover a longer time period, namely from 1991-2000, and take into consideration more detailed information on individual work and family life. Since there is no other comparable panel survey of Spain that would allow for an analysis of life course decision-making from a longitudinal perspective, data for all Spanish analyses will come from the ECHP. In doing so, the observation period will be confined to 1994-1997. Also, data for any pooled analysis comes from the ECHP. Since it is not possible to reconcile the three data sources in some important respects (Section 6.2), this study prefers to use the original ECHP sample rather than converted GSOEP and BHPS data. Hence, pooled analyses are restricted to the time period from 1994-1996. Table 6.1 summarises the sampling and survey methods in each of the three surveys. Using these three longitudinal panel surveys, the analyses are limited to original sample members with full interview, no disabilities, and aged 16 and older.[38]

Depending on the analytical purpose at hand, different sub-samples have to be considered: a sub-sample of gainfully employed and unemployed for the analysis of transitions into and out of employment; a sub-sample of singles and cohabitants for the study of partnership decisions; and a sub-sample of childless individuals for the investigation of the decision to have a first child. Chapters Seven to Nine will therefore detail further sample selection criteria. A principal goal of this study is to harmonise data from the three data sources, but some shortcomings can only be partly remedied. Hence, at several places, the presented analysis is not comparable in a methodically strict sense. The purpose of the following section is to focus on transitions and variables of interest and their data comparability.

6.1 Transitions and variables of interest

This section is structured as follows. Section 6.2.1 describes the employment, partnership, and parenthood transitions under study. The variables are then defined. To this end, Section 6.2.2 explains the measurement of employment

---

[38] The GSOEP, BHPS, and ECHP data analysed for the research to be presented in Chapter Seven and Eight exclude foreigners. Moreover, analyses based on the GSOEP use the samples for West Germans and East Germans. Examinations for Great Britain are based on original BHPS sample members only, thus excluding the sub-sample of the United Kingdom European Community Household Panel (ECHP), the low-income sample as well as the two additional samples in Scotland and Wales.

and unemployment, a crucial distinction for the analysis to follow. Against this background, Section 6.2.3 illustrates the measurement of labour market insecurity and individual resources. The discussion ends with other variables that are related to the processes under study.

6.2.1 Employment, partnership and parenthood transitions

Recall from Chapter Two that this study focuses on three main life course decisions, namely employment, partnership, and parenthood decisions. Employment decisions encompass decisions about whether or not to continue at school, which educational or occupational track to follow, whether or not to enter gainful employment and part-time or full-time work, in particular. Yet, embarking on a research strategy which focuses on the above employment decisions only would not do justice to employment careers in globalising labour markets. Rather, this study inquires into risks of insecure employment and labour market exclusion and transitions under study are the following:

- *risk of insecure employment at labour market entry and the hazard of being hit by unemployment during early labour market career*, to scrutinise whether some labour market entrants are more likely than others to directly enter the labour market and find a stable position,
- *entry into unemployment and exit from unemployment along with chances of upward mobility and risks of downward occupational mobility in adult work life*, to investigate whether and to what extent labour market insecurity extends well into adult life,
- *entry into unpaid homemaking and exit from unpaid homemaking*, since we do not yet exactly know how labour market flexibility affects women's work and family careers, and,
- *satisfaction with job security*, to gauge the subjective perception of insecurity.

Partnership decisions involve decisions about timing and kind of partnership. The focus of this study is on first partnership formation and the empirical investigation centres on:

- *entry into first partnership* (marriage versus cohabitation), to analyse whether labour market insecurity leads to a deferment of partnership formation and, furthermore, to a growing propensity to enter into less binding relationships, and,
- *the transformation of cohabitation into marriage*, to explore whether labour market insecurity makes individuals less likely to transform cohabitation into marriage.

Lastly, as became clear in Chapter Two, parenthood decisions entail decisions about childlessness, timing of first birth, and number of children. This study focuses on *entry into parenthood* as an irreversible, life-shaping transition that constraints behaviour of both partners, particularly of women.

6.2.2 Measurement of employment and unemployment

In assessing the repercussions of labour market insecurity on the work and family life of men, women, and youth in particular, a shared definition and measurement of employment and unemployment in the three data sources at hand is of vital importance. For instance, the unemployment rate may vary considerably depending on whether registered unemployment, self-defined unemployment or the number of persons actively searching for a job is measured. The following analyses rest upon the International Labour Organisation (ILO) guidelines on measuring employment and unemployment.

Table 6.2 Measurement of employment and unemployment

Variable name	Definition	Countries' Particularities
Employed	performed some work during the reference week; or had a job but was away from it during reference week	GSOEP: self-defined activity status[39]
Unemployed	during the reference week without work and actively seeking paid employment or self-employment within last four weeks	GSOEP: only from 1994 onwards, actively seeking within last three months (1994-97)
In education	enrolled in education (self-defined activity status)	
Not economically active	during the reference week without work, not actively seeking and not homemaking	
Homemaking	during the reference week without work and not actively seeking, family care and maternity leave (self-defined activity status)	

[39] All three surveys include a measure of the self-defined activity status (i.e. respondents were asked to describe their current situation). Some may consider themselves as unemployed or doing housework while they are employed according to the ILO guidelines and vice versa. The BHPS and the ECHP also ask the respondent to state whether they performed some work during the reference week or had a job from which they were temporarily away from. Yet, this type of information is not available in most waves of the GSOEP.

A first distinction is made between labour force and economically inactive. Following the ILO definition, the labour force is subdivided as employed and unemployed. Those in *paid employment* are either persons who during a given reference period did any paid work or persons with a job that they were away from. According to this ILO definition any person who works at least one hour a week is a gainful worker. The measurement used for this study also considers the main activity of persons and separates those gainfully employed persons with more than 15 hours a week from those working less than 15 hours (Section 6.2.3). The *unemployed* includes all individuals above age 16 who during the reference period were jobless, currently available to take up work, and actively searching for gainful employment in a given period. *Not economically active* are persons who are not in the labour force, that is all persons who were not employed or unemployed during the defined reference period because of educational enrolment, homemaking, annuity, or other reasons such as illness or disability.

Extracting data from the GSOEP, the BHPS, and the ECHP, the above guidelines can only be partly met (see also Table 6.2 on the previous page). While the ECHP collects all the necessary information, measurement of employment and unemployment does not comply with the ILO guidelines in the other two surveys. In particular, the availability criterion and the active search criterion do not measure up to the criteria in the ECHP.[40] To conciliate the three data sources, the ILO definition has therefore to be slimmed. Unemployed persons are not gainfully employed during the last week but have actively searched for a new job within the previous four weeks.[41] Thus, the availability criterion does not come into consideration.[42] Apart from data availability and comparability, this decision may also be justified on substantive grounds. As to the above sketched ILO guidelines, the active search criterion is assumed to be the pivotal criterion. The availability criterion is much more difficult to fulfil for women who may actively search for work but face considerable hurdles to

---

[40] Between 1991 and 1997 the corresponding question in the GSOEP asks whether the respondent would be immediately able to start a new job. By contrast, in the ECHP and the BHPS availability is defined as being able to start a new job within two weeks. The BHPS data provide the relevant information only from 1996 onwards. See also Table 6.2.

[41] One could also study persons who are out of work and signed on at unemployment benefit office. But these persons are not necessarily ILO unemployed. In comparing the ILO unemployment rate and this so-called Claimant Count it can be shown that the rates have been much the same during high unemployment, while the Claimant Count is slightly smaller than the ILO rate during more prosperous economic times (for Britain see Nickell, 1999).

[42] In line with the ILO guidelines, respondents who did no paid work during the reference week but have already found a job and are waiting to start in this job in the future are considered unemployed.

entering a job since they take major responsibility in child-rearing and domestic work, and thus, have to arrange for day care. It is vital to bear in mind that this modified measurement is likely to lead to an overestimation of unemployment as compared to ILO unemployment.

To thoroughly analyse work and unemployment, transitions into and out of economic inactivity are of vital empirical importance. More precisely, it is an open research question whether, and if so, how exactly labour market deregulation and flexibility impact education-to-work transitions and the work-family linkage. To capture the mutual interdependence of work, unemployment, education, and inactivity, it is furthermore distinguished between persons in education and those not economically active for other reasons. Despite the attempt to bring in line the three data sources, the constructed variables are not strictly comparable due to variant wording in the three surveys along with changes in questionnaires over consecutive panel waves (see Table 6.2).

6.2.3 Measurement of labour market insecurity and individual resources

The theoretical framework has elaborated the prime importance of flexible forms of employment and risks of labour market exclusion as indicators of labour market insecurity. Recall from Chapter Three that this analysis primarily focuses on three measures. First, as detailed in the previous section, the individual *activity status* is looked at. A distinction is made between being enrolled in education, being employed, being unemployed, and being out of the labour force. Second, among the employed different *employment statuses* have to be taken into account and the analysis differentiates between employees, employers, and own-account workers. Third, the *employment relationship* of employees is described on the basis of their working hours and employment contract. As suggested by Hakim (1998), part-time employment comprises a very heterogeneous set of jobs, such as half-time jobs and marginal jobs. This analysis distinguishes between full-time, part-time, and marginal part-time work. All jobs of 15 to less than 30 hours per week are defined as part-time and marginal work involves less than 15 hours a week. With respect to the type of employment contract, the analysis separates permanent employment contracts from fixed-term work and seasonal contracts, respectively. Table 6.5 on the next page summarises variables, definitions, and countries' particularities.

Apart from this objective measure, this study also employs a subjective measure of insecurity. Again, data comparability turned out to be difficult to access. In the ECHP satisfaction with job security has been measured annually as part of a set of job items that can be rated on a 1-to-6 response scale, whereby 1 corresponds to '*not satisfied at all*' and 6 to '*fully satisfied*'. In the BHPS, however, a 1-to-7 response scale has been used so that this data-set can not be easily harmonised with ECHP data. In the GSOEP respondents are asked to evaluate their worries in various areas of life (e.g., job security, economic development, increase of crime, peace in the world), ranking themselves as very worried, slightly worried, or not worried. Due to this variant measurement it is not possible to conciliate the GSOEP with the other two data sources. A table giving more details on measurement of satisfaction with job security is annexed to this chapter.

Table 6.5 Measurement of labour market insecurity and individual resources

Variable name	Definition	Countries' Particularities
Type of contract	distinguishes between 1 'permanent employment contract', 2 'fixed-term or short-term contract' and 3 'casual work with no contract / some other arrangement', employees only	GSOEP: no casual contracts ECHP: not measured in the first panel wave, only available for ILO employed normally working more than 15 hours a week
Working hours	measured as hours per week normally worked in main job or business: 1'marginal: 1-14' 2 'part-time: 15-29' 3 'full-time: more than 30'	
Satisfaction with job security	1-to-6 response scale where 1 corresponds to '*not satisfied at all*' and 6 to '*fully satisfied*'	GSOEP: worries about job security BHPS: 1-to-7 response scale
Highest educational level achieved	Low: less than second stage of secondary education (ISCED 0-2) Medium: second stage of secondary level education (ISCED 3) High: recognised third level education (ISCED 5-7)	ECHP: measured only at entry into the survey, not annually updated BHSP / GSOEP: collapses
Occupation	1 'higher-grade professional', 2 'lower-grade professional', 3 'routine non-manual', 4 'petty bourgeoisie', 5 'farm workers', 6 'skilled manual', 7 'Semi- and unskilled manual'	GSOEP: four digit ISCO88-classification and occupational status BHPS: four digit ISCO88-classification and employment status ECHP: two digit ISCO88-classification and employment status

A main argument developed in this study is that individual degrees of job insecurity are substantially mediated by individual resources. Hence the analysis controls for the highest educational level achieved and the occupation. Chapter Four has shown how country-specific educational systems differ. Due to this institutional diversity, the comparative study of education requires a methodology which translates country-specific education levels into a comparable set of categories. To this end, various typologies have been developed, such as the *CASMIN classification* and the *International Standard Classification of Education* (ISCED).[43] Given the choice of data sources included in the analyses, this study applies the ISCED. While the GSOEP and the BHPS provide rich information and also allow for other classifications, the ECHP only separates recognised third level education (ISCED 5-7), second stage of secondary level education (ISCED 3), and less than second stage of secondary education (ISCED 0-2).[44] Various education variables provided in the GSOEP and the BHPS have been used to derive a similar three-level collapsed ISCED classification. This comparative measurement and taxonomy of education does not permit full allowance for within-country variety in educational careers. The analyses to be presented in Chapter Nine apply a more refined classification which is meant to better reflect institutional diversity.

In order to more completely capture the influences of individual resources this study also considers the role of occupations and uses a classification of occupational classes which rests on the EGP class schema that distinguishes positions within labour markets by means of the employment relations that they involve (Erikson and Goldthorpe, 1992; see Table 6.4 in the appendix of this chapter). To recode occupations, the *International Standard Classification of Occupations* (ISCO) along with available information on the employment status have been used.[45] It is, though, relevant to note that data on kind of occupational

---

[43] The CASMIN classification has been developed in the research project '*Comparative Analysis of Social Mobility in Industrial Nations*'. Interested readers may have a look at Müller *et al.* (1989) or Braun and Müller (1997). Readers interested in definitions, concepts, and operational instructions of ISCED are referred to UNESCO (1975), OECD (1999) and: http://www.unesco.org/education/docs/isced_1997.htm [05.08.03].

[44] A further major drawback of the measurement of education in the ECHP is that this information is collected only when respondents enter the survey. The highest educational level has not been updated over the first four consecutive panel waves even though young sample members may still upgrade their skills.

[45] The analysis uses the conversion tools provided by Ganzeboom H.B.G.; Treiman, D.J., International Stratification and Mobility, File: Conversion Tools. Utrecht: Department of Sociology, Summer 1994, which can be downloaded at: http://home.fsw.vu.nl/hbg.ganzeboom/. [18.11.03]. More information on ISCO codes can be found at http://www.ilo.org/public/english/bureau/stat/class/isco.htm [05.08.03] and http://www.warwick.ac.uk/ier/isco/brit/grplist.html [05.08.03].

activity and occupational position vary considerably not only between the three data sources, but have also been subject of amendments over successive observation years. Hence, analysts encounter difficulties in meeting requirements for data comparability.

6.2.4 Other variables

It is of vital empirical importance to study the effects of labour market insecurity and individual resources in the context of other individual characteristics and labour market influences on the work and family life of men and women. Previous research has extensively focused on various aspects of young people's transitions to the adult life course and their work and family life later on (Section 2.4). Starting from this body of literature, the analysis also controls for a series of other explanatory variables which are assumed to be important predictors of the processes under study. Since this study does not explicitly inquire into their impact, this section does not set out the measurement of these variables, but a short description can be found in the data and methods sections of Chapters Seven to Nine.

6.3 Methods

This study applies a combination of descriptive and multivariate analyses to investigate the impact of labour market insecurity on the work and family life of men and women. In doing so, it follows two analytical strategies. Firstly, whenever possible and theoretically justified this study pools data for the three countries and pursues joint analyses. In other analyses, separate models are estimated and room is left in order to take into account some unique features of each country under study. Nonetheless, this study aims to present highly standardised country-specific contributions that share a common structure and research focus, very similar methods, measures, graphical representations, and tables. While the various chapters to follow include data and method sections that brief these various descriptive and multivariate analyses, this section aims to introduce the statistical method applied to study life course transitions. To this end, let us first reiterate the transition processes under study and thereby derive what technique is needed to approach the various research questions.

The prime focus of this study is on employment, partnership, and parenthood decisions. Individuals are seen as rational actors who intentionally decide between various courses of action. Individuals may make these life course decisions at any point in their lifetime and this decision-making process is related to their previous and present life history. But we can not observe the decision-making process with social survey data. What we can measure, however, are the outcomes of this processes which are life course transitions. To put it into other words, survey data may yield information on the timing of employment, partnership, and parenthood transitions.

What we need is a statistical method that allows the prediction of the propensity of individuals to make these life-shaping transitions. While the various dependent and explanatory variables can change their state at any time, the panel data at hand provides annual data for various processes while providing monthly, retrospective information for others. Hence, the three data sources only allow the study of the probability of making certain life course transitions between each pair of panel waves. Given this rather crude measurement, discrete-time transition models are useful and this statistical method and its terminology is now described in some detail.

With discrete-time transition models one can analyse the transition rate of experiencing a particular event at time *t*. *Event* is a byword for an individual's transition from one discrete state to one (of several) potential discrete state(s) within a well-defined interval of time. Individuals in a specific discrete state who have a chance to switch to a specific outcome state during this period of time belong to the *risk set*. The time period that a person is at risk of event occurrence is defined as the *risk period*. In discrete-time analysis, the *hazard rate h(t),* or interchangeably *transition rate,* is defined as the conditional probability that an individual will experience an event at a particular time t_i, given that this event did not occur before time t_i and hence the individual still belongs to the risk set. In other words, in discrete-time methods time can take on only positive integer values and the hazard rate is given as:

$$h(t) = P(T = t_i | T \geq t_i) \text{ where } t_i \text{ (i=1,2,...) indicates the } i^{th} \text{ discrete time point} \qquad (6.1)$$

To model this conditional probability, one can specify a logit model in which the dependent variable indicates event occurrence at a specific point in time and is expressed as a logit (Allison, 1982, 1984; Yamaguchi, 1991). As an illustration, in the bivariate case the corresponding function reads:

$$Log\left(\frac{P(t)}{1-P(t)}\right) = a(t) + b_1 x_1 \qquad (6.2)$$

where $\frac{P(t)}{1-P(t)}$ gives the odds for a given probability P and the natural logarithm

of $\frac{P(t)}{1-P(t)}$ the logit of P.

As can be seen from Equation 6.2, in letting the intercept vary by the length of time in which the individual has been at risk, the discrete-time model permits the analysis of changes in the transition rate over time. Depending on the underlying assumption, one may either introduce duration as a continuous variable (e.g., linear duration effect) or include a set of dummy variables in the specified logit model (categorical duration effect). Estimates resulting from maximum-likelihood logit estimation provide the change in the logit of discrete-time transition models. Alternatively, one may display odds ratios from logistic regression that can be interpreted as follows: a one unit increase in an explanatory variable increases or decreases the odds of experiencing the event under study. Notice that, interchangeably, this study refers to risks, chances, and odds.

In order to apply this technique the data-set has to be set up in a specific way. The input data uses multiple records for each sample member. More precisely, in the so-called person-period record file, each period an individual belongs to the risk set is treated as a distinct observation. Since the analyses use annual panel waves of three longitudinal surveys, each record refers to one panel wave. Related to this, analysts also have to decide upon balanced versus unbalanced design during data extraction and processing. The longitudinal sample shrinks due to sample attrition over consecutive panel waves, but new sample members enter the survey according to the follow-up rules. While the so-called *balanced design* is conditional on the presence of sample members in all panel waves under study, the *unbalanced design* allows sample members to leave the sample while it adds new entrants to the sample. In this study all analyses are based on unbalanced longitudinal samples.

Let us now discuss some important extensions of the above specified statistical model. *First*, some variables to be considered in the analysis are time-constant. For instance, labour market entry cohort and birth cohort are fixed. Other covariates, however, may vary over time. To illustrate, individuals may upgrade their occupational grade or change a job position. These events may increase or decrease the transition rate under study. To disregard the time-relatedness of such parallel processes would mean to oversimplify the statistical model and to inaccurately estimate the hazard rate. Hence it may yield inadequate causal inferences. This brings us to an important point at issue in causal analysis. When analysing social processes, the disentanglement of cause and effect is not always straightforward.[46] Various social processes are not only mutually interdependent. Events may also seem to occur simultaneously given a crude time measurement (see Blossfeld, 1996). With respect to the life course transitions under study in this work, it is vital to keep in view that employment, partnership, and parenthood transitions are highly interconnected so that life events in one life domain are likely to have a reciprocal impact on the others and vice versa. It is therefore necessary to update time-varying information

[46] Readers interested in concepts and techniques of causal inference may consult two recent publications by Goldthorpe (2001b) and Pötter and Blossfeld (2001). For a thorough discussion of causes and time-dependent covariates consult Blossfeld (1996).

throughout the observation period. A technical question that arises at this point is how can one incorporate such explanatory variables in discrete-time transition models? Recall from the previous paragraph that annual panel data is arranged as a person-period file. This data structure allows the updating of time-varying variables from one time unit to another. Hence, to analyse the impact of a change in one explanatory variable in year t on the transition rate the following year such time-varying covariates can enter the equation as variables lagged by one panel wave. In the trivariate case with one time-constant and one time-varying variable, the logit function can be expressed as follows:

$$Log\left(\frac{P(t)}{1-P(t)}\right) = a(t) + b_1 x_1 + b_2 x_{2_{t-1}} \tag{6.3}$$

where x_1 is time constant and x_2 is time-varying.

A *second* extension of the discrete-time transition model takes into account alternative destination states. In various social processes potential destination states are competing and the occurrence of one event removes the individual from risk of the other events. To simplify matters, one may consider the transitions under study once more. Transitions from employment to non-employment may refer to either becoming unemployed or to exiting out of the labour market; unemployed may enter a job or leave the labour force. In the analysis of first partnership formation, the two competing risks are entry into cohabitation and entry into marriage. With respect to transformations of cohabitation into marriage, one has to consider marriage and union dissolution as competing risks. In the analysis of first parenthood there are no competing risks. Unlike in continuous-time event history models, the discrete-time likelihood function can not be factored into a set of single transition rates (Allison, 1982; Vermunt, 1997). Tto control for alternative outcomes in the multiple-risk model, multinomial logistic regressions have to be estimated, in which the dependent variable is coded zero for non-occurrence and 1, ..., j for event occurrence of the *j* competing risks.[47] The discrete-time, competing risks transition model can be expressed as follows:

---

[47] Alternatively, it is also feasible to pursue analyses for each destination state separately (Allison, 1995; see also Begg and Gray, 1984). The researcher then focuses on one specific event type, excludes all the person-years in which competing risks occur from the estimation sample and specifies a simple binomial logit model for the event of interest. This conditional maximum likelihood estimation yields parameter estimates that are unbiased, consistent, and asymptotically normal. The results diverge only insignificantly from those generated by multinomial logistic regression.

$$Log\left(\frac{P_j(t)}{1-\sum P_j(t)}\right) = a_j(t) + b_{j1}x_1 + b_{j2}x_{2t-1} \qquad \text{with } j= 1,2,\ldots \text{ discrete outcomes} \tag{6.4}$$

More advanced discussions of discrete-time transitions models are available in Allison (1982, 1984) and Yamaguchi (1991). Those who wish to gain a fuller understanding of event history techniques may also consult Blossfeld and Rohwer (2001).

Box 6.1 A note on autocorrelation of residuals in panel regressions and the Huber/White/sandwich estimator of variance

Autocorrelation violates an important assumption of regression analysis (Ostrom, 1978). To put the matter briefly, any regression model will almost certainly omit some measures that influence the dependent variable apart from all the explanatory variables included in the model specification. These uncontrolled influences are absorbed in the error term of the regression equation. In cases in which the error terms are correlated, autocorrelation is present and it is no longer assured that the standard errors are unbiased estimators of the actual standard deviations. As a consequence of autocorrelation, tests of statistical significance will yield invalid inferences.

It can be easily shown that autocorrelation is likely to occur in panel regressions which are based on person-period record files. To put it into words, in data-sets with repeated records on individuals, observations are not independent. If the analysis uses multiple records for each sample member, and the error associated to the specified regression model is the same for each period an individual belongs to the sample, the error terms will be correlated. To accurately specify regressions models, the statistical package STATA therefore allows the estimation of robust standard errors by using the so-called Huber/White/sandwich estimator of variance (White, 1980, 1982). While the estimated regression coefficients remain unchanged, this procedure will yield estimated standard errors that are robust to arbitrary forms of correlation within individuals. Notice that standard errors from binary and multinomial logistic regressions as well as ordered probit regressions to follow result from the Huber/White/sandwich estimator of variance.

Lastly, weighting procedures merit mention. All three data sources provide the analyst with various weights. Let us first consider what these weights are good for.[48] To begin with, for the panel data at hand, cross-sectional and longitudinal weights can be distinguished. As to the former, design and redressement weights can be used to compensate for disparate sample selection probabilities (for instance due to stratified sampling or cluster sampling). Furthermore, weights can be applied to adjust for non-response at the household and individual level. By contrast, with longitudinal weights, analysts attempt to correct for sample

[48] For an advanced treatment of survey sampling and weighting procedures refer to Gabler *et al.* (1994), Kish (1965), Kalton (1983), and Chaudhuri and Stenger (1992).

loss between consecutive panel waves due to sample attrition.[49] In the descriptive analyses this study makes use of weighting procedures to reflect the structure of the population.[50] However, all discrete-time analyses are pursued without weighting. This decision can be justified on substantive grounds. To put the matter briefly, all three surveys are based on a multistage, complex sample selection procedure. In order to estimate unbiased parameters for the survey population, design weights can be used. However, when using weights for complex samples, statistical packages tend to overstate or understate standard errors of survey estimates, and hence, inferences drawn from the survey population may not be valid (Kalton, 1983; Lipsmeier, 1999). For while statistical packages deal with simple random sampling, they usually can not handle such complex sample designs. There has been a great deal of discussion among statisticians, economists, and sociologists and it remains a controversial issue whether, and if so, how to use weights in analytical models based on complex samples. From a practical standpoint, however, one may argue that the longitudinal analyses pursued in this study take account of sample attrition in that they control for various social-demographic characteristics that are correlated with attrition.[51]

6.4 Summary and outlook

The goal of this chapter was straightforward. It detailed the data, variables, and methods used in this analysis and discussed issues of data comparability. The chapter pointed to some flaws in terms of data comparability, some of which are generally associated with systematic international comparisons, while others are clearly related to the longitudinal and life course approach of this study and, more particularly, the choice of countries and data sources. The chapter therewith provided the necessary background knowledge to follow the empirical investigations to be presented in Chapters Seven to Nine. These chapters aim to uncover the repercussion of labour market insecurity on the work and family life of men and women. More specifically, the remainder of the empirical part of

---

[49] It can be distinguished between survey related attrition (e.g., temporary drop-outs) and attrition that is not related to the survey (e.g., decease).

[50] The various analyses to follow are pursued using STATA (7.0) (see Kohler and Kreuter, 2001). This statistical package allows for so-called analytical weights. In doing so, weights are re-scaled so that the sum of all weights equals the number of observations. For a detailed discussion of the usage of weighted samples and tests of significance see Lipsmeier (1999). For more information on STATA refer to http://www.stata.com [02.05.03].

[51] For an overview on non-response in panel surveys and various explanatory factors refer to Schräpler (2000) and Mika (2002).

this study is structured as follows. A first goal of the empirical part of this study is to inquire into *labour market insecurity and its impact on the work life of young adults*. Chapter Seven presents a set of comparisons of patterns of labour market integration in Germany, Great Britain, and Spain with a particular focus on risks of insecure employment and labour market exclusion along with individual's perception of job security. This chapter provides an important insight into labour market insecurity of young adults in the three countries under study and serves as the impetus for the further analyses. A second aim is to investigate *the repercussions of labour market insecurity on the family life of young adults*. More precisely, Chapter Eight delves into partnership and parenthood decisions and asks whether and to what extent there is empirical evidence to suggest that labour market insecurity leads to a deferment of first partnership formation and entry into first parenthood. Chapters Seven and Eight therewith attempt to further our understanding of the consequences of labour market insecurity in early adult life. Yet, if we are to fully understand whether, and if so, how exactly labour market insecurity shapes the work and family life of men and women, adult life has to become a further issue of interest. A third objective is therefore to investigate *labour market insecurity and its consequences on work and family life of adult workers* and Chapter Nine gives a deeper understanding of whether and to what extent labour market insecurity extends into adult life.

Appendix

Table 6.3 Measurement of satisfaction with job security

	Question wording	Response scale
SOEP	1991-1997: What about the following areas: Do they worry you? If employed, the security of your job.	1-to-3 response scale, where 1 corresponds to '*very worried*', 2 to '*slightly worried*' and 3 to '*not worried*'
	1998-2000: What is your attitude towards the following areas - are you concerned about them?	1-to-3 response scale, where 1 corresponds to '*very concerned*', 2 to '*somewhat concerned*' and 3 to '*not concerned at all*'
BHPS	I'm going to read out a list of various aspects of jobs, and after each one I'd like you to tell me from this card which number best describes how satisfied or dissatisfied you are with that particular aspect of your own present job. Your job security...	1-to-7 response scale, where 1 corresponds to '*not satisfied at all*', 4 to '*Not satisfied / dissatisfied*' and 7 to '*fully satisfied*'
ECHP	How satisfied are you with your present job or business in terms or earnings, hours of work, working conditions etc.? Using the scale 1 to 6 please indicate your degree of satisfaction in each case. Position '1' means that you are not satisfied at all, and '6' that you are fully satisfied. Job security...	1-to-6 response scale, where 1 corresponds to '*not satisfied at all*' and 6 to '*fully satisfied*'

Source: GSOEP (1991-2001), BHPS (1991-2000), ECHP (1994-1997).

Table 6.4 The EGP class schema

Classes	Include
I	Higher-grade professionals, administrators, and officials; managers in large industrial establishments; large proprietors
II	Lower-grade professionals, administrators, and officials; higher-grade technicians; managers in small industrial establishments; supervisors of non-manual employees
IIIa	Routine non-manual employees, higher grade (administration and commerce)
IIIb	Routine non-manual employees, lower grade (sales and services)
IVa	Small proprietors, artisans, etc., with employees
IVb	Small proprietors, artisans, etc., without employees
IVc	Farmers and smallholders; other self-employed workers in primary production
V	Lower-grade technicians; supervisors of manual workers
VI	Skilled manual workers
VIIa	Semi- and unskilled manual workers (not in agriculture)
VIIb	Agricultural and other workers in primary production

Note: The starting point of this schema is the distinction between employees, self-employed, and employers. Class positions are further sub-divided on the basis of (i) number of employees and sector of employment within the class of employers, (ii) sector of employment within the class of self-employed workers, and, (iii) the type of labour contract and the conditions of employment within the class of employees.

Source: Erikson and Goldthorpe (1992: 38f.).

7 Labour market insecurity and its impact on labour market entry and early career

7.1 Introduction

Over the last decades, a growing deregulation and flexibility of labour markets in Europe can be observed, leading to an increase in various precarious employment relationships. Transitions from school to work appear increasingly complex and involve periods of temporary and part-time employment, unemployment, economic inactivity, job experimentation along with gainful employment during educational upgrading. Hence, labour market integration appears more and more fragmented and has extended well into adult work life. The theoretical discussion in the previous chapters established why and how labour market insecurity is assumed to shape individual life courses. Growing insecurity during labour market entry and early career may not only question the current economic standing of individuals. It may also impede their future labour market stability, and thus, their career maturity accumulation and long-run socio-economic standing. Fragmentation and uncertainty in early careers possibly mould individual life-shaping employment, partnership, and parenthood decisions.

Starting from these theoretical considerations, this chapter focuses on youth labour market integration in Germany, Great Britain, and Spain in the 1990s. More precisely, this chapter has a three-step endeavour. Firstly, it offers a description of the transition into employment and outlines whether and to what extent labour market entrants are confronted with job insecurity. Secondly, it relates individual degrees of satisfaction with job security with actual employment relationships. Thirdly, it describes longitudinal employment profiles in early labour market careers and inquires into patterns of instability.

The remainder of this chapter is structured as follows. A reiteration of the main lines of the theoretical framework, research questions, and hypotheses is given first, followed by data and statistical methods used in the analysis. The principal part of this chapter inquires into labour market insecurity and its impact on labour market entry and early career in Germany, Great Britain, and Spain. Section 7.5 includes the presented findings in a broader picture of labour market integration of young job seekers in Europe. Section 7.6 summarises the major findings, implications for the further analyses, and concluding remarks.

7.2 Theoretical background and research hypotheses

The starting point of this work is the assumption that the recent restructuring process of European labour markets lowers individual degrees of life course security, and hence, leads individuals to postpone life course decisions. The previous chapters stressed the key role of labour market integration and career stability for life course decision-making in modern societies. Through secure employment, so the argument, rational decision-makers seek to gain long-run certainty about their labour market career and socio-economic standing, which allows them to make life-shaping decisions. In order to uncover whether, and if so, how exactly labour market insecurity and partnership and parenthood decisions are interrelated, it is vital to gain an insight into individual patterns of insecurity and labour market exclusion. The central purpose of this chapter is therefore to understand how labour market insecurity interferes with individual's labour market entry and early career.

To approach individual career entry and subsequent labour market profile various transition processes and transition outcomes have to be considered. Firstly, one may study the movement of labour market entrants between educational enrolment, gainful employment, unemployment, and economic inactivity. Secondly, among those gainfully employed, one may trace transitions between secure and insecure job positions. In respect thereof, successful labour market entries and early careers may be captured by two main career indicators: chances to gain stable full-time employment and risks of unemployment. From a different angle, individual's perception and expectation about his or her future labour market career can be grasped as a further indicator of career stability. This chapter focuses on two research questions. Are some labour market entrants more likely than others to enter directly the labour market and find a stable position? And, to what extent are labour market entrants unsatisfied with their job security?

The key objective of this chapter is to describe similarities and dissimilarities of individual degrees of actual and perceived labour market insecurity in the three countries under study. According to the country-specific hypothesis it is proposed that insecurity is highly confined to entrants in the Spanish insider-outsider labour market, and hence, job precariousness and perceived job insecurity should be highest. Insecurity is expected to be more equally spread in Great Britain, but young adults presumably experience higher degrees of job insecurity and perceive their job as more insecure than Germans due to the British hire-and-fire system and a less well-defined education-to-work transition. One may also expect rather modest risks in terms of job insecurity in Germany, where flexibility has been introduced as a controlled experiment and the educational system is strongly coupled with the labour market. As compared to their West German counterparts, however, prior research has already revealed that East Germans are exposed to more insecurity (Chapter Four). It remains an open research question whether East Germans also perceive their job as less secure.

The chapter also draws attention to the role of individual resources and asks whether chances of secure gainful employment and risks of unemployment are stratified by educational attainment and occupational class. As formulated in more detail in Chapter 5, it is maintained that risks of labour market insecurity and exclusion are channelled to low-qualified individuals and those in semi- and unskilled occupational class. In summary, the theoretical discussion of Chapters Four and Five proposed that institutional filters and individual resources should absorb labour market insecurity with varying repercussions on individual career profiles. The following sections tackle upon this issue.

7.3 Data and methods

The data analysed come from two samples selected using annual panel waves of the European Community Household Panel (ECHP) and the German Socio-economic Panel Study (GSOEP) (see Section 6.1). More precisely, the analysis uses pooled ECHP data for the observation period 1994-96 and is limited to original sample members who were born after 1967 (thus aged at most 29 in 1996, the last available survey year in the ECHP), are not disabled, and reported complete information on all the variables of interest.[52] Since the ECHP data does not allow the differentiation between East and West German employees, the analysis is complemented by a comparable sample drawn from the GSOEP.[53] The study employs an unbalanced longitudinal sample and Table 7.1 gives some details on the survey population.

The principal focus of the analysis is on the type of job at labour market entry and early career, not the timing of labour market entry.[54] Several rationales are behind this. The previous chapters have shown that labour market integration

---

[52] Since information on the type of contract has only been collected from 1995 onwards, some analyses are confined to the time period 1995-1996. For the following analyses the modified ILO guidelines on measuring employment and unemployment are used (Chapter Six). Small case numbers and the questionnaire route in the ECHP do not permit an analysis of secondary part-time jobs.

[53] Recall from Section 6.1.4 that the analysis uses the samples for West and East Germans. Foreigners have been excluded.

[54] With labour market entry the analysis refers to school-to-work transitions as well as transitions from non-employment. The labour market entry – as studied within the confines of this chapter – is thus not necessarily the first entry into the primary labour market. The analysis of this chapter controls for important aspects of the early labour market career, such as labour force experience and previous spells of unemployment.

can no longer be understood as a single-step transition out of school and into work (see Section 2.2.1). Rather, young job seekers are increasingly moving between employment, unemployment, and further education, and it is therefore intricate to fix the moment when they manage to settle in the labour market. A second reason for this can be attributed to cross-national differences in institutional arrangements and job search strategies (Section 4.3). Likewise, for the purpose of this study the timing of labour market entry is not a useful indicator since it does not yield information on the type of job position and the degree of insecurity attached to it. This relates to another important issue to be kept in view. A salient transition route from school to work is often through an intermediate status as an apprentice. The analysis to follow, however, does not inquire into these intermediate statuses and also this decision can be sustained on substantive grounds. Firstly, vocational training is considered as part of the education period and not as first employment. Secondly, depending on the country-specific context under study, these intermediate roles have a different meaning and hence also different impacts on labour market integration of young job seekers (see Sections 2.2.1, 3.1.3, 4.3).

Table 7.1 Synopsis of survey population

		ECHP		GSOEP
	Germany	Great Britain	Spain	Germany
Number of individuals	1,678	1,768	4,859	3,695
Person-wave observations	4,316	3,800	11,746	9,630
in percent by gender				
% men	52.6	48.0	51.4	49.2
in percent by sample				
% East Germans				37.7
in percent by activity status				
% employed	63.0	66.2	36.2	55.2
% unemployed	4.8	9.1	18.1	5.6
% economically inactive	6.2	10.0	8.0	12.3
% in education	26.0	14.8	37.7	26.9

Source: ECHP (1994-1996), men and women aged 16-29. GSOEP (1994-1996), men and women aged 16-29.

The analysis of this chapter is divided into three distinct aspects of labour market integration and proceeds as follows:

Transition into employment: Section 7.4.1 deals with transitions into employment and inquires into chances to enter gainful employment and risks of entry into insecure jobs, in particular. Respondents who enter a job position directly after having left the educational system are separated from those who enter the labour market after having been out of the labour force (either unemployed or economically inactive). The models estimated in this section are multinomial logistic regressions (Aldrich and Nelson, 1984).

Perceived job security and employment relationship: Through a series of simple bivariate comparisons, Section 7.4.2 pinpoints individual characteristics of young job holders and identifies who is more likely to experience risky work relationships at the beginning of the labour market career. In the core part of this section, the analysis focuses on satisfaction with job security and estimates ordered probit regressions to unravel actual and perceived job insecurity (see Box 7.1).

Longitudinal employment profiles: Section 7.4.3 examines longitudinal employment profiles. The first aspect of concern is whether insecure entry-level jobs are stepping-stones to secure employment. An analysis of the risk of entering into unemployment follows. This issue is studied by means of a discrete-time competing risks model for exit from employment into either unemployment or economic inactivity.

Box 7.1 A note on maximum-likelihood ordered probit estimation

Satisfaction with job security has been measured on a 1-to-6 response scale in the ECHP, while worries about job security have been measured on a 1-to-3 response scale in the GSOEP. These two dependent variables are ordinal variables and the analysis therefore uses maximum-likelihood ordered probit estimation which allows the estimation of associations between a categorical and ordered dependent variable and one or more independent variables (Greene, 2003). The ordered probit estimation procedure gives an underlying score estimated by a function of the independent variables and a set of *i-1* cut points, where *i* is the number of possible outcomes of the dependent variable.

$$\Pr(outcome = i) = \Pr\left(\tau_{i-1} < \beta_1 x_1 + \beta_2 x_2 + \ldots + \beta_k x_k + u \le \tau_i\right) \qquad (7.1)$$

As illustrated in Figure 7.1, in the six-outcome probit model one estimates the coefficients $\beta_1, \beta_2, \ldots, \beta_k$ together with five cut points. The probability of observing a specific outcome *i* corresponds to the probability that the estimated linear function falls between two cut points of the area under a standard normal distribution. Putting it another way, the thresholds estimated for a particular outcome represent the point at which the preference to agree with one outcome of the response scale changes.

Figure 7.1 An illustration of the standard normal distribution and cut points in ordered probit models

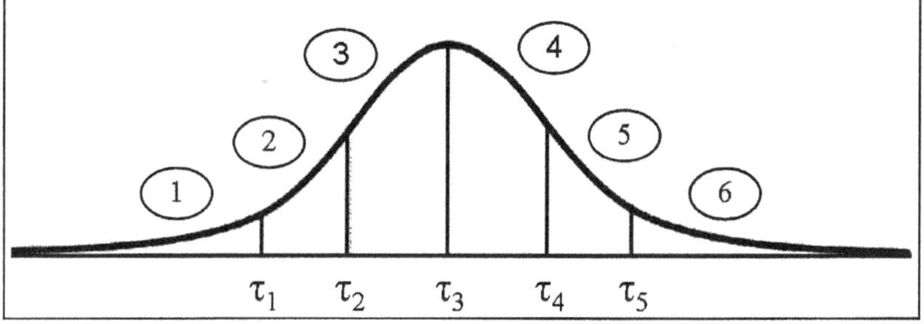

7.4 Findings: Labour market integration in Germany, Great Britain, and Spain

7.4.1 A description of the transition into employment

The school-to-work transition is important to individuals' subsequent life opportunities. Prior research analysing young people's transitions into employment has already focused on the effects of labour market segmentation, human capital, and cross-national variations in institutional arrangements (Shavit and Müller, 1998). We also begin to accumulate some knowledge of the impact of labour market insecurity on various types of uncertainty in early employment transitions (Golsch, 2001, 2003; Francesconi and Golsch, forthcoming; Kurz *et al.*, forthcoming; Kurz and Steinhage, 2001). This section moves beyond these country-specific and descriptive results to multivariate data analysis with pooled data. The research interest here is the cross-national variation in labour market entry patterns of young job seekers. More precisely, two issues are dealt with: the probability to find a job and the risk to enter into an insecure employment relationship.

The first analysis of this section uses a conditional sample of men and women who are enrolled in education in 1994 or 1995 and leave the educational system into employment, unemployment, or economic inactivity the subsequent year.[55] The following discussion rests on the results from multinomial logistic regression models and concentrates on the odds to enter gainful employment rather than unemployment. This analysis of the school-to-work transition is pursued for men and women separately and controls for:

- *Age*, to grasp duration effects,
- *country*, to test for cross-country variations,
- *highest educational qualification* (three-level collapsed ISCED classification, base=medium), to scrutinise to what extent educational attainment eases labour market integration as suggested in human capital theory and signalling theory (e.g., Rosenbaum *et al.*, 1990),
- *interaction between country and education*, to investigate whether the impact of educational attainment varies with the country-specific educational system, and,
- whether a person has been in a *paid apprenticeship* the previous year, to capture the role of intermediate statuses.

---

[55] One concern that arises in this analysis is that this sample is likely to be positively selected since some people with poor labour market prospects may be more prone to extend their participation in the educational system rather than becoming unemployed (see e.g., Offe, 1977).

Figure 7.2 Education-to-work transitions in Germany, Great Britain, and Spain by gender, education, and age (Conditional Effects Plots)

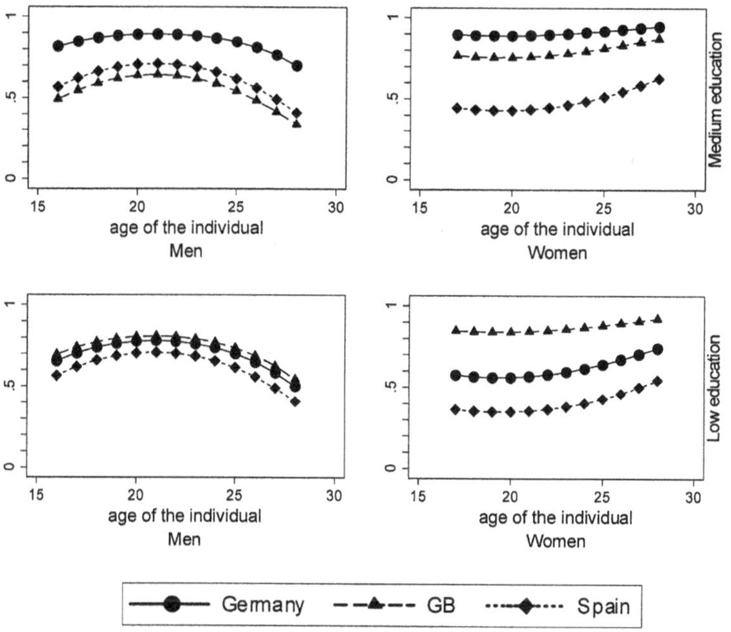

Note: Results from multinomial logistic regressions (see Table 7.2). Predicted probabilities of being employed rather than unemployed one year after leaving education.
Source: ECHP (1994-1996), men and women aged 16-29.

Figure 7.2 demonstrates the employment probabilities for men and women with medium or low educational qualification, respectively, by country and age. Table 7.2 in the appendix reports the coefficients of the full model. The results pinpoint significant differences between countries, men and women, and individuals with medium and low educational attainment. First, as to the upper panel of Figure 7.2, particularly educated German men have high chances to enter directly the labour market while employment probabilities are considerably lower in Great Britain and Spain. This cross-national variation seems insignificant, however, for men with low educational qualification. The picture changes somewhat once we study women. Employment probabilities of qualified women seem lowest in Spain and highest in Germany. Chances to hold a job one year after leaving education are also comparably high for women in Great Britain. In Germany, the odds to be gainfully employed, however, are considerably lower for women with low educational qualification. But this does not hold true for low-qualified women in Great Britain. These results are in line with the descriptive findings presented in Chapters Two and Three. In Germany, the education-to-work transition is smooth and the larger part of German education leavers enter gainful employment in a very short time. Educational qualification and paid apprenticeship are salient to young adults' labour market entry in Germany (see also Brauns *et al.*, 1999; Kurz and Steinhage, 2001). It is worthy to note though that employment probabilities are lower in the Eastern part of Germany, a within-country variation that could not be studied with the data at hand. Quite the opposite, the school-to-work transition is inherently unstable in the Spanish insider-outsider labour market and the greater part of young job seekers is hit by unemployment, no matter their educational attainment (see also Klijzing, forthcoming; Simó *et al.*, forthcoming). Particularly women are likely to become outsiders in the Spanish labour market. Great Britain represents yet another unique case. Educational qualification does not seem to be a significant mechanism through which labour market entries are determined. Yet, this finding may also be attributable to the imprecise measurement of educational qualification in the ECHP. Over and above, chances to enter gainful employment are higher for women than for men in Great Britain – a result that points to gender-segregated first entry patterns into the labour market (OECD, 1998).

A smooth education-to-work transition does not necessarily imply high degrees of job security and hence life course security. The second crucial question is which type of entry-level job young labour market entrants hold. In what follows, the enquiry concentrates on a conditional sample of persons who are not employed in 1994 or 1995 but hold a job the following year.[56] The analysis estimates separate multinomial logistic regression models for men and women in which the type of employment contract becomes the dependent variable (fixed-term contracts and casual work, permanent contract=comparison group). The study considers the following explanatory variables:

- *Age*, to gauge life cycle effects,
- *country*, to control for cross-country variations,
- *educational qualification*, since education is a determinant of employment probabilities,
- *interaction between country and education*, to evaluate whether the impact of educational attainment varies between the three countries,

---

[56] Again, this sample is likely to suffer from positiv selection because some people may be more hesitant to enter the labour market if they perceive that their chances to enter a secure insider position are small.

- *previous activity status* (two dummies for unemployment-to-work and inactivity-to-work, base=school-to-work), to capture whether the type of contract obtained at labour market entry varies with the previous status, and,
- a dummy variable for whether this is the *first entry into the labour market,* since labour market entrants lack career maturity which is meant to play a crucial role in job allocation processes.

Figure 7.3 Risk of having a fixed-term contract at labour market (re-)entry in Germany, Great Britain, and Spain by gender, labour force experience, and age (Conditional Effects Plots)

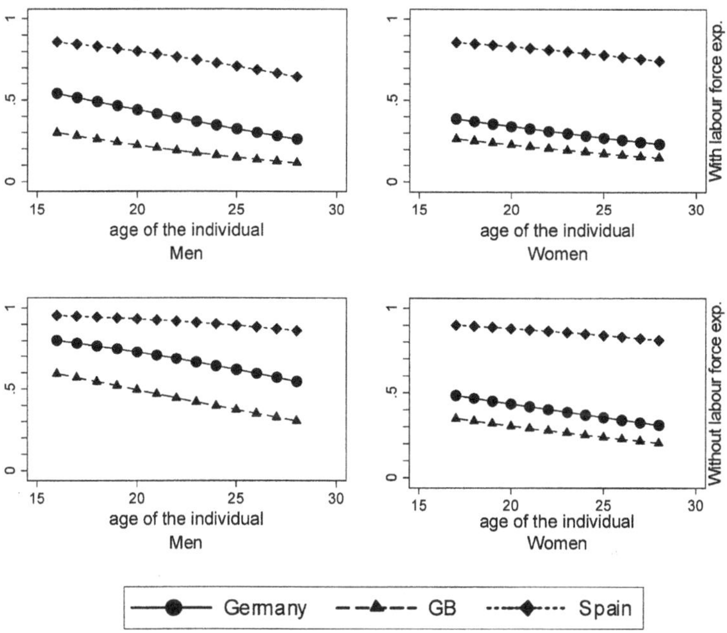

Note: Results from multinomial logistic regressions (See Table 7.3). Predicted probabilities of having a fixed-term contract rather than a permanent contract one year after leaving education for persons with medium educational qualification.
Source: ECHP (1994-1996), men and women aged 16-29.

The results from multinomial logistic regression are reported in Table 7.3, annexed to this chapter. From this it becomes evident that, independent from the transition made, the proportion of labour market entrants contracted on a fixed-term basis is highest in Spain and lowest in Great Britain. The following discussion concentrates on education-to-work transitions and Figure 7.3 presents the conditional effects plots for men and women, with and without labour force experience, respectively.

Figure 7.3 reveals further cross-national variations. As one would expect from the theoretical framework of this study, the risk to be employed on a fixed-term basis is particularly high in Spain. As compared to the highly flexible labour market in Great Britain, the odds to be contracted on a time-limited basis are also comparatively higher in Germany and there appears to be no statistically significant difference between young West and East Germans (Kurz *et al.*, forthcoming). Figure 7.3 also illustrates an interesting similarity. For men, the risk to enter the labour market as a fixed-term employee is generally higher for labour market entrants without labour force experience. This is particularly so for German men. This result is further substantiated by the finding that direct school-to-work transitions end more often in fixed-term employment as compared to unemployment-to-job and inactivity-to-job shifts (see Table 7.3).

To conclude, despite small case numbers and a short observation period, this section already evidenced some important cross-country differences which reside in the country-specific flexibility routes and institutional arrangements in education. But the findings also raise important questions. In Spain, labour market entrants are faced with pronounced uncertainty in work life, no matter their labour force experience or educational attainment. It remains an open research question, though, whether, and if so, for whom this insecurity is of a temporary nature only. By comparison, the degree of uncertainty faced by their German counterparts is considerably lower. However, young adults more often hold fixed-term jobs than their counterparts in Great Britain, particularly if this is their first job. What we do not yet know is whether these uncertain entry-level jobs are due to a recruitment strategy rather than a hire-and-fire strategy. If so, chances are high that, after an initial training and screening period, these positions will be converted into more secure employment relationships. Even though previous studies emphasise the increased prevalence of unemployment, part-time work, and inactivity among new labour market entrants in Great Britain during the 1990s (Taylor, 2000), the comparative analysis of this section revealed comparatively high employment probabilities and showed that education-to-work transitions less often result in fixed-term employment than in the other two countries. This is an outcome of the open employment system in Great Britain and the above analysis points to two other important research areas. First, problems faced by young people while entering the labour market may be linked to the less well-defined on-the-job training, and hence, leading to intense mobility and prolonged job-seeking to find an appropriate and lasting vacancy. Second, even though job seekers may enter the labour market quickly within the hire-and-fire system, the risk of job loss may be high, and this introduces uncertainty in individual life courses. The remainder of this chapter refers to these various issues.

Figure 7.4 Type of contract by other individual characteristics in Germany, Great Britain, and Spain (percent)

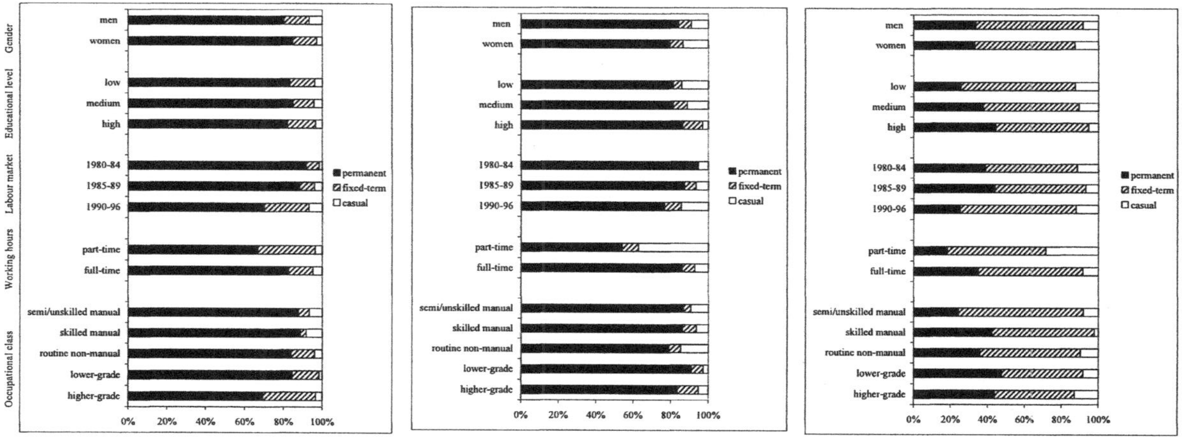

Germany Great Britain Spain

Note: High educational level – recognised third level education (ISECD 5-7); medium – second stage of secondary level education (ISCED 3), low – less than second stage of secondary education (ISCED 0-2). Weighted by cross-sectional weights of interviewed persons.

Source: ECHP (1996), men and women aged 16-29, employees only.

7.4.2 Perceived job security and employment relationship

A second dimension of uncertainty is perceived job insecurity, here measured by satisfaction with job security. Are those in obviously insecure positions also less satisfied with job security?

Before focusing on the results obtained from the multivariate analyses, this section first offers a useful description of who are the temporary employees. An important question within the comparative framework of this study is this: Are there differences in the composition of temporary employees in the selected countries? This information provides us with the background against which to interpret cross-country variations in job satisfaction and longitudinal employment profiles. Figure 7.4 shows the proportion of men and women having a permanent, fixed-term, or casual contract in 1996 by gender, educational level, labour market entry cohort, working hours, and occupational class. These stacked bar charts reveal two salient pieces of information.

First, there is a fair amount of heterogeneity across workers in Germany, Great Britain, and Spain. When studying a larger age group, the charts reveal even more clear patterns with respect to educational attainment, occupational standing, and labour market entry cohorts (Golsch, 2003). This indicates more pronounced differences across workers if older, and hence, more experienced and better qualified individuals are included in the analysis. As to the sample used for this study, few have already completed third level education and the larger part is at the very beginning of their occupational career. Yet, as young adults advance in their jobs, some seem more likely than others to gain stable employment, an issue which it is turned to in Section 7.4.3.

Second, country differences prevail. A first striking variation is this: In Spain, only 34 and 33 percent of men and women, respectively, have a permanent contract. Women are more often casual workers while men hold more often fixed-term posts. Quite the opposite, in Germany and Great Britain more than 80 percent of young adults are permanent workers. Yet, the proportion of fixed-term employees is higher in Germany than in Great Britain. While there are no pronounced differences with respect to educational qualification in Germany, the results for Spain reveal a clear pattern: the proportion of permanent workers is highest within the group of high-qualified. As compared to those with lower educational level (25 percent), 38 percent of men and women with middle and 44 percent of those with high educational qualification are permanent employees. By contrast, particularly employees with high educational attainment hold fixed-term contracts in Great Britain. Figure 7.4 suggests a similar pattern for occupational class. In Spain, labour market insecurity appears particularly channelled towards low qualified and semi- and unskilled workers, a finding that is further substantiated by previous studies (Simó *et al.*, forthcoming). While 68 percent of all semi- and unskilled employees have a fixed-term contract, this is only the case for 43 percent of all higher-grade and 44 percent of all lower-grade professional workers. Hence, education and occupation seem to function as a significant buffer for increased labour market flexibility in Spain. In Great Britain, differences with respect to occupational standing are much less clear-cut, indicating that occupation is a less distinct shield against insecurity. Yet, semi- and unskilled employees as well as non-manual employees are more often casual workers and fixed-term contracts seem more prevalent in higher-grade professional occupations (see also Francesconi and Golsch, forthcoming). In Germany then, the proportion of fixed-term employees is remarkably high among higher-grade professionals. Other studies have already shown that low-qualified employees but also university graduates more often occupy fixed-term positions (Bielenski *et al.*, 1994; Kurz *et al.*, forthcoming). The latter result has been attributed to the fact that many university graduates hold a job in the public sector, where fixed-term contracts are more widely-used than in private firms. This is in stark contrast to Spain and a revealing result inasmuch as in Spain insecurity is directed towards the inherently unstable positions in the lower segments of the labour market, whereas in Germany a good deal of fixed-term employees is in rather protected and well-paid positions that offer good career prospects. Figure 7.4 also shows that fixed-term and casual posts are first and foremost part-time positions. So, a lack in contractual security seems to go hand in hand with lower incomes in either part-time positions or low occupational classes. Lastly, the proportion of fixed-term contracts is especially in the youngest labour market entry cohort (1990-96). Figure 7.4 exhibits further cross-country variations, however. While in Spain only 25 percent of the most recent labour market entry cohort has a permanent position, this relates to 70 and 76 percent in Germany and Great Britain, respectively. Looking at the cohort 1980-84, over 90 percent have entered a permanent post in Germany and Great Britain. By contrast, in Spain 50 percent in the cohort 1980-84 are fixed-term employees and 11 percent perform some casual work without contract. In this respect, other investigations reveal a clear age and cohort effect for temporary employment in Spain: young, and the more recent labour market entry cohorts in particular, hold precarious jobs (Golsch, 2003).

In summary, in respect of the various important between-country variations, we may reckon that labour market insecurity has a potentially different meaning for young workers and their professional career in Germany, Great Britain, and Spain. Based on these findings, the analysis now tries to unravel perception, type of employment relationship, and country. Unfortunately, the ECHP data that has been used thus far does not allow the separation of East and West German employees. The following analysis makes a two-step endeavour. First, using the harmonised ECHP data it provides an examination of satisfaction with job security in Germany, Great Britain, and Spain. Second, the analysis explores data from the GSOEP and provides some illustrative results on Germany. Due to different questions and answers in the ECHP and GSOEP questionnaire, however, the results are not directly comparable (see Chapter Six). To give a picture of the degree of satisfaction, Figure 7.5 shows Box-and-Whisker plots by country and type of employment contract.

Figure 7.5 Degree of satisfaction with job security by type of contract in Germany, Great Britain, and Spain (Box-and-Whisker Plots)

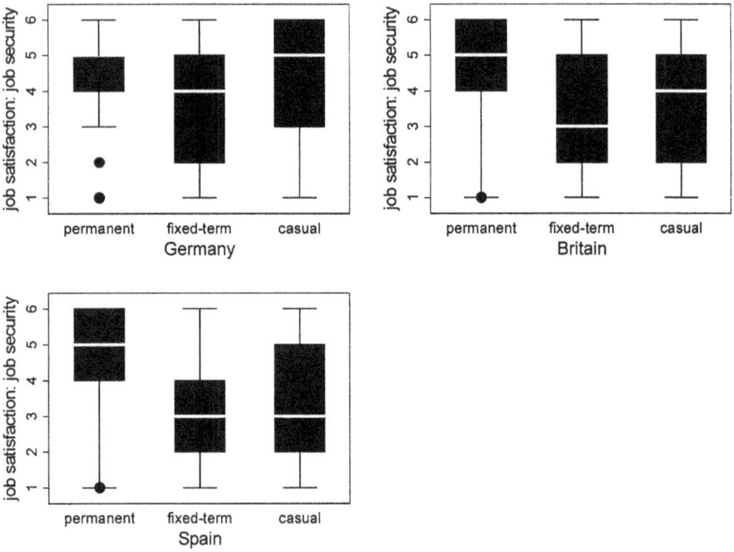

Note: 1 stands for '*not satisfied at all*', 6 for '*fully satisfied*'. Weighted by cross-sectional weights of interviewed persons.
Source: ECHP (1995-1996), men and women aged 16-29, employees only.

In all three countries permanent employees rate their job as more secure compared to those in temporary positions (see also Golsch, 2003). Further investigations summarised in Table 7.4 in the appendix of this chapter reveal statistically significant mean differences in satisfaction with job security by type of employment contract in all three countries. Yet, Figure 7.5 also shows important variations between Germany, Great Britain, and Spain. The inter-quartile range is smallest for permanent employees in Germany. By contrast, the upper and lower quartiles are larger in Great Britain and Spain. Hence, holding a permanent job in Germany generally implies higher degrees of satisfaction with job security. Yet, in comparing the mean satisfaction of permanent employees, Spaniards feel significantly more secure than their counterparts in Germany and Great Britain (Table 7.4). Figure 7.5 also exhibits pronounced differences between non-permanent employees. While fixed-term and casual employees rate their job as comparatively insecure in Spain, the median and inter-quartile range is larger in the other two countries. Particularly German fixed-term employees are more satisfied.

The descriptive results in Figure 7.5 already provide support for the hypothesis that subjective degrees of insecurity vary across countries. In order to test more fully for between-country variations, the following analysis runs ordered probit regressions, which treat satisfaction with job security as the outcome variable. A single model for all three countries has been specified that controls for:

- *Country*, which is meant to reflect country-specifics,
- *type of employment contract*, to capture the impact of objective job insecurity on satisfaction with job security,
- *interaction between employment relationship and country*, to scrutinise country-specific differences in the impact of employment relationships, and,
- a set of *control variables* (age and age square[57], occupational class, working hours, and marital status) that have been shown to determine job satisfaction (Chapter 3.1.5).

This section presents separate models for men and women to take into account potential gender differences. Figure 7.6 shows conditional effects plots that show predicted probabilities to be fully satisfied with job security by employment relationship, country, and gender. The upper panel displays the results for men, the lower panel refers to women. Table 7.5, annexed to this chapter, reports the coefficients.

---

[57] Somewhat surprisingly, the results of this specification suggest that satisfaction with job security declines with increasing age of men. Further analyses (not shown here) revealed offsetting effects. While the effect of age is large, negative, and significant in Spain, the reversed effect can be observed in Germany, and the effect is insignificant in Great Britain. We cannot detect any significant effect of age on women's satisfaction with job security. Again, this is due to the fact that the effect of age is positive in Germany and negative in Spain, while it does not have any significant impact in Great Britain.

Figure 7.6 Satisfaction with job security by type of contract, gender, and age in Germany, Great Britain, and Spain (Conditional Effects Plots)

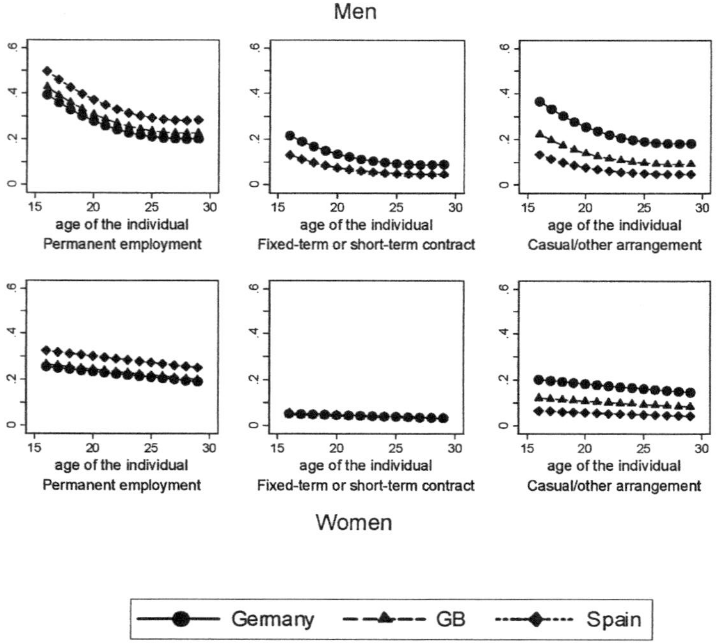

Note: Results from ordered probit regressions (See Table 7.5). Predicted probabilities of being completely satisfied with job security for married, skilled manual, and full-time workers.

Source: ECHP (1995-1996), men and women aged 16-29, employees only.

Figure 7.6 reveals that permanent employees are generally more satisfied than fixed-term employees. Spaniards feel more secure than their counterparts holding a permanent job in Germany or Great Britain. Interestingly, there are no significant differences between permanent workers in the latter two countries. The picture is different for fixed-term employees and it is a captivating finding that German employees appear now more satisfied than their counterparts in Great Britain and Spain. A reasonable explanation for this result refers to the closed employment system in Germany, where temporary contracts are more likely to function as a screening tool to recruit workers for permanent posts. However, as can be seen from the lower panel of Figure 7.6, this finding does not show up for women. With the exemption of Germany, men who perform some casual work are significantly less likely to be fully satisfied. Although not significantly different, this holds also true for women.

Figure 7.7 Worries about job security by type of contract in East and West Germany (Stacked bar chart)

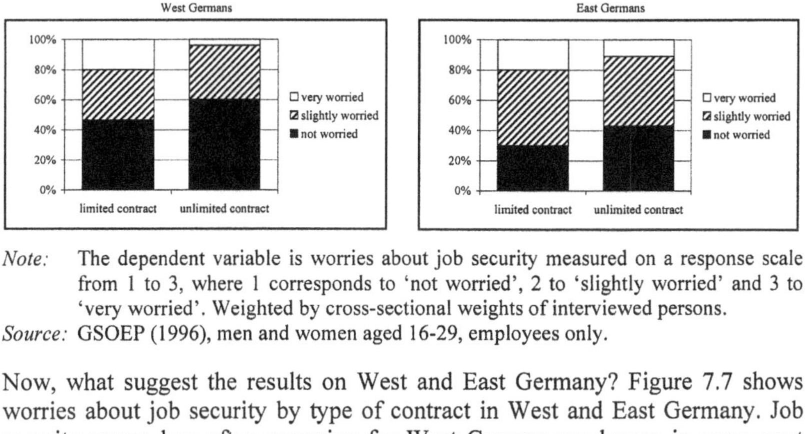

Note: The dependent variable is worries about job security measured on a response scale from 1 to 3, where 1 corresponds to 'not worried', 2 to 'slightly worried' and 3 to 'very worried'. Weighted by cross-sectional weights of interviewed persons.

Source: GSOEP (1996), men and women aged 16-29, employees only.

Now, what suggest the results on West and East Germany? Figure 7.7 shows worries about job security by type of contract in West and East Germany. Job security seems less often worrying for West German employees in permanent employment: about 58 percent do not worry and some 37 percent have only slight worries. By contrast, East German employees on a temporary contract are by 10% points more often very worried, while they are by 14% points less often not worried than those in permanent positions.

Figure 7.8 Worries about job security by type of contract, gender, and age in East and West Germany (Conditional Effects Plots)

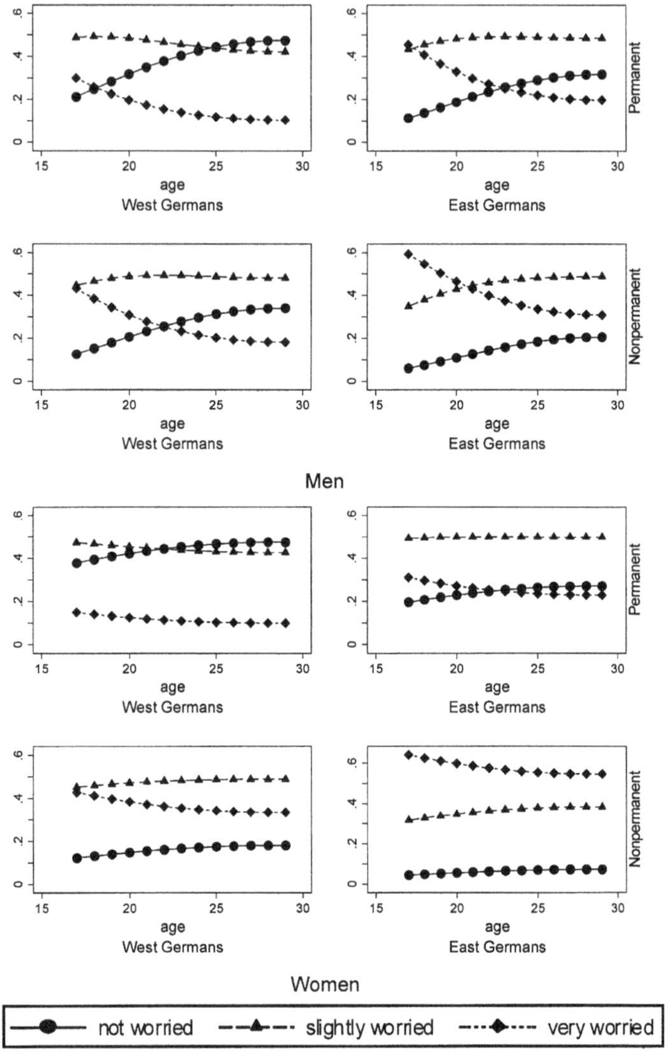

Note: Results from ordered probit regressions (See Table 7.5). Predicted probabilities for married, skilled manual, and full-time workers.

Source: GSOEP (1995-1996), men and women aged 16-29, employees only.

Next, the analysis runs ordered probit regressions and estimates the probability to be worried about job security. The underlying statistical model is the same that has been used for the above analysis with pooled ECHP data. Figure 7.8 on the previous page shows the results for men (upper panel) and women (lower panel) and for all three outcomes of the dependent variable (the estimates are presented in Table 7.5, annexed to this chapter). Notice that various characteristics are held constant in the specific sub-sample to show the predicted probabilities for permanent and non-permanent employees, respectively. At the core of the following discourse are the conditional effects for whether individuals are very worried about their job security, indicated by a large square in Figure 7.8.

Two important results can be stressed. Firstly, in line with the above analysis, permanent employees are less likely to be very worried as compared to non-permanent employees. Secondly, East Germans are much more prone to be very concerned, an expected within-country variation given the dim job prospects in the tight East German labour market (Chapter Four).

In concluding this section, the presented descriptive analyses revealed common factors that account for variation in job satisfaction. Permanent employees generally feel more secure. Yet, this is even more pronounced in the Spanish insider-outsider labour market where strong legal obligations protect permanent employees from dismissal. In contrast, temporary employees in Germany seem more satisfied with their job security than their counterparts in Great Britain and Spain. Taken on their own, details of perceived job security and employment relationships can say relatively little about whether, and if so, for whom insecurity at first entry into the labour market has a serious impact on the professional career during early adult life. More precisely, the different conclusions reached by the above analysis raise two important questions. Are temporary jobs dead-end roads or rather stepping-stones to better, more secure employment? And, to what extent does job insecurity increase the risk of social exclusion? The following section will therefore inquire into longitudinal employment profiles.

7.1.1 Longitudinal employment profiles in early labour market careers

Having entered work, individuals experience different patterns of labour market mobility and success. The discussion of the results of this section is arranged around two central indicators of career stability, which are transitions from insecure to permanent employment and risk of job loss.

Longitudinal employment profiles give us a better understanding of how long temporary employment can last. Table 7.6 on the following page presents row percentages for type of contract in 1995 by type of contract one year later. In all three countries, the great majority of permanent employees remain in their position. In Spain, about 88 percent are still in permanent employment. This is even more often the case in Great Britain (95 percent) and Germany (96 percent). Also, in all three countries there is considerable annual change with respect to temporary employees, indicating that a substantial proportion of non-permanent employees succeed in entering permanent employment. However, this probability seems much higher in Germany and Great Britain, whereas temporary employment in Spain is more long-term. For instance, while only 47 percent of British employees holding fixed-term posts in 1995 are still in this position one year later and about 42 percent manage to enter a permanent position, the respective percentages for Spain amount to 75 and 19 percent. Among casual employees we observe even more annual movement. These transition rates are particularly high in Germany, where it is much more uncommon to perform some casual work during the early labour market career. All in all, in Germany and Great Britain temporary employment functions more often as a stepping-stone to permanent employment.

Table 7.6 Transitions between different employment contracts in Germany, Great Britain, and Spain between 1995 and 1996 (percent)

	in 1996		
	permanent	fixed-term	casual
in 1995			
Germany			
permanent	96.05	1.87	2.08
fixed-term	48.69	49.72	1.59
casual	77.67	4.43	17.90
Great Britain			
permanent	94.58	2.62	2.80
fixed-term	42.17	46.58	11.25
casual	44.90	2.89	52.21
Spain			
permanent	88.30	9.27	2.43
fixed-term	18.70	75.35	5.94
casual	11.45	50.28	38.27

Note: Row percentages for type of contract. Weighted by base weights of interviewed persons.
Source: ECHP (1995-1996), men and women aged 16-29, employees only.

Further analyses provide support for the assumption that transition rates into permanent employment significantly differ between countries. Table 7.7, annexed to this chapter, presents the findings of a multinomial logistic regression model for leaving an insecure job position, controlling for labour force experience, country, type of employment contract, occupational class, sector, and gender. Keeping constant all other covariates, the transition rate into permanency is lowest in the Spanish insider-outsider market whereas the highest odds are found in the flexibly co-ordinated German labour market. Various other findings merit mention. The more employment experiences individuals have gained, the higher their transition rate into secure gainful employment. After an initial rise in labour force experience, however, this effect will tend to level off. Chances to escape from insecure employment also vary with respect to occupational class and sector of employment. Yet, these effects are country-specific. Vis-à-vis employees in skilled manual positions, workers in lower-level but also higher-level occupations have lower chances to transform an insecure contract into a permanent one. Compared to semi- and unskilled manual workers in Germany, however, transitions into permanent employment are even more improbable in Great Britain and in Spain, in particular. At the same time, there appears to be no significant difference between higher- and lower-grade professionals in the three countries under study. Yet, although not significantly different, the transition rate into permanent employment appears to be comparatively higher for professional workers in Spain. This result is tentative, yet linked to the above finding that insecurity is channelled towards the inherently unstable positions in the lower segments of the Spanish labour market. Finally, the public sector in Germany inhibits routes into permanent work. In Great Britain and Spain the reverse is true; here employees in the public sector are not worse off as compared to those employed in the private sector. Why is this the case? Again, this finding is tentative and should be judged in the context of previous research. In Germany, the risk of temporary employment is considerably higher in the public sector (Kurz *et al.*, forthcoming). While public sector employees with a permanent contract are better shielded against unemployment than their counterparts in the private sector, temporary workers are more often hit by unemployment than those occupying a temporary post in the private sector (Kurz and Steinhage, 2001). Hence, holding a fixed-term contract in the German public sector seems to go hand-in-hand with greater insecurity for young workers.

A higher labour market turnover is inherently associated with non-permanent employment. A related question, however, is whether labour market insecurity at labour market entry has any impact on transitions to unemployment. The latter mobility event is important to individual labour market careers, since unemployment has a severe penalty on subsequent job tenure (Böheim and Taylor, 2000; Golsch, 2002; Gregg and Wadsworth, 2000): Individuals who enter a job after a spell of unemployment are more likely to be in uncertain positions, such as temporary employment and low-paid occupations. Past unemployment spells also increase the risk to re-enter unemployment and unemployment risks are considerably higher for non-permanent workers (see Francesconi and Golsch, forthcoming; Golsch, 2003; Kurz *et al.*, forthcoming).

In what follows, the analysis goes a step forward and specifies a statistical model that allows the test for between-country variation in unemployment risks. The analysis uses annual observations on employees at risk to be hit by unemployment or exit the labour market the ensuing year. The discrete-time competing risks transition model for entry into unemployment includes the following explanatory variables:

- *Labour force experience and labour force experience squared*, to control for duration effects,
- *country*, which is meant to reflect country-specifics,
- *type of employment contract*, to capture the impact of job insecurity on the probability to enter unemployment,
- *interaction between country and type of employment contract*, to scrutinise cross-country differences in the impact of employment relationships,
- *occupational class*, which is meant to reduce heterogeneity between individuals,
- *unemployment experience* during the past five years, since previous unemployment spells have been shown to increase the probability of future unemployment,
- *interaction between country and unemployment experience*, since the effect of past unemployment spells may depend on the country-specific context,
- *gender*, and
- *interaction between country and gender*.

Table 7.7 in the appendix shows the estimates obtained from the above model and Figure 7.9 on the subsequent page presents conditional effects plots for transitions into unemployment by gender, type of employment contract, labour force experience, and unemployment experience. Regardless of the other explanatory variables, the risk of experiencing unemployment is substantially greater for flexi-workers than for workers in permanent employment. Over and above these effects, the estimates document that workers who have been previously unemployed are also exposed to a higher hazard of unemployment experience. Hence, temporary employment is likely to destabilise the professional career of young adults. Yet, cross-country variation exists. As one would expect from the discussion in Chapters Three and Four, the transition rate into unemployment is highest in Spain and lowest in Germany. More importantly, temporary employment and previous spells of joblessness emerge as having a country-specific effect on the risk to be hit by unemployment. In Spain, the hazard rate is generally high, no matter the type of employment contract or past unemployment experiences. This is a captivating finding since holding a permanent contract in the Spanish insider-outsider labour market was expected to shield labour market insecurity. The results of this analysis, however, demonstrate that few have already filled a permanent job and these employees are not yet significantly less likely to be hit by unemployment than those occupying fixed-term jobs. This may be due to a significant age and cohort effect of temporary employment in Spain. If the analysis includes older and hence more experienced workers, permanent employment functions as a protective factor (Golsch, 2003).

By contrast, permanent employees face a considerably lower redundancy risk in Germany and Great Britain. Yet, as can be seen from Figure 7.9, this between-country variation is less pronounced when studying fixed-term employees. This is even more obvious for temporary employees with unemployment experiences. Hence, in Germany and Great Britain, insecurity appears particularly funnelled to flexi-workers with previous unemployment spells. Independent of the other explanatory factors, occupational class plays a significant role and this gives support to the assumption that individual resources serve to shield risks in insecure times (Table 7.7).

Figure 7.9 Risk to be hit by unemployment in Germany, Great Britain, and Spain by type of employment contract, unemployment experience, labour force experience, and gender (Conditional Effects Plots)

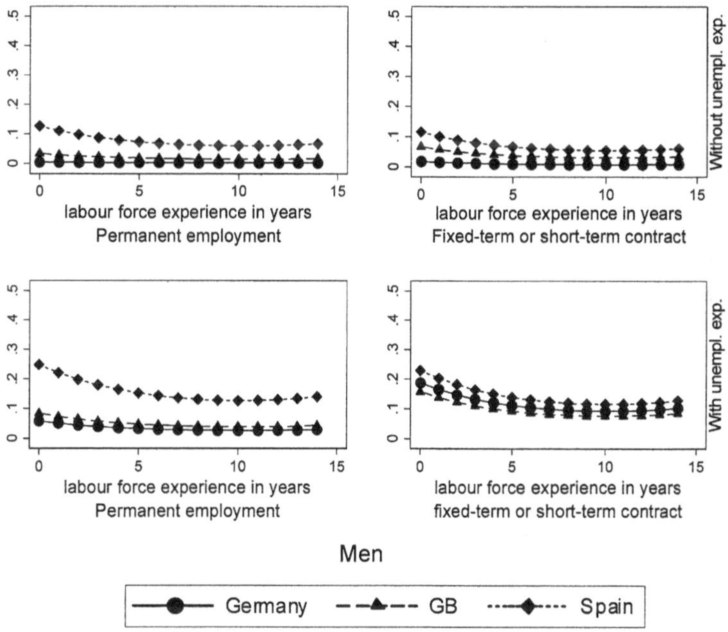

Figure 7.9 *continued*

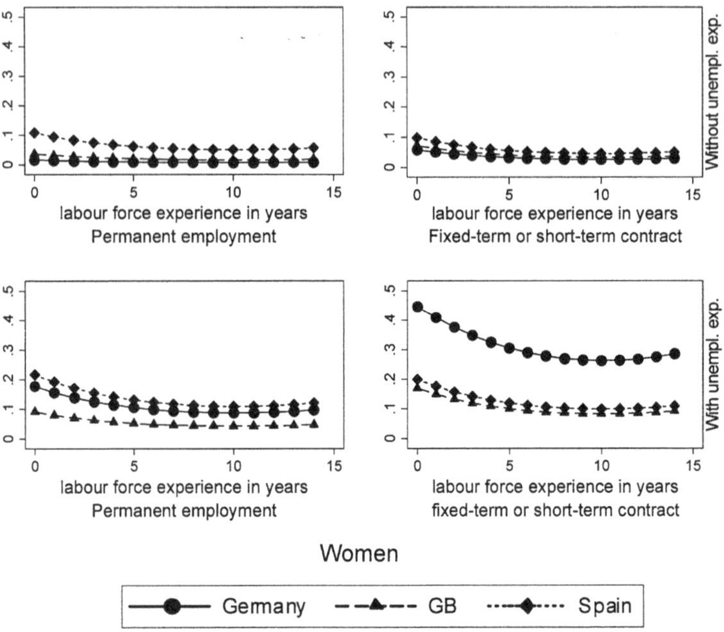

Note: Results from specification [2] in Table 7.6. Predicted probabilities for skilled manual workers in the private sector.

Source: ECHP (1995-1996), men and women aged 16-29, employees only.

In summary, this section provides further evidence to suggest that labour market deregulation and flexibility have serious repercussions on young adult's labour market entry. From a comparative perspective, however, the important result to stress is that – as already seen in the previous sections – young Spaniards are exposed to more uncertainty, whereas young adults in Germany and, to a lesser extent, in Great Britain seem less affected by increasing insecurity. This difference roots in distinct country-specific institutional packages (Chapter Four). Due to this institutional entrenchment labour market insecurity has presumably also very different implications for individual's early labour market career and hence their life course security and life course decisions.

7.5 Crossing the border – Central findings from other country-specific studies

This chapter has a further goal beyond the analysis of labour market entry and early career in Germany, Great Britain, and Spain. This is a short review of central findings from other country-specific studies. This endeavour implies two strong points. Firstly, it permits to make an estimate whether, and if so, to what extent the identified repercussions and individual adaptation strategies are the same in other countries that have entered upon comparable flexibility routes and institutionalised similar arrangements in education and welfare. In this vein, this section seizes a chance to corrobate the belief that institutional arrangements serve to mitigate or intensify the negative effects of labour market insecurity. Secondly and related to this, this review extends the scope of the empirical analysis that was regionally limited due to time and space limitations of this project. While there have been numerous cross-national comparative studies that inquire into similarities and dissimilarities across countries as well as a huge amount of country-specific studies that describe determinants and changes in timing, sequencing, and prevalence of mobility events in early labour market careers across birth cohorts, few have tried to gauge the impact of labour market insecurity from a comparative perspective. This section zooms in on the outcomes of selected comparative analyses that discuss at greater length the role of intervening variables and seek to identify common factors along with international differences in labour market integration.

In accord with the theoretical framework of this study, various other studies reveal that young adults are more and more exposed to labour market insecurity (Blossfeld *et al.*, forthcoming). This becomes evident in progressively more uncertain employment relationships such as temporary employment contracts. There is further empirical evidence that such flexible jobs tend to be more precarious than permanent insider positions (e.g., Giesecke and Groß, 2003; DiPrete *et al.*, 2001). Yet, from the cross-national comparison, important differences have been identified in terms of unemployment entry, share of flexible labour, chances to end unemployment or insecure employment, chances to re-enter the labour market from non-employment as well as poverty risks. In respect thereof, the manpower who seems the strongest affected is the one in Southern European labour markets (Muffels and Fourage, 2000). Against this background, prior research has demonstrated that nation-specific flexibility tracks and institutional arrangements in employment relations, education, and welfare fulfil the function to shield labour market insecurity to varying degrees and with unique repercussions for distinct groups of young job holders (Blossfeld *et al.*, forthcoming). As already discussed in Section 4.3, previous studies have extensively focused on the important role of educational systems for the smoothness of education-to-work transitions (Allmendinger, 1989;

Gangl, 2001; Shavit and Müller, 1998). The findings of cross-national research furthermore show that so-called 'linkage structures' which bridge transitions into and out of employment along with transitions into and out of formal education lower the risk to lose one's job whereas unemployment rates are considerably higher in countries where these transitions are more unstructured (Sackmann, 2001). Other studies have pointed out differences in employment demand, active labour market policies and rigidity of employment protection systems that account for cross-national variation in unemployment-to-job shifts (Russell and O'Connell, 2001). Moreover, strict employment protection legislation decreases job mobility rates and reduces status returns to mobility among young labour market entrants, particularly in the Southern European countries. Hence, in these latter countries chances are high that young workers remain trapped in insecure positions (Gangl, 2003). As also suggested by the findings of this chapter, insecurity appears directed to outsiders in insider-outsider labour markets of closed employment systems. Quite the opposite, risks of insecure employment and unemployment are more spread in the open employment system and job insecurity seems of short duration (Blossfeld *et al.*, forthcoming). We may, however, be surprised to see some long-term effects of insecurity on the adult employment career in the highly flexible British labour market (see Chapter Nine). As to micro-level factors, individual resources have been shown to determine youth labour market integration in increasingly insecure times (see also Section 4.3). Drawing on the insights of the comparison of fourteen countries from five welfare regimes, an important result of the volume by Blossfeld *et al.* (forthcoming) is the so-called 'inequality of uncertainty': In line with the results discussed in this chapter, the findings reveal an increasing segmentation of the labour force in as far as globalisation pressures are generally shifted to outsiders such as youth and, more particularly, young adults with less human capital and working in semi- and unskilled professions.

The results of this chapter are interesting and revealing in their own right. Yet, they gain even more importance and empirical strength when seen in the context of these studies, which employ other data sources, methodological approaches, and countries. Taken together, this chapter provides evidence in support of the country-specific hypothesis of this study and the final section of this chapter summarises the principal conclusions of the analysis.

7.6 Discussion and concluding remarks

This chapter examined labour market entry patterns and early career profiles of young adults in the 1990s. The focus was on individual patterns of insecurity and labour market exclusion, captured by transitions into employment, perceived job security and employment relationship along with longitudinal employment profiles. The chapter presented findings from the ECHP and the GSOEP and embedded these in results from previous research. To conclude this analysis and review, one may raise two important questions. Firstly, to what extent are labour market entrants confronted with job insecurity and what are the differences across the three countries under study? And secondly, to what extent do institutional filters and individual resources help young people more or less successfully into secure jobs? The following three key conclusions can be drawn.

First, the material presented in this chapter demonstrates that young adults face high degrees of labour market insecurity during their early labour market career. Temporary employment appears to be an important route into the labour market, independently of whether this is a direct school-to-work transition or a transition from non-employment. At the same time, flexible employment increases unemployment risks. Yet, there is some indication that precarious employment does not entrap employees. Rather, there is considerable year-to-year movement from fixed-term as well as casual employment.

Second, however, as contended in the country-specific hypothesis, important types of variation can be identified in terms of labour market integration and risk of labour market exclusion. The youth who are hardest hit by labour market insecurity are the ones in the Spanish insider-outsider labour market. These points are illustrated by lower employment probabilities, precarious entry-level jobs, lower transition rates into permanent employment, and a high risk of unemployment. This is in stark contrast to labour market profiles of young labour market entrants in Germany and Great Britain. In these latter two countries it seems much easier to get a foot into the labour market. Yet, compared to their German counterparts the youth in the highly flexible labour market of Great Britain bear a higher unemployment risk, are more dissatisfied with their job security and certain workers in lower-level occupations do have longer odds to convert insecure employment relationships into permanent ones. In summary, labour market flexibility is thus likely to come at the cost of greater instability in the early stages of young people's careers, particularly in Spain.

And *third*, there is support but also some contrary evidence for the individual resources hypothesis. On the one hand, the results of the above analysis reveal that educational and occupational qualification matter. Lower skilled entrants are faced with a higher risk of holding temporary contracts and those being employed in the lower-level occupations are more likely to be hit by unemployment. Furthermore, semi- and unskilled manual workers have a slim chance to escape from insecure employment. On the other hand, however, there is also some evidence to suggest that German employees in higher-level occupations hold fixed-term positions and have an off-chance to transform these insecure job positions into permanent ones.

There are shortcomings and areas of research that could not be studied within the confines of this chapter. Firstly, this study detailed an important cross-country variation in terms of who are the temporary employees. The fact that insecurity is directed towards low qualified and in semi- and unskilled positions in Spain, whereas a great deal of German temporary workers occupy professional occupations, is a revealing finding in itself. Over and above, this result opens a further empirical door which is the study of income differentials. Prior research has already revealed that flexible employment has a severe penalty on income (see for instance, Booth *et al.*, 2002; Gallie *et al.*, 1998; Gregg and Wadsworth, 2000). Unfortunately, due to time and space limitations it was not possible to inquire into this research area and it would obviously be of great promise to devote future analyses to the linkage between income security and contractual security in a comparative perspective. Related to this, it was beyond the scope of this study to investigate whether some individuals accept temporary employment if they accomplish higher earnings as a compensation for temporal uncertainty (see also Korpi and Levin, 2001). In this respect, future research should elaborate on the rational actor perspective in the course of increasing labour market insecurity. Lastly, a careful note on two important issues with respect to data limitations and methodological approach is necessary. Since the analysis of this chapter used data from the first three panel waves of the ECHP, the observation period was confined and case numbers small. With regard to the former, employment probabilities, satisfaction with job security, transitions from insecure to permanent employment and risk of job loss are likely to vary with the business cycle. Likewise, over the 1990s employment legislation has been subject of modifications in all three countries under study. A further shortcoming of the ECHP data is the limitation of regional information and the measurement of educational qualification. To measure more adequately cross-country variations in early career patterns, a more disaggregated analysis with harmonised data is highly valuable. Moreover, the three-level collapsed ISCED classification used in the ECHP does not permit full allowance for within-country variety in educational qualifications. In summary, inferences drawn should be taken as tentative and progress should be made to collect further empirical evidences by using other data sources.

Summarising the results and conclusions from this chapter shows that the issue of institutional filters and individual resources is essential. This is an important finding to bear in mind when studying the repercussions of labour market insecurity on partnership and parenthood decisions. The next research question to pose is this: Beyond its impact on labour market integration and exclusion during early labour market career, what comparative inference can be drawn from the analysis of labour market insecurity and life course decision-making of young adults? The succeeding chapter touches upon this issue.

Appendix

Table 7.2 Activity status of young adults one year after leaving education in Germany, Great Britain, and Spain by gender (Multinomial logistic regression)

	Men				Women			
	From education to				From education to			
	employment		inactivity		employment		inactivity	
Age								
Age	1.069	*	1.143		-0.423		-0.136	
Age square	-0.026	**	-0.029	*	0.011		0.007	
Country								
Germany (base)								
Great Britain	-1.522	***	-1.710	*	-0.957		-0.444	
Spain	-1.215	***	0.463		-2.372	***	-1.552	*
Educational qualification								
High education	-0.065		-0.607		-0.041		0.408	
Medium education (base)								
Low education	-0.845		1.097		-1.840	**	-1.610	
Country * education								
Great Britain * low education	1.701	**	-1.365		2.373	**	2.142	
Spain * low education	0.835		-1.046		1.501	**	2.459	*
Apprenticeship	0.805	***	-0.362		1.075	***	-0.377	
Constant	-9.082		-11.399		6.182		-0.709	
Log Likelihood	-457				-423			
Number of person wave observations	523				529			
Number of events	312		103		292		44	

Note: Obtained from multinomial logistic regression. Entries into unemployment = comparison group. ***p<0.01, **p<0.05, *p<0.10.

Source: ECHP (1995-1996), men and women aged 16-29, employees only.

Table 7.3 Type of contract at labour market (re-)entry in Germany, Great Britain, and Spain by gender (Multinomial logistic regression)

	Men		Women	
	Fixed-term	Casual	Fixed-term	Casual
Age				
Age	-0.100 **	-0.070	-0.067	-0.026
Labour force experience				
No experience	1.230 ***	1.216 **	0.398	0.624
Country				
Germany (base)				
Great Britain	-1.009 **	1.103 *	-0.560	1.813 **
Spain	1.635 ***	1.672 ***	2.261 ***	2.997 ***
Educational qualification				
High education	-0.182	-0.394	0.272	-0.700
Medium education (base)				
Low education	-0.617	-0.140	0.089	-0.678
Country * education				
GB * low education	-0.757	-0.954	-0.845	0.227
Spain * low education	1.012 *	0.572	0.448	1.505
Previous activity status				
In education (base)				
Unemployed	-0.616 *	-0.577	-0.205	-0.094
Economically inactive	-1.745 ***	-1.090 **	-1.019 **	-0.303
Constant	1.759	-0.657	0.676	-2.322
Log Likelihood	-477		-430	
Number of person wave observations	594		522	
Number of events	327	90	255	99

Note: Obtained from multinomial logistic regression. Permanent employment = comparison group. ***p<0.01, **p<0.05, *p<0.10.

Source: ECHP (1995-1996), men and women aged 16-29, employees only. GSOEP (1995-96), men and women aged 16-29, employees only.

Table 7.4 Mean satisfaction with job security by type of employment relationship in Germany, Great Britain, and Spain

	Mean	Mean difference	*t*-test	H_A	N
Germany					
Permanent	4.466				
Fixed-term	3.667	.799	7.28	Diff>0 ***	1,193
Casual	4.236	.230	1.32	Diff>0 *	1,083
Great Britain					
Permanent	4.596				
Fixed-term	3.325	1.271	8.60	Diff>0 ***	988
Casual	3.856	.740	5.70	Diff>0 ***	1,019
Spain					
Permanent	4.703				
Fixed-term	3.160	1.543	22.71	Diff>0 ***	1,961
Casual	3.240	1.463	13.84	Diff>0 ***	903

Note: Satisfaction has been measured on a response scale from 1 to 6 where 1 corresponds to '*not satisfied at all*' and 6 to '*fully satisfied. N* is the number of person-wave observations. The column labelled "*t*-test" reports the *t*-test for two-sample t test with equal variances. H_0: mean(permanent and full-time)–mean(non-standard)=diff=0. ***p<0.01, **p<0.05, *p<0.10.

Source: ECHP (1995-1996), men and women aged 16-29, employees only.

Table 7.5 Satisfaction with job security in Germany, Great Britain, and Spain by gender (Ordered probit regression)

	Satisfaction with job security		Worries about job security	
	Men	Women	Men	Women
Country				
Germany (base)				
Great Britain	0.085	0.032		
Spain	0.258 ***	0.201 **		
West Germany (base)				
East Germany			0.411 ***	0.545 ***
Type of employment contract				
Permanent (base)				
Fixed-term	-0.516 ***	-0.957 ***		
casual	-0.073	-0.181		
Unlimited contract (base)				
Limited contract			0.350 *	0.855 ***
Country * contract				
Great Britain * fixed-term	-0.414 *	-0.088		
Great Britain * casual	-0.508 *	-0.363		
Spain * fixed-term	-0.596 ***	-0.175		
Spain * casual	-1.029 ***	-0.874 **		
East Germany * limited contract			-0.729 **	0.139

	Satisfaction with job security				Worries about job security			
	Men		Women		Men		Women	
Age								
Age	-0.225	**	-0.017		-0.304		-0.109	
Age square	0.004	*	0.000		0.005		0.002	
Occupational class								
Higher-grade professional	0.257	**	0.334		-0.056		-0.820	***
Lower-grade professional	0.194	**	0.302		-0.198		-0.542	***
Routine non-manual	0.173	**	0.274		-0.202		-0.561	***
Skilled manual (base)								
Semi- and unskilled manual	-0.061		0.024		0.052		-0.397	*
Agricultural and other workers	-0.151		-0.128		-0.981	*	-0.451	
Working hours								
Full-time (base)								
Part-time	-0.218	*	0.059		0.463		-0.029	
Marital status								
Never married	-0.191	***	-0.057		-0.359	***	-0.089	
Cohabiting	-0.178	*	0.031		-0.224	*	0.110	
Married (base)								
Separated/divorced/widowed	0.361		-0.081		-0.762		-0.085	
Log Likelihood	-3840		-3045		-758		-671	
Number of person wave obs.	2,377		1,900		813		776	

Note: Coefficients obtained from ordered probit regression. Satisfaction with job security is measured on a response scale from 1 to 6. 1 corresponds to '*not satisfied at all*' and 6 to '*fully satisfied*'. The other dependent variable is worries about job security measured on a response scale from 1 to 3, where 1 corresponds to '*not worried*', 2 to '*slightly worried*' and 3 to '*very worried*'. Standard errors have been adjusted using the Huber/White/sandwich estimator of variance. ***p<0.01, **p<0.05, *p<0.10.

Source: ECHP (1995-1996), men and women aged 16-29, employees only. GSOEP (1995-1996), men and women aged 16-29, employees only.

Table 7.7 Transition from insecure to permanent contract and risk to be hit by unemployment in Germany, Great Britain, and Spain (Multinomial logistic regression)

	Entry into secure job		Entry into unemployment	
Labour force experience				
Labour force experience in years	0.308	***	-0.161	**
Labour force experience squared	-0.015	*	0.008	
Country				
Germany (base)				
Great Britain	-0.385		1.992	**
Spain	-1.865	**	3.410	***
Type of employment contract				
[1] Fixed-term (base) [2] Permanent (base)				
Fixed-term			1.317	**

	Entry into secure job		Entry into unemployment	
Casual	0.361		0.838	***
Country * employment contract				
Great Britain * fixed-term			-0.605	
Spain * fixed-term			-1.421	**
Unemployment experience			2.565	***
Country * unemployment experience				
Great Britain * unemployment experience			-1.599	**
Spain * unemployment experience			-1.739	**
Occupational class				
Higher- /lower-grade professional	-1.534	*	-0.940	*
Routine non-manual	-0.645		0.348	
Skilled manual (base)				
Semi- and unskilled manual	-0.071		0.327	
Agricultural and other workers	-1.768	**	0.839	*
Country * occupational class				
Great Britain * higher- /lower-grade prof.	-0.268			
Spain * higher- /lower-grade professional	1.393			
Great Britain * semi- and unskilled manual	-3.037	*		
Spain * semi- and unskilled manual	-1.790	*		
Sector				
Private sector (base)				
Public sector	-2.254	***		
Country * sector				
Great Britain * public	2.285	**		
Spain * public	2.003	**		
Gender				
Men (base)				
Women	0.507		1.248	**
Country * gender				
Great Britain * women	-0.540		-1.157	
Spain * women	-1.099		-1.424	**
Constant	0.522		-5.347	***
Log Likelihood	-663		-1077	
Number of person wave observations	747		2,167	
Number of events	147		181	

Note: Obtained from multinomial logistic regression for leaving an insecure job position (the two risks are entry into a permanent job and entry into non-employment) and discrete-time competing risk transition model for entry into unemployment (with the other risk being that of economic inactivity). All variables lagged by one period except country and gender. Standard errors have been adjusted using the Huber/White/sandwich estimator of variance. *** p<0.01, ** p<0.05, * p<0.10.

Source: ECHP (1995-1996), men and women aged 16-29, employees only.

8 Labour market insecurity and its repercussions on partnership and parenthood decisions

8.1 Introduction

The last chapter explored the nature of employment relationships of young adults and revealed to what extent labour market entry patterns have become more complex and insecure. It shed important light on individual chances to find a secure full-time position along with risks to lose one's job. Starting from these results one may ask: is there evidence to suggest that labour market deregulation and flexibility does have an impeding impact on partnership and parenthood decisions? Within the transition process from youth to adulthood, entry into the labour market gains particular importance. This is so as a stable job position ensures high income stability, thus providing individuals with a certain degree of economic security and good career prospects, a basis that is seen as a prerequisite for partnership formation and parenthood. By contrast, insecure gainful employment and risks of labour market exclusion may question such an economic basis and career outlook.

The objective of this chapter is twofold. First, it contributes to our understanding of whether and to what extent a solid economic basis through gainful employment serves as an important prerequisite for partnering and parenting. Hence, the chapter aims to grasp the consequences of economic insecurity in terms of non-employment or reduced working hours. Second, the chapter asks: Apart from economic insecurity, is there also evidence to suggest that job insecurity as gauged by precarious employment relationships and individuals' perception of job insecurity has an impact on life course decision-making in Germany, Great Britain, and Spain during the 1990s?

The chapter begins by reiterating the main lines of the theoretical background, research questions, and hypotheses. This is followed by a brief description of data, methods, and measures used. The chapter then presents the empirical results. In Section 8.5 the issue of labour market insecurity and life-shaping decisions is broadened towards other country-specific contexts. A discussion of major findings and concluding remarks complete the chapter.

8.2 Theoretical background and research hypotheses

The previous theoretical chapters developed a theoretical framework for understanding how labour market insecurity and life course decisions appear interrelated via the concept of life course security. In the empirical part of this study the attention first turned to patterns of labour market insecurity and exclusion of young employment-seekers. Chapter Seven provided empirical evidence for the increasing turbulence of labour market entry and early career and demonstrated that nation-specific institutional arrangements filter risks to varying degrees. At the same time, individual resources operate and lead to a cumulation of risks within the group of low-qualified workers. Against this background this chapter investigates the effects of labour market insecurity on partnership and parenthood decisions. More precisely, the chapter aims to deliver answers to the following key research questions. Is job insecurity and perceived job insecurity systematically related to men's and women's early living arrangements and partnership formation? And, how does job precariousness and perceived job insecurity affect young people's decision to become parents? As elaborated in Chapter Three, it is maintained that temporary positions impede predictions of one's future labour market career, while unemployment implies a high degree of economic insecurity. Facing great difficulties in settling in the labour market, individuals may also perceive their job as comparatively insecure. The insecurity hypothesis suggests that individuals in insecure labour market positions lack the ability to envisage future developments and to plan ahead, thus implying less life course security. It is proposed that job precariousness and perceived job insecurity will make a postponement of life course transitions more likely. More precisely, with respect to partnership and parenthood decisions, the transition-specific hypothesis contended that job insecurity increases the propensity to remain single rather than partner, and to cohabit rather than marry. The effect of job insecurity is assumed to be considerably higher for transitions into first parenthood. The chapter also addresses the issue of risk profiles and communicates the role of institutional filters and individual resources throughout its different sections. Chapters Four and Five described institutional filters and the importance of individual resources and outlined a set of risk profile hypotheses. Firstly, gender-specific adaptations strategies are expected and it is maintained that the overall effects of job insecurity are stronger for men than for women. Yet, it is expected that gender-specific adaptation strategies are always country- and transition-specific. Insecurity should have the most adverse effect in Spain, whereas the effect of job insecurity is rather intermediate in Germany, and comparatively weak in Great Britain. The empirical analysis of this chapter aims to disentangle the complex interrelation between country-specific, transition-specific, and gender-specific adaptation strategies.

8.3 Data, methods, and measures

The data used are from the German Socio-economic Panel Study (GSOEP, 1994-2000), the British Household Panel Survey (BHPS, 1994-2000), and the Spanish European Community Household Panel (ECHP, 1994-1997). The analyses are confined to an unbalanced longitudinal sample of men and women aged 16 to 40 years. The analyses are furthermore limited to original sample members with a full interview, no disabilities, and at least two years of observation. Table 8.1 gives a summary of the survey population in each of the three surveys.

Table 8.1 Synopsis of survey population

	Germany GSOEP 1994-2000	Great Britain BHPS 1994-2000	Spain ECHP 1994-1997
Number of individuals	4,850	3,860	7,144
Person-wave observations	26,449	21,247	24,983
in percent by gender			
% men	48.9	47.9	50.4
in percent by sample			
% East Germans	38.7		
in percent by activity status			
% employed	60.2	77.5	47.8
% unemployed	5.2	4.4	16.7
% inactive	12.5	9.0	12.8
% in education	22.1	9.1	22.7

Source: GSOEP (1994-2000), BHPS (1994-2000), ECHP (1994-1997), men and women aged 16-40.

As outlined in Chapter Six, this chapter focuses on two types of life-shaping decisions, namely partnership and parenthood decisions. The analysis pursues discrete-time (competing risks) transition models for men and women separately. In each of these models, the dependent variable is defined as a change in marital and family status, respectively, between two consecutive panel waves. The group of individuals exposed to partnership and parenthood transitions are different. The following paragraphs therefore outline areas of research, sample selection criteria, and definition of events.

First partnership formation[58]*:* In the analysis of first partnership formation the risk set is defined as everyone who is unpartnered in one particular year and the

[58] The ECHP does not provide life history data on the family and marital biography of a person. In the BHPS such information has only been collected in the second sweep in 1992. Thus, the analysis for Great Britain and Spain uses the self-reported marital status to identify transitions to first partnership.

two possible destination states are entry into first cohabitation and entry into first marriage. This investigation disregards cohabitation after marriage.

The outcome of cohabiting unions: This analysis uses a sub-sample of cohabiting couples and the two risks under consideration are marriage and dissolution of the union. Since the decision to convert cohabitation into marriage is a joint decision, the examination rests on cohabiting women and aims to capture the role of the partnership context. It addresses the question of whether the respondent stays with the same partner and ignores cohabitation after marital dissolution.

First parenthood as a single decision: The examination uses a sample of childless persons and the dependent variable in the discrete-time models distinguishes between staying childless and becoming a parent between two panel waves. Respondents whose first child was born before the start of the panel and step-parents are excluded from the analysis.[59]

First parenthood as a joint decision: In most countries marriage and parenthood are endogenous processes and parenthood decisions are largely joint decisions. This is to say that the employment status and job security of the partner may be very important determinants of parenthood decisions. This is especially the case in the analysis of entry into first motherhood, and in countries where the male-breadwinner model reigns in particular. The above outlined analysis of first parenthood will therefore be supplemented by an examination of the partnership context. This study includes cohabiting and married women only and, as detailed above, concentrates on moves from being childless in one year to having a child the subsequent panel wave.

A number of complications and concerns that arise in the analysis of partnership and parenthood decisions merit mention. Unlike the previous chapter, the analysis of this chapter runs parallel models for Germany, Great Britain, and Spain separately. This decision can be sustained on various substantive grounds. A first argument refers to the feasibility of the analysis. Due to the diverse country-specific trends in life course transitions, it is not possible to analyse the same transitions in Germany, Great Britain, and Spain. For instance, as seen in Chapter Two, non-marital unions still play a minor role in Spain and this is mirrored in very small case numbers of cohabitants in the Spanish ECHP. By contrast, in Great Britain the greater part of parental home leavers are cohabiting rather than marrying. In this latter country, therefore, the panel data does not allow the examination of direct entries into first marriage. In

---

[59] In the analyses based on the BHPS and the Spanish ECHP, the birth of the first child can only be identified if the child lives in the same household at the time of the interview. Here, the dependent variable has been constructed by using the information on the household composition. In the GSOEP, by contrast, the occurrence of family events has been measured annually as part of the survey.

various model specifications the number of alternative outcomes is too small to permit a multinomial logistic regression analysis. This problem was remedied by estimation of separate binomial logit models for each event type. This procedure leads to the same conclusions as in multinomial logistic regression analysis but allows for event-specific specifications (Chapter Six; see also Allison, 1995; Begg and Gray, 1984). A further pitfall is the different meaning of insecure job positions for young workers and the disparate repercussions on their professional career in Germany, Great Britain, and Spain (see Chapter Seven). While in the former two countries the proportion of flexi-workers is comparatively low and employees escape from insecure job positions more quickly, insecure employment is by far more spread and long-term in Spain. Over and above, Chapter Seven evidenced the disparate composition of the group of flexi-workers and Chapter Three highlighted important sectoral differences. Furthermore, given that part of the analysis concentrates on the gainfully employed and knowing that female labour force participation rates differ considerably in Germany, Great Britain, and Spain (Chapter Three), the analysis of pooled data is likely to compare differently composed groups of women. For these various reasons, it seems more accurate to model insecurity in the three countries under study separately.

The theoretical framework of this study has emphasised the centrality of objective and subjective measures of labour market insecurity. The models to be presented in the following sections control for the following proxy variables:

- *Activity status* (three dummy variables for unemployed, in education, not economically active, base=employed), which is meant to reflect economic insecurity that is likely to result from insecure employment relationships (Chapter Seven),
- *type of employment relationship*, two dummy variables for flexi-worker (type of employment contract: permanent and non-permanent[60] and working hours: part-time and full-time), to capture the effect of insecure job positions,
- *interaction between age and flexi-worker,* since not only the intensity but also the timing of partnership and parenthood decisions may depend on job security, and
- *satisfaction with job security,* to gauge the impact of subjective measures of job insecurity.

[60] The GSOEP does not allow the separation of fixed-term and casual employees. Hence, for reasons of data comparability, this chapter presents a more aggregated analysis than Chapter Seven and separates permanent from non-permanent workers. It furthermore excludes marginal part-timers due to the specific questionnaire route in the ECHP. Notice also that the analysis of gainfully employed is confined to employees.

Over and above these proxy variables for insecurity, the specified models include various other measures that are inherently related to the transition processes under study. These are

- *Age and age square* (centred effects), to control for life cycle effects,
- *birth cohort* (three dummy variables for 1960-64, 1965-69, 1970-74, base=1975-83) to capture cohorts effects,
- *highest educational qualification* (three-level collapsed ISCED classification, base=medium)[61], to capture the well-known impact of opportunity costs (Section 2.4.1; Becker, 1981),
- *interaction between age and education,* to disentangle timing and education effects (Section 2.4.1; Blossfeld, 1995; Blossfeld and Huinink, 1991),
- *marital status,* (three dummies for never married, cohabiting, separated/divorced/widowed, base=married),
- *presence of children,* and
- *region (*in the case of Germany, one dummy for East Germany).

The analyses of the outcome of cohabiting unions and first parenthood as a joint decision use couple data and implement a classification that allows the separation of more secure from more insecure couples. Unfortunately, case numbers are too small to permit a differentiation between insecure labour market positions. Table 8.2 presents the employed variables and their definitions.

Table 8.2 Gender organisation of paid work and insecurity at the household level

Variable name	Definition
Secure traditional family	man holds a secure full-time job and woman does the housework
Secure modified family	man holds a secure full-time job and woman is a flexi-worker
Secure dual earner family	man and woman work in secure full-time positions
Insecure family (base)	various insecure positions: man is a flexi-worker and woman is employed; woman is unemployed or currently enrolled in education; both partners are not working; man is not working and woman holds a job

[61] Further analyses (not shown here) included a collapsed EGP class schema as a control variable. The estimates from this specification provide support for the assumption that individual resources matter. The models presented here do not include both, educational qualification and occupational class, since these two covariates are highly correlated.

Analyses are conducted through a series of steps. First, a specification is estimated which includes the measures for economic insecurity only. In the next step, the attention shifts to the role of flexible work arrangements. It is well-known that partnership and parenthood decisions are highly interrelated. Men and women are more prone to become a parent if they are married and pregnancies make a marriage more likely. For that reason, the analysis of the transition to first partnership and entry into first parenthood specifies two models, one that excludes and one that includes information on the presence of children and marital status, respectively. Since this book is primarily interested in the impact of positions of insecurity, and not so much in the well-known effects of children and marital status, the discussion of this chapter does not go into details of these latter models. However, important findings from this additional analysis will be indicated at the relevant points in the text.

8.4 Findings: Family formation in Germany, Great Britain, and Spain

The discussion first turns to the results for the transition to first partnership and the outcome of cohabiting unions. It then proceeds to the impact of insecurity on entry into first parenthood.

8.4.1 The transition to first marital or non-marital union and its evolution

The decision to form a union and to transform cohabitation into marriage is a life-shaping decision. There is a large body of research examining the role of different socio-economic and demographic characteristics in accounting for variations among persons in partnership decisions (see Section 2.4). In this section the question is raised whether there is also empirical evidence to suggest that labour market insecurity leads individuals to postpone or even forgo such decisions. First union formation is considered first. The section then explores whether and when young people convert their cohabitation into marriage.

The results of discrete-time transition models for the transition into first partnership (consensual union versus marriage) and pursued for men and women separately are reported in Tables 8.3 and 8.4, respectively. Both tables document the estimates obtained for Germany, Great Britain, and Spain, and for two different specifications. The first model focuses on the role of the activity status, the second model differs from the first for dealing with job insecurity of employees. The focus is on entry into cohabitation in Germany and Great Britain, whereas the analysis of Spain deals with entry into first marriage (see Section 8.3). The estimation provides some evidence that men and women who lack life course security are less likely to enter a first partnership. Country differences prevail, however.

Table 8.3 The relationship of first partnership formation, activity status and job insecurity in Germany, Great Britain, and Spain (Logistic regression), Men

	Germany		Great Britain		Spain	
	Entry into cohabitation		Entry into cohabitation		Entry into marriage	
Activity status						
Employed (base)						
In education	-0.176		-1.201 ***		-1.823 ***	
Economically inactive	-0.264		-0.533		-1.256 **	
Unemployed	-0.364		-0.130		-0.790 ***	
Type of employment contract						
Permanent (base)						
Temporary		-0.725		-1.104 *		-0.107
Working hours						
Full-time (base)						
Part-time		-0.569		-1.481 **		-0.946
Age * flexi-worker		0.215 **		-0.094		0.103
Satisfaction with job security				-0.498 *		0.905 *
Worries about job security						
Not worried (base)						
Slightly worried		-0.231				
Very worried		-0.412				
Educational qualification						
High education	-0.215	-0.618	0.121	0.150	-0.207	-0.641
Medium education (base)						
Low education	-0.635	-0.390	-0.279	-0.170	0.188	0.170
Educational qualification * age						
High education * age	0.119	0.172	0.020	0.058	-0.030	0.108
Low education * age	-0.069	-0.024	-0.110 *	-0.108	-0.083	-0.083
Age (centred effects)						
Age	1.294 ***	1.171 **	1.156 ***	1.031 ***	1.819 ***	2.470 ***
Age square	-0.026 ***	-0.023 ***	-0.022 ***	-0.020 ***	-0.031 ***	-0.045 ***

	Germany Entry into cohabitation		Great Britain Entry into cohabitation		Spain Entry into marriage	
Birth cohort						
1960-64	0.223	-0.390	0.320	0.334	0.111	-0.619
1965-69	-0.038	-0.249	0.002	0.068	0.073	-1.223
1970-74	0.144	0.020	-0.108	-0.051	-0.252	-1.340
1975-83 (base)						
Region						
West Germany (base)						
East Germany	-0.152	-0.625 **				
Constant	-3.834 ***	-3.104 ***	-2.543 ***	-2.164 ***	-3.449 ***	-3.121 ***
Log Likelihood	-741	-390	-832	-615	-671	-239
Number of person wave observations	6,554	3,434	3,344	2,014	5,583	1,140
Number of events	168	93	253	195	181	69

Note: Obtained from binomial logit regressions. Standard errors have been adjusted using the Huber/White/sandwich estimator of variance. All variables lagged by one period except birth cohort and region. *** $p<0.01$, ** $p<0.05$, *$p<0.10$.

Source: GSOEP (1994-2000), BHPS (1994-2000), ECHP (1994-1997), men and women aged 16-40.

Table 8.4 The relationship of first partnership formation, activity status, and job insecurity in Germany, Great Britain, and Spain (Logistic regression), Women

	Germany		Great Britain		Spain	
	Entry into cohabitation		Entry into cohabitation		Entry into marriage	
Activity status						
Employed (base)						
In education	-0.179		-0.647 ***		-1.360 ***	
Economically inactive	-1.053 ***		0.341		0.337	
Unemployed	-1.442 **		-0.291		-0.355 *	
Type of employment contract						
Permanent (base)						
Temporary		0.088		-0.540		-0.233
Working hours						
Full-time (base)						
Part-time		-1.623 **		-0.141		0.409
Age * flexi-worker		-0.041		-0.001		0.025
Satisfaction with job security				-0.294		-0.022
Worries about job security						
Not worried (base)						
Slightly worried		0.694 **				
Very worried		0.821 **				
Educational qualification						
High education	0.682 **	0.806 **	0.017	-0.075	0.005	-0.305
Medium education (base)						
Low education	0.181	0.020	-0.323	0.168	0.068	-0.316
Educational qualification * age						
High education * age	0.080	0.057	-0.043	-0.071	-0.054	-0.040
Low education * age	0.052	0.057	-0.067	-0.001	-0.100 **	-0.038
Age (centred effects)						
Age	0.392	-0.722	0.704 ***	0.305	1.369 ***	1.064 *
Age square	-0.011	0.011	-0.014 ***	-0.006	-0.024 ***	-0.019 *

	Germany Entry into cohabitation		Great Britain Entry into cohabitation		Spain Entry into marriage	
Birth cohort						
1960-64	-1.750 **	-2.452 **	-0.142	-0.247	-0.131	-0.618
1965-69	-0.365	0.230	0.124	0.315	-0.043	-0.571
1970-74	0.275	0.421	0.268	0.463 *	-0.210	-0.763
1975-83 (base)						
Region						
West Germany (base)						
East Germany	-0.081	-0.558 *				
Constant	-3.657 ***	-3.596 ***	-2.460 ***	-2.134 ***	-2.860 ***	-1.654 **
Log Likelihood	-721	-264	-808	-503	-707	-214
Number of person wave observations	6,742	2,847	2,758	1,453	4,583	718
Number of events	183	70	257	168	194	66

Note: Obtained from binomial logit regressions. Standard errors have been adjusted using the Huber/White/sandwich estimator of variance. All variables lagged by one period except birth cohort and region. *** $p<0.01$, ** $p<0.05$, *$p<0.10$.

Source: GSOEP (1994-2000), BHPS (1994-2000), ECHP (1994-1997), men and women aged 16-40.

In Germany, the estimates document that economic insecurity – as approximated by the activity status – has no impact on the transition to cohabitation for men, whereas economically inactive or unemployed women seem significantly less likely to enter a consensual union. Yet, it is worthy to note that the results are somewhat different when studying entries into first marriage (results not shown). Here, men who are unemployed, economically inactive or currently enrolled in education are less prone to marry, while gainful employment does not seem to be a significant prerequisite of this transition for women. Part-time employment lowers the transition rate for women; yet, it should be noted that it is very unusual for unpartnered women to work part-time. Being in temporary employment does not have any significant impact on women's probability of entering into first cohabitation according to the estimates of model 2 in Table 8.4. Yet, as can be seen from the main effect of temporary work (which does not quite reach the 10 percent level of significance) and the significant interaction effect between temporary work and age in Table 8.3, there is some indication that men in such insecure positions defer union formation at young ages. The estimates for worries about job security, instead, are negative but not statistically significant for men. Interestingly, women who are worried about their job security are more likely to enter a union.

In Great Britain, the estimation also provides us with some evidence that men and women in insecure labour market positions are less likely to cohabit. While individuals who are currently enrolled in education seem less likely to cohabit, the estimates for economic inactivity and unemployment are not statistically significant. However, compared to those in permanent jobs, men in temporary jobs are less likely to enter a consensual union, particularly at older ages (model 4). As can be seen from Table 8.4, the corresponding estimates for women are not statistically significant, suggesting that insecure employment does not reduce their chance of cohabiting. Moreover, the individual perception of insecurity has no impact on the odds that women will enter a cohabiting union. Yet, the more satisfied men are, the less likely they seem to partner. This result is tentative and may indicate that highly satisfied men are more career-oriented.

In Spain then, model 5 in Table 8.3 reveals that employment is obviously an important prerequisite for men's entry into first marriage (see also Golsch, 2003; Simó *et al.*, 2002b; Ahn and Mira, 2001). Women's unemployment and educational enrolment also lower the probability to marry (Table 8.4). But once we focus on employees only, is there evidence to suggest that the type of employment relationship and the perception of job security have an impact on the studied transitions? Although men in part-time and temporary employment are less likely to enter a marital union than men in full-time or permanent employment, this difference is not statistically significant. Yet, it becomes obvious that satisfaction with job security is an important predictor of men's entry into first marriage: the more satisfied they are, the more likely they are to marry (see also Golsch, 2003). At the same time, the measures of insecurity do not play any significant role for women.

Apart from the insecurity measures, Tables 8.3 and 8.4 document some further findings. With respect to educational qualification, we do not find any educational gradient for men, indicating that cohabitation is a common form of partnership among all educational groups. It is only in Great Britain that the results provide an indication of how men with higher educational qualification postpone this partnership decision and catch up at older ages. For women, the results reveal no impact of educational qualification in Great Britain and Spain, whereas the highly educated women in Germany are more likely to cohabit. The results furthermore reveal the well-known age effect: with increasing age the probability to enter a first union increases, but this will tend to level off at older ages. Younger cohorts of German women seem more prone to enter a consensual union than women born earlier. This finding suggests that cohabitation has become a common mode of first partnership. However, there is no such indication of a cohort effect for women in Great Britain and Spain and for men. Lastly, as outlined in Chapter Four, since the reunification, East Germans are confronted by far more uncertainties and this renders life-shaping decisions more difficult for East Germans than for West Germans. Interestingly, the results presented in Tables 8.3 and 8.4 show that East Germans are indeed less likely to enter a consensual union, even though the model controls for positions of insecurity. This effect is insignificant under model 1 and again negative but significant under model 2.

Figure 8.1 The transformation of cohabitation into marriage in Germany and Great Britain by labour market position of the couple and age (Conditional Effects Plots)

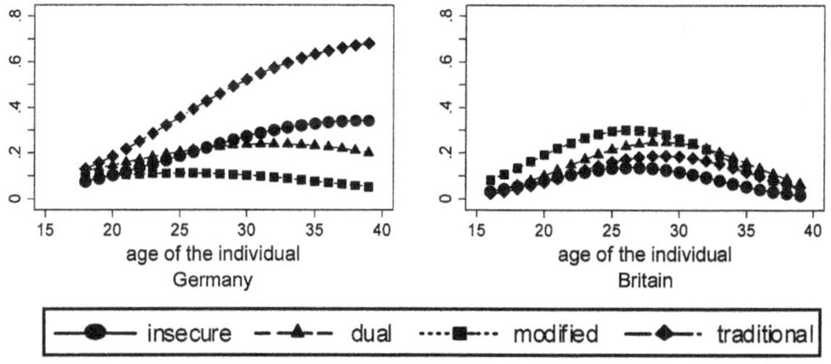

Note: Results from binomial logistic regressions (see Table 8.5). Predicted probabilities of marrying relative to remaining in the cohabiting union for childless women with medium education and belonging to the youngest birth cohort.

Source: GSOEP (1994-2000), BHPS (1994-2000), cohabiting women aged 16-40.

Before drawing some tentative conclusions from this analysis, this section reports on the results obtained from a regression analysis on the outcome of cohabiting unions. To what extent does labour market insecurity impact the transformation of cohabitation into marriage? The above analysis on Germany and Great Britain considered the entry into consensual unions. Table 8.5 in the appendix of this chapter gives the results for a discrete-time transition model for whether these persons convert their cohabiting union into marriage. Prior research analysing this transition revealed very few significant predictors for women, whereas cohabiting men in insecure positions appeared to be less likely to marry their partners (Francesconi and Golsch, forthcoming). But these studies have not taken into account the couple context and its various types of uncertainty. The analysis of this chapter tries to fill this gap up and Figure 8.1 presents conditional effects plots for cohabiting women by security, gender division of labour, and age in Germany and Great Britain.

In Germany, minor differences between couples in secure or insecure positions can be observed at young ages. Yet, at older ages we find that the odds of converting cohabitation into marriage are highest for couples in which the male breadwinner holds a secure full-time job and the woman stays at home. Conversely, the odds of marrying the partner relative to remaining in the cohabiting union are lowest in the modified model, in which women contribute to the household income through their part-time work while men work full-time. This result is surprising, yet linked to the fact that it is very unusual for childless women to work part-time in this early phase of their employment career. Women in dual earner couples and couples in insecure positions are always less likely to transform their cohabitation into marriage than those in traditional partnerships. But there is no real difference in behaviour between the former two types of partnerships. The picture is different for couples in Great Britain. Here, dual earner couples in secure job positions and couples where the man holds a secure full-time job while the woman works part-time are more prone to marry. Quite the contrary, male breadwinner families and couples in insecure labour market positions, in particular, are less likely to do so.

Some further results are noteworthy. Prior research has shown how pregnancy and childbirth within a consensual union as well as the presence of children before the start of the union are interrelated with the odds of transforming cohabitation into marriage (see Blossfeld *et al.*, 1999; Ermisch and Francesconi, 2000a; Francesconi and Golsch, forthcoming). In line with these studies, the above analysis reveals that being a mother reduces the odds of converting the union into marriage (the estimate does not quite reach the 10 percent level of significance in Great Britain). The presented model is a parsimonious one, however. Prior research has investigated the role of different socio-economic and demographic characteristics in accounting for variations among persons in partnership dissolution patterns (e.g., Berrington and Diamond, 2000; Ermisch and Francesconi, 2000a and 2000b). For instance, we know from various other publications that religious affiliation impacts the outcome of cohabiting unions. Yet, it is important to note that these other determinants do not rule out the effect of the insecurity measures (see Francesconi and Golsch, forthcoming).

In summary, the above analysis gives some support to the hypotheses of this study, but also raises important questions. The first central finding is that insecurity seems to delay the entry into first union for men, but it has no such clear-cut impact on partnership formation for women. At the same time, the results suggest that the labour market insecurity of cohabiting men and women spills over into their family life. This gender-specific impact of insecurity on life-shaping decisions was fully expected. Assuming that the male breadwinner model is still in place, men consolidate the economic basis of a household through their permanent full-time employment. Yet, with the increasing insecurity of employment relationships in contemporary societies, men are likely to confront essential barriers to meet such preconditions. Conversely, women do not perceive their instability in the labour market as a factor that impacts partnership decisions. Over and above, there is also some evidence to suggest that being employed in a job position with little protection and career prospects, women are even more likely to start a first union, suggesting that marriage functions as a safety net for women in insecure labour market positions. Another striking finding is that the repercussions of insecurity are nation-specific. In support of the country-specific hypothesis, labour market insecurity has a strong and negative effect for men in Spain. As seen in Chapter Seven, chances are high that job seekers enter the labour market as temporary workers. At the same time, workers in temporary positions are more likely to be hit by unemployment. Joblessness, in turn, will make it difficult to establish a solid economic household basis. Hence, labour market flexibility is likely to come at the cost of security in the early stages of young Spaniards' careers, be it due to flexible employment or unemployment. Yet, the findings for Germany and Great Britain are more mixed. Confirming the expectations discussed in Chapter Five, the estimates document that labour market insecurity has a less distinct impact on partnership life in Germany. Men's unemployment, economic inactivity, and educational enrolment have no effect on entry into first cohabitation but only on entry into first marriage. This may suggest that labour market insecurity does not determine less self-binding partnership decisions. However, despite the generally better job prospects of temporary workers in Germany and the speedy transformation of temporary positions into permanent ones (see Chapter Seven), temporary employment leads men to defer partnership decisions. This is in stark contrast to the findings by Kurz *et al.* (forthcoming) who show that men in temporary job positions are equally likely to form a union as compared to permanent workers. One explanation for these diverse outcomes refers to the different observation period and survey population. The study by Kurz *et al.*

covers the time span 1984-1998 and includes only individuals aged 16 to 35, who have left full-time education between 1984 and 1997 and started employment within five years after having left education. The disappearance of the 'deterrent' effect of job insecurity may also be attributable to the different model specification used by Kurz *et al.* (forthcoming). While this study focuses on employees only, Kurz *et al.* study all individuals, be they in employment or not, and introduce dummy variables for activity status, employment status, and insecure employment positions. Moreover, their specification does not control for interaction effects between age and flexible employment. It is not possible to give a final answer here, but the difference in results denotes that the findings depend on the methodological approach and conceptualisations used. The findings presented for Great Britain are also somewhat unexpected. This is because in the British low-trust labour market, differences between permanent and temporary contracts are much less pronounced than in the Spanish insider-outsider market for instance. The results of the above analysis indicate that insecurity impedes the transition to first partnership and the transformation of cohabitation into marriage, providing support for the insecurity and transition-specific hypothesis (Francesconi and Golsch, forthcoming). With short job tenure in temporary employment, employees on temporary posts may judge their current position as a stepping-stone to permanent, and thus, better paid employment. One may assume that they are waiting for a permanent job before making important life course decisions – an issue that will be picked up below. The analysis of a related life course transition, the entry into first parenthood, will shed more light on the interplay of labour market insecurity and life course decision-making.

8.4.2 The transition to first parenthood and the couple context

The last section established to what extent labour market insecurity interferes with men's and women's partnership decisions in all three countries, albeit in different veins. Here the attention turns to the decision of having the first child as an irreversible, long-term joint project that constraints behaviour of both partners, particularly of women. The analysis is conducted through a series of steps. Firstly, this section reviews the findings from the analysis of entries into first fatherhood and motherhood, respectively. In the next step, the section presents the findings from an analysis of couples. Table 8.6 documents the results for a discrete-time transition model for entry into first fatherhood; Table 8.7 reports the same type of information for women. The analysis compares the results from two different specifications. The first model considers the activity status, whereas the second model examines employees only.

Table 8.6 The relationship of entry into first fatherhood, activity status, and job insecurity in Germany, Great Britain, and Spain (Logistic regression)

	Germany		Great Britain		Spain	
Activity status						
Employed (base)						
In education	-0.767 ***		-1.862 **		-1.604 **	
Economically inactive	-0.051		0.065		-1.344 *	
Unemployed	-0.332		0.203		-1.041 ***	
Type of employment contract						
Permanent (base)						
Temporary		-0.163		-0.733		-1.166 ***
Working hours						
Full-time (base)						
Part-time		-1.424		-0.078		-0.592
Age * flexi-worker		-0.017		0.156 **		0.110
Satisfaction with job security				0.112		-1.010 **
Worries about job security						
Not worried (base)						
Slightly worried		-0.098				
Very worried		0.199				
Educational qualification						
High education	-0.123	0.051	-0.390 **	-0.297 *	0.070	-0.716
Medium education (base)						
Low education	0.149	0.188	-0.244	-0.130	0.889 ***	1.338 ***
Educational qualification * age						
High education * age	0.109	0.047	0.075 **	0.092 **	-0.076	0.033
Low education * age	0.026	0.051	0.069	0.081	-0.207 ***	-0.234 **
Age (centred effects)						
Age	1.189 ***	1.117 ***	1.048 ***	1.183 ***	1.453 ***	2.061 ***
Age square	-0.021 ***	-0.020 ***	-0.017 ***	-0.019 ***	-0.020 ***	-0.030 **
Birth cohort						

	Germany		Great Britain		Spain	
1960-64	1.070 **	0.918	-1.078 **	-1.317 **	0.793	0.296
1965-69	0.715	0.483	0.749 *	-1.023 **	0.920	0.342
1970-74	0.422	0.430	0.439	-0.581 *	0.593	-0.017
1975-83 (base)						
Region						
West Germany (base)						
East Germany	0.112	-0.122				
Constant	-4.022 ***	-3.720	-2.433 ***	-2.405 ***	-5.155 ***	-3.941 ***
Log Likelihood	-944	-651	-915	-724	-579	-249
Number of person wave observations	6,277	3,099	5,423	3,740	6,338	1,453
Number of events	239	173	242	194	152	75

Note: Obtained from binomial logit regressions. Standard errors have been adjusted using the Huber/White/sandwich estimator of variance. All variables lagged by one period except birth cohort and region. *** p<0.01, ** p<0.05, *p<0.10.

Source: GSOEP (1994-2000), BHPS (1994-2000), ECHP (1994-1997), men and women aged 16-40.

Table 8.7 The relationship of entry into first motherhood, activity status, and job insecurity in Germany, Great Britain, and Spain (Logistic regression)

	Germany		Great Britain		Spain	
Activity status						
Employed (base)						
In education	-1.238 ***		-2.506 ***		-1.113 ***	
Economically inactive	-0.504		1.075 ***		1.200 ***	
Unemployed	-0.045		0.101		-0.116	
Type of employment contract						
Permanent (base)						
Temporary		-0.051		-1.139 ***		-0.020
Working hours						
Full-time (base)						
Part-time		0.237		0.291		0.364
Age * flexi-worker		0.043		-0.042		-0.005
Satisfaction with job security				0.028		1.174 *
Worries about job security						
Not worried (base)						
Slightly worried		0.005				
Very worried		-0.186				
Educational qualification						
High education	0.248 *	0.280 *	-0.332 **	-0.253 *	-0.126	-0.204
Medium education (base)						
Low education	0.078	0.036	-0.228	0.272	0.374 *	0.068
Educational qualification * age						
High education * age	0.051	0.043	0.047	0.025	0.052	0.006
Low education * age	-0.095 *	-0.056	-0.179 *	-0.126	-0.089 *	-0.222
Age (centred effects)						
Age	0.867 ***	0.775 **	0.580 ***	0.608 ***	0.801 **	2.243 **
Age square	-0.015 ***	-0.014 **	-0.010 ***	-0.010 **	-0.012 *	-0.035 **
Birth cohort						

	Germany		Great Britain		Spain	
1960-64	-0.113	-0.505	0.191	-0.191	0.012	-1.150
1965-69	0.024	-0.195	0.120	-0.164	0.195	-0.932
1970-74	0.085	-0.208	0.039	-0.308	-0.005	-0.816
1975-83 (base)						
Region						
West Germany (base)						
East Germany	0.150	0.006				
Constant	-2.713 ***	-2.376 ***	-2.700 ***	-2.433 ***	-3.610 ***	-3.997 ***
Log Likelihood	-1135	-776	-959	-820	-620	-173
Number of person wave observations	5,025	2,550	4,727	3,361	5,258	931
Number of events	325	237	267	232	160	48

Note: Obtained from binomial logit regressions. Standard errors have been adjusted using the Huber/White/sandwich estimator of variance. All variables lagged by one period except birth cohort and region. *** $p<0.01$, ** $p<0.05$, *$p<0.10$.

Source: GSOEP (1994-2000), BHPS (1994-2000), ECHP (1994-1997), men and women aged 16-40.

The estimates give some further support to the insecurity hypothesis. At the same time, the analysis also reveals different impacts on men and women and points to further country differences. In Germany, the transition to first parenthood does not seem to be influenced by men's and women's activity status. Although men and women who are either unemployed or not economically active are always less likely to become a parent than their employed counterparts, this difference is never statistically significant. Only men and women who are still in full-time education have a lower probability of becoming a parent one year later. Furthermore and in line with other studies (Kurz *et al.*, forthcoming; Tölke and Diewald, 2002), the type of employment relationship does not seem to matter for the transition to parenthood in Germany. Likewise, the individual perception of job insecurity appears to have no effect on the decision to have a child. Again the picture for men and women in Great Britain and Spain is different.

In Great Britain, the estimates document a negative relationship between the probabilities of becoming a father while being in full-time education but there is no significant effect of the other activity states. Women who are out of the labour force are more likely to have their first child than women who are in employment. Conversely, women who are still in full-time education have a lower probability of becoming mothers one year later. In support of the insecurity hypothesis, a precarious employment relationship has a negative impact on entry into first fatherhood in Great Britain: holding a temporary job decreases the likelihood to become a father (the estimate does not quite reach the 10 percent level of significance). As can be seen from the significant interaction effect between temporary work and age, this effect tends to level off with increasing age. Yet, this insecurity effect found in specification [4] vanishes when marital status is included in the regression analysis (results not shown). Somewhat surprisingly, we do find the same negative relationship between the probability of becoming a mother and temporary work (Table 8.7). Tables 8.6 and 8.7 furthermore document that the estimates for satisfaction with job security are positive for men and women, yet statistically insignificant.

Lastly, in support of the expectations of Chapter Five, the transition to first parenthood is heavily influenced by the activity status of men and women in Spain. Compared to gainfully employed men, those currently enrolled in education, unemployed or not economically active are less likely to become a father. In turn, unemployment and educational enrolment lead women to defer first motherhood while this transition is highly probable for inactive women, who are likely to have already decided to embark on a family career. As to model 6, we see that Spaniards who hold a permanent job have the highest probability to become fathers. Conversely, men on temporary posts have children less often and at later ages (the interaction effect between flexi-work and age does not quite reach the 10 percent level of significance). At the same time, the estimates document that insecure employment has no impact on the transition to first motherhood. Surprisingly, the higher the degree of satisfaction, the lower the probability to become a father. For women we observe the opposite effect. The more they think that their job is secure the more likely they are to become mothers.

There are some other results of the analysis of entry into first fatherhood and motherhood that are noteworthy. The estimates for age and age square reveal that the odds of becoming mothers and fathers, respectively, rise with increasing age. Yet, as can be seen from the significant quadratic term, this will tend to level off at higher ages. In line with the literature discussed in Section 2.4.1, educational qualification plays a significant role for transitions to first parenthood. In Germany, highly qualified women postpone this parenthood decision and seem to catch up with their less educated counterparts. Quite the contrary, there is no such timing effect for men in Germany. In Great Britain, there is also evidence that well educated men and women adjourn the decision to have a child. In Spain then, men and women with low educational qualification are more likely to become fathers and mothers, respectively. Yet, with increasing age this effect will tend to level off. Lastly, as also seen in the study be Kurz *et al.* (forthcoming), we cannot detect a significant effect of region: Despite the dim job prospects in the tight East German job market, East Germans make this parenthood decision at the same rate as West Germans. This result is somewhat unanticipated, yet conceivably linked to the fact that child-care facilities remain more widespread in East Germany and that women are more job oriented and more willing to combine full-time work with child-rearing.

The results presented so far demonstrate that labour market insecurity determines the decision to become a parent. Yet, a careful note on the results of the above analysis has to be made. Since the male breadwinner model prevails, it might not be women's labour market position that matters, but rather the one of their partner. So one may ask: How does this picture change once we study couples only? The remainder of this section focuses on childless couples and investigates the impact of insecure labour market positions on their parenthood decisions. To this end, the analysis uses a set of dummy variables that describe different types of households (see Section 8.3). The estimates and standard errors of this analysis are summarised in Table 8.8, annexed to this chapter.

To visualise differences in the probability to parent, Figure 8.2 on the next page presents conditional effects plots for married women. The most important general finding is that in all three countries secure male breadwinner families, and, complementary, female homemaker families are most likely to become parents. Quite the opposite, in dual earner couples, couples in insecure positions and couples where the woman contributes to the household income through her part-time work. However, there are eye-catching differences between countries.

Figure 8.2 Entry into first parenthood in Germany, Great Britain, and Spain by labour market position of the couple and age (Conditional Effects Plots)

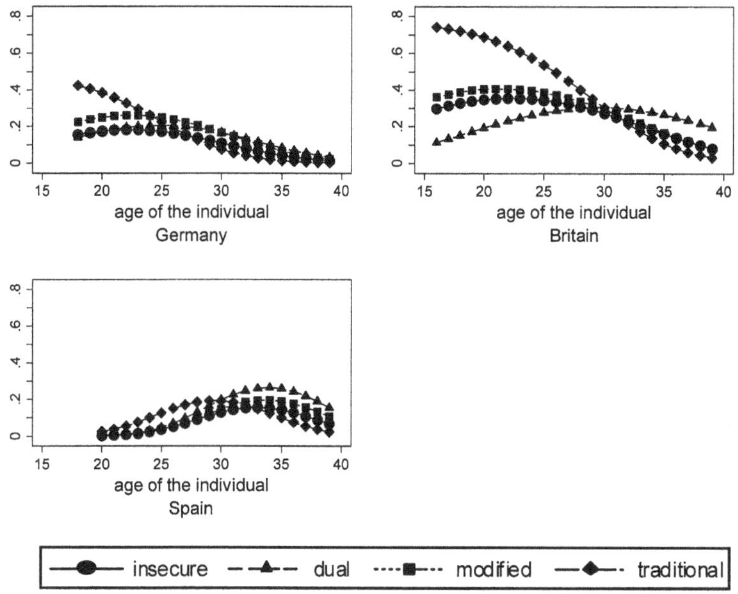

Note: Obtained from binomial logit regressions (see Table 8.5). Predicted probabilities for married women with medium educational qualification and belonging to the younges birth cohort.

Source: GSOEP (1994-2000), BHPS (1994-2000), ECHP (1994-1997), men and women aged 16-40.

In Germany, the most striking finding is that differences between the other types of family are small. It is only at very young ages that the odds of entering first parenthood are higher for male breadwinner families. In Great Britain, insecure labour market positions imply a lower probability to parent at young ages, as does the modified model. Dual earners are even less likely to have a child. As can be seen in Figure 8.2, dual earner couples, couples where women supplement the household income through part-time work and couples in insecure positions defer the decision to have a first child in Spain. Yet, differences between these types of gender division are small. Since case numbers are small the results are tentative. It is revealing, however, that around 50 percent of the sample included in the analysis of Spain is in insecure labour market positions. Another clear finding across all three countries is that cohabiting couples are less likely to have a child, indicating that being married is a key variable in explaining the transition to first parenthood. This result suggests that the indirect effect of labour market insecurity looms potentially large: As the analysis of partnership formation revealed, young people in insecure labour market positions stay single longer and tend to remain cohabiting instead of marrying. The former is particularly the case of Spain. A further postponement of parenthood through the impact of increasing labour market insecurity is therefore likely to be observed. Lastly, as we have also seen in the separate regression models for men and women (Tables 8.6 and 8.7), the findings from the analysis of the couple context point to a significant effect of educational qualification: Women with high educational qualification are prone to defer this parenthood decision.

So what are the principal conclusions to be drawn from the above analysis? In Germany, insecurity does not seem to interfere with parenthood decisions. Even though the country-specific hypothesis conjectured that the impact of insecurity is weakest in Germany, this result is somewhat surprising. We may observe this statistical insignificance of both objective and subjective measures of insecurity for three principal reasons. First, since martial status is the most powerful predictor of entry into parenthood this may be due to a mediated effect of insecurity on partnership formation, an issue that has already been tackled above. A second explanation is the high transition rate of temporary workers into permanent employment along with the fact that temporary workers are more often found in higher-grade occupations which are better paid and offer better job prospects (Chapter Seven). Third, the finding may also result from methodological weaknesses since the data at hand do not allow the separation of trainees and 'regular' fixed-term employees (see also Kurz *et al.*, forthcoming). It is by no means less unreckoned that insecurity looms large for men and women in Great Britain. Since employees are generally exposed to a higher degree of insecurity, the type of employment contract was expected to be of little importance. As already argued in the previous section, young Britons tend to bide until they have entered a secure and reasonably paid job position. Interestingly, if women hold a temporary job in the British low-trust environment, they will take this into consideration when making the decision to have a first child. Lastly, from the analysis of Chapter Seven we know that in Spain temporary employment is extraordinarily high, long lasting, and alternating with unemployment spells. It is therefore hard to establish and solidify an economic basis through permanent employment, particularly at younger ages. As a consequence, Spaniards in insecure labour market positions are less likely to become fathers and more likely to postpone it until they become an 'insider'. Yet, if they do not manage to live up to this expectation, they seem to catch up with their counterparts on permanent posts (see Golsch, 2003). With a large absence of social security and a lack of security in terms of maternity leave and re-entry after employment disruption in Spain, not only the type of men's employment contract but also women's perception of job security matter.

8.5 Making the bridge – Central findings from other country-specific studies

This chapter identified country-specific and gender-specific ways of how men and women cope with labour market insecurity. Before the last section summarises the principal conclusions of this analysis, the discussion now turns to some important findings of other country-specific studies. To this point, there has been little empirical evidence regarding the repercussions of labour market insecurity on partnership and parenthood decisions from a comparative perspective. The volumes by Blossfeld *et al.* (forthcoming) and Corijn and Klijzing (2001) put this research into a broader context of more than ten different countries. Precisely because these two studies analyse a different set of countries and employ other data sources, samples, methodological approaches, and conceptualisations, both volumes may serve as a first yardstick to evaluate whether the results of the above analysis also apply to other countries with similar contextual settings.

By and large, the results of this research are very much in line with the findings of this chapter. Insecurity – as approximated by activity status, employment relationship and economic cycle – adversely affects young adults. Prior research has revealed that educational enrolment and family formation seem incompatible, particularly for women, young adults, and people living in nations where social welfare policy is weak (Corijn and Klijzing, 2001; see also Blossfeld, 1995). Moreover, non-employment and temporary work result in higher uncertainty and lead individuals to defer life-shaping decisions (Blossfeld *et al.*, forthcoming; Corijn and Klijzing, 2001). A further dimension that could not be studied within the confines of this study are 'multiple roles': as a consequence of insecurity young adults seem also more likely to combine what used to be mutually exclusive roles, such as educational enrolment and gainful employment (Blossfeld *et al.*, forthcoming). Yet, these previous studies have evidenced different types of coping strategies for men and women and identified country-specific adaptation strategies that are shaped by nation-specific institutional arrangements in education, labour market, and welfare. These gender-specific and country-specific adaptation strategies are interwoven and can thus not be discussed separately. As contended in the gender-specific hypothesis of this work, particularly women's responses to insecurity appear strongly linked to welfare state support, gender division of labour, and career orientation. The two selected studies show how unemployment impacts men's partnership and parenthood decisions whereas the corresponding results are mixed for women. Depending on the welfare regime under study, unemployment may keep women from forming a union and becoming a mother. Yet, women in insecure labour market positions may also be more prone to marry and have a child (Blossfeld *et al.*, forthcoming; see also Corijn and Klijzing, 2001). Such gender-specific responses to insecurity are especially obvious in the male-breadwinner societies, such as Germany, the Netherlands, Italy, and Spain. Quite the contrary in the liberal and social-democratic welfare regimes. In these latter countries where the dual earner model is more spread, gender-specific adaptation strategies are much less prevalent. At the same time and in line with the considerations on the mediating role of institutional filters in Chapter Four, the volume by Blossfeld *et al.* (forthcoming) reveals that the impact of labour market insecurity is strongest in countries such as Italy and Spain that are characterised by a conspicuous absence of help from the welfare state. The social-democratic welfare regime presents yet another unique case. As an illustration, the case of Sweden exhibits how a comparatively secure social safety net counteracts the postponement of life-shaping decisions in the course of increasing labour market insecurity (Bygren *et al.*, forthcoming). In summary, these results deliver a first insight into labour market insecurity and individual partnership and parenthood decisions and offer a promising perspective for future comparative life course research.

8.6 Discussion and concluding remarks

Two central research questions guided the discussion of this chapter. Firstly, is there empirical evidence to suggest that increased levels of insecurity have an impact on partnership and parenthood decisions of men and women? And secondly, how do the observed differences in the degree of job satisfaction, composition of temporary employees and longitudinal employment profiles translate into country-specific adaptation strategies? The analysis considered objective and subjective measures of insecurity and was divided into four distinct aspects of family formation. By using data from the German Socio-economic Panel Study, the British Household Panel Survey, and the Spanish European Community Household Panel, the focus was on first partnership formation, the outcome of cohabiting unions, and parenthood decisions from a single actor and a couple perspectives. The principal conclusions can be synthesised as follows.

First, labour market insecurity adversely affects all of the transitions by generating an environment characterised by more job insecurity and hence less life course security. This becomes evident in lower transition rates into first marriage or consensual union and lower odds of marrying the partner relative to remaining in the cohabiting union. Over and above, insecurity leads individuals to postpone the entry into first parenthood. Yet, this effect of labour market insecurity seems largely mediated via the entry into marriage. Since young adults in precarious employment tend to defer first marriage and are more prone to live in cohabiting unions instead of marital ones, a postponement of first parenthood becomes more likely. In summary, through secure employment rational decision-makers seek to gain long-run certainty about their labour market career and socio-economic standing which allows them to make life-shaping decisions. But this conclusion is oversimplified since gender-specific and country-specific responses to labour market insecurity are unconsidered.

The *second* central finding that emerges is that men and women react to insecurity in different ways. In support of the gender-specific hypothesis, the results suggest that if the labour market position of men is marked by insecurity, then this is will impact their family life. Firstly, holding a job is an important predictor for union formation and parenthood among men. The increasing postponement of first partnership and parenthood is thus not only due to a higher school leaving age but also to difficulties in finding a first job. Yet, the important point to note is that, once men have successfully entered the labour market, uncertainty may take the form of flexi-work and this will also result in a deferment of life-shaping decisions. The impact of insecurity was expected to result in different responses for women, a hypothesis which generally gained strong support, particularly for women in Spain. Educational enrolment keeps women from forming a union and becoming a mother through increased opportunity costs. Furthermore, being unemployed reduces their chance of entering a first union. Yet, job insecurity appeared to have no impact on women's first union formation. Rather, there is some evidence to suggest that women in insecure positions are more prone to enter a union. This implies that women may want to contribute to the household budget but men need to consolidate it through their permanent full-time employment. Marriage may thus serve as a safety net for women in insecure labour market positions. Yet, if it comes to the decision to have a child, women's employment outlook matters: As suggested in the gender-specific hypothesis, if women face a high degree of insecurity in the labour market, this will delay their entry into first motherhood.

Third, as Chapter Seven identified diverse implications of increased labour market insecurity for labour market integration of young adults in Germany, Great Britain, and Spain, so does this chapter point to different consequences on family life in the three countries under study. In support of the country-specific hypothesis, the youth who confront the strongest detriments of increased labour market insecurity are the ones living in Spain (see also Golsch, 2003; Simó *et al.*, 2002b; Ahn and Mira, 2001). A stable job position ensures high income stability, thus providing individuals with a certain degree of economic security and good career prospects, a prerequisite for partnership formation and parenthood. Yet, young Spaniards face many hurdles on their way to economic independence, be it due to unemployment or temporary work. As to Germany and Great Britain, there is limited support and considerable contrary evidence for the country-specific hypothesis, however. There were mixed findings of the impact of insecurity for Germany. While the above analysis of partnership decisions provided clear support for the insecurity hypothesis, other investigations have not found such consequences of labour market insecurity on family formation (Kurz *et al.*, forthcoming). With respect to parenthood decisions, however, the relative importance of security was not prevalent. By and large, the results suggest that it is essential whether a man holds a job or not, but it does not seem to matter whether this job is a permanent one or not (Kurz *et al.*, forthcoming; Tölke and Diewald, 2002). It remains to be seen whether this unexpected finding is due to the methodological approach or whether there is indeed no impact of labour market insecurity on family life in Germany. Unfortunately, this issue could not be adequately approached within the comparative and therefore highly standardised analysis of this chapter. Lastly, the results for Great Britain evidence that temporary work impedes life course decision-making of young adults, even though job insecurity is assumed to be of short duration and more evenly spread among workers (see also Francesconi and Golsch, forthcoming). One rationale behind this unexpected finding may be that Britons in insecure labour market positions defer life-shaping decisions because they judge their current position as a stepping-stone to more secure and better paid employment. Quite the contrary in Spain, where job prospects are dim and young adults are moving between flexible employment and unemployment. It is possible to test this hypothesis with the BHPS data by reconstructing the past employment career. Yet, it was not possible to trace this research question within the confines of this comparative study and future research on this issue is therefore needed. Nonetheless, we may be curious to see the results of Chapter Nine which goes into labour market insecurity, career maturity and the work and family life of adult workers in Great Britain. In summary, this chapter has delivered some important insights into life course decision-making of men and women, but also pointed to desirable further extensions of the above presented analysis. This section therefore concludes with a discussion of some strong points and shortcomings of this analysis.

A first strong point is the consideration of subjective measures of insecurity, which is obviously a further dimension in the analysis of the transition to adulthood. Yet, further elaboration is needed to disentangle the effects of employment relationship and perceived job security. A second strength of this study is the attempt to study life course decision-making from a couple perspective. Even though the results remain tentative due to small case numbers, the chapter suggested to what extent the partner's job security impacts women's partnership and parenthood decisions. This model specification seems more adequate since the decision to convert a cohabiting union into marriage as well as the decision to have a first child is largely a joint decision. At the same time, this strength relates to an important drawback of the analysis. The data at hand do not permit a detailed classification of different types of insecure labour market positions of couples. Undoubtedly, individual responses are likely to differ depending on whether the two partners, the man or the woman are in an insecure labour market position. Therefore future research should be devoted to a more disaggregated analysis. A further strength of this chapter is that the country-specific contributions are highly standardised in that they share a common research focus, methods, measures, graphical representations and tables. Again, this strength is also a weakness. The chapter would have been stronger with a more thorough and explicit study of why temporary employment plays a prominent role in Great Britain. The same can be said for the mixed results on Germany. Lastly, the presented analysis obviously disregarded several other determinants of partnership and parenthood decisions that have been shown to play a crucial role in individual life course decision-making (see Chapter Two). However, these weaknesses should not distract from the fact that, as a whole, this chapter provides evidence of how labour market insecurity interferes with individual decision-making.

Appendix

Table 8.5 The transition from cohabitation into marriage in Germany and Great Britain (Logistic regression)

	Germany		Great Britain	
Labour market position of couples				
Secure dual earner family	-0.049	(0.264)	0.703	(0.230)
Secure traditional family	0.981	(0.439)	0.347	(0.379)
Secure modified family	-0.917	(0.572)	0.995	(0.267)
Insecure family (base)				
Interaction between labour market position and age				
Secure dual earner family * age	-0.059	(0.072)	0.063	(0.052)
Secure traditional family * age	0.038	(0.099)	0.065	(0.080)
Secure modified family * age	-0.117	(0.147)	-0.001	(0.059)
Educational qualification				
High education	-0.011	(0.299)	-0.060	(0.156)
Medium education (base)				
Low education	-0.216	(0.410)	-0.029	(0.353)
Age (centred effects)				
Age	0.336	(0.458)	0.759	(0.257)
Age square	-0.004	(0.008)	-0.014	(0.005)
Birth cohort				
1960-64	-1.948	(0.897)	0.171	(0.542)
1965-69	-0.030	(0.565)	-0.039	(0.419)
1970-74	0.095	(0.451)	-0.017	(0.313)
1975-83 (base)				
Has a child	-0.722	(0.385)	-0.287	(0.196)
Region				
West Germany (base)				
East Germany	-0.309	(0.252)		
Constant	-1.332	(0.529)	-2.368	(0.378)
Log Likelihood	-268		-612	
Number of person wave observations	740		1,438	
Number of events	100		231	

Note: The figures are coefficients from binomial logit regressions. Standard errors (in parentheses) have been adjusted using the Huber/White/sandwich estimator of variance. All variables lagged by one period except birth cohort and region.

Source: GSOEP (1994-2000), men and women aged 16-35. BHPS (1994-2000), ECHP (1994-1997), men and women aged 16-40.

Table 8.8 The transition to first parenthood and the labour market position of couples in Germany, Great Britain, and Spain (Logistic regression)

	Germany	Great Britain	Spain
Labour market position of couples			
Secure dual earner family	0.366 (0.199)	-0.124 (0.250)	0.349 (0.380)
Secure traditional family	-0.055 (0.876)	0.524 (0.728)	1.011 (0.436)
Secure modified family	0.484 (0.305)	0.153 (0.327)	0.018 (0.427)
Insecure family (base)			
Interaction between labour market position and age			
Secure dual earner family * age	0.051 (0.055)	0.097 (0.053)	0.048 (0.096)
Secure traditional family * age	-0.150 (0.182)	-0.125 (0.149)	-0.176 (0.111)
Secure modified family * age	0.004 (0.078)	-0.013 (0.071)	0.040 (0.128)
Educational qualification			
High education	0.434 (0.182)	-0.347 (0.164)	0.032 (0.449)
Medium education (base)			
Low education	0.019 (0.383)	-0.186 (0.573)	0.476 (0.382)
Educational qualification * age			
High education * age	0.068 (0.053)	0.071 (0.038)	-0.036 (0.106)
Low education * age	0.016 (0.079)	-0.035 (0.111)	-0.290 (0.103)
Age (centred effects)			
Age	0.453 (0.349)	0.296 (0.280)	1.672 (0.860)
Age square	-0.010 (0.006)	-0.007 (0.005)	-0.025 (0.015)
Birth cohort			
1960-64	0.001 (0.596)	-0.668 (0.554)	0.888 (1.131)
1965-69	0.154 (0.455)	-0.555 (0.455)	0.993 (1.411)
1970-74	0.195 (0.365)	-0.535 (0.355)	1.380 (1.439)
1975-83 (base)			
Marital status			
Married (base)			
cohabiting	-1.002 (0.168)	-1.243 (0.180)	-1.416 (0.620)
Region			
West Germany (base)			
East Germany	-0.029 (0.183)		
Constant	-2.140 (0.422)	-0.984 (0.406)	-3.665 (1.180)
Log Likelihood	-541	-611	-192
Number of person wave obs.	1,493	1,803	412
Number of events	192	211	86

Note: The figures are coefficients from binomial logit regressions. Standard errors (in parentheses) have been adjusted using the Huber/White/sandwich estimator of variance. All variables lagged by one period except birth cohort and region.

Source: GSOEP (1994-2000), men and women aged 16-35. BHPS (1994-2000), ECHP (1994-1997), men and women aged 16-40.

9 Labour market insecurity and its consequences on the work and family life of adult workers

9.1 Introduction

The previous two chapters explored the impact of labour market insecurity on labour market entry and early career and established to what extent job insecurity hampers partnership and parenthood decisions. Chapters Seven and Eight thereby added to our current understanding of life course decision-making in insecure times and, more particularly, the mediating role of institutional filters and individual resources. Thus far, however, the research focus was limited to early adult life. What we do not yet know is whether and to what extent insecurity of career-entry processes spills over well into adult work and family life, determining long-run chances of occupational mobility and risks of labour market exclusion. Increased labour market deregulation and flexibility may also result in gender-specific strategies, an idea that runs through the various previous chapters. The purpose of this chapter is to ask whether job insecurity is equally spread over men's and women's entire labour market career; or is it confined only to early labour market positions? Are some individuals more likely to 'lose' in the highly flexible, deregulated labour markets such as Great Britain? Moreover, does job insecurity at early stages of the labour market career induce serious repercussions on adult work life? And, how exactly do labour market deregulation and flexibility influence job satisfaction of men and women?

To take account for the complexity of career patterns of adult job holders, and to advance our knowledge of the role of institutional filters and individual resources in mediating deregulation and flexibility pressures, the consequences of labour market insecurity on the work and family life of adult workers will be exemplified in Great Britain. From a European perspective, Great Britain stands out as a country that has long had a relatively high degree of flexibility and change in the labor market. The British employment regulation system is the least protective in Europe (Deakin and Reed, 2000; Chapter Four). So, if there is an overall decrease of job stability, Great Britain should be at the forefront from a European perspective. For the purpose of this chapter, Great Britain therefore appears to be a challenging country for a case study of the transformation of employment relationships. Despite this country-specific focus, however, the chapter leaves room to take findings for other countries into account and aims to motivate further investigations on other countries.

The chapter is structured as follows. The next section recapitulates the underlying research questions and hypotheses. Section 9.3 reviews the large body of research contributions that tackle this topic and scrutinises whether and to what extent stable, life-long employment relationships have eroded in Great Britain. This is followed by a description of data, methods, and measures used. The following section delves deeper into job insecurity of adult Britons in the 1990s. More specifically, Section 9.5.1 synthesises the results for work and unemployment of adult job holders. Section 9.5.2 addresses the work-family linkage of women in Great Britain. Section 9.5.3 explores chances of upward mobility and risks of downward mobility, and Section 9.5.4 focuses on satisfaction with job security, total pay, and promotion prospects. Section 9.6 brings together empirical evidence from Germany and Spain in order to broaden these issues towards other country-specific contexts. The final section summarises the principal conclusions.

9.2 Theoretical background and research hypotheses

The theoretical framework of this study developed how labour market insecurity is mediated by institutional filters and individual resources, likely to interfere with individual life-course decision-making. To gauge the extent to which adult workers experience labour market insecurity, this chapter studies career profiles of men and women in the highly flexible British labour market and will shed more light on adult workers' risk profiles coupled with country of residence, gender, career maturity, and individual resources. To describe individual degrees of insecurity and risks of labour market exclusion, the primary focus is on the following interrelated mobility events: (i) *risks of entry into unemployment and chances to exit from unemployment*, (ii) *transitions into and out of unpaid homemaking*, and, (iii) *risks of downward and upward occupational mobility*.

This study proposes that labour market insecurity is filtered through *country-specific institutions* (Chapter Four). Great Britain is an example of a 'liberal' welfare regime (Esping-Andersen, 1999) and has as such already experienced increased levels of deregulation and flexibility of the labour market. With the dominance of 'open' employment relationships, a comparatively market-driven economy, a weak employment protection system, and the decline in trade unions and coverage by collective bargaining, workers are minimally shielded against labour market pressures (see Section 4.2.2). In contrast to countries with rather 'closed' employment relationships and predominant vacancy competition, Great Britain is best described as a rather individualistic mobility regime, where employees compete for wage increments and premiums and where differences in wages reflect the marginal productivity of employees (Sørensen and Tuma, 1981). Employer-led flexibility, relatively unconstrained competition, and a 'hire-and-fire' system lead to comparatively low wages, short duration of unemployment but high rates of job mobility, and less predictability of occupational moves. All in all, the analysis expects that occupational moves are less predictable and include both, occupational up- and downward mobility. Overall job insecurity is assumed to be more evenly spread among British workers than among workers, say, in the closed labour markets of Germany and Spain. However, as elaborated in more detail in Chapter Five, flexibility is expected to have a different impact on the work and family life of men and women and career maturity and individual resources should function as significant buffers against labour market pressures. The remainder of this section comments on the potential effect of gender, career maturity, and individual resources.

The previous chapters already established *gender-specific effects* of labour market insecurity on life course decision-making of young adults. Here the question is raised to what extent increasing deregulation and flexible measures induce similar repercussions for adult men and women. While for men flexible work should destabilise their employment career, different hypotheses can be put forward for women. Comparing men and women, female careers used to be more flexible and fragmented by virtue of the integration of work and family life. Increased labour market flexibility may help some women to reconcile work and family life but is likely to introduce further instability in their employment careers. Others may not seek a permanent place in the labour market. Having said that, it generally proves that women increasingly extend their educational enrolment, are more career-oriented, and appear better equipped for job competition than ever before (Chapter Two). Labour market insecurity creates work incentives for some women since the economic basis of dual-earner households provides more resources and de-couples the long-run economic prospects of a household and the stability of male job careers. How exactly flexibility impacts women's work and family career is therefore an open research question. In Great Britain, employment probabilities of school leavers seem higher for women while they have worsened (Chapter Two); men are also more often hit by unemployment than women (see Section 9.3). Yet, child-care facilities and leave entitlements are poor (Chapter Four), and hence, the British welfare state renders gainful employment of mothers with young children difficult. While the separate taxation system may work as an inducement for some women to be gainfully employed and to hold a full-time job in particular, the means-tested benefit system will possibly create incentives to reduce working hours or exit the labour force for others. At the same time, the expanded British part-time labour market opens flexible job opportunities and will foster women's mobility between homemaking and employment.

According to a further fundamental idea of this study, *career maturity* is assumed to be a crucial employee benefit (see Chapter Five). In other words, this study presumes that the young – who have gained little experience and have developed only weak ties to the labour market – experience higher degrees of insecurity while those already settled in the labour market should remain comparatively sheltered against new market risks. As argued in more detail in Section 5.4, employers make increasing use of flexible work arrangements not only to screen the work potential of labour market entrants (recruitment strategy), but also to adjust to labour market shifts, thereby lowering their firing costs. In return, the school-to-work transition is becoming more and more insecure, as can be seen in the increased prevalence of flexible kinds of work arrangements and longer job search processes characterised by intervening unemployment and inactivity spells (Chapter Seven; Francesconi and Golsch, forthcoming; Taylor, 2000). It is presumably more difficult for recent labour market entrants to make career advancements and insecurity at early stages of the labour market career may induce serious repercussions on adult work life. By contrast, in the British low-trust environment with the hire-and-fire system in particular, career maturity may only have a modest impact (Section 5.4).

Lastly, *individual resources* should significantly shield workers from labour market insecurity. This study does not only anticipate that the degree of insecurity faced by employees belonging to the service class differs from that faced by unskilled workers. The educational qualification of individuals may also identify differences in ability and income prospects that influence the transitions under study and cannot be explained by differences in occupation. These differential degrees of insecurity will become revealed in terms of higher unemployment risks, lower re-entry probabilities for unemployed, and increased risks of downward mobility. However, due to national differences in flexibility paths and institutional arrangements in education, individual resources may offer better protection from job insecurity in some countries, less so in others. Previous studies have already examined the role of the individual's resources and established that individual resources are more important determinants of career opportunities in countries with weaker employment protection and weaker labour market boundaries (DiPrete *et al.*, 1997). In the British low-trust environment, workers should gain stability through their own personal characteristics. From another viewpoint, the practical on-the-job training in Great Britain and the weak connection between educational certificates and entry-level jobs should enhance mobility to find an appropriate and lasting job match (Blossfeld and Stockmann, 1998/1999; Steinmann, 1998/1999; see Section 4.3.2).

9.3 Are there signs of employment (in)stability in Great Britain?

From Chapter Seven and various other empirical studies, we know that labour market entry patterns of youth are becoming more and more insecure (Francesconi and Golsch, forthcoming; Scherer, 2001; Taylor, 2000). School-to-work transitions are less often direct and less often lead to permanent full-time positions. There has been a substantial increase in the proportion of youth moving between short-term jobs, unemployment spells, and training programmes. While time-limited contracts are not extensively used in Great Britain, young labour market entrants, particularly those previously unemployed or economically inactive, are often forced to accept these contracts. Tthere is also evidence that suggests an increase in own-account workers and part-timers among the youth. How does the picture of increasing employment instability change once we study job stability over the life course? Are those already settled in the labour market relatively protected? Or is there evidence to suggest a decline in job stability of mid-career workers? Several empirical studies on the British case provide counterfactual evidence. Despite the highly debated increase in job insecurity, average *job tenure* – understood as an indicator for employment stability – has not declined during the last three decades (Gregg and Wadsworth, 1999a). However, there are several offsetting effects. First, these studies point to strong age effects (Gregg and Wadsworth, 1999a). The median job tenure fell for those at both ends of the labour market career, young labour market entrants and those over 50. This has been related to the increase in short-term contracts among young labour market entrants and the less clear-cut school-to-work transition in Great Britain. As to those older than 50, there is some evidence that the decline in job tenure is not so much linked to early retirement but to a decrease in long-term jobs. Second, the decline in youth and older men's job tenure is offset by an increase in women's job tenure (Gregg and Wadsworth, 1999a; Gregg *et al.*, 2000). This is mainly driven by the increasing tenure of women with dependent children, in particular in the age group from 35 to 49 years. Looking at the share of short-term jobs (less than one year), it can be shown that since the mid-1980s the proportion of men in short-term jobs has increased independently of educational degree. However, this was most strongly in the age group from 16 to 24 years. Yet, the main drawback of this indicator is that reasons for ending a job are not taken into account. Has job tenure among men declined because of quits (worker-initiated separations) or layoffs (firm-initiated separations)? Putting it another way, are we looking at job-to-job shifts, promotions, shifts to unemployment, or inactivity? To answer the question of whether labour market careers are increasingly insecure, it is not sufficient to show that job tenure has decreased.

Looking at *unemployment flows*, men face substantially higher unemployment risks than women (Booth *et al.*, 1999) and it is important to note that individual resources play a far more crucial role for men (see Figure 9.1). Over the last decades, men's labour market position has worsened, in particular for men with a low educational level and those in low occupational classes (Booth *et al.*, 1999; Gallie *et al.*, 1998; Nickell, 1999). The risk of firm-initiated separations is much higher for more recent cohorts (Booth *et al.*, 1999). Also, it has become harder to move out of unemployment (Nickell, 1999), earnings losses have increased (Gregg *et al.*, 1999b; Gregg and Wadsworth, 2000; Nickell *et al.*, 2002), and, for both men and women, unemployment spells have enduring negative impacts on subsequent labour market careers (Gallie *et al.*, 1998). At the same time, inactivity rates have generally risen for men, particularly for those 50 and older (Gregg and Wadsworth, 1999b).

Figure 9.1 Unemployment rates in Great Britain by level of education, social class, and gender, 1990-1998

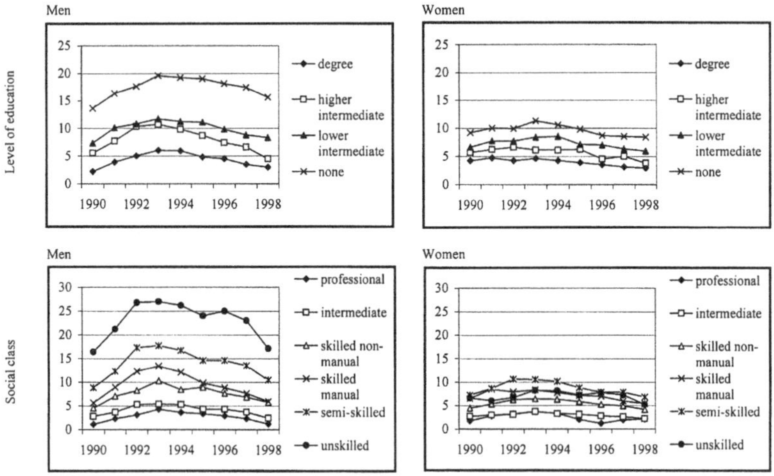

Source: Nickell (1999). Spring LFS, ILO definition.

As previously argued, the *incidence of temporary employment* is rather low and has grown little. Also, there is no evidence to suggest that employment conditions of temporary workers have worsened. Rather, there appears to be some degree of convergence in the job insecurity of temporary and permanent workers (Gallie *et al.*, 1998). Yet, it is important to stress that some temporary workers are much less likely to move out of temporary employment, are poorly paid, and face higher unemployment risks (Booth *et al.*, 2002).

Apart from tenure, unemployment in- and outflows, and incidence of short-term contracts, *income mobility* can serve as another indicator for employment stability. Even long-term positions may be insecure due to a high probability of wage loss. Some recent empirical investigations indicate that wage cuts are no longer restricted to female and youth labour markets. From the early 1980s onwards, the risk of wage loss seems to have spread to men and all age groups (Nickell *et al.*, 2002; Stewart, 1999). Also, the probability has gone up for the highly skilled. Still, over the last three decades, wage inequality appears to have risen (Machin, 1999). Short-term wage mobility rates have fallen, which has exacerbated the rise in inequality. The well-educated and highly-skilled still seem to be rather protected, while those in semi- and unskilled positions are most affected by the fast and intense technological shifts, as well as the decline in union membership and coverage by collective bargaining. Furthermore, poorly skilled and badly paid workers are much more likely to experience unemployment and inactivity spells, entrapping them in a 'low pay – no pay' cycle (Dickens, 1999; Stewart, 1999).

In summary, this evidence suggests that over the last decades, men are likely to have seen more substantial changes in job insecurity than women. Even though the insecurity of employment relationships appears to be the strongest among the young, there is also a decline in job stability among 50- to 60-year-olds and, to a lesser extent, among male mid-career workers. Yet educational and occupational qualifications still seem to function as important determinants of job stability. But why do women seem to be performing better in recent times? Several authors argue that women's increase in long-term employment is connected to their increasing tendency to take maternity leave and to less often withdraw from labour force participation (Gallie *et al.*, 1998; Desai *et al.*, 1999). Interestingly, there are strong differences between different industrial sectors with respect to job instability (Doogan, 2001). Yet these findings are not in line with the commonly made distinction between traditional industries and new industries, as well as production industries and new service industries. It is probably not so much technological advancements and increased global competition that account for increasing job insecurity in Great Britain. Rather, several authors suggest that the increase in men's job instability is mainly due to the dramatic decline in union memberships and coverage by collective bargaining and the radical privatisation (Abercrombie and Warde, 2000; Doogan, 2001). In view of these empirical findings, the discussion now turns to a more detailed analysis of job insecurity over the 1990s.

9.4 Data, methods, and measures

The outlined research questions will be addressed by using longitudinal data from the British Household Panel Survey (BHPS), covering 1991-2000 (Section 6.1.2). At issue here are mobility events during the early labour market career vis-à-vis career profiles of mid-career workers. For the purpose of this chapter, the analysis is therefore confined to men and women born in 1950 and after (thus aged at most 50 in 2000, the last available survey year).[62] The analysis is furthermore limited to original sample members who are not disabled, provided complete information at each interview date, have entered a first job after full-time education, with at least two years of panel data, and an identifiable labour market entry year. These sample selection criteria lead to an unbalanced longitudinal sample of 3,173 men and 3,169 women with 21,770 and 23,573 person-wave observations, respectively. The analysis runs discrete-time competing risks transition models for men and women separately (see Section 6.3). The dependent variable in the multinomial logit models is the occurrence of a given mobility event between two panel waves, coded as 1, ..., *m* for occurrence of the *m* alternative outcomes and 0 for non-occurrence. Let us first make plain the terminology to be used, the mobility events and alternative outcomes of interest, and the specific sub-samples under study.

Risks of entry into unemployment and chances to exit from unemployment: In the analysis of work and unemployment, the two mobility events are employment entry and employment exit. Employment entry refers to transitions from unemployment to job and the competing risk is exit out of the labour market. Employment exit is a change from employment either to unemployment or out of the labour force. It is vital to bear in mind that this study applies a modified version of the ILO guidelines for measuring employment and unemployment as detailed in Chapter Six.

Transitions into and out of unpaid homemaking: As to work and family, the analysis focuses on women only and describes employment exit as a change from job to unpaid homemaking, considering unemployment as a competing risk. Employment entry is a change from unpaid homemaking to employment or unemployment. In the analyses to follow unpaid homemaking is measured as a self-reported activity status (either family care or maternity leave) (Chapter Six).

Risks of downward and chances of upward occupational mobility: With work and job mobility this chapter refers to risks of downward and chances of upward occupational mobility.[63] Changes in the occupational standing are defined by the Standard International Socio-Economic Index of Occupational Status (ISEI).[64]

---

[62] The analysis does not take into account mobility events that occur at the end of the labour market career. This is because these events are likely to be driven by other explanatory variables and time dependency. Such an analysis would also have to take into account other competing risks (early retirement) and a potentially different meaning of flexible work.

[63] This analysis does not separate 'within-employer mobility' from 'between-employer mobility'. Likewise, it does not distinguish between 'within-industry mobility' and 'industrial mobility' (for a discussion refer to DiPrete *et al.*, 1997).

[64] To derive the ISEI the analysis uses four digit ISCO-88 codes and applies the conversion tools provided by Ganzeboom, H. B.G.; Treiman, D. J., International Stratification and

To differentiate between upward and downward occupational mobility, this study uses two different approaches. First, upward and downward mobility is defined to occur when a respondent's ISEI score increases or decreases by at least ten percent, respectively. Changes on the ISEI score of less than 10 percent are referred to as 'lateral' moves and considered the comparison group.[65] This approach can be challenged on at least two substantive grounds. This 10 percent threshold value is arbitrary. A further potential shortcoming is the fact that a 10 percent increase or decrease has a different meaning depending on whether a person has already a high or rather low occupational standing.[66] The second approach of this chapter is therefore to study occupational mobility defined as any change in ISEI-score between two panel waves. This approach also has some considerable limitations since a change in ISEI-score between two consecutive panel waves may be owed to recall errors or coding errors. By pursuing analyses for both approaches, this study attempts to evaluate whether the results remain robust across varying specifications.

Satisfaction with job security, total pay and promotion prospects: The study of mobility events will be supplemented by an examination of individual degrees of job satisfaction. In line with the conceptualisation of job insecurity, this chapter studies satisfaction with three items, namely job security, total pay, and promotion prospects, measured on a 1-to-7 response scale, where 1 corresponds to 'not satisfied at all' and 7 to 'completely satisfied'. The former is meant to reflect the fear of job loss or uncertainty about the continuation of employment contracts. Satisfaction with total pay does not capture insecurity in terms of the probability of income loss but only the satisfaction with present pay. It may therefore be determined by other factors not discussed in the context of this chapter. Nonetheless, in a context of extensive wage competition and high incentives for wage flexibility, satisfaction with total pay is an important aspect to keep in mind. Lastly, this chapter studies satisfaction with promotion prospects since labour market insecurity may not only lead to less predictability of the employment relationship, but also impacts the long-run career mobility.

Mobility, File: Conversion Tools. Utrecht: Department of Sociology http://home.fsw.vu.nl/hbg.ganzeboom/. [18.11.03], Summer 1996. For an overview on various occupational scales that have been developed to facilitate cross-national comparative stratification research see Ganzeboom and Treiman (1996) and Ganzeboom and Treiman (2003).

65 For both men and women the ISEI-index in this sample varies between 16 and 88. Those already in good position can hardly move further up, those in very bad positions can not move further down. Respondents with an ISEI-score between 80 and 88 and 16 and 17, respectively, are therefore excluded from the analysis.

66 To illustrate this consider the following example. For a person with an ISEI-score of 20 a 10 percent increase corresponds an increase by 2 points on the ISEI-scale. For a person with an ISEI-score of 60 a 10 percent increase would be equivalent to an increase by 6 points on the ISEI-scale.

To disentangle the complex interplay between labour market insecurity, national adaptation strategies, and the moderating impact of career maturity and individual resources, the analysis includes the following explanatory variables:

- *Type of employment relationship* of employees (described through working hours and employment contract)[67], to gauge the impact of flexible forms of employment, and,
- *career maturity*[68] to disentangle employment experiences and labour market insecurity experiences. Career maturity is approximated by:
  a. *employment experience* and *employment experience squared,* operationalised as variables that count the number of years in which individuals are employed, to capture the effect of labour force experience and accumulation of occupation- and firm-specific knowledge,
  b. *flexi-worker experience*[69] which represents the number of years a person has been in an insecure employment relationship and is meant to run counter to employment experiences, and,
  c. *unemployment experience* (dummy variable that indicates whether respondents have been unemployed at least once in the previous panel waves) to investigate whether previous unemployment spells determine future mobility events.

---

[67] The analysis uses slightly different specifications for men and women. Due to small case numbers, the models for men separate full-time and fixed, full-time and casual, part-time and marginal part-time jobs. This operationalisation is well-founded since for men any part-time or marginal post, whether permanent or non-permanent, should involve considerable degrees of insecurity (see Chapter Three and Five). For women, the latter two flexible forms of employment are further sub-divided into permanent and non-permanent job positions. Here one may expect that insecurity is attached to non-permanent positions while women on permanent posts should be in comparatively secure positions, no matter whether these are full-time, part-time, or marginal part-time.

[68] Career maturity is a complex theoretical construct and therefore difficult to grasp in the empirical analysis. It is difficult to fix a specific point in time when a person has settled in the labour market. The timing of labour market integration does not only depend on the country-specific educational system (Section 4.2). Rather, with the increasing turbulence during early labour market careers, researchers lack a reliable threshold value. The onset of the 'clock' in discrete-time models one, three or five years after first labour market entry is an arbitrary threshold value for the analysis of mobility events. Also, such an research strategy would not permit to study in full the most recent labour market entry cohort with the panel data at hand and to analyse whether instability during the first labour market years has any impact on the subsequent career, in particular.

[69] For men any part-time, marginal part-time, full-time and fixed-term or full-time and casual job is considered a flexi-worker experience. For women, only experiences in non-permanent jobs are added while permanent marginal and permanent part-time jobs are not counted (see the definition of flexible employment).

In summary, these indicators allow for a more clear description of the individual employment career. Various practical issues of data handling merit mention at this point, all of which are discussed in some detail in Box 9.1.

Box 9.1 A note on censoring and its potential impact on estimates

The panel data at hand allows the reconstruction of employment careers between 1991 and 2000. However, the analysis has to deal with different types of censoring (Andreß, 1992; Blossfeld and Rohwer, 2001), some of which necessitate assumptions about the underlying censoring process as well as duration dependence. In general, spells are censored if there is no or incomplete information about their beginning and ending times. All spells that started and ended before the first sweep in 1991 are *fully censored* and this results in a sample selection bias. One solution to this is to assume that the transition rate does not depend on the duration in the origin state (i.e., assumption of a Markov process). However, as for the mobility events under study this assumption is barely justified. Other spells are *left censored* which means that the spell started before the first panel wave. One way to deal with this type of censoring is to exclude these spells and consider only those that begin during the observation period. However, this strategy would also lead to a specific sample selection. As an illustration, the analysis of unemployment risks would then be conditional on previous employment interruptions. Alternatively, by using retrospective data one could attempt to reconstruct the employment career before the panel start. In the BHPS, retrospective data on employment status spells have only been collected in wave 2 (1992) while information on jobs held in employment has been gathered in wave 3 only (1993) and from respondents who were already interviewed in the previous wave and have ever had a paid job other than their current employment. Using this information would mean to select only those sample members who have provided complete information in this particular panel wave. Moreover, life history data are less reliable since respondents tend to understate short spells and spells that started a long time before the interview in particular (Dex and McCulloch, 1998; Becker, 2001; Middendorff, 2000). Also, in the retrospective data employment and unemployment spells are self-defined, whereas this study applies the ILO guidelines. The analysis of combined life history and panel data may therefore suggest changes in transitions rates across cohorts and historical time that are simply due to differences in data quality.

To verify to what extent left truncated spells bias the estimates for the transition processes under study, further analyses (not shown here) have been pursued in which (i) left censored spells have been excluded, (ii) the starting point for employment and flexi-worker experiences was the first panel wave present in the BHPS, and, (iii) information on the start of an employment status spell in the first panel wave has been used to reconstruct the beginning date for left censored spells. These three different approaches yield to a great extent the same conclusions. As one would expect, however, in the Markov model various estimates do not reflect distinct conditions at labour market entry. Rather, some covariates partly capture uncontrolled past employment experiences. The analysis to follow therefore fills the gap for left truncated spells but disregards fully left-censored spells. This approach also has potential shortcomings and it seems reasonable to assume that the analysis underestimates the impact of past employment experiences and labour market insecurity.

The analysis also has to deal with *right censored* spells. Under the assumption that this censoring process is random and therefore not related to the transition rates under study, these right censored spells do not cause any problems in the analysis. Yet, right censoring may also be due to panel attrition and hence cause a selectivity bias. Recall from above that this study is based on an unbalanced longitudinal sample. As explained in Section 6.3 the analyses are pursued without weighting. To correct for sample loss between consecutive panel waves the analyses control for various social-demographic characteristics that are correlated with attrition. However, some of the analyses to follow include only few control variables due to considerable multicollinearity with other explanatory variables. A related question is how to handle gaps for temporary drop-outs. In these cases, we do not know whether a person has already made the transition under study or stayed in the same activity status. Here the study makes the practical assumption that the activity status remained the same.

The analysis also inquires into whether and to what extent educational qualification and occupational standing offset increased levels of insecurity.[70] To this end, the analysis applies

- a more refined classification of *educational qualification* than in the previous two chapters which is meant to better reflect the educational system in Great Britain (five dummies to differentiate higher and first university degree, higher vocational qualification, A level or equivalent, GCSE/O level or equivalent=base, less than O level and no qualification; see Section 4.3.2 for a description of the British educational system), and,
- studies a person's *occupational standing* (four dummy variables separating very low, low=base, high and very high ISEI-scores by using quartiles).

Box 9.2 The construction of a gender index

Table 9.2 Items measuring gender roles in the BHPS

Variable	Description
OPFAMA*	A pre school child is likely to suffer if his or her mother works
OPFAMB*	Family suffers if woman works full-time
OPFAMC	A woman and her family would all be happier if she goes out to work
OPFAMD	Both the husband and wife should contribute to the household income
OPFAME	Having a fulltime job is the best way for a woman to be an independent person
OPFAMF*	A husband's jobs is to earn money; a wife's job is to look after the home

Source: BHPS (1991-2000), all respondents, waves 1, 3, 5, 7, 9. * indicates reverse scoring. Table 9.2 summarises the items that have been used for the construction of the gender index. Respondents were asked to rate these items on a 1-to-5 response scale, where 1 corresponds to 'strongly agree' and 5 to 'strongly disagree' (Likert, 1932). Scorings for statements that are negatively correlated with the gender roles being measured have been reversed and the individual item scores for this battery have been summed for all respondents. To determine if all items fit this summative rating scale, the interitem correlations for all pairs of variables

[70] The presented models do not include both, educational qualification and occupational class, in a model because of high correlation.

have been computed. Apparently, the selected items do not correlate strongly with each other.

Table 9.3 Interitem correlations

	OPFAMA	OPFAMB	OPFAMC	OPFAMD	OPFAME	OPFAMF
OPFAMA	1.000					
OPFAMB	0.684	1.000				
OPFAMC	0.235	0.286	1.000			
OPFAMD	0.144	0.210	0.349	1.000		
OPFAME	0.112	0.200	0.366	0.400	1.000	
OPFAMF	0.441	0.512	0.198	0.172	0.094	1.000

Source: BHPS (1991-2000), women only, wave 1, 3, 5, 7, 9, pair wise case deletion.

To assess the reliability of the additive scale, Cronbach's alpha (Cronbach, 1951) has been calculated and Table 9.4 summarises the results of the reliability analysis. Item E 'Having a fulltime job is the best way for a woman to be an independent person' does not fit in the scale well. The item-test and item-rest correlations are lower than for the other items and the average interitem correlation increases by dropping it from the scale. Cronbach's alpha does not substantially decrease if this item is removed; the other five items seem to be more well-fitting.

Table 9.4 Results from reliability analysis

Item	Observations	Sign	Item-test correlation	Item-rest correlation	Average inter-item corr.	alpha
OPFAMA	16,081	+	0.6801	0.4970	0.2785	0.6587
OPFAMB	16,095	+	0.7513	0.5968	0.2511	0.6263
OPFAMC	16,076	+	0.6325	0.4330	0.2969	0.6786
OPFAMD	16,089	+	0.5915	0.3800	0.3127	0.6947
OPFAME	16,092	+	0.5649	0.3460	0.3230	0.7046
OPFAMF	16,089	+	0.6292	0.4274	0.2985	0.6803
Test scale					0.2935	0.7136

Source: BHPS (1991-2000), women only, wave 1, 3, 5, 7, 9, standardised items.

Item E has been omitted and the resulting Cronbach's alpha (0.7046) indicates fairly good reliability. The derived index is the sum of the individual item scores for five variables:

Table 9.5 Summary statistics for the item battery and the derived scale

Variable	Mean	Std Dev	Min	Max
OPFAMA	2.901	1.097	1	5
OPFAMB	2.790	1.117	1	5
OPFAMC	3.098	.756	1	5
OPFAMD	2.495	.912	1	5
OPFAMF	2.149	.997	1	5
Gender index	13.432	3.362	5	25

Source: BHPS (1991-2000), women only, wave 1, 3, 5, 7, and 9.

Though the following discussion will focus on the impact of labour market insecurity, career maturity, individual resources, and gender, it is important to study these effects in the context of some other labour market influences. These include:

- *Labour market entry cohorts* since not all cohorts have been similarly affected by globalisation pressures[71],
- yearly *unemployment rate* by gender[72], to capture variations in the macroeconomic conditions and the business cycle,
- *industrial sector* (see Table 9.1 in the appendix), since not all sectors have been affected to the same extent by intense technological advancement and enhanced global competition (Golsch, 2002),
- *unemployment duration* and *homemaking duration,* to control for well-known duration effects in the case of exit from unemployment and in the analysis of transitions from unpaid homemaking to employment, respectively,
- *marital status*, the *number of children by age,* and *partner's educational qualification, activity status, and employment relationship,* because various transition rates under study are also likely to depend on previous partnership decisions and the family cycle, and,
- a *gender index,* to capture women's work orientation. The scale varies between 5 and 25, where high scores indicate more traditional gender roles (see Box 9.2 on page 218).

9.5 Findings: Experiencing insecurity in a highly flexible labour market

The discussion of the results is subdivided into four main sections. Patterns of work and unemployment are discussed first, followed by an analysis of work and family, then work and occupational mobility. The analysis is complemented by an examination of individual degrees of job satisfaction.

9.5.1 Work and unemployment in Great Britain

Table 9.6 documents the estimates obtained from a discrete-time competing

---

[71] Labour market entries of the studied sample occurred during distinct phases: labour market entries before 1970, a period characterised by low unemployment, slow and predictable economic development and policies that were introduced to guarantee male full-time employment; 1970-1979, when new technologies and information and communication possibilities started to spread, calling into question economic policies governments previously adhered to; 1980-1990, characterised by strong restrictions on welfare policies and the deregulation of the traditional British unionism; 1990 and later, a period typified by increased levels of insecurity resulting from the deregulation and flexible measures introduced over the 1980s.

[72] Unemployment rates were obtained from the following website: http://www.statistics.gov.uk/ [30.05.03].

risks transition model for *entry into unemployment* (see Section 6.3). The analysis uses annual observations of employees at risk either to become unemployed or to exit the labour market in the following year. Table 9.6 reports the results from a parsimonious specification, controlling for employment relationship, employment and flexi-worker experiences, unemployment spells, labour market entry cohorts, unemployment rate, and industrial sector. Model 1 shows the results for men; model 2 presents the estimates for women.

The estimates document that the insecurity measures play a crucial role. Flexi-workers – as approximated by type of employment relationship – face much higher unemployment risks, even after controlling for their previous employment career, occupational standing, and industrial sector. Only women in permanent part-time positions do not seem more likely to be hit by unemployment as compared to their counterparts in permanent full-time positions. However, the more employment experience individuals have gained, the lower their redundancy risk, regardless of their employment relationship. After an initial rise in employment experiences this shielding effect will tend to level off for men. Previous career instability – as gauged by flexi-worker experiences and unemployment spells – plays a significant role. The more flexi-worker experience men have accumulated, the higher their odds of entry into unemployment. For women, previous spells of precarious employment do not seem to increase their transition rate into unemployment. Yet, earlier unemployment spells heighten such risk for both men and women. Table 9.6 further shows that high occupational standing lowers, low occupational standing increases the unemployment risk of employees. Yet, these estimates are not significant for women.

The results presented in Table 9.6 indicate that the type of employment relationship matters irrespective of a person's career maturity. To analyse more clearly to what extent there is evidence to suggest that also adult workers – who were expected to be shielded by seniority and experience – are comparatively unprotected, further analyses have been run for two separate age groups. A first model specification covers the age span from 16 to 29 years. It refers to individuals who are likely to be in their early labour market stages and hence have accumulated little experience and presumably established only weak ties to the labour market. A second specification deals with individuals aged 30 to 49. It is meant to reflect risks of employment-to-unemployment transitions of mid-career workers who are likely to have already settled in the labour market and have therefore accumulated knowledge and experience and developed stronger ties. Table 9.7 on page 223 summarises the obtained results for men (models 1and 2) and women (models 3 and 4), controlling for the same covariates used for the overall model presented in Table 9.6.

Table 9.6 Risk of entry into unemployment by gender (Multinomial logistic regression)

	Men		Women	
Type of employment relationship				
Permanent and full-time (base)				
Fixed-term and full-time	1.038	***	0.840	**
Casual and full-time	1.186	***	1.233	***
Part-time	0.678	**		
Part-time and permanent			-0.042	
Part-time and non-permanent			1.357	***
Marginal	1.716	***		
Marginal and permanent			0.413	*
Marginal and non-permanent			1.053	***
Employment experience (in years)	-0.245	***	-0.105	*
Employment experience squared	0.007	***	0.002	
Flexi-worker experience (in years)	0.124	***	0.081	
Unemployment experience (dummy)	0.432	***	0.630	***
Labour market entry cohort				
< 1970	-0.067		-0.465	
1970-79	0.121		-0.081	
1980-89 (base)				
1990-	0.245		0.153	
Occupational standing (ISEI score)				
Very low (1st quartile)	0.519	***	0.239	
Low (2nd quartile) (base)				
High (3rd quartile)	-0.518	**	-0.219	
Very high (4th quartile)	-0.615	***	-0.291	
Unemployment rate	0.132	***	0.203	**
Industrial Sector				
Extractive	-0.492		-0.650	
Transformative (base)				
Social services	-0.599		-0.717	**
Distributive services	0.233		-0.072	
Producer services	-0.011		-0.337	
Personal services	-0.014		0.010	
Public	-1.111	***	-0.909	***
Constant	-4.232	***	-4.593	***
Log Likelihood	-2229		-4263	
Number of person wave observations	12,936		13,458	
Number of events	332		269	

Note: Obtained from discrete-time competing risks transition model for leaving a job position. The figures are coefficients from multinomial logistic regressions. Standard errors have been adjusted using the Huber/White/sandwich estimator of variance. All variables lagged by one period except labour market entry cohort. *** p<0.01, ** p<0.05, *p<0.10.

Source: British Household Panel Study, 1991-2000, employees only.

Table 9.7 Risk of entry into unemployment by gender and age (Multinomial logistic regression)

	Men				Women			
	Age 16-29		Age 30-49		Age 16-29		Age 30-49	
Type of employment relationship								
Permanent and full-time (base)								
Fixed-term and full-time	0.839	***	1.225	***	0.906	*	0.946	*
Casual and full-time	0.993	***	1.438	***	1.162	***	1.519	***
Part-time or marginal	1.151	***	0.038					
Part-time and permanent					0.382		-0.336	
Part-time and non-permanent					1.958	***	0.745	*
Marginal and permanent					0.712	*	0.279	
Marginal and non-permanent					0.072		1.349	***
Employment experience (in years)	-0.272	***	-0.255	***	-0.004		-0.119	*
Employment experience squared	0.012		0.007	***	-0.009		0.002	
Flexi-worker experience (in years)	0.224	**	0.092		-0.007		0.118	
Unemployment experience (dummy)	0.188		1.056	***	0.479	**	0.781	***
Labour market entry cohort								
< 1970			0.339				-0.259	
1970-79	0.964	**	0.355		0.125		0.076	
1980-89 (base)								
1990-	0.282		0.523		0.125		0.338	
Occupational standing (ISEI score)								
Very low (1st quartile)	0.590	***	0.465	**	0.506	**	-0.071	
Low (2nd quartile) (base)								
High (3rd quartile)	-0.458	*	-0.516		-0.165		-0.279	
Very high (4th quartile)	-1.032	***	-0.173		-0.311		-0.337	
Unemployment rate	0.165	***	0.096		0.192		0.179	
Industrial Sector								
Extractive	-2.266	**	0.489		-0.335		-1.046	
Transformative (base)								
Social services	-0.362		-0.387		-0.416		-1.096	**
Distributive services	0.269		0.218		0.259		-0.520	
Producer services	0.127		-0.060		-0.627	*	-0.098	
Personal services	-0.152		0.163		0.063		-0.142	
Public	-1.184	***	-0.953	**	-0.908	***	-0.949	***
Constant	-4.490	***	-4.368	***	-4.833	***	-4.286	***
Log Likelihood	-1336		-857		-2070		-2121	
Number of person wave observations	5,340		7,596		5,371		8,087	
Number of events	217		115		140		129	

Note: Obtained from discrete-time competing risks transition model for leaving a job position. The figures are coefficients from multinomial logistic regressions. Standard errors have been adjusted using the Huber/White/sandwich estimator of variance. All variables lagged by one period except labour market entry cohort. *** $p<0.01$, ** $p<0.05$, *$p<0.10$.

Source: British Household Panel Study, 1991-2000, employees only.

Table 9.7 reveals that flexible employment relationships carry a considerable degree of insecurity for both young adults and mid-career workers. Men on fixed-term or casual posts and those in job positions with reduced working hours (though not statistically significant under model 2) face much higher unemployment risks. Likewise, transition rates into unemployment are higher for women in the categories of fixed-term and full-time, and casual and full-time. Part-time, non-permanent employment and marginal work (though insignificant for temporary employees under model 3 and permanent workers under model 4) also increase unemployment risks for women. In contrast, permanent posts seem to protect women from unemployment, even if they are only part-timers.

There are also some meaningful differences between young and mid-career workers as well as between men and women. Employment experiences do matter for men, not for women. Also, flexi-worker experience is a significant predictor of entries into unemployment for young men but not for women and men aged 30 to 49. Quite the contrary, previous unemployment spells increase unemployment risks for all but young men. Surprisingly, a person's occupational standing plays a significant role for young men while in the other specifications a significant impact shows up only for men aged 30 to 49 and young women with very low ISEI-scores.

To summarise, the analysis of risks of entry into unemployment leads to the following conclusions. Labour market flexibility is likely to come at the cost of greater instability in labour market careers. Flexible employment relationships increase unemployment risks net of previous employment experiences, gender, and age. Notwithstanding this result, it is vital to stress that with increasing employment experience, male employees are more and more protected. However, turbulence during their previous labour market career increases men's risk of becoming unemployed. Hence, insecurity during their early labour market career seems to induce repercussions on men's adult work life. These results may be seen as a further indication of how growing labour market insecurity may be considered a particular dilemma for young men. Individual resources function as important buffers against unemployment risks for men, particularly for those in their early labour market stages. Interestingly, for women previous career experiences do not matter apart from past unemployment spells and we do not observe a mediating effect of their occupational standing. Thus, women in Great Britain do not only seem less often hit by unemployment (see Section 9.3), but instead it is the case that previous career instability and individual resources do not determine women's unemployment risks. But once unemployed, who is more likely to re-enter the labour market swiftly and into comparatively secure positions?

In what follows, the discussion centres on a sub-sample of unemployed men and women. Table 9.8 presents the results of a discrete-time competing risks transition model for *exit from unemployment* using a parsimonious model controlling for previous employment career, unemployment duration, labour market entry cohort, educational qualification, and unemployment rate.

Table 9.8 Chances to exit from unemployment by gender (Multinomial logistic regression)

	Men				Women			
	All exits		Insider		All exits		Insider	
Employment experience (in years)	0.152	***	0.163	***	0.137		0.068	
Employment experience squared	-0.004	*	-0.005		-0.009		-0.004	
Flexi-worker experience (in years)	0.050		-0.092		-0.259	*	-0.438	**
Unemployment duration (in years)								
Up to 1 year (base)								
1-2 years	-0.840	***	-0.988	***	-0.529	**	-0.871	***
2 years and longer	-0.880	***	-1.017	***	-0.681	***	-1.028	***
Labour market entry cohort								
< 1970	-0.127		-0.412		0.140		0.152	
1970-79	-0.298		-0.427	*	0.082		-0.415	
1980-89 (base)								
1990-	0.040		0.053		0.031		0.332	
Educational qualification								
Higher and first degree	0.735	**	0.839	**	0.944	***	1.191	***
Vocational degree	0.271		0.377		0.013		-0.089	
A Level (or equiv.)	0.635	***	0.747	***	0.258		0.340	
GSCE/O Level (or equiv.) (base)								
Less than O Level	-0.311		-0.213		-0.159		-0.214	
Unemployment rate	-0.099	***	-0.136	***	-0.198	*	-0.289	**
Constant	1.238	***	1.036	**	2.135	**	1.779	*
Log Likelihood	-1,238		-1,753		-1,023		-1,378	
Number of person wave observations	1,314		1,314		1,010		1,008	
Number of events	582		337		458		157	

Note: Obtained from discrete-time competing risks transition model for exiting unemployment. The figures are coefficients from multinomial logistic regressions and the alternative outcomes are exit the labour force (model 1 and 3) and economic inactivity, flexible entry-level job, and self-employment (model 2 and 4). Standard errors have been adjusted using the Huber/White/sandwich estimator of variance. All variables lagged by one period except labour market entry cohort. *** $p<0.01$, ** $p<0.05$, *$p<0.10$.

Source: British Household Panel Study, 1991-2000, employees only.

Table 9.8 reports the results from four different specifications. A first specification studies chances to exit into a job or exit the labour force the following year (models 1 and 3). For the purpose of this chapter, Table 9.8 only provides the estimates for exits into employment. This model may be seen as unsatisfactory since empirical evidence points to high risks of re-entry into badly paid, insecure jobs (see Chapter Three; Section 9.3). An interesting question in the competing risks framework is therefore whether speedy re-employment goes hand in hand with secure employment relationships. Hence, to model exit-to-employment transitions, a second specification separates insiders – men who obtain a permanent and full-time post, women who conclude a permanent contract – from those who enter the labour market as flexi-workers or self-employed (models 2 and 4). Table 9.8 only shows the estimates for exits into secure employment.

The estimates in Table 9.8 display the significant role of previous employment experiences for men. Employment experience does not only protect against unemployment risks (see Table 9.6), but the more experience men have accumulated, the more likely they are to exit from unemployment (model 1) and to enter permanent full-time employment respectively (model 2). Preceding spells of flexible employment do not seem to impact men's chances to exit from unemployment. Yet, flexi-worker experience lowers women's transition rate into employment and into permanent full-time jobs in particular. Table 9.8 further reveals a strong effect of unemployment duration on the chances of leaving unemployment. Already after one year of unemployment the transition rate into employment decreases significantly. As reflected in Table 9.8, higher educational qualification increases the probability to rapidly re-enter the labour market.

Table 9.9 on the next page presents the findings for the same model specification by sex and age group. Distinguishing between the above two defined age groups leads to some different conclusions about the effects of the explanatory variables. As to men, employment experiences matter for young workers, but not for those aged 30 to 49 years. Noteworthy, among men aged 16 to 29 previous spells in flexible jobs lower the chances to be re-employed in a permanent full-time position. An extended length of unemployment brings about great difficulties in re-entering the labour market. Aside from their previous employment career, labour market entry cohort, age, and educational qualification determines men's chances to enter a job and increases their chances to be contracted on a permanent full-time base, respectively.

The picture is slightly different for women (models 5 to 8). Employment experiences raise chances to exit unemployment for women aged 30 to 49 but do not seem to play any significant role for their younger counterparts. Yet, the more flexi-worker experience these women have accumulated the less likely they are to exit out of unemployment and to find a secure full-time position, though these coefficients do not quite reach the 10 percent level of significance due to the small number of observations. Chances to exit into a permanent job seem higher for young women with high educational qualification, but high educational qualification does not seem to matter for transitions into secure employment for women aged 30 to 49. However, case numbers are small, and hence, inferences drawn from models 7 and 8 should be taken as tentative.

Table 9.9 Chances to exit from unemployment by gender and age (Multinomial logistic regression)

	Men				Women			
	Age 16 to 29		Age 30 to 49		Age 16 to 29		Age 30 to 49	
	All exits	Insider	All exits	Insider	All exits	Insider	All exits	Insider
Employment exp. (in years)	0.433 ***	0.462 ***	0.096	0.081	-0.179	-0.103	0.282 **	0.163
Employment exp. squared	-0.039 *	-0.037	-0.002	-0.001	0.026	0.020	-0.015 *	-0.008
Flexi-worker exp. (in years)	-0.124	-0.316 *	0.133	0.055	-0.091	-0.207	-0.282	-0.807
Unemployment exp. (in years)								
Up to 1 year (base)								
1-2 years	-0.752 ***	-0.844 ***	-0.895 ***	-1.147 ***	-0.612 **	-1.038 ***	-0.253	-0.344
2 years and longer	-0.502 **	-0.500 **	-1.431 ***	-2.088 ***	-0.832 ***	-1.056 ***	-0.420	-0.968 *
Labour market entry cohort								
< 1970			-0.481	-0.625			-0.266	0.390
1970-79	-0.234	-0.258	-0.668 **	-0.722 *	0.192	0.229	-0.077	0.032
1980-89 (base)								
1990-	0.176	0.186	-0.725 *	-0.837 *	-0.296	0.046	0.947	0.630
Educational qualification								
Higher and first degree	1.231 ***	1.397 ***	0.097	0.036	0.779 *	1.193 ***	1.070 *	0.705
Vocational degree	-0.020	0.154	0.718 *	0.757	0.238	0.441	-0.090	-1.319 *
A Level (or equiv.)	0.319	0.386	1.336 **	1.574 ***	0.286	0.534	0.510	-0.416
GSCE/O Level (base)								
Less than O Level	-0.442 **	-0.355	-0.057	0.050	-0.405	-0.301	0.181	-0.109
Unemployment rate	-0.105 **	-0.159 ***	-0.083	-0.094 **	-0.522 ***	-0.546 ***	0.261	0.018
Constant	1.131 **	1.069 *	1.449 *	1.026 **	4.636 ***	3.647 ***	-1.133	-0.596
Log Likelihood	-841	-1161	-371	-549	-631	-843	-375	-496
Number of person wave obs.	895	895	419	419	637	636	373	372
Number of events	392	239	190	98	277	124	181	33

Note: Obtained from discrete-time competing risks transition model. Standard errors have been adjusted using the Huber/White/sandwich estimator of variance. The figures are coefficients from multinomial regression. All variables lagged by one period except labour market entry cohort. *** p<0.01, ** p<0.05, *p<0.10.

Source: British Household Panel Study, 1991-2000.

In summary, these results of the risks of entry into and chances to exit from unemployment demonstrate that past career experiences matter for young men. Flexible work arrangements and previous labour market insecurity experiences increase young men's unemployment risks. Even though chances are high that temporary employment is converted into permanent employment (Chapter Seven), past spells in flexible employment and less employment experience seems to lower their chances to re-enter the labour market after unemployment spells and into secure full-time employment. This gives some support to the above discussed assumption that increased deregulation and flexibility is likely to entrap young men in a '*flexible employment – unemployment – flexible employment cycle*'. However, regardless of their career maturity or individual resources, adult temporary workers also face a higher degree of insecurity. For future research, it could therefore prove fruitful to inquire into whether and for whom precarious jobs are likely to lead to chains of insecure employment. Other examinations have shown such a relationship for temporary employees in Germany (Giesecke and Groß, 2003). For women, the findings of this section suggest a different impact of flexible employment measures. In contrast to men, past career experiences affect adults' but not young women's chances to exit out of unemployment. It seems reasonable to link this career instability to women's family commitments, as that may impede the integration of work and family life. Other investigations (not shown here) revealed that employment and flexi-worker experience lose their predictive power once the analysis controls for martial status and number of children. The above assumption is further supported by the finding that insecurity experiences do not determine entry into unemployment apart from past unemployment experiences. Yet, just as for men, we also observe an increased degree of insecurity for women currently in flexible work arrangements regardless of their age, individual resources of past employment experience.

9.5.2 Work and family in Great Britain

This section focuses on women only and investigates the impact of flexible employment on their work and family life. The discussion first draws on the results from a discrete-time competing risks transition model for leaving a job position into unpaid homemaking. Transitions into unemployment or economic inactivity are considered competing risks. The section then explores chances to exit from unpaid homemaking. Again, redundancy and changes into inactivity are studied as competing risks but the following paragraphs do not report on the estimates for these alternative outcomes.

Table 9.10 shows the estimates for *transitions into unpaid homemaking*. The first model takes into account a sub-sample of female employees whereas the second model examines women in partnerships only.

Table 9.10 Transitions into unpaid homemaking (Multinomial logistic regression)

	All women	Women in partnerships
Type of employment relationship		
Permanent and full-time (base)		
Fixed-term and full-time	0.989 *	1.201 *
Casual and full-time	0.942 **	1.095 *
Part-time and permanent	0.639 ***	0.446 *
Part-time and non-permanent	0.952 **	0.627
Marginal and permanent	1.170 ***	1.197 ***
Marginal and non-permanent	1.642 ***	1.086 **
Employment experience (in years)	-0.271 ***	-0.236 ***
Employment experience squared	0.011 ***	0.009 ***
Flexi-worker experience (in years)	-0.173	-0.083
Unemployment experience (dummy)	0.011	-0.093
Labour market entry cohort		
< 1970	-0.857 ***	-0.800 **
1970-79	-0.712 ***	-0.704 ***
1980-89 (base)		
1990-	0.149	-0.006
Educational qualification		
Higher and first degree	-0.150	
Vocational degree	-0.148	
A Level (or equiv.)	-0.322	
GSCE/O Level (or equiv.) (base)		
Less than O Level	0.416 **	
Industrial Sector		
Private (base)		
Public	-0.588 ***	-0.458 **
Marital status		
Never married	-1.157 ***	
Married (base)		
Cohabiting	-0.078	-0.258
Separated/divorced/widowed	-0.041	
Number of children by age		
No children (base)		
Children aged 0 to 4	0.474 ***	0.265
Children aged 5 to 15	-0.059	-0.272 **
Gender index	0.120 ***	0.141 ***
Educational qualification		
Equal qualification (base)		
Partner higher qualification		0.109
Partner lower qualification		-0.604 **
Partner's activity status		
Employed (base)		
Unemployed		0.941 **
Economically inactive		1.418 ***
Partner's employment relationship		

	All women	Women in partnerships
Employer		0.518
Own account worker		0.733 ***
Permanent full-time employee (base)		
Flexi-worker		0.821 **
Constant	-3.924 ***	-4.239 ***
Log Likelihood	-2,262	-1,184
Number of person wave observations	7,356	4,380
Number of events	253	166

Note: Obtained from discrete-time competing risk transition model for leaving a job position. The figures are coefficients from multinomial logistic regressions. Standard errors have been adjusted using the Huber/White/sandwich estimator of variance. All variables lagged by one period except labour market entry cohort. *** $p<0.01$, ** $p<0.05$, *$p<0.10$.

Source: British Household Panel Study, 1991-2000, women, employees only.

The first model provides evidence that women in flexible employment are much more likely to discontinue their employment career as compared to their counterparts in permanent full-time positions. As one would expect, increasing work experience makes transitions into unpaid homemaking less probable. However, after an initial decrease in the transition rate, the impact of employment experiences tends to level off. Previous experience in flexible employment and past unemployment experience does not seem to have repercussions on women's transition rates into unpaid homemaking. This is surprising, since one might expect that career instability discourages women and hence makes them less prone to opt for continuous employment. Several further results are worthy of noting. Women with low educational qualification are significantly more likely to interrupt their work career in order to carry the brunt of responsibility for domestic work and childrearing. Women with pre-school children seem more often to suspend their gainful occupation to take care of the household. Finally, women with more traditional work orientations – as captured by the gender index – are significantly more likely to abdicate.

Referring to model 2 in Table 9.10, the estimates reveal that it is essential to incorporate partners' characteristics. Keeping constant all other explanatory variables, the partner's educational qualification, activity status, and employment relationship turn out to be significant predictors of women's transitions into unpaid care giving. If the woman is better qualified than her partner, she is less likely to suspend gainful employment in order to do unpaid domestic work, which likely reflects stronger career orientations of women. Yet other results are intriguing, such as the higher transition rates into unpaid homemaking for women whose partner is unemployed or economically inactive. Likewise, exits into unpaid homemaking seem more probable if the partner is an own account worker or holds a flexible job. Why is this the case?

Table 9.11 Chances to exit from unpaid homemaking (Multinomial logistic regression)

	All women			Women in partnerships		
	All exits	Insider	Flexi-worker	All exits	Insider	Flexi-worker
Employment experience (in years)	0.078 **	0.096 *	0.050	0.078	0.153 **	0.030
Employment experience squared	-0.003	-0.005 *	0.000	-0.003	-0.012 **	0.002
Flexi-worker experience (in years)	0.191 **	0.061	0.307 ***	0.099	-0.222	0.454 **
Unemployment experience (dummy)	0.316 **	0.176	0.465 **	0.367 **	0.339 *	0.430
Homemaking experience (in years)						
Up to 1 year (base)						
1-2 years	-0.240 *	-0.157	-0.949 ***	-0.287	-0.111	-1.476 ***
2-3 years	-0.517 ***	-0.440 **	-0.970 **	-0.545 **	-0.300	-1.203 **
3 years and longer	-0.816 ***	-1.013 ***	-0.500 **	-0.770 ***	-0.953 ***	-0.434
Labour market entry cohort						
< 1970	-0.733 ***	-1.035 ***	0.067	-0.726 ***	-1.004 ***	-0.016
1970-79	-0.031	-0.168	0.139	-0.135	-0.140	-0.292
1980-89 (base)						
1990-	0.161	0.102	0.496 *	0.031	0.059	0.226
Educational qualification						
Higher and first degree	-0.021	-0.489	0.522			
Vocational degree	0.028	-0.035	0.078			
A Level (or equiv.)	0.330 *	0.061	0.544 *			
GSCE/O Level (or equiv.) (base)						
Less than O Level	0.041	0.029	-0.167			
Marital status						
Never married	-0.371 *	-0.369	-0.195			
Married (base)						
Cohabiting	-0.130	-0.153	-0.047	-0.160	-0.210	0.047
Separated/divorced/widowed	-0.194	-0.180	-0.057			
Number of children by age						
No children (base)						
Children aged 0 to 4	-0.281 ***	-0.318 ***	-0.145	-0.183 *	-0.226 *	0.008
Children aged 5 to 15	0.040	-0.003	0.189 *	0.151 *	0.096	0.374 ***

	All women			Women in partnerships		
	All exits	Insider	Flexi-worker	All exits	Insider	Flexi-worker
Educational qualification						
Equal qualification (base)						
Partner higher qualification				-0.929 ***	-1.357 ***	-0.371
Partner lower qualification				0.042	0.068	0.049
Partner's activity status						
Employed (base)						
Unemployed				-0.695 ***	-0.469 *	-2.026 ***
Economically inactive				-0.755 ***	-0.985 ***	-0.628
Partner's employment relationship						
Employer				0.087	0.136	-0.560
Own account worker				-0.159	-0.231	-0.597
Permanent full-time employee (base)						
Flexi-worker				-0.169	0.166	-1.526 *
Constant	-0.882 ***	-1.024 ***	-2.905 ***	-0.730 ***	-1.051 ***	-2.567 ***
Log Likelihood	-2,368	-2,587		-1,410	-1,572	
Number of person wave observations	2,847	2,847		1,830	1,830	
Number of events	511	330	115	332	216	78

Note: Obtained from discrete-time competing risks transition model for exiting unpaid care giving in the 1990s. Standard errors have been adjusted using the Huber/White/sandwich estimator of variance. The figures are coefficients from multinomial regression. All variables lagged by one period except labour market entry cohort. *** $p<0.01$, ** $p<0.05$, *$p<0.10$.

Source: British Household Panel Study, 1991-2000.

Before attempting an answer, we can look at a similar analysis of transitions from unpaid homemaking into employment. Table 9.11 gives the results for a discrete-time competing risks transition model for chances to *exit out of unpaid homemaking*. It reports the estimates from four different specifications, with the first two referring to all women, and the latter focusing on couples only. The analysis first examines exits into employment (models 1 and 3). It then studies the type of entry-level job and distinguishes between permanent job positions (insiders) and flexible work arrangements.

The main effects to note are the following. As can be seen from model 1, the more employment experiences a woman has already accumulated the more likely she is to re-enter the labour market. Interestingly, once we control for the type of entry-level job, this only holds true for exits into temporary employment (model 2). Previous career instability – as gauged by flexi-worker experiences and previous unemployment spells – raises chances to exit from unpaid homemaking. However, women with previous spells of flexible employment or past unemployment experiences seem significantly more likely to accept a temporary rather than a permanent post, and one may assume that these two indicators reflect stronger work orientations. This is particularly clear for previous unemployment spells, operationalised as not working but actively searching for a job. By and large, the results may be seen as a further hint that career instability has a qualitative different meaning for men and women in Great Britain. Related to this, earlier examinations (not shown here) revealed that more traditional orientations measured on the gender index seem to lower the transition rate into employment but the estimates were insignificant under all specifications. Since the items measuring gender roles have only been biannually part of the survey (Box 9.2) and hence the study would be based on considerably less person wave observations, the specifications of Table 9.11 do not include the gender index. Nonetheless, it is noteworthy that the estimates for flexi-worker spells and past unemployment experiences remain significant even if the analysis controls for gender orientation. The estimates from models 1 and 2 furthermore document that the transition rate into employment declines the longer women interrupt their employment career. As expected, women with young infants are significantly less likely to re-enter gainful employment and to find a permanent job position in particular. At the same time, women with schoolchildren are significantly more likely to re-enter the labour market as flexi-workers.

Turning to the results for couples (models 3 and 4), we again find that the more employment experience, the higher the chances to exit from unpaid homemaking into permanent employment. By contrast, past spells of flexible work arrangements increase the transition rate into flexi-worker positions. Just as under models 1 and 2, the number of children by age determines women's prospects to find a job and their chances to enter secure employment in particular. But what can we conclude from the estimates for partner's characteristics? If the partner has a higher educational qualification, chances are small that women re-enter the labour market and take up a permanent job in particular. While the partner's employment relationship does not seem to matter, Table 9.11 reveals the intriguing result that women of unemployed or economically inactive men are also significantly less likely to re-enter the labour market. One would expect that if the husband is unemployed, economically inactive women should be more likely to search for a job to compensate for the loss of income. When holding a job, women should be less prone to resign if the husband is hit by unemployment, and in the literature this has been called an '*added worker effect*'. The analysis here provides considerable contrary evidence. Prior research indicates that in Great Britain the labour force participation rate of the wives of jobless men is markedly lower than that of wives of working men. McGinnity (2002) presents evidence to suggest that wives of unemployed men are significantly less likely to make inactivity-to-employment transitions, though they do not have a higher propensity to exit gainful employment. She links these results to a potential disincentive effect of the means-tested benefit system, flat-rate entitlements, and a low earnings disregard in Great Britain. By contrast, the same study by McGinnity (2002) provides support for an 'added worker effect' in Germany, where the greater part of the unemployed receives insurance-based benefits. As most of the unemployed in Great Britain receive means-tested benefits, these results cast some important light on the documented rise in workless households (Section 9.2; Gregg *et al.,* 1999a). The findings of this section seem to be in accordance with previous studies. It is noteworthy though that a more adequate analysis on the impact of partner's characteristics would have to take length of unemployment spell, previous labour-market history and benefit type into account. In these terms the analysis by McGinnity (2002) is much more elaborate.

9.5.3 Work and occupational mobility in Great Britain

As outlined in Chapter Three, increasing insecurity may not only become visible in the form of high unemployment risks and low chances to exit from unemployment. Insecurity may also be attached to the level of remuneration, particularly the risk of income loss. This may be especially meaningful in the British context, which is characterised by strong incentives to introduce wage flexibility in labour relations (see Chapter Four). In the following section, attention is paid to changes in socio-economic status in order to examine the risks of downward and upward occupational mobility. Firstly, the focus is on the estimates of a discrete-time competing risks transition model for chances of upward and risks of downward mobility by gender regardless of the age window (Table 9.12). Subsequently, the discussion moves on to the results according to the two aforementioned age groups (Table 9.13). In all specifications, leaving the labour market into unemployment or economic inactivity is regarded as a competing risk but this section does not report on the results for these latter transitions. The debate concentrates on the obtained findings for a specification in which mobility is gauged by a 10 percent increase or decrease in ISEI-score between two panel waves. Tables that document the estimates for an alternative approach in which mobility is defined as any change in ISEI-score are annexed to this chapter.

Table 9.12 Chances of upward, risks of downward occupational mobility by gender (Multinomial logistic regression, 10% threshold)

	Men		Women	
	upward	downward	upward	downward
Type of employment relationship				
Permanent and full-time (base)				
Fixed-term and full-time	0.199	0.345 *	0.434 **	0.699 ***
Casual and full-time	0.663 ***	0.880 ***	0.539 ***	0.856 ***
Part-time	0.598 ***	0.199		
Part-time and permanent			-0.424 ***	0.100
Part-time and non-permanent			0.290	0.753 ***
Marginal	0.472	1.038 ***		
Marginal and permanent			-0.448 ***	0.403 ***
Marginal and non-permanent			0.068	0.705 ***
Employment experience (in years)	-0.144 ***	-0.185 ***	-0.074 ***	-0.137 ***
Employment experience squared	0.004 ***	0.006 ***	0.002 *	0.005 ***
Mobility experience (dummy)	1.205 ***	1.163 ***	1.020 ***	1.059 ***
Flexi-worker experience (in years)	-0.072 *	-0.062	-0.097 **	0.003
Unemployment experience (dummy)	0.007	0.351 ***	0.013	0.107
Labour market entry cohort				
< 1970	-0.071	-0.376 ***	0.082	-0.086
1970-79	-0.049	-0.109	-0.088	0.005
1980-89 (base)				
1990-	0.052	0.120	0.018	0.123
Previous occupation (ISEI score)				
Very low (1st quartile)	0.523 ***	-0.804 ***	-0.022	-0.881 ***
Low (2nd quartile) (base)				
High (3rd quartile)	-0.469 ***	0.742 ***	-1.142 ***	0.823 ***
Very high (4th quartile)	-2.626 ***	1.280 ***	-2.478 ***	1.533 ***
ISEI score 1st job	0.015 ***	-0.016 ***	0.016 ***	-0.017 ***
Educational qualification				
Higher and first degree	0.637 ***	-0.890 ***	0.625 ***	-0.840 ***
Vocational degree	0.245 ***	-0.367 ***	-0.235 ***	-0.358 ***
A Level (or equiv.)	0.179 *	-0.309 ***	0.072	-0.243 **
GSCE/O Level (or equiv.) (base)				
Less than O Level	-0.113	0.248 **	-0.344 ***	0.296 ***
Unemployment rate	0.014	0.017	-0.065 *	-0.020

	Men				Women			
	upward		downward		upward		downward	
Industrial sector								
Extractive	-0.004		0.140		0.323		-0.376	
Transformative (base)								
Social services	0.301	*	0.123		-0.246	*	-0.216	
Distributive services	0.028		-0.041		-0.005		-0.109	
Producer services	0.553	***	-0.347	***	0.468	***	-0.421	***
Personal services	0.051		-0.076		0.033		0.072	
Public	0.202	**	-0.149		-0.363	***	-0.379	***
Constant	-2.119	***	-1.080	***	-1.142	***	-1.105	***
Log Likelihood	-9,803				-10,926			
Number of person wave observations	12,014				12,399			
Number of events	1,813		1,539		1,713		1,556	

Note: Obtained from discrete-time competing risks transition model. The figures are coefficients from multinomial regression. Standard errors have been adjusted using the Huber/White/sandwich estimator of variance. All variables lagged by one period except labour market entry cohort. *** p<0.01, ** p<0.05, *p<0.10.

Source: British Household Panel Study, 1991-2000, employees only.

The above analysis leads to the following principal conclusions. The proxy variables for flexible employment clearly determine occupational mobility. The results indicate that men with fixed-term contracts are more likely to move downward but do not seem more likely to make upward career moves as compared to their counterparts in permanent posts. In contrast, casual full-time employees are more likely to be mobile in either direction. Furthermore, men in part-time positions have high chances of accomplishing a higher socio-economic status whereas marginal employees seem significantly more likely to experience downward moves. Referring to model 2, holding a fixed-term or casual full-time job significantly increases chances of upward but also risks of downward occupational mobility for women. By contrast, those in permanent job positions with reduced working hours seem less likely to be upwardly mobile. At the same time, non-permanent part-time posts and marginal work generally make downward moves more probable for women. From this it can be concluded, that flexible work arrangements bring a considerable degree of career instability, not only in terms of unemployment risks, but also with respect to downward occupational mobility. Furthermore, the estimates for employment experience exhibit that chances of upward but also risks of downward mobility are higher during the first years of employment. The more experience men and women have accumulated the lower the probability to move in either direction. The significant quadratic term of employment experiences indicates that after an initial decrease in the transition rate, this impact levels off. Furthermore, previous mobility experiences (whether up- or downward) make future career moves more likely for men and women. More importantly, the longer a person has been in insecure, flexible employment relationships, the less likely they are to make upward occupational moves. Moreover, past unemployment experiences significantly increase risks of downward mobility for men. Taken together, career instability seems to come at a cost for the future occupational career. This finding is further substantiated by the other results in Table 9.12. The ISEI-score of the first job after completing full-time education plays a significant role in the study of men's and women's occupational mobility. The better the entry-level job, the higher the chances of ensuing upward mobility; and, accordingly, the lower the risk to experience any downward move. This result underpins the distinct relevance of entry-level jobs in globalised labour markets.[73] As discussed in the previous chapters, there is evidence to reveal that the school-to-work transition becomes more precarious. This is particularly evident in the highly flexible British labour market, characterised by weak employment protection, a 'hire-and-fire' system, and a great deal of 'job hoppers' among the youth. This lends further support to the hypothesis that increased insecurity during the early labour market career is linked to increased instability during the subsequent career. We may therefore envisage higher degrees of insecurity of mid-career workers for the future.

Previous socio-economic status and educational qualification also have a clear effect. The better the previous occupation – again approximated by the ISEI-score – the lower the chances of upward and the higher the risks of downward mobility. In addition, the higher the educational qualification, the lower the downward mobility risks. The highly skilled seem to have better chances with the poorly skilled having significantly lower chances to experience any upward occupational move.

But how does this picture change once we analyse different age groups? The estimates from a more disaggregated analysis for the same model specification discussed above are shown in Table 9.13 on page 239. This table gives further support to the hypothesis that the type of employment relationship matters irrespective of career maturity, gender, and age. For young men, we find evidence that flexible jobs increase both chances of being upwardly mobile and the risk of experiencing any downward career move (model 1). However, the transition rates for young men in fixed-term and full-time positions are no more significantly different from permanent full-time employees. Interestingly, the estimates for the various types of flexible employment relationships are insignificant for men aged 30 to 49, except for casual full-time employees who are more likely to move upward- and downward (model 2). Just as for men, the

[73] Empirical evidence for this relationship between entry-level jobs and subsequent career opportunities has also been provided for other countries. Interested readers are referred to Blossfeld (1987) for a review of theories and a discussion of the German case.

estimates for women aged 16 to 29 suggest that, with the exception of permanent fixed-term and marginal work, flexible employment increases risks of downward occupational mobility (model 3). Note, however, that young temporary full-time workers and their counterparts on temporary part-time job positions are also more likely to move upward. Referring to model 4, we see that female employees in permanent part-time or permanent marginal posts are significantly less likely to move up the occupational ladder while this does not hold true for their younger counterparts. It proves that, apart from permanent part-time employees, also female flexi-workers aged 30 to 49 are generally more likely to experience a downward move. In summary, the important point to be noted with regard to occupational mobility is that flexible employment also has significant repercussions for women's careers, notwithstanding their age, previous employment career, and individual resources.

As already seen in Table 9.12, employment experience significantly determines current mobility events. We furthermore observe lower risks of upward and downward mobility for persons with past mobility experience. Moreover, previous unemployment spells increase the risks of downward occupational mobility for men. However, this does not hold true for women. While significant in Table 9.12, the estimates for flexi-worker experience lose their predictive power for men and young women once the models are run separately by age group. Yet, chances of upward mobility are significantly lower the more flexi-worker experience women aged 30 to 49 have accumulated.

Comparing these estimates with the ones from the alternative approach which treats mobility as any change in ISEI-score (Tables 9.15 and 9.16, annexed to this chapter), we largely arrive to similar conclusions about the impact of flexible work arrangements, past career experiences, individual resources, gender, and age. Some results, however, are different and hence noteworthy. Referring to the results for men, we find some indication that holding a full-time but fixed-term job markedly increases the risk of any decrease in ISEI-score (Table 9.15, model 1; Table 9.16, model 1) whereas the corresponding estimate is insignificant when using the 10 percent threshold value (Table 9.13). Hence, we may assume that fixed-term positions carry increased degrees of insecurity. However, as compared to the other types of flexible work arrangements, the potential loss in ISEI-score seems smaller. A second notable point is that past unemployment experiences appears to be an important predictor of men's downward occupational mobility in Table 9.12 and 9.13, but much less so when studying any change in the ISEI-score (Table 9.15, model 1; Table 9.16, models 1 and 2). Here it is reasonable to assume that previous unemployment spells not only increase the future risk of unemployment. Unemployment experience also increases future risk of serious downward occupational mobility for men.

Table 9.13 Chances of upward, risks of downward occupational mobility by gender and age (Multinomial logistic regression, 10% threshold)

	Men				Women			
	Age 16 to 29		Age 30 to 49		Age 16 to 29		Age 30 to 49	
	upward	downward	upward	downward	upward	downward	upward	downward
Type of empl. relationship								
Permanent and full-time (base)								
Fixed-term and full-time	0.067	0.158	0.100	0.308	0.462 *	0.277	0.180	1.005 ***
Casual and full-time	0.548 **	0.785 ***	0.502 *	0.781 **	0.570 **	0.865 ***	0.241	0.741 **
Part-time or marginal	0.642 ***	0.480 *	0.070	0.063				
Part-time and permanent					-0.164	0.582 ***	-0.500 ***	-0.094
Part-time and non-permanent					0.652 **	0.970 ***	0.089	0.619 **
Marginal and permanent					-0.246	0.427	-0.524 ***	0.362 **
Marginal and non-permanent					0.026	1.040 **	0.054	0.529 *
Employment exp. (in years)	-0.309 ***	-0.445 ***	-0.108 ***	-0.144 ***	-0.105 *	-0.244 ***	-0.049	-0.107 ***
Employment exp. squared	0.018 ***	0.029 ***	0.003 **	0.005 ***	0.004	0.012 **	0.001	0.004 ***
Mobility experience (dummy)	0.877 ***	0.993 ***	1.513 ***	1.340 ***	0.761 ***	0.879 ***	1.216 ***	1.204 ***
Flexi-worker exp. (in years)	-0.034	-0.022	-0.034	-0.035	-0.007	0.083	-0.116 **	-0.016
Unemployment exp. (dummy)	0.039	0.268 **	-0.035	0.452 ***	-0.168	0.077	0.187	0.141
Labour market entry cohort								
< 1970			-0.026	-0.324 **			0.023	-0.092
1970-79	-0.169	0.300	0.001	-0.092	0.647 **	0.021	-0.163	0.007
1980-89 (base)								
1990-	-0.102	0.062	0.101	0.056	-0.091	0.112	0.102	0.174
Educational qualification								
Higher and first degree	0.690 ***	-0.912 ***	0.590 ***	-0.879 ***	0.902 ***	-1.046 ***	0.383 **	-0.755 ***
Vocational degree	0.315 **	-0.297 **	0.228 *	-0.381 ***	-0.141	-0.396 ***	-0.292 ***	-0.335 ***
A Level (or equiv.)	0.115	-0.377 **	0.247 *	-0.278 *	0.251 **	-0.150	-0.086	-0.384 **
GSCE/O Level (base)								
Less than O Level	0.038	0.379 **	-0.191	0.172	-0.153	0.217	-0.413 ***	0.346 ***
Unemployment rate	-0.035	-0.026	0.059 ***	0.060 **	-0.154 **	-0.032	0.017	0.010

	Men				Women			
	Age 16 to 29		Age 30 to 49		Age 16 to 29		Age 30 to 49	
	upward	downward	upward	downward	upward	downward	upward	downward
Controls for:								
Previous occupation (ISEI)	√	√	√	√	√	√	√	√
ISEI-score 1st job	√	√	√	√	√	√	√	√
Industrial sector	√	√	√	√	√	√	√	√
Constant	-1.486 ***	-0.286	-2.720 ***	-1.640 ***	-0.557	-0.296	-1.805 ***	-1.725 ***
Log Likelihood	-4,354		-5,380		-4,445		-6,385	
Number of person wave obs.	4,689		7,325		4,823		7,576	
Number of events	835	652	978	887	724	593	989	963

Note: Obtained from discrete-time, competing risk transition model. Standard errors have been adjusted using the Huber/White/sandwich estimator of variance. The figures are coefficients from multinomial regression. All variables lagged by one period except labour market entry cohort. *** p<0.01, ** p<0.05, *p<0.10.

Source: British Household Panel Study, 1991-2000, employees only.

What are the principal conclusions that we can draw from the analysis on work and mobility in Great Britain? In summary, insecurity adheres to flexible employment relationships. At the same time, individual resources not only protect against downward mobility but foster upward occupational mobility for both men and women. However, as already seen in the analysis on work and unemployment (Section 9.5.1), flexible work arrangements particularly increase employment instability for young men. Downward occupational moves are very likely and chances of obtaining a higher socio-economic status are also high. It is important to note that past unemployment spells generally increase risks of downward mobility for men. The results on work and unemployment revealed that flexible employment and flexi-worker experiences increases unemployment risks and lower the chances of re-entering the labour market into secure job positions. Young men thus seem to confront much greater risks of increased deregulation and flexibility than male mid-career workers. By contrast, as also seen in Section 9.5.1, the repercussions of flexible employment seem higher for mid-career women. Upward career paths are blocked and the chance of loss in socio-economic status high. Moreover, the longer adult women hold flexible jobs, the less likely upward career moves become. The previous section has revealed that such women are largely switching between flexible work and homemaking, so one may conjecture that flexibility has a different meaning for women than for men, inasmuch as it facilitates combining work and family life. However, this comes at the cost of a highly unstable work career.

9.5.4 Work and job satisfaction in Great Britain

The previous sections investigated whether and to what extent there is empirical evidence for an increase in job insecurity, which is captured by unemployment risks, chances to exit from unemployment, and risk of experiencing downward occupational mobility. The results point to significant differences in the degree of insecurity according to the type of employment relationship, past employment experiences, age, gender, and individual resources. Yet, as elaborated in Chapter Three, increasing deregulation and flexibility are likely to affect not only labour market careers, but also people's psychological wellbeing, perceptions, and expectations about their labour market career and social life. Chapter Eight established how subjective perceptions of insecurity determine life course decisions. What remains is the question of whether we can also observe differences in the perception of insecurity, particularly for those in obviously insecure positions. Independent of their actual labour market positions, individuals' evaluation of the likelihood and consequences of job or income loss may be quite different. This section aims to briefly comment on who is more likely to feel insecure in a highly flexible labour market.

Table 9.14 Satisfaction with job security, total pay, and promotion prospects (Ordered probit regression)

	Men			Women		
	Job security	Total pay	Promotion	Job security	Total pay	Promotion
Type of employment relationship						
Permanent and full-time (base)						
Fixed-term and full-time	-0.883 ***	-0.131 **	-0.288 ***	-0.894 ***	-0.121 *	-0.114
Casual and full-time	-1.258 ***	-0.154 **	-0.527 ***	-1.164 ***	0.071	-0.400 ***
Part-time	-0.079	0.029	-0.199 **			
Part-time permanent				0.085 **	0.164 ***	0.091 **
Part-time non-permanent				-0.856 ***	0.213 ***	-0.097
Marginal	-0.399 ***	0.142	-0.337 **			
Marginal permanent				0.268 ***	0.501 ***	0.159 **
Marginal non-permanent				-0.483 ***	0.328 ***	-0.008
Flexi-worker experience (in years)	-0.028 **	-0.059 ***	-0.031 *	-0.032 **	-0.025	-0.014
Unemployment experience (dummy)	-0.065 *	-0.061	-0.041	0.067 *	-0.105 **	-0.022
Labour market entry cohort						
< 1970	-0.007	-0.163 **	0.196 **	-0.055	0.063	0.046
1970-79	-0.079	-0.131 ***	0.051	-0.023	0.025	0.012
1980-89 (base)						
1990-	0.012	0.062	0.139 ***	0.068	0.031	0.082 *
Age	-0.064 ***	-0.027 *	-0.061 ***	-0.057 ***	0.022	-0.054 ***
Age square	0.001 ***	0.001 **	0.001 **	0.001 ***	0.000	0.002 **
Unemployment rate	-0.055 ***	-0.038 ***	-0.015 **	-0.038 ***	-0.082 ***	-0.043 **

	Men			Women		
	Job security	Total pay	Promotion	Job security	Total pay	Promotion
Controls for:						
Occupational standing (ISEI score)	√	√	√	√	√	√
Industrial sector	√	√	√	√	√	√
Marital status	√	√	√	√	√	√
Number of children by age	√	√	√	√	√	√
Log Likelihood	-25,793	-26,684	-17,667	-25,226	-27,282	-17,202
Number of person wave observations	15,263	15,311	9,526	15,637	15,729	9,234

Note: Coefficients obtained from ordered probit regression. Standard errors have been adjusted using the Huber/White/sandwich estimator of variance. The dependent variable is satisfaction with job security, total pay, and promotion prospects, measured on a response scale from 1 to 7, where 1 corresponds to 'not satisfied at all' and 7 to 'completely satisfied'. The other variables included in the regressions are: current occupational standing (quartiles, 2nd quartile=base), industrial sector (extractive, transformative=base, distributive, producer, social, personal, public), marital status (never married, separated/divorced/widowed, cohabiting, married=base) and number of children by age (number of children aged 0 to 4, number of children aged 5 to 15, no children=base). *** p<0.01, ** p<0.05, *<p0.10.

Source: British Household Panel Study, 1991-2000, employees only.

Table 9.14 shows the results of ordered probit regressions (Long, 1999; Greene, 2003) for satisfaction with job security, total pay, and promotion prospects by type of employment relationship, flexi-worker and unemployment experiences, labour market entry cohort, age, and unemployment rate. (Further covariates included are occupational standing, industrial sector, marital status, and number of children by age, estimates of which are not shown here).

Three principal findings are noteworthy. First, fixed-term and casual full-time employees are less satisfied with job security, total pay, and promotion prospects (though partly insignificant for women under models 5 and 6). This is in line with the above result that temporary employees confront a higher risk of unemployment and decreases in socio-economic status. This result also confirms findings of other studies showing high wage differentials (see for instance Booth *et al.*, 2002). By and large, the analysis lends further support to the assumption that a lack in contractual security goes hand in hand with income insecurity. In relation to the other types of flexible employment, individual degrees of job satisfaction obviously differ for men and women. Reduced working hours generally lead to less satisfaction with job security and promotion prospects for men, whereas for women it is vital to distinguish between permanent and temporary job positions. Women in permanent posts, whether part-time or marginal part-time, are significantly more satisfied with their job security, total pay, and promotion prospects as compared to their counterparts in permanent full-time posts. Reduced working hours in temporary employment seem to lower women's satisfaction with job security. However, women with short working hours are generally more satisfied with their total pay. Here we presumably observe voluntary part-timers, that is young at the beginning of their labour market career and therefore likely to shift to full-time employment or women who combine work and family career.

Second, it is particularly noteworthy that for men satisfaction with job security, total pay, and promotion prospects decline with increasing flexi-worker experiences. For women, this holds true for perception of job security. Similarly, women with past unemployment episodes report lower degrees of satisfaction with total pay. Men who have been hit by unemployment perceive their current job as less secure. Surprisingly, we find the opposite effect for women. Also, we cannot detect any significant differences in the individual degree of satisfaction with promotion prospects among people with or without previous unemployment experience. By and large, these results lead to the conclusion that previous career instability not only has serious repercussions on future job insecurity, but it also moderates subjective perceptions and expectations about ones future labour market career.

Third, the estimates reveal that high unemployment reduces individual levels of job satisfaction. The subjective perception seems thus linked to increased numerical, wage, and functional flexibility during economic downturns.

9.6 Bringing the context in: Central findings from other country-specific studies

The previous sections offered an examination of labour market insecurity and its consequences for the work and family life of adult workers in Great Britain. The empirical scope of this chapter is therefore regionally limited. Before summarising the principal conclusions, this section intends, firstly, to reiterate a set of country-specific hypotheses for Germany and Spain and, secondly, to develop a synthesis of results from other country-specific contributions in this field. The impetus for this endeavour is the following. European countries have entered upon distinct flexibility routes and various country-specific institutions mediate labour market pressures (Chapter Four). Due to institutional entrenchment, flexible employment may have a markedly different meaning and the risk of job or income loss and its consequences vary between countries. A key question is therefore whether and to what extent the results on mobility and job satisfaction of adult workers apply to Great Britain only or translate into other contextual settings.

The *German mobility system* has been characterised by smooth education-to-work transitions and a strong linkage between educational achievement and labour market outcomes (Chapter Four; Blossfeld and Stockmann, 1998/1999; Shavit and Müller, 1998; Scherer, 2001). Hence, insecurity should be significantly filtered by educational qualification and occupational class. The mobility system is furthermore characterised by rather secure employment careers and a low degree of occupational mobility determined by seniority rules in internal labour markets (Carroll and Mayer, 1986). One may therefore expect that career maturity is potentially more determining in the German occupationally segmented labour market where long-term relationships based on trust prevail and flexible employment mainly functions as a recruitment strategy rather than a hire-and-fire strategy (Chapter Four). Yet, it is vital to stress that the above discourse applies to men, but not necessarily to women. While for men deregulation and flexibility should erode the standard employment relationship – which was typically a permanent full-time position –, the effect on women's careers is less clear. In Germany, social policy is oriented towards men's standard employment relationship (Dombois, 1999; Hinrichs, 1996; Pfau-Effinger, 1996), and hence, provides strong incentives for women to carry the brunt of household and child-care responsibilities. By and large, for women it is hard to combine family and work life other than through discontinuous and part-time employment. In the past, the German mobility system did therefore barely present upward career paths for women and mothers in particular. At the same time, the bulk of part-time jobs are positions with at least 15 hours of work per week and therefore protected by employment legislation. On the other hand, the educational expansion is particularly pervasive for women and reflects their growing desire to invest in human capital and participate in the labour market, as well as their improved labour market chances and promotion prospects (Chapter Two; Blossfeld, 1985, 1988, 1995). As already discussed for women in Great Britain, it is difficult to derive an expectation about whether deregulation and flexibility introduce an even higher degree of insecurity and instability in female work life, or whether more continuous –though more flexible – career paths open-up, some women may have always been looking for.

Which repercussions of increasing labour market pressures on adult work life can be expected for Spain? Recall from the previous chapters that the *Spanish mobility system* is highly segmented. Job security is first and foremost attached to the type of contract and one may presume that permanent contracts increase in value with increasing job tenure. In other words, the insider-outsider labour market channels labour market risks towards outsiders and new labour market entrants who are affected most by labour market insecurity (Bentolila and Dolado, 1994). By contrast, insiders in permanent job positions are highly sheltered, and thus, likely to accumulate career maturity which in turn will make their job career increasingly more secure. Given that the transition rate into permanency is comparatively low (Chapter Seven), the timing of becoming an insider in the Spanish mobility system is crucial. However, it remains an open research question whether young workers are immediately sheltered once they obtain a permanent post, or whether previous career instability spills over into an insider's work life. Again, it must be stressed that these various arguments apply to men, but will not hold true for women. As pointed out in Chapters Two and Three, the female labour force participation remains comparatively low and part-time positions are rare. In a context of high unemployment and low support by the welfare state, labour market insecurity may be considered a particular dilemma for women. While young Spanish men face considerable hurdles to establish long-run economic prospects for the household, chances are small that women can compensate potential earnings losses of their partners. Even when women find jobs, the chances are high that it is a temporary arrangement, low-paid, and inherently unstable.

Recent investigations give us some first answers to the underlying research questions. For Germany, there is limited support and considerable contrary evidence for the hypothesis of a sweeping decrease in men's employment stability (Kurz *et al.*, 2002; Erlinghagen and Knuth, 2002; see also Jann and Diekmann, 2003). There is only evidence in support of the former hypothesis inasmuch that unemployment risks have grown larger across birth cohorts (Kurz *et al.*, 2002). With respect to occupational mobility and re-entry after periods of unemployment men's employment careers do not seem increasingly unstable. Educational qualification and occupational class still matter in that insecurity is largely channelled towards low qualified workers and in low occupational classes (Kurz *et al.*, 2002). But young employment seekers meet with significant obstacles to enter permanent job positions and therefore appear as the losers of increased labour market flexibility in Germany (Chapter Seven; Kurz and Steinhage, 2001; Kurz *et al.*, forthcoming). Quite the opposite to men, the preliminary results from a working paper by Grunow and Buchholz (2003) give strength to the hypothesis that adult women also confront significant detriments of increased labour market insecurity, and hence, bear costs of deregulation and flexibility. Women's careers have grown more precarious across birth cohorts and are characterised by seesaw changes between unemployment, inactivity, marginal, and temporary work. Another striking finding is that educational qualification and occupational class do not shelter recent birth cohorts of women from unemployment or downward occupational mobility. From their preliminary results Grunow and Buchholz (2003) conclude that the individual protection of institutional arrangements against labour market risks seems to have evaporated for women in Germany.

A study by Simó *et al.* (2002a) on men's job mobility in Spain reveals that labour market risks are indeed channelled towards low educated, semi- or unskilled adult male workers. Other studies have also shown that the duration of employment spells has very much decreased, resulting in high job turnover rates (Bentolila and Dolado, 1994; Dolado *et al.*, 2002). Age and individual resources seem key factors determining career opportunities, though they lose some of their importance across labour market entry cohorts (Simó *et al.*, 2002a). A further finding of the same study is that individual resources condition transitions from fixed-term to permanent employment. Unfortunately, at the time of writing this study, a similar analysis on female career opportunities in Spain was not available. We shall therefore be anxious to see how recent transformation in the Spanish mobility system impact women.

Connecting the various results of this chapter with other major country-specific contributions, between-country variation does by no means have grown smaller. It is a captivating result that German men do not seem to lose in increasingly uncertain times while the opposite holds true for British men. Further research is needed to bring together a series of country-specific studies on labour market careers in an age of globalisation and, thus, to shed more light on how labour market insecurity impacts the work and family life of adult men and women.

9.7 Discussion and concluding remarks

This chapter had the goal of investigating whether and to what extent there is empirical evidence to support the hypothesis of an overall decline in job security in Great Britain. It first asked if there are signs of employment (in) stability. Other research has argued that young adults, in particular, turn out to be the 'losers' in highly flexible labour markets. However, a review of major findings from recent empirical investigations suggested that job insecurity has spread somewhat to adult men. While men are likely to have seen substantial decreases in employment stability women's careers seem to have become more stable over the last decades.

The second part of this chapter provided a more detailed picture of job insecurity of British men and women in the 1990s. Here the question was raised as to whether insecurity is equally spread among all employees alike. Using longitudinal data from the first ten waves of the British Household Panel Survey, the chapter analysed three interrelated mobility events, risks of entry into unemployment and chances to exit from unemployment, transitions into and out of unpaid homemaking, and risks of downward and chances of upward occupational mobility. The chapter also examined subjective degrees of job satisfaction. The main attention was devoted to the interplay between labour market insecurity, gender, career maturity, and individual resources. The salient findings for this chapter can be summarised as follows.

The analysis of this chapter revealed important *gender differences*. At first view it is intriguing that men seem to bear much greater costs of flexibility than women. But the difference may lie in the gender-specific role of flexible work, career maturity, and individual resources in the British mobility system. Flexible work arrangements do not only influence men's and women's careers differently. Also, career maturity and individual resources have different implications for men and women. In beginning to understand what is behind these gender differences, the following paragraphs therefore extrapolate these related findings.

As expected, *labour market insecurity* deeply impacts job stability. A central finding is that flexible employment introduces a high degree of insecurity into work careers independent of a person's *career maturity*. Regardless of employment experience and age, flexi-workers are more likely to be hit by unemployment and confront higher risks of downward occupational mobility. Given the low-trust environment of Great Britain, this result is less surprising. On the other hand, employment experience is a vital source of security, whereas previous spells of flexible work or unemployment destabilise the future labour market career and that irrespective of a person's current employment relationship. To summarise, the less employment experience and the more insecurity experience a person has, the more likely he or she is to enter a *'low pay – no pay cycle'*. However, there is an important gender differences here. For men, career maturity protects against unemployment, increases young men's chances to re-enter the labour market, and determines their career opportunities in adult working life. However, the examination of labour market insecurity experiences showed that flexible work arrangements and unemployment spells during the early labour market career induce repercussions on men's adult work life. The principle of responsibility and reciprocity and certain in-work benefits create incentives for men to re-enter the labour market quickly, even though chances are high that entry-level jobs are inherently insecure. Overall, the results indicate that insecurity at labour market entry entraps men in a *'flexible employment – unemployment – flexible employment cycle'* and may thus be seen as the onset of an unstable job career. For women, flexibility has a different meaning, inasmuch as career maturity does not determine women's employment-to-unemployment transitions but appears instead to be an important predictor of re-entry into the labour market by unemployed mid-career women. Career maturity is likely to be a crude approximation of women's work orientation, which is substantiated by the finding that it is an important parameter for exits into unpaid homemaking along with rehiring after periods of unpaid homemaking. Moreover, mid-career women with flexi-worker experiences face fewer career opportunities. A further striking finding of the chapter is that men's career instability shapes women's employment decisions, making them less prone to be gainfully employed – perhaps due to the disincentives to work built into the means-tested benefit system. By the same token, flexible work arrangements may well fit with women's work orientations and their family life, thereby increasing their labour market attachment and job tenure. In these terms, flexible work may introduce more stability in women's careers, even though it often means being employed in the lower segments of the labour market. For women, one can suggest that they thus switch between *'flexible employment, homemaking, and flexible employment'*. In summary, the results presented in this chapter hint how growing labour market insecurity might be considered a specific dilemma for young men and mid-career women.

Gender differences exist in *individual resources* as well, though the expectation was that they functioned as important buffers against labour market insecurity. While such resources indeed determine men's and women's work careers, it was in different veins. With regard to the risk of job loss, high occupational standing looms large for men, particularly with regard to young job holders. At the same time, individual resources play a decisive role in men's chances to re-enter the labour market, particularly into permanent full-time employment. The same applies for men's career mobility. For women, however, individual resources do not make any difference with respect to unemployment risks and seem of little account for chances to exit into a job. Individual resources merely matter for women's career mobility. All in all, we can extrapolate that particularly young men with low educational qualification and those employed in precarious occupations appear to particularly be the losers in terms of a higher degree of job insecurity.

Lastly, the chapter investigated the *subjective degree of job satisfaction* as approximated by satisfaction with job security, total pay, and promotion prospects. The results revealed that temporary employees are generally less satisfied with their current job. Moreover, past labour market insecurity experience and high unemployment lower the degree of job satisfaction. So in beginning to understand the relationship between flexible employment and job satisfaction, we can conclude that labour market insecurity is likely to introduce uncertainty in an individual's life, impacting perceptions and expectations about one's labour market career and social life.

The presented analysis has delivered some important insights into career mobility of men and women in Great Britain, but raised also some important questions. Let us therefore conclude by pointing out some desirable further extensions of the above presented analysis. Further examinations are required to give additional empirical strengths to the findings of this chapter. This should be done by using other measures and model specifications as well as different data-sets. To put the matter briefly, it could prove fruitful to apply a different measurement of labour market insecurity and career maturity. Above that, the analysis of this chapter was temporally limited in scope. Future research should therefore inquire into retrospective data and study individual degrees of insecurity and risks of labour market exclusion across labour market entry cohorts and historical time. Further elaboration is also needed on couples' employment careers to scrutinise more clearly how employment instability of men impacts women's careers and work orientations. Lastly, the discourse of the previous section developed some first tentative hypotheses in a comparative framework. In future research, it would be interesting to extend the analysis presented in this chapter to investigate inter-country variation in labour market insecurity and its impact on work and family life of adult workers.

Appendix

Table 9.1 The Browning-Singelmann classification of sectors and industries

Sectors	Include
Extractive	Agriculture, fishing, and forestry; Mining
Transformative	Construction; Food; Textile; Metal; Machinery; Chemical; Miscellaneous manufacturing; Utilities
Distributive services	Transportation and storage; Wholesale trade; Retail trade (except eating and drinking places)
Producer services	Communication; Banking, credit, and other financial services; Insurance; Real estate; Engineering and architectural services; Accounting and bookkeeping; Miscellaneous business services; Legal services
Social services	Medical and health services; Hospitals; Education; Welfare and religious services; Non-profit organisations; Postal services; Government; Miscellaneous professional and social services
Personal services	Domestic services; Hotels and lodging places; Eating and drinking places; Repair services; Laundry and dry cleaning; Barber and beauty shops; Entertainment and recreational services; Miscellaneous personal services

Source: Browning and Singelmann (1978: 487).

Table 9.15 Chances of upward, risks of downward occupational mobility by gender (Multinomial logistic regression, any change in ISEI score)

	Men				Women			
	upward		downward		upward		downward	
Type of employment relationship								
Permanent and full-time (base)								
Fixed-term and full-time	0.218		0.450	**	0.391	**	0.595	***
Casual and full-time	0.783	***	0.944	***	0.558	***	0.740	***
Part-time	0.524	**	0.080					
Part-time and permanent					-0.302	***	0.119	
Part-time and non-permanent					0.248		0.755	***
Marginal	0.441		0.976	***				
Marginal and permanent					-0.381	***	0.424	***
Marginal and non-permanent					0.162		0.656	***
Employment experience (in years)	-0.152	***	-0.183	***	-0.087	***	-0.140	***
Employment experience squared	0.004	***	0.006	***	0.002	*	0.005	***
Mobility experience (dummy)	1.197	***	1.171	***	1.023	***	1.013	***
Flexi-worker experience (in years)	-0.053		-0.033		-0.073		-0.020	
Unemployment experience (dummy)	-0.053		0.174	*	0.049		0.086	
Labour market entry cohort								
< 1970	-0.134		-0.307	**	0.088		-0.094	
1970-79	-0.125	*	-0.145	*	-0.050		0.016	
1980-89 (base)								
1990-	0.017		0.124		-0.003		0.062	
Previous occupation (ISEI score)								
Very low (1st quartile)	0.383	***	-0.868	***	-0.036		-0.749	***
Low (2nd quartile) (base)								
High (3rd quartile)	-0.241	***	0.495	***	-0.723	***	0.857	***
Very high (4th quartile)	-1.736	***	0.978	***	-1.574	***	1.565	***
ISEI score 1st job	0.012	***	-0.012	***	0.013	***	-0.014	***
Educational qualification								
Higher and first degree	0.505	***	-0.709	***	0.639	***	-0.518	***
Vocational degree	0.212	***	-0.342	***	-0.150	*	-0.327	***
A Level (or equiv.)	0.150	*	-0.300	***	0.155	*	-0.163	*
GSCE/O Level (or equiv.) (base)								
Less than O Level	-0.114		0.142		-0.313	***	0.208	**
Unemployment rate	0.008		0.018		-0.048		-0.032	
Industrial sector								
Extractive	-0.016		0.016		0.255		-0.503	*
Transformative (base)								
Social services	0.130		-0.126		-0.370	***	-0.341	**
Distributive services	-0.082		-0.212	**	-0.182	*	-0.276	**
Producer services	0.390	***	-0.334	***	0.224	**	-0.458	***
Personal services	-0.148		-0.245	**	-0.129		-0.135	
Public	-0.017		-0.398	***	-0.500	***	-0.602	***
Constant	-1.490	***	-0.562	**	-0.953	***	-0.727	**

	Men		Women	
	upward	downward	upward	downward
Log Likelihood	-11,301		-12,090	
Number of person wave observations	12,014		12,399	
Number of events	2,286	2,093	2,058	1,957

Note: Obtained from discrete-time competing risk transition model. Standard errors have been adjusted using the Huber/White/sandwich estimator of variance. The figures are coefficients from multinomial regression. All variables lagged by one period except labour market entry cohort. *** p<0.01, ** p<0.05, *p<0.10.

Source: British Household Panel Study, 1991-2000, employees only.

Table 9.16 Chances of upward, risks of downward occupational mobility by gender and age (Multinomial logistic regression, any change in ISEI score)

	Men				Women			
	Age 16 to 29		Age 30 to 49		Age 16 to 29		Age 30 to 49	
	upward	downward	upward	downward	upward	downward	upward	downward
Type of empl. relationship								
Permanent and full-time (base)								
Fixed-term and full-time	0.242	0.502 **	-0.089	0.126	0.445 *	0.261	0.162	0.831 ***
Casual and full-time	0.676 ***	0.749 ***	0.711 **	1.064 ***	0.556 **	0.795 ***	0.371	0.598 *
Part-time or marginal	0.587 **	0.398	0.094	0.015				
Part-time and permanent					-0.147	0.491 ***	-0.335 ***	-0.012
Part-time and non-permanent					0.558 *	0.982 ***	0.082	0.631 **
Marginal and permanent					-0.187	0.529 **	-0.444 ***	0.379 ***
Marginal and non-permanent					0.381	1.507 ***	0.068	0.294
Employment exp. (in years)	-0.305 ***	-0.442 ***	-0.111 ***	-0.137 ***	-0.141 **	-0.282 ***	-0.053 *	-0.106 ***
Employment exp. squared	0.017 ***	0.028 ***	0.003 ***	0.005 ***	0.005	0.015 ***	0.001	0.003 ***
Mobility experience (dummy)	0.908 ***	1.083 ***	1.477 ***	1.301 ***	0.903 ***	0.967 ***	1.136 ***	1.071 ***
Flexi-worker exp. (in years)	-0.047	-0.018	-0.015	-0.004	-0.022	0.022	-0.078	-0.026
Unemployment exp. (dummy)	-0.033	0.102	-0.084	0.255 *	-0.068	0.096	0.167	0.082
Labour market entry cohort								
< 1970			-0.086	-0.267 *			0.057	-0.040
1970-79	-0.367	0.338	-0.068	-0.138	0.535 *	-0.257	-0.096	0.068
1980-89 (base)								
1990-	-0.145	-0.022	0.007	0.145	-0.126	0.070	0.050	0.044
Educational qualification								
Higher and first degree	0.535 ***	-0.763 ***	0.483 ***	-0.678 ***	0.927 ***	-0.632 ***	0.418 ***	-0.479 ***
Vocational degree	0.244 **	-0.330 **	0.223 *	-0.321 ***	-0.094	-0.299 **	-0.173 *	-0.329 ***
A Level (or equiv.)	0.090	-0.396 ***	0.187	-0.242 *	0.320 **	-0.064	0.015	-0.293 **
GSCE/O Level (base)								
Less than O Level	0.021	0.247 *	-0.173	0.092	-0.058	0.268	-0.389 ***	0.202 *
Unemployment rate	-0.045 *	-0.040	0.050 **	0.065 ***	-0.123 **	-0.006	0.017	-0.031

	Men				Women			
	Age 16 to 29		Age 30 to 49		Age 16 to 29		Age 30 to 49	
	upward	downward	upward	downward	upward	downward	upward	downward
Controls for								
Previous occupation (ISEI)	√	√	√	√	√	√	√	√
ISEI-score 1st job	√	√	√	√	√	√	√	√
Industrial sector	√	√	√	√	√	√	√	√
Constant	-0.808 **	0.404	-2.139 ***	-1.198 ***	-0.299	-0.333	-1.593 ***	-1.061 **
Log Likelihood	-4,873		-6,358		-4,868		-7,134	
Number of person wave obs.	4,689		7,325		4,823		7,576	
Number of events	1,036	872	1,250	1,221	864	758	1,194	1,199

Note: Obtained from discrete-time competing risk transition model. Standard errors have been adjusted using the Huber/White/sandwich estimator of variance. The figures are coefficients from multinomial regression. All variables lagged by one period except labour market entry cohort. *** p<0.01, ** p<0.05, *p<0.10.

Source: British Household Panel Study, 1991-2000, employees only.

10 Conclusion

The goal of this study was to develop a theoretical framework for enhancing our understanding of when individuals make life course decisions and to analyse explicitly and thoroughly in how far new structural constraints due to the recent restructuring process of European labour markets have an effect on life course decision-making. To this end, the impact of labour market insecurity on individual life courses has been gauged in three selected countries, namely Germany, Great Britain, and Spain during the 1990s. Two pivotal research questions guided the discussion. The first research question of this study asked to what extent young adults are confronted with job insecurity and whether there is empirical evidence for an impeding impact on transitions to adulthood. Throughout the theoretical part of this study this research question has been further elaborated and the second research question asked: is it possible to identify certain risk profiles coupled to country of residence, gender, career maturity, and individual resources? The comparative, longitudinal, and life course approach of this study provided not only special insights into the role of institutional filters in mediating labour market insecurity. Besides distinct institutional entrenchment on the aggregate level, this work also demonstrated the crucial role of individual resources, gender, and career maturity.

Within the theoretical framework of this study, this chapter synthesises and discusses the main findings of the preceding chapters to achieve four objectives. First, Section 10.1 summarises the results of the analysis and outlines whether there is empirical evidence to support the hypotheses. In doing so, this section examines how each analysis has contributed to the theoretical framework of this study for understanding how labour market insecurity and life course decisions appear interrelated via the concept of life course security. Second, the chapter reflects upon the implications of these findings in Section 10.2. Third, Section 10.3 debates on some important flaws of the explanatory approach and the empirical analysis of this study, establishes the trade-offs attached to its comparative approach, and expresses various suggestions for future research. The final section outlines the key lessons that can be drawn from this study.

10.1 Central findings – insecurity and risk profiles

The analysis of this study provided ample evidence in support of the *insecurity hypothesis*. Insecurity may take the form of slim chances to find a job and a higher risk to enter into an insecure employment relationship, high risks of entry into unemployment and low chances to end unemployment, low transition rates from insecure to permanent employment, and higher risks of downward occupational mobility. A second dimension of insecurity is the subjective perception of job insecurity. The impact of insecurity was expected to result in less life course security, and hence, job precariousness and perceived job insecurity were assumed to make a deferment of transitions to adulthood more likely. Indeed, labour market flexibility was likely to come at the cost of greater instability in the labour market career and as a consequence of insecure labour market positions individuals tended to postpone family formation and entry into parenthood. The mere fact of labour market insecurity, however, will not do to adequately describe and explain individual life course decision-making. An idea that runs explicitly through the various chapters of this work is that labour market insecurity does not operate quasi detached from contextual settings and individual characteristics. Rather, as suggested in the *risk profile hypothesis*, individual degrees of job insecurity were substantially filtered by institutional arrangements in one's country of residence, gender, career maturity, and individual resources. The results of this study revealed that these various filters are highly interdependent; they determine life course security and shape men's and women's work and family life. Depending on the context under study the empirical analysis identified diverse adaptation strategies and the following sections address the five hypotheses that are behind the idea of risk profiles.

10.1.1 Country-specific adaptation strategies

In the comparative framework of this study, country-specific institutions were assumed to mediate structural changes on the macro-level. More precisely, this study examined nation-specific, historically grown flexibility routes along with arrangements in educational systems and welfare state provisions. The *country-specific hypothesis* suggested that cross-country differences in these institutional contexts will shape individual-level decision-making processes. This hypothesis generally gained support. More particularly, in the context of the transition into employment, three important findings emerged. Firstly, men and women were the hardest hit in Spain, where an insider-outsider labour market prevails and government support to ease the transition from school to work is weak. This was illustrated by the fact that the young shared low employment probabilities, the experience of flexible entry-level jobs and job loss, and low transition rates into permanent employment. Quite the contrary in Germany and Great Britain. In these latter two countries it was much easier to get a foot into the labour market. Yet, compared to their German counterparts the youth in the British low trust labour market bore a higher unemployment risk, were more dissatisfied with their job security, and certain workers in lower-level occupations had longer odds to convert insecure employment relationships into permanent ones. But if degrees and repercussions of insecurity differ in these three countries, then we should also expect other adaptation strategies of rational actors. This is exactly what the empirical evidence from this study tells us. In support of the country-specific hypothesis, the youth who confronted the strongest detriments of increased labour market insecurity were the ones living in Spain. Insecurity also loomed large for men and women in Great Britain, even though job insecurity was of short duration and more evenly spread among workers. One rationale behind this unexpected finding may be that Britons in insecure labour market positions defer life-shaping decisions because they judge their current position as a stepping-stone to more secure and better paid employment. The findings for Germany were mixed. While the analysis of partnership decisions provided support for the insecurity hypothesis, insecurity does not seem to interfere with parenthood decisions. By and large, the results suggested that it is essential whether a man holds a job or not, but it does not seem to matter whether this job is a permanent one or not. However, the empirical results showed that these effects are also transition-specific. At the same time, important gender-specific strategies emerged.

10.1.2 Transition-specific effects of insecurity

According to the *transition-specific hypothesis* job insecurity was expected to increase the propensity to remain single rather than partner, and to cohabit rather than marry. The effect of job insecurity should be considerably higher for transitions into first parenthood. In line with these considerations, the results of this study revealed that insecure labour market positions meant lower transition rates into first marriage or consensual union. There was also evidence that labour market insecurity tends to decrease the odds of marrying the partner relative to remaining in the cohabiting union, albeit case numbers were small and it is therefore better not to draw too definitive conclusions from this analysis. Over and above, the analysis evidenced that insecurity leads individuals to postpone the decision to become a parent. Yet, this latter effect of labour market insecurity seemed largely mediated via the entry into marriage. Since young adults in precarious employment tend to defer first marriage and are more prone to live in cohabiting unions instead of marital ones, a postponement of first parenthood becomes more likely.

10.1.3 Gender-specific impact of insecurity

The findings of this study confirmed the *gender-specific hypothesis*, which argued that overall the effects of job insecurity are stronger for men than for women. Men in all three countries were negatively affected by labour market insecurity. By contrast, women did not perceive their instability in the labour market as an element that deters union formation. There was rather some evidence that women in insecure position are more prone to enter a union, suggesting that marriage functions as a safety net for women in insecure labour market positions. But the story appeared to be different for transitions into first motherhood. In line with the expectations of Chapter Five, a central finding was that if the labour market position of employed women in Great Britain and Spain is characterised by insecurity, then this is an element that deters first motherhood. In summary, what catches the eye is the male-breadwinner view of the relationship between employment career and family formation, whereby men are more likely to marry and parent when they are able to establish and solidify a solid economic household basis.

10.1.4 Concentrated risks in early careers

The *career maturity hypothesis* contended that career maturity is a crucial employee's benefit that filters insecurity. This study provided support, but also some contrary evidence for this hypothesis. Labour market insecurity was particularly channelled towards the young who have gained little experience and have developed only weak ties to the labour market. They were largely swapping between temporary employment and unemployment and it took more time to find a first job and to transform a temporary contract into a permanent one. Yet, another central finding of this work was that flexible employment introduced high degrees of insecurity in work careers independent of a person's career maturity. On the other hand, employment experiences were a vital source of security, whereas previous spells of flexible work or unemployment destabilised the future career. Yet, this analysis was confined to Great Britain and we may expect stronger effects of career maturity in the closed labour markets of Germany and Spain.

10.1.5 Educational attainment and occupational status as buffers

The final striking finding was support for the *individual resources hypothesis*. Educational qualification and occupational class were two mechanisms through which labour market insecurity appears funnelled. Lower skilled entrants were faced with a higher risk of holding temporary contracts and those being employed in the lower-level occupations were more likely to lose their job. Furthermore, chances to escape from insecure employment were smaller and risks of downward occupational mobility higher for employees in the lower-grade occupations. However, due to national differences in flexibility paths and institutional arrangements in education, there were also some important country-specific differences. Insecurity was directed towards low qualified and in inherently unstable occupations in Spain, whereas a great deal of German temporary workers held higher-level occupations and had an off-chance to transform these insecure job positions into permanent ones.

10.2 Implications of research

From looking at the findings presented in the foregoing chapters, the discussion now turns to their implications. First and foremost, policy makers should have a vested interest in easing labour market integration and improving the employment prospects of young adults, who are hardest hit by increasing labour market insecurity. Youth is not only confronted with insecure entry-level jobs, and thus, often moving between temporary employment, unemployment, and further education. There is also some evidence that increased insecurity faced by young people while entering the labour market has a serious impact on their future labour market career. A significant finding is that individual resources and career maturity serve as insecurity shields whereas previous spells of unemployment or insecure gainful employment funnel insecurity. This important result points to specific challenges for future education policy and labour market policy. In today's learning societies, a key goal of education policy should be the upgrading of the work force. Furthermore, one may intuitively argue that with increasing labour market insecurity the social security system seems more and more outdated in many European countries. More precisely, as to employment- and welfare-sustaining policies, benefits and eligibility requirements have to be adjusted to the increasingly flexible work force and employment-creation measures need to be launched to re-integrate the unemployed more speedily and into secure positions. The analysis furthermore pinpoints the repercussions of labour market insecurity on family life. It is a salient finding that individuals in uncertain positions are prone to defer or even forgo partnership and parenthood decisions. This casts additional light on the above discussed demands for labour market policy and welfare-sustaining policy. Moreover, future actions of policy makers should be directed to the extension of child-care facilities, family-friendly work arrangements, and family-oriented benefits, and hence, ease the combination of work and family career. It will thus de-couple the long-run economic prospects of a household and the stability of the main breadwinner's job career, thereby lowering social risks.

Yet, it is not immediately obvious whether such measures will gain their end in the three respective countries under study. This book evidenced that European countries have entered on disparate paths and that their country-specific responses to globalisation are multifaceted. Institutional entrenchment may impose certain rigidities and the whole institutional package of a country has to be considered to derive policy implications. In the flexibly co-ordinated German economy, institutions serve to lower social and economic risks; persons are highly decommodified. Yet, high unemployment indicates that the system remains too rigid to allow for fast and efficient adjustments to new challenges in a globalising world. This implies that Germany is not succeeding in preventing risky mobility events. Hence, in the future German policy makers will have to break new ground in social policy and labour legislation. Yet, they may be reluctant to follow the British track. In the open employment system in Great Britain where flexibility is employer-led, institutions neither protect against labour market risks nor do they absorb economic and social hazards during times of need. Due to its laissez-faire policy, Great Britain lacks social solidarity and we can observe some long-term negative consequences of flexible change in the labour market. Hence, Great Britain demonstrates an example of how flexibility as the general principle can serve to exacerbate insecurity and increase inequality. Due to marginal flexibility in the closed Spanish labour market, risks are almost exclusively concentrated in labour market outsiders while insiders remain highly sheltered. Spain is a revealing example of how flexible measures can fail to remedy the rigidity of an employment system and the high prevalence of unemployment, in particular. With the deep restructuring process and profound flexible change, the high level of economic insecurity due to high unemployment during the early 1980s turned into an equally high level of temporal and economic insecurity in the 1990s. One may therefore speculate that the described repercussions of labour market insecurity would also have been arisen in the case of no deregulation and flexibility. In any case, the high degree of uncertainty and its implications for young adult's life course decision-making will solely but surely question the future functioning of the family-oriented welfare system.

The previous chapters also stressed the oversimplification and biasedness of a focus on the negative outcomes of flexible measures only. Rather, deregulation and flexibility serve as a required tool to adapt to new challenges in the course of globalisation. They create new job positions and conditions (which are more commensurate with women's careers), and hence, ease labour market integration for many people. But the two important points to note are the following: Firstly, in most European countries social security systems still need to be adjusted to new labour market risks and the new labour force stratum of flexi-workers. Secondly, governments need to contravene the concentration of risks on workers with certain characteristics. It is difficult to foresee future actions that policy makers may want to make but it is evident that the repercussions of labour market insecurity on the work and family life of men and women can not be disregarded. As suggested by the vogue word 'Flexicurity', both flexibility and security have to become the theme of the debate.

10.3 Suggestions for further research

This study aimed to give insights into life course decision-making under labour market insecurity. In order to keep this study focused, various decisions about a purposeful research design have been made. More precisely, four issues deserve further attention. These concern (i) *country selection and observation period*, (ii) *the theoretical model*, (iii) *the choice of life course transitions under study*, and, (iv) *methodology*. The theory-driven decisions determine the validity and scope of this study and may be challenged on substantive grounds. In the following, the conceptualisation of the research design of this study and its salient shortcomings will be discussed in some depth to derive suggestions for progress and further research.

A first question to start with in this study was this: How to select countries for comparison? And, how many countries have to be studied? For the purpose of this study three countries have been chosen that have entered on disparate and rather fast-paced flexible paths that are deeply rooted in their country-specific institutional context. The empirical scope of this work is therewith regionally limited. Above that, this study has deliberately restricted all analyses to the 1990s. This *regional and temporal limitation* is an important aspect to be kept in view when debating validity and scope of the causal approach of this study. A crucial question within the comparative framework of this study is: To what extent is labour market insecurity filtered by country-specific institutional arrangements? The theoretical framework elaborated the pivotal role of a country's flexibility route, educational system, and welfare state provision. Based on profound country descriptions, the three countries under study were juxtaposed along two main dimensions of security: the property of jobs and the environment of jobs. The country-specific hypothesis established whether each of the countries under study is secure or insecure on one or the other of these dimensions. Beyond question, the real world is by far more complex and the research focus of this study leaves out many more institutional packages. One would need to cover many more countries in order to inquire into the role of institutional filters and a research agenda with the objective to fully cross-classify countries along the two suggested dimensions of security may even be insolvable. This book provides only selective case studies and it is therefore highly desirable to extend the analysis towards other nation-specific contexts. From another view point, the research question of whether and to what extent labour market insecurity interferes with individual life course decision-making could have been approached by means of a cohort analysis. Institutions, flexible measures, and potential sources of insecurity are continuously subject to change. Hence, for future research it is promising to pursue a dynamic analysis of individual life courses and respective changes across history, lifetimes, and birth cohorts.

Second, the *theoretical model is limited in scope*. The purpose of this work was not to develop an all-embracing theoretical framework that puts into perspective the various determinants of individual life course decision-making. Rather, the principal goal was to enhance our understanding of labour market insecurity and its repercussions on individual life course decisions. In addition to the voluminous body of research contributions on the work and family life of men and women, this study gives significant hints that labour market insecurity matters in individual employment careers and that the type of employment relationship and the perception of job security are further determinants of life course decision-making. The results of this study are therefore interesting and revealing in their own right. However, the key goal of a global theory of elements of decision-making processes needs to be kept firmly in sight. A strongpoint of this study is the theoretical consideration and empirical implementation of both actual and perceived security. Yet, this theme deserves further exploration. Firstly, not all types of labour market flexibility could be studied within the confines of this study. More precisely, the analysis presented here discounts the so-called internal flexibility. With the rise in demand for multi-skilled and experienced labour, functional flexibility gains importance in today's learning societies. Likewise, wage flexibility remains largely unconsidered in this study, as are outsourcing and subcontracting. To complete the picture of labour market deregulation and flexibility, an analysis of these other types of flexibility is required. Secondly, qualitative interviewing could provide further insights into how people perceive insecurity and deal with lacking life course security, an issue that will be picked up below.

Third, the presented research is *restricted on selected life course transitions*, namely entry into the labour market and some cardinal kinds of mobility events during the subsequent career, partnership formation, and birth of the first child. Further progress could be made in several respects. If we are to fully understand the long-term impact of career maturity, youth and adult life have to become an issue of research. To this point, the question whether job insecurity at early stages of the labour market career impacts adult work life has only been addressed for the British context. Furthermore, to make the picture of labour market insecurity and its repercussions on the work life of men and women more comprehensive, future research may explore transitions into retirement. In the previous chapters lifetime is analytically broken down into various interrelated transitions during youth and adulthood. The role of labour market flexibility on leaving the labour force remains untouched, however. Moreover, in today's low-fertility societies one may expect a potentially large impact of labour market insecurity on the decision to have a second child. This is because bringing up more than one child escalates the financial obligations and hampers the integration of work and family life. It may thus jeopardise the economic basis of a household in increasingly insecure times. Also, in the future it could prove fruitful to focus on the employment decisions of specific disadvantaged groups such as single parents or the working poor.

Last but not least, there are also some pitfalls with respect to *methodology*. As in any empirical study, and in comparative research programs in particular, the results of this study need to be tested against other data sources and operationalisations. It would also be beneficial to run different specifications of the models. Without qualitative interviewing and data analysis, we do not quite understand individual's life planning and their decision-making process remains a black box. Further research is therefore needed to study individual employment careers and biographical insecurity by means of biographical data (e.g., Strünck, 2003). This study has also not progressed far enough as to couple data analysis. Even though the employed data sources entail information on the partner, small case numbers did not always permit a couple analysis so that partner's characteristics had to be disregarded. With further sweeps to come shortly such an endeavour seems promising. In particular, analysts will gain the chance to exploit more fully the harmonised ECHP data. Notwithstanding these various limitations, this study stands as an important contribution to the cross-national study of life course decision-making and sheds important light on labour market insecurity and the work and family life of men and women, in particular. So, what lessons are to be drawn from this comparative study?

10.4 Concluding remarks – winners and losers in increasingly insecure labour markets

The flexible change in European labour markets opens up new options for rational decision-makers but also interpolates new sources of insecurity in individual life courses. Deregulation and flexibility run moving stairs into and out of gainful employment as well as into and out of secure jobs and this restructuring process leads to passages for some people, yet to impassages for others. Insecurity in work life translates into serious repercussions on life-shaping decisions in family life. From the results of this study it is not possible to derive a simple polarity of winners and losers in the course of deregulation and flexibility, because it fails to reveal how institutional filters and individual characteristics serve to mitigate insecurity. In beginning to understand the detrimental effects of labour market insecurity, we can extrapolate that the youth is hardest hit. Young job holders lack stability and security in employment careers, thus implying less life course security. This is particularly evident in the Spanish insider-outsider labour market where we may expect serious long-term consequences on adult work and family life. It is much easier to overcome periods of insecure employment in the flexible labour market of Britain, but the price paid for this is higher levels of overall employment insecurity. The flexibly co-ordinated economy of Germany then does not succeed in preventing risky mobility events in the course of globalisation. Yet, a more extensive and generous social security system mitigates social risks. Lastly, the lower skilled and those in lower-level occupations bear the brunt of increased insecurity.

In conclusion, this book can only cast some light on the complex mutual interdependence of macro-level changes that impact national labour markets; certain risk profiles coupled to country of residence, gender, career maturity, and individual resources; and life course decision-making. To fully gauge the implications of deregulation and flexible change, much more additional research has to be pursued in the future.

References

Abercrombie, N. and Warde, A. (2000) *Contemporary British Society*. Cambridge, Polity Press.

Ahn, N. and Mira, P. (2001) Job bust, baby bust?: Evidence from Spain, *Journal of Population Economics*, 14, 505-521.

Alasuutari, P. (2000) Globalisation and the Nation-State: An Appraisal of the Discussion, *Acta Sociologica*, 43, 3, 259-269.

Alba-Ramírez, A. (1998) Re-employment probabilities of young workers in Spain, *Investigaciones Económicas*, XXII, 2, 201-224.

Aldrich, J. and Nelson, F. (1984) *Linear Probability, Logit, And Probit Models*. Newbury Park/ London/ New Delhi, Sage Publications.

Allison, P. (1982) Discrete-time Methods for the Analysis of Event Histories, in Leinhard, S. (ed) *Sociological Methodology*. San Francisco, Jossey Bass, 61-98.

Allison, P. (1984) *Event History Analysis. Regression for Longitudinal Event Data*. Beverly Hills/ London/ New Delhi, Sage Publications.

Allison, P. (1995) *Survival analysis using the SAS system. A practical guide*. Cary, North Carolina, USA, SAS Institute Inc.

Allmendinger, J. (1989) Educational System and Labour Market Outcomes, *European Sociological Review*, 3, 231-250.

Allmendinger, J. and Hinz, T. (1997) Mobilität und Lebensverlauf: Deutschland, Großbritannien und Schweden im Vergleich, in Hradil, S. and Immerfall, S. (eds) *Die Westeuropäischen Gesellschaften im Vergleich*. Opladen, Leske und Budrich, 247-285.

Andreß, H.-J. (1992) *Einführung in die Verlaufsdatenanalyse. Statistische Grundlagen und Anwendungsbeispiele kategorialer Daten*. Köln, Zentrum für Historische Sozialforschung.

Aragón Medina, J. and Cachón Rodríguez, L. (1999) Mercado de trabajo, empleo y políticas de empleo: Consideraciones desde una perspectiva europea, *Cuadernos de Relaciones Laborales*, 15, 51-76.

Armer, J. M. and Marsh, R. (1982) *Comparative sociological research in the 1960s and 1970s*. Leiden, Brill.

Arulampalam, W. (2000) *Is Unemployment Really Scarring?* Mimeo, University of Warwick.

Ashton, D., Maguire, M. and Spilsbury, M. (1990) *Restructuring The Labour Market: The Implications For Youth*. London, Macmillan.

Atkinson, J. (1984) Manpower strategies for flexible organizations, *Personel Management*, 15, 28-31.

Baizán, P. (1998) Transitions vers l'âge adulte des générations espagnoles nées en 1940, 1950 et 1960, Genus, 54, 3-4, 233-263.

Baizán, P. (2001) Transitions to adulthood in Spain, in Corijn, M. and Klijzing, E. (eds), *Transitions to Adulthood in Europe*. Dordrecht/ Boston/ London, Kluwer Academic Publishers, 279-312.

Banco de España (1994) *Informe Anual 1993*. Madrid, Banco de España.

Bardasi, E. and Gornick, J. (2000) Women and part-time employment: Worker's 'Choices' and Wage Penalties in Five Industrialized Countries, *Working Papers of the Institute for Social and Economic Research*, paper 2000-11, Colchester, University of Essex.

Beck, U. (1986) *Risikogesellschaft. Auf dem Weg in eine andere Moderne*. Frankfurt am Main, Suhrkamp, 1. Auflage.

Beck, U. (1999) *Was ist Globalisierung?* Frankfurt am Main, Suhrkamp, 6. Auflage.

Becker, G. (1973) A Theory of Marriage, Part 1, *Journal of Political Economy*, 81, 813-846.

Becker, G. (1981) *A Treatise on the Family*. Cambridge, Havard University Press.

Becker, R. (2001) Reliabilität von Retrospektiven Berufsverlaufsdaten. Ein Vergleich zwischen der Privatwirtschaft und dem öffentlichen Dienst anhand von Paneldaten, *ZUMA-Nachrichten*, 49, 25, 29-56.

Begg, C. and Gray, R. (1984) Calculation of polychotomous logistic regression parameters using individualized regressions, *Biometrika*, 71, 1, 11-18.

Bentolila, S. and Dolado, J. (1994) Labour flexibility and wages: lessons from Spain, *Economic Policy*, 28, 53-100.

Berger, P. and Luckmann, T. (1980) *Die gesellschaftliche Konstruktion der Wirklichkeit. Eine Theorie der Wissenssoziologie*. Frankfurt am Main, Fischer.

Bernardi, F. (2000) Globalisation, Recommodification and Social Inequality: Changing Patterns of early Careers in Italy, *GLOBALIFE Working Paper Series*, No. 7, Bielefeld, University of Bielefeld.

Bernardi, F. and Nazio, T. (2001) Globalisation and the transition to adulthood in Italy, *GLOBALIFE Working Paper Series,* No. 19, Bielefeld, University of Bielefeld.

Berrington, A. (2001) Transition to adulthood in Britain, in Corijn, M. and Klijzing, E. (eds), *Transitions to Adulthood in Europe*. Dordrecht/ Boston/ London, Kluwer Academic Publishers, 67-102.

Berrington, A. and Diamond, I. (2000) Marriage or Cohabitation: A Competing Risks Analysis of First Partnership Formation Among the 1958 British Birth Cohort, *Journal of the Royal Statistical Society,* Series A, 163, 2, 127-151.

Bielby, W. T. and Bielby, D. D. (1989) Family Ties: Balancing Commitments to Work and Family in Dual-Earner Households, *American Sociological Review*, 54, 776-789.

Bielenski, H. (1997) Deregulierung des Rechts befristeter Arbeitsverträge. Enttäuschte Hoffnungen, unbegründete Befürchtungen, *WSI-Mitteilungen*, 8/199, 532-537.

Bilbao, A. (1999) La globalización y las relaciones laborales, *Cuadernos de Relaciones Laborales*, 15, 123-137.

Billari, F. C., Castiglioni, M., Castro Martín, T., Michielin, F. and Ongaro, F. (2002) Household and union formation in a Mediterranean fashion: Italy and Spain, in Klijzing, E. and Corijn, M. (eds) *Dynamics of fertility and partnership in Europe. Insights and lessons from comparative research.* New York/ Geneva, United Nations, 17-41.

Bispinck, R. (1997) Deregulierung, Differenzierung und Dezentralisierung des Flächentarifvertrags. Eine Bestandsaufnahme neuerer Entwicklungstendenzen der Tarifpolitik, *WSI-Mitteilungen*, 8/199, 551-561.

Blossfeld, H.-P. (1985) *Bildungsexpansion und Berufschancen*. Frankfurt am Main, Campus.

Blossfeld, H.-P. (1987) Entry into the Labor Market and Occupational Career in the Federal Republic. A Comparison with American Studies, *International Journal of Sociology*, 17, 1-2, 86-115.

Blossfeld, H.-P. (1988) Bildungsverläufe im historischen Wandel, in Boudenhöfer, H. J. (ed) *Bildung, Beruf, Arbeitsmarkt*. Duncker und Humblot, 259-302.

Blossfeld, H.-P. (ed) (1995) *The New Role of Women. Family Formation in Modern Societies*. Boulder/ San Francisco/ Oxford, Westview Press.

Blossfeld, H.-P. (1996) Macro-sociology, Rational Choice Theory, and Time. A Theoretical Perspective on the Empirical Analysis of Social Processes, *European Sociological Review*, 12, 2, 181-206.

Blossfeld, H.-P. (2002) Globalisation, social inequality and the role of country-specific institutions. Open research questions in a learning society, in Conceicao, P., Heitor, M. and Lundvall, B.-A. (eds) *Innovation, Competence Building and Social Cohesion in Europe: Towards a Learning Society*, Cheltenham/Lyme: Edward Elgar.

Blossfeld, H.-P. and Drobnič, S. (eds) (2001) *Careers of Couples in Contemporary Societies. A Cross-National Comparison of the Transition From Male Breadwinner to Dual-Earner Families*. Oxford, Oxford University Press.

Blossfeld, H.-P. and Hakim, C. (eds) (1997a) *Between Equalization and Marginalization. Women Working Part-Time in Europe and the United States of America*. Oxford, Oxford University Press.

Blossfeld H.-P. and Hakim, C. (1997b) Introduction: A comparative perspective on part-time work, in Blossfeld, H.-P. and Hakim, C. (eds) *Between equalization and marginalization. Part-time working women in Europe and the United States*. Oxford, University Press, 1-21.

Blossfeld, H.-P. and Huinink, J. (1989) Die Verbesserung der Bildungs- und Berufschancen von Frauen und ihr Einfluß auf den Prozeß der Familienbildung, *Zeitschrift für Bevölkerungswissenschaft*, 15, 4, 383-404.

Blossfeld, H.-P. and Huinink, J. (1991) Human capital investments or norms of role transitions? How women's schooling and career affect the process of family formation, *American Journal of Sociology*, 97, 143-168.

Blossfeld, H.-P. and Huinink, J. (2001) Lebensverlaufsforschung als sozialwissenschaftliche Forschungsperspektive. Themen, Konzepte, Methoden und Probleme, *BIOS*, 14, 2, 5-31.

Blossfeld, H.-P. and Jaenichen, U. (1990) Bildungsexpansion und Familienbildung – wie wirkt sich die Höherqualifikation der Frauen auf ihre Neigung zu heiraten und Kinder bekommen aus? *Soziale Welt*, 41, 454-476.

Blossfeld, H.-P., Klijzing, E., Mills, M. and Kurz, K. (eds) (forthcoming) *The losers in a globalizing world: becoming an adult in uncertain times*. London/ New York, Routledge.

Blossfeld, H.-P., Klijzing, E., Pohl, K. and Rohwer, G. (1999) Why do cohabiting couples marry? An example of a causal event history approach to interdependent systems, *Quality and Quantity*, 33, 229-242.

Blossfeld, H.-P. and Müller, R. (1996) Sozialstrukturanalyse, Rational Choice Theorie und die Rolle der Zeit, *Soziale Welt*, 17, 382-410.

Blossfeld, H.-P. and Nuthmann, R. (1988) *Strukturelle Veränderungen der Jugendphase als Kohortenprozeß*, Arbeitspapier Nr. 271. Goethe-Universität Frankfurt und Universität Mannheim, Sonderforschungsbereich 3, Mikroanalytische Grundlagen der Gesellschaftspolitik.

Blossfeld, H.-P. and Prein, G. (1998) The relationship between rational choice theory and large-scale data analysis – Past developments and future perspectives, in Blossfeld, H.-P. and Prein, G. (eds) *Rational choice theory and large-scale data analysis*. Boulder, Westview Press, 3-28.

Blossfeld, H.-P. and Rohwer, G. (1997) Part-time work in West Germany, in Blossfeld, H.-P. and Hakim, C. (eds) *Between equalization and marginalization. Women working part-time in Europe and the United States of Amerika*. Oxford, Oxford University Press, 164-190.

Blossfeld, H.-P. and Rohwer, G. (2001) *Techniques of Event History Modeling. New Approaches to Causal Analysis*. Mahwa, New Jersey, Lawrence Erlbaum Associates.

Blossfeld, H.-P. and Shavit, Y. (1993) Dauerhafte Ungleichheiten. Zur Veränderung des Einflusses der sozialen Herkunft auf die Bildungschancen in dreizehn industrialisierten Ländern, *Zeitschrift für Pädagogik*, 30, 25-52.

Blossfeld, H.-P. and Stockmann, R. (1998/1999) The German Dual System in Comparative Perspective, *International Journal of Sociology*, 28, 4, 3-28.

Blossfeld, H.-P. and Timm, A. (1997) Der Einfluß des Bildungssystems auf den Heiratsmarkt, *Kölner Zeitschrift für Soziologie und Sozialpsychologie*, 49, 440-476.

Böheim, R. and Taylor, M. (2000) Unemployment duration and exit states in Britain, *Working Papers of the Institute for Social and Economic Research*, paper 2000-1, Colchester, University of Essex.

Booth, A. and Francesconi, M. (1999) Job Mobility in 1990s Britain: Does Gender Matter? *Working Papers of the Institute for Social and Economic Research*, paper 1999-26, Colchester, University of Essex.

Booth, A. and Francesconi, M. (2003) Union coverage and non-standard work in Britain. *Oxford Economic Papers*, 55, 383-416.

Booth, A., Francesconi, M. and Garcia-Serrano, C. (1999) Job tenure and job mobility in Britain, *Industrial and Labor Relations Review*, 53, 1, 43-70.

Booth, A., Francesconi, M. and Frank, J. (2002) Temporary Jobs: Stepping Stones Or Dead Ends? *The Economic Journal*, 112, 480, 189-213.

Braun, M. and Müller, W. (1997) Measurement of Education in Comparative Research, *Comparative Social Research*, 16, 163-201.

Brauns, H., Gangl, M. and Scherer, S. (1999) Education and Unemployment: Patterns of Labour Market Entry in France, the United Kingdom and West Germany, *Arbeitspapiere – Mannheimer Zentrum für Europäische Sozialforschung*, 6, Mannheim, Mannheimer Zentrum für Europäische Sozialforschung.

Breen, R. (1997) Risk, recommodification and stratification, *Sociology*, 31, 473-489.

Browning, H. and Singlemann, J. (1978) The Transformation of the U.S. Labor Force: The Interaction of Industry and Occupation, *Politics & Society*, 8, 3-4, 429-480.

Buck, N. and Gershuny, J. (1996) Changing families in changing circumstances. ESRC Research Centre on Micro-Social Change in *MRS Conference Papers*.

Bumpass, L. (1990) What's Happening to the Family? Interactions between Demographic and Institutional Change, *Demography*, 27, 483-498.

Burchell, B., Dale, A. and Joshi, H. (1997) Part-Time Work among British Women, in Blossfeld, H.-P. and Hakim, C. (eds) *Between Equalization and Marginalization.* Oxford, Oxford University Press, 210-246.

Burchell, B., Ladipo, D. and Wilkinson, F. (eds) (2002) *Job Insecurity and Work Intensification.* London/ New York, Routledge.

Burgess, K. (2000) Unemployment and Union Strategies in Spain, in Bermeo, N. (ed), *Unemployment in Southern Europe. Coping with the Consequences.* London, Frank Cass, 1-31.

Bygren, M., Duvander, A.-Z. and Hultin, M. (forthcoming) Elements of uncertainty in life courses: Transitions to adulthood in Sweden, in Blossfeld, H.-P., Klijzing, E., Mills, M. and Kurz, K. (eds) *Globalization, Uncertainty, and Youth in Society.* London/ New York, Routledge.

Caldwell, J. C. (1976) Towards a Restatement of Demographic Transition Theory, *Population and Development Review*, 2, 321-366.

Caldwell, J. C. (1982) *Theory of Fertility Decline.* London, Academic Press.

Carneiro, I. and Knudsen, L. B. (2001) Fertility and Family Surveys in Countries of the ECE Region, Country Report Denmark, Comparable FFS-data, Economic Studies No. 10t, Geneva, United Nations Economic Commission for Europe.

Carrilho, M. J. and Magalhães, G. (2000) Fertility and Family Surveys in Countries of the ECE Region, Standard Country Report Portugal, Economic Studies No. 10p, Geneva, United Nations Economic Commission for Europe.

Castells, M. (1996) *The Rise of the Network Society. The Information Age: Economy, Society and Culture*, Volume I. Oxford, Blackwell Publishers.
Castro Martín, T. (1992) Delayed childbearing in contemporary Spain: trends and differentials, *European Journal of Population*, 8, 217-246.
Cebulla, A. (2001) Flexibilität und soziale Sicherung in Großbritannien unter besonderer Berücksichtigung des "New Deal", in Klammer, U. and Tillmann, K. (eds) *Flexicurity: Soziale Sicherung und Flexibilisierung der Arbeits- und Lebensverhältnisse*, Forschungsprojekt im Auftrag des Ministeriums für Arbeit und Soziales, Qualifikation und Technologie des Landes Nordrhein-Westfalen, Düsseldorf, WSI, 585-636.
Chaudhuri, A. and Stenger, H. (1992) *Survey Sampling. Theory and Methods*. New York/ Basel/ Hong Kong, Marcel Dekker.
Cherlin, A. J., Kiernan, K. E. and Chase-Lansdale, P. L. (1995) Parental Divorce in Childhood and Demographic Outcomes in Young Adulthood, *Demography*, 32, 3, 299-318.
Clark, A. (1997) Job satisfaction and gender: Why are women so happy at work? *Labour Economics*, 4, 341-372.
Clark, A. (1998) Measures of job satisfaction. What makes a good job? Evidence from OECD countries, Labour market and social policy, occasional papers No. 34, France, OECD.
Clark, A., Oswald, A. and Warr, P. (1996) Is job satisfaction U-shaped in age? *Journal of Occupational and Organizational Psychology*, 69, 57-81.
Cleland, J. and Wilson, C. (1987) Demand Theories of the Fertility Transition: An Iconoclastic View, *Population Studies*, 41, 1, 5-30.
Coleman, J. and Husén, T. (1985) *Becoming adult in a changing society*. Paris, OECD.
Corijn, M. and Klijzing, E. (eds) (2001) *Transitions to Adulthood in Europe*. Dordrecht/ Boston/ London, Kluwer Academic Publishers.
Council of Europe (2001) *Recent demographic developments in Europe*. Strasbourg, Council of Europe Publishing.
Cousins, C. (1994) A comparison of the labour market position of women in Spain and the UK with reference to the "flexible" labour debate, *Work, Employment and Society*, 8, 1, 45-67.
Cronbach, L. (1951) Coefficient alpha and the internal structure of test, *Psychometrika*, 16, 297-334.
Davis, K. (1963) The Theory of Change and Response in Modern Demographic History, Population Index, 29 (October), 345-366.
Deacon, A. (2000) Learning from the US? The influence of American ideas upon 'new labour' thinking on welfare reform, *Policy & Politics*, 28, 1, 5-18.
Deakin, S. and Reed, H. (2000) River Crossing or Cold Bath? Deregulation and Employment in Britain in the 1980s and 1990s, in Esping-Anderson, G. (ed) *Why deregulate Labour Markets?* Oxford, Oxford University Press, 115-147.
Dearden, L., Machin, S. and Reed, H. (1997) Intergenerational Mobility in Britain, *Economic Journal*, 107, 47-64.
Delgado, M. (1995) Spain, in Blossfeld, H.-P. (ed) *The New Role of Women. Family Formation in Modern Societies*. Oxford, Westview Press, 191-243.
Delgado, M. and Castro Martín, T. (1998) Fertility and Family Surveys in Countries of the ECE Region, Standard Country Report Spain, Economic Studies No. 10i, Geneva, United Nations Economic Commission for Europe.
De Miguel Castaño, C. (1993) Profesión y Género, in Garrido Medina, L. and Gil Calvo, E. (eds) *Estrategias familiares*. Madrid, Alianza Universidad, 95-112.

Desai, T., Gregg, P., Steer, J. and Wadsworth, J. (1999) Gender and the labour market, in Gregg, P. and Wadsworth, J. (eds) (1999) *The State of Working Britain*. Manchester/ New York, Manchester University Press, 168-184.

De Sandre, P., Ongaro, F., Rettaroli, R. and Salvini, S. (2000) Fertility and Family Surveys in Countries of the ECE Region, Standard Country Report Italy, Economic Studies No. 10o, Geneva, United Nations Economic Commission for Europe.

Dex, S. and McCullogh, A. (1995) Flexible Employment in Britain: A Statistical Analysis, *Research Discussion Series No. 15*, Equal Opportunity Commission.

Dex, S. and McCullogh, A. (1998) The Reliability of Retrospective Unemployment History Data, *Work, Employment and Society*, 12, 3, 497-509.

Dickens, R. (1999) Wage mobility in Great Britain, in Gregg, P. and Wadsworth, J. (eds) *The State of Working Britain*. Manchester/ New York, Manchester University Press, 206-224.

Dickens, R. and Ellwood, D. (2001) Whither Poverty in Great Britain and the United States? The Determinants of Changing Poverty and Whether Work Will Work. *National Bureau of Economic Research Working Paper No. 8253*, April.

Diewald, M., Huinink, J., Solga, H. and Sørensen, A. (1995) Umbrüche und Kontinuitäten – Lebensverläufe und die Veränderungen von Lebensbedingungen seit 1989, in Huinink, J., Mayer, K. U., Diewald, M., Solga, H., Sørensen, A. and Trappe, H. (1995) *Kollektiv und Eigensinn. Lebensverläufe in der DDR und danach*. Berlin, Akademie, 307-348.

Dingeldey, I. (1998) Arbeitsmarktpolitische Reformen unter New Labour, *Aus Politik und Zeitgeschichte*, 11, 32-38.

DiPrete, T., de Graaf, P., Luijkx, R., Tahlin, M. and Blossfeld, H.-P. (1997) Collectivist versus Individualsit Mobility Regimes? Structural Change and Job Mobility in Four Countries, *American Journal of Sociology*, 103, 2, 318-358.

DiPrete, T., Goux, D., Maurin, E. and Tahlin, M. (2001) Institutional determinants of employment chances. The structure of unemployment in France and Sweden, *European Sociological Review*, 17, 3, 233-254.

Dolado, J., García-Serrano, C. and Jimeno, J. (2002) Drawing Lessons From The Boom Of Temporary Jobs In Spain, *The Economic Journal*, 112, 721, 270-295.

Dombois, R. (1999) Der schwierige Abschied vom Normalarbeitsverhältnis, *Aus Politik und Zeitgeschichte*, 37, 13-20.

Doogan, K. (2001) Insecurity and Long-term Employment, *Work, Employment and Society*, 15, 3, 419-441.

Elster, J. (1989) *Solomonic Judgements – studies in the limitations of rationality*. New York, New York University Press.

Erikson, E. H. (1950) *Childhood and Society*. London, Hogarth Press.

Erikson, R. and Goldthorpe, J. (1992) *The Constant Flux. A Study of Class Mobility in Industrial Societies*. Oxford, Clarendon Press.

Erlinghagen, M. and Knuth, M. (2002) Auf der Suche nach dem "Turbo-Arbeitsmarkt". Zwischenbericht an die Deutsche Forschungsgemeinschaft (DFG) zum Projekt "Restrukturierung des Arbeitsmarktes. Disaggregierte Längsschnittanalysen mit der IAB-Beschäftigtenstichprobe", *Graue Reihe des Instituts Arbeit und Technik*, 2002-03.

Ermisch, J. (1999) *Cohabitation and Childbearing Outside Marriage in Britain*, Paper presented at the Institute for Research on Poverty Conference on Non-marital Fertility, University of Wisconsin-Madison, 29-30 April.

Ermisch, J. and Di Salvo, P. (1997) The Economic Determinants of Young People's Household Formation, *Economica*, 64, 627-644.

Ermisch, J. and Francesconi, M. (2000a) Patterns of household and family formation, in Berthoud, R. and Gershuny, J. (eds) *Seven Years in the Lives of British Families. Evidence on the dynamics of social change from the British Household Panel Survey*. Bristol, Policy Press, 21-44.

Ermisch, J. and Francesconi, M. (2000b) Cohabitation in Great Britain: Not for Long, but Here to Stay, *Journal of the Royal Statistical Society*, Series A, 163, 2, 153-171.

Ermisch, J. and Francesconi, M. (2001a) *The Effects of Parents' Employment on Children's Lives*. London, Family Policy Study Centre for the Joseph Rowntree Foundation.

Ermisch, J. and Francesconi, M. (2001b) Family Matters: Impacts of Family Background on Educational Attainments, *Economica*, 68, 137-156.

Esping-Andersen, G. (1993) (ed) *Changing Classes. Stratification and Mobility in Post-industrial Societies*. London/ Newbury Park/ New Dehli, Sage Publications.

Esping-Andersen, G. (1996) *Welfare states in transition. National adaptations in global economies*. London/ Thousands Oaks/ New Delhi, Sage Publications.

Esping-Andersen, G. (1999) *Social foundations of postindustrial economics*. Oxford, Oxford University Press.

Esping-Andersen, G. and Regini, M. (2000) *Why Deregulate Labour Markets?* Oxford, Oxford University Press.

European Commission Eurostat (1996) The European Community Household Panel (ECHP): Survey Methodology and Implementation, Vol. 1, Luxembourg.

Eurostat (1998) Labour Force Survey, Principal Results 1997, Statistics in focus, Theme 3 (Population and Social Conditions).

Eurostat (1999) Labour Force Survey, Principal Results 1998, Statistics in focus, Theme 3 (Population and Social Conditions).

Eurostat (2000) Labour Force Survey, Principal Results 1999, Statistics in focus, Theme 3 (Population and Social Conditions).

Eurostat (2001) Labour Force Survey, Principal Results 2000, Statistics in focus, Theme 3 (Population and Social Conditions).

EURYDICE/CEDEFOP (1995) *Structures of the Education and Initial Training System in the European Union*. Brussels, Eurydice.

Falguera i Baró, M. A. (1999) *La nova regulació de la contractació a temps parcial: vells problemes, noves solucions*. 2n Premi Cirera i Soler, 1999. Barcelona, Quaderns, Unió de Treballadors Democratacristians de Catalunya.

Ferarra, M. (1996) The 'Southern Model' of Welfare in Social Europe, *Journal of European Social Policy*, 6, 1, 17-37.

Francesconi, M. and Golsch, K. (forthcoming) The Process of Globalisation and Transitions to Adulthood in Britain, in Blossfeld, H.-P., Klijzing, E., Mills, M. and Kurz, K. (eds) *Globalization, Uncertainty, and Youth in Society*. London/ New York, Routledge.

Frejka, T. and Calot, G. (2001) Contemporary cohort reproductive patterns in low fertility countries, *Population and Development Review*, 27, 1, 103-132.

Fuchs, S. and Schettkat, R. (2000) Germany: A Regulated Flexibility, in Esping-Anderson, G. (ed) *Why deregulate Labour Markets?* Oxford, Oxford University Press, 211-244.

Gabler, S., Hoffmeyer-Zlotnik, J. and Krebs, D. (1994) (eds) *Gewichtung in der Umfragepraxis*. Opladen, Westdeutscher Verlag.

Gallie, D., White, Y. and Tomlinson, M. (1998) *Restructuring the Employment Relationship*. Oxford, Clarendon Press.

Gangl, M. (2001) European patterns of labour market entry. A dichotomy of occupationalized vs. Non-occupationalized systems? *European Societies*, 3, 4, 471-494.

Gangl, M. (2003) The only way is up? Employment Protection and job mobility among recent entrants to European labour markets, *European Sociological Review*, 19, 5, 429-449.

Ganzeboom, H. and Treiman, D. (1996) Internationally Comparable Measures of Occupational Status for the 1988 International Standard Classification of Occupations, *Social Science Research*, 25, 201-239.

Ganzeboom, H. and Treiman, D. (2003) Three Internationally Standardised Measures for Comparative Research on Occupational Status, in Hoffmeyer-Zhlotnik, J. and Wolf, C. (eds) *Advances in Cross-National Comparison. A European Working Book for Demographic and Socio-economic Variables*. New York, Kluwer Academic/ Plenum Publishers.

Garrido Medina, L. (1992) *Las dos biografías de la mujer en España*. Madrid, Instituto de la Mujer, Ministerio de Trabajo y Asuntos Sociales.

Gauthier, A. H. (1996) *A Comparative Analysis of Family Policies in Industrialized Countries*. Oxford, Clarendon Press.

Gauthier, A. H. (2000) The promises of comparative research, *Working papers of the European Panel Analysis Group*, Paper 16, Colchester, University of Essex.

Geißler, R. (1996) *Die Sozialstruktur Deutschlands. Zur gesellschaftlichen Entwicklung mit einer Zwischenbilanz zur Vereinigung*. Opladen, Westdeutscher Verlag.

Giddens, A. (2000) *Runaway World. How Globalization is Reshaping our Lives*. London, Profile Books.

Giesecke, J. and Groß, M. (2003) Temporary Employment: Chance or Risk? *European Sociological Review*, 19, 2, 161-177.

Goldin, C. and Katz, L. F. (2000) The Power of the Pill: Oral Contraceptives and Women's Career and Marriage Decisions, *National Bureau of Economic Research Working Paper No. 7527*, February.

Goldscheider, F. and Waite, L. J. (1991) *New Families, No Families?* Berkeley, University of California Press.

Goldthorpe, J. (1997) Current issues in comparative methodology: a debate on methodological issues, *Comparative Social Research*, 16.

Goldthorpe, J. (2001a) Globalization and Social Class, Mannheimer Vorträge 9, Mannheim, Universität Mannheim.

Goldthorpe, J. (2001b) Causation, Statistics, and Sociology, *European Sociological Review*, 17, 1, 1-20.

Golsch, K. (2001) Transition to adulthood in Great Britain and the process of globalization, *GLOBALIFE Working Paper Series*, No. 17, Bielefeld, University of Bielefeld.

Golsch, K. (2002) Globalisation, Labour Market Flexibility and Job Insecurity A tale on Britain, *GLOBALIFE Working Paper Series*, No. 36, Bielefeld, University of Bielefeld.

Golsch, K. (2003) Employment flexibility in Spain and its impact on transitions to adulthood, *Work, Employment and Society*, 17, 4, 713-740.

González López, M. (1998) Do Modern Welfare States Foster Democratic Family Arrangements? Comparative Case Studies of Britain and Spain, *Southern European Society and Politics*, 3, 2, 98-123.

González López, M. (2001) *The Interplay between Occupational Career and Family Formation in Spain*. Florence, European University Institute, unpublished thesis.

Goossens, L. (2001) Transition to adulthood: developmental factors, in Corijn, M. and Klijzing, E. (eds) *Transitions to Adulthood in Europe*. Dordrecht/ Boston/ London, Kluwer Academic Publishers, 27-42.

Gornick, J. and M. Meyers (2003) Families that Work. Policies for Reconciling Parenthood and Employment. New York: Russell Sage Foundation.

Granström, F. (1997) Fertility and Family Surveys in Countries of the ECE Region, Standard Country Report Sweden, Economic Studies No. 10b, Geneva, United Nations Economic Commission for Europe.

Greene, W. H. (2003) *Econometric Analysis* (Fourth edition). Upper Saddle River, NJ, Prentice Hall.

Gregg, P. and Wadsworth, J. (1996) More Work in Fewer Households? In Hills, J. (ed) *Income and Wealth: New Inequalities*. Cambridge, Cambridge University Press.

Gregg, P. and Wadsworth, J. (1999a) Job tenure, 1975-98, in Gregg, P. and Wadsworth, J. (eds) *The State of Working Britain*. Manchester, University Press, 109-126.

Gregg, P. and Wadsworth, J. (1999b) Economic Inactivity, in Gregg, P. and Wadsworth, J. (eds) *The State of Working Britain*. Manchester, University Press, 47-57.

Gregg, P. and Wadsworth, J. (2000) Mind the Gap, Please: The Changing Nature of Entry Jobs in Britain, *Economica*, 67, 499-524.

Gregg, P., Hansen, K. and Wadsworth, J. (1999a) The rise of the workless household, in Gregg, P. and Wadsworth, J. (eds) *The State of Working Britain*. Manchester, University Press, 75-89.

Gregg, P., Knight, G. and Wadsworth, J. (1999b) The cost of job loss, in Gregg, P. and Wadsworth, J. (eds) *The State of Working Britain*. Manchester, University Press, 249-258.

Gregg, P., Knight, G. and Wadsworth, J. (2000) Heaven knows I'm miserable now: job insecurity in the British labour market, in Heery, E. and Salmon, J. (eds) *The Insecure Workforce*. London/ New York, Routledge, 39-56.

Grunow, D. and Buchholz, S. (2003) Changing Female Careers? Women's Career Mobility, Unemployment and Transitions to Unpaid Care Giving in West Germany, *GLOBALIFE Working Paper Series*, Faculty of Social Sciences and Economy, Bamberg, Otto-Friedrich-University.

Haisken-DeNew, J. and Frick, J. (2001) *DTC Desktop Companion to the German Socio-Economic Panel Study (GSOEP)*, Version 5.0, Updated to Wave 17 (Q), Berlin, DIW.

Hakim, C. (1991) Grateful slaves and self-made women: fact and fantasy in women's work orientations, *European Sociological Review*, 7, 2, 101-121.

Hakim, C. (1998) *Social Change and Innovation in the Labour Market*. Oxford, Oxford University Press.

Hakim, C. (2000) *Work-lifestyle choices in the 21st century. Preference theory*. Oxford, Oxford University Press.

Hamermesh, D. (2001) The Changing Distribution of Job Satisfaction, *The Journal of Human Resources*, XXXVI, 1, 1-30.

Hanefeld, U. (1987) *Das Sozio-Ökonomische Panel*. Campus, Frankfurt.

Hannan, D., Raffe, D. and Smyth, E. (1997) Cross-National research on school to work transitions: An analytic framework, in Werqzin, P., Breen, R. and Planas, J. (eds) *Youth Transitions in Europe: Theories and Evidence*. Documents Séminaires No. 120, Marseille, CEREQ.

Haskey, J. and Kiernan, K. E. (1989) Cohabitation in Great Britain: Characteristics and Estimated Numbers of Cohabiting Partners, *Population Trends*, 58, 23-32 (Winter).

Heath, A. and Cheung, S. Y. (1998) Education and Occupation in Britain, in Shavit, Y. and Müller, W. (eds) *From School to Work: A Comparative Study of Educational Qualifications and Occupational Destinations*. Oxford, Clarendon Press, 71-101.

Heery, E. and Abbott, B. (2000) Trade unions and the insecure workforce, in Heery, E. and Salmon, J. (eds) *The insecure Workforce*. London/ New York, Routledge, 155-180.

Heery, E. and Salmon, J. (eds) (2000) *The Insecure Workforce*. London/ New York, Routledge.

Heinz, W. (ed) (1999) *From Education to Work: Cross-National Perspectives*. Cambridge, Cambridge University Press.

Held, D., McGrew, A., Goldblatt, D. and Perraton, J. (1999) *Global Transformations. Politics, Economics and Culture*. Oxford, Polity Press.

Helen, R. and O'Connell, P. J. (2001) Getting a Job in Europe: The Transition from Unemployment to Work among Young People in Nine European Countries, *Work, Employment and Society*, 15, 1, 1-24.

Hillmert, S. (2001) *Ausbildungssysteme und Arbeitsmarkt. Lebensverläufe in Großbritannien und Deutschland im Kohortenvergleich*. Wiesbaden, Westdeutscher Verlag.

Hinrichs, K. (1996) Das Normalarbeitsverhältnis und der männliche Familienernährer als Leitbilder der Sozialpolitik. Sicherungsprobleme im sozialen Wandel, *Sozialer Fortschritt*, 4, 102-107.

Hirst, P. and Thompson, G. (1996) *Globalization in Question*. Cambridge, Polity Press.

Hobcraft, J. (2002) Moving Beyond Elaborate Description: Towards Understanding Choices About Parenthood, in Macura, M. and Beets, G. (eds) *Dynamics of fertility and partnership in Europe. Insights and lessons from comparative research*, Volume I. New York/ Geneva, United Nations, 131-143.

Hobcraft, J. and Kiernan, K. (1995) Becoming a parent in Europe, Plenary paper for European Population Conference, EAPS / IUSSP European Population Conference Proceedings, Milan.

Hoem, J. M. (1986) The impact of education on modern family-union initiation, *European Journal of Population*, 2, 113-133.

Hoffmann, E. and Walwei, U. (1998) Normalarbeitsverhältnis: ein Auslaufmodell? Überlegungen zu einem Erklärungsmodell für den Wandel der Beschäftigungsformen, *Mitteilungen aus der Arbeitsmarkt- und Berufsforschung*, 3, 409-425.

Hogan, D. and Astone, N. (1986) The Transition to Adulthood, *Annual Revue of Sociology*, 12, 109-130.

Holdsworth, C. (2000) Leaving Home in Britain and Spain, *European Sociological Review*, 16, 2, 201-222.

Holdsworth, C. and Irazoqui Solda, M. (2002) First Housing Moves in Spain: An Analysis of Leaving Home and First Housing Acquisition, *European Journal of Population*, 18, 1-19.

Holzer, J. and Kowalska, I. (1997) Fertility and Family Surveys in Countries of the ECE Region, Standard Country Report Poland, Economic Studies No. 10d, Geneva, United Nations Economic Commission for Europe.

Hotz, V. J., Klerman, J. A. and Willis, R. J. (1997) The Economics of Fertility in Developed Countries, in Rosenzweig, M. R. and Stark, O. (eds) *Handbook of Population and Family Economics*. Amsterdam/ Lausanne/ New York/ Oxford/ Shannon/ Tokyo, Elsevier Science, 275-347.

Huinink, J. and Wagner, M. (1995) Partnerschaft, Ehe und Familie in der DDR, in Huinink, J., Mayer, K. U., Diewald, M., Solga, H., Sørensen, A. and Trappe, H. (eds) *Kollektiv und Eigensinn. Lebensverläufe in der DDR und danach*. Berlin, Akademie, 145-188.

Huinink, J., Mayer, K. U. and Trappe, H. (1995a) Staatliche Lenkung und individuelle Karrierechancen: Bildungs- und Berufsverläufe, in Huinink, J., Mayer, K. U., Diewald, M., Solga, H., Sørensen, A. and Trappe, H. *Kollektiv und Eigensinn. Lebensverläufe in der DDR und danach*. Berlin, Akademie, 89-144.

Huinink, J., Mayer, K. U., Diewald, M., Solga, H., Sørensen, A. and Trappe, H. (1995b) *Kollektiv und Eigensinn. Lebensverläufe in der DDR und danach*. Berlin, Akademie.

Hullen, G. (2001) Transitions to adulthood in Germany, in Corijn, M. and Klijzing, E. (eds) *Transitions to Adulthood in Europe*. Dordrecht/ Boston/ London, Kluwer Academic Publishers, 153-172.

Hullen, G. (forthcoming) Fertility and Family Surveys in Countries of the ECE Region, Standard Country Report Germany, Economic Studies, Geneva, United Nations Economic Commission for Europe.

Iacovou, M. (2001) Leaving Home in the European Union, *Working Papers of the Institute for Social and Economic Research*, paper 2001-18, Colchester, University of Essex.

Iannelli, C. and Soro-Bonmatí, A. (2001) The Transition from School to Work in Southern Europe: the Cases of Italy and Spain, Working papers of the TSER project, Comparative Analysis of Transitions from Education to Work in Europe, Mannheim, MZES.

ILO (1999) *Key indicators of the labour market: KILM*. Geneva, International Labour Organisation.

ILO (2001-2002) *Key Indicators of the Labour Market*. Geneva, International Labour Organisation.

Irwin, S. (1995) *Right of Passage. Social Change and The Transition From Youth To Adulthood*. London, UCL Press Limited.

Jann, B. and Diekmann, A. (2003) Das Ende der Normalarbeit: Mythos oder Wirklichkeit?, in Allmendinger, J. (ed) *Entstaatlichung und Soziale Sicherheit*, Verhandlungen des 31. Kongresses der Deutschen Gesellschaft für Soziologie in Leipzig 2002. Beiträge aus Arbeitsgruppen, Sektionssitzungen und den Ad-hoc-Gruppen (CD-ROM). Opladen, Leske und Budrich.

Jenkins, S. (2000) Trends in the UK income distribution, in Hauser, R. and Becker I. (eds) *The Personal Distribution of Income in an International Perspective*. Berlin, Springer Verlag.

Jenkins, S. and Rigg, J. (2001) *The Dynamics of Poverty in Britain: Routes In and Out of Poverty*. University of Essex, unpublished paper.

Jimeno, J. F. and Toharia, L. (1994) *Unemployment and labour market flexibility: Spain*. Geneva, International Labour Office.

Jurado Guerrero, T. (1995) Legitimation durch Sozialpolitik? Die spanische Beschäftigungskrise und die Theorie des Wohlfahrtsstaates, *Kölner Zeitschrift für Soziologie und Sozialpsychologie*, 47, 4, 727-752.

Jurado Guerrero, T. (1999) *Why do Spanish young people stay longer at home than the French? The role of employment, housing and social policies*. Florence, European University Institute, unpublished thesis.

Kaiser, L. (2002) Job Satisfaction: A Comparison of Standard, Non-Standard, and Self-Employment Patterns across Europe with a Special Note to the Gender/Job Satisfaction Paradox, *Working papers of the European Panel Analysis Group*, Paper 27, Colchester, University of Essex.

Kalton, G. (1983) *Introduction to Survey Sampling*. Beverly Hills/ London/ New Delhi, Sage Publications.

Katus, K., Puur, A. and Sakkeus, L. (2000) Fertility and Family Surveys in Countries of the ECE Region, Standard Country Report Estonia, Economic Studies No. 10n, Geneva, United Nations Economic Commission for Europe.

Katz, H. (1993) The decentralisation of collective bargaining, *Industrial and Labor Relations Review*, 47, 1, 3-22.

Kerckhoff, A. (1990) *Getting started. Transition to adulthood in Great Britain*. Boulder, Co/ Oxford, Westview Press.

Kerckhoff, A. (2000) Transition from school to work in international perspective, in Hallinan, M. (ed) *Handbook of the Sociology of Education*. New York, Kluwer.

Kiernan, K. (1992) The Impact of Family Disruption in Childhood on Transitions Made in Young Adult Life, *Population Studies*, 46, 213-234.

Kiernan, K. (1997) Becoming a young parent: a longitudinal study of associated factors, *British Journal of Sociology*, 48, 3, 406-428.

Kiernan, K. (1999) Cohabitation in Western Europe, *Population Trends*, 96, 25-32.

Kiernan, K. (2001) The rise of cohabitation and childbearing outside marriage in Western Europe, *International Journal of law, policy and the family*, 15, 1-21.

Kiernan, K. (2002) The state of the European Union: An analysis of FFS data on partnership formation and dissolution, in Macura, M. and Beets, G. (eds) *The dynamics of fertility and partnership in Europe: insights and lessons from comparative research*, Volume I. Geneva/ New York, United Nations, 57-76.

Kiernan, K. and Diamond, I. (1983) The age at which childbearing starts – a longitudinal study, *Populations Studies*, 58, 23-31.

Kiernan, K. and Eldridge, S. (1987) Age at marriage: Inter and intra cohort variation, *British Journal of Sociology*, 37, 363-380.

Kiernan, K. and Hobcraft, J. (1997) Parental Divorce during Childhood: Age at First Intercourse, Partnership and Parenthood, *Population Studies*, 51, 41-55.

Kish, L. (1965) *Survey Sampling*. New York/ London/ Sydney, John Wiley & Sons.

Klammer, U. and Tillmann, K. (2001) *Flexicurity: Soziale Sicherung und Flexibilisierung der Arbeits- und Lebensverhältnisse*. Forschungsprojekt im Auftrag des Ministeriums für Arbeit und Soziales, Qualifikation und Technologie des Landes Nordrhein-Westfalen. Düsseldorf, WSI.

Klijzing, E. (forthcoming) Globalization and the early life course: A description of selected economic and demographic trends, in Blossfeld, H.-P., Klijzing, E., Mills, M. and Kurz, K. (eds) *Globalization, Uncertainty, and Youth in Society*. London/ New York, Routledge.

Kohler, H.-P. (1997) Learning in Social Networks and Contraceptive Use, *Demography*, 34, 3, 369-383.

Kohler, U. and Kreuter, F. (2001) *Datenanalyse mit Stata: allgemeine Konzepte der Datenanalyse und ihre praktische Anwendung*. München, Oldenbourg.

Kohli, M. (1985) Die Institutionalisierung des Lebenslaufs. Historische Befunde und theoretische Argumente, *Kölner Zeitschrift für Soziologie und Sozialpsychologie*, 37, 1-29.

Kohn, M. (1989) Cross-National Research as an Analytic Strategy, in Kohn, M. (ed) *Cross-national research in sociology*. American Sociological Assocation Presidential Series, Newbury Park/ London/ New Delhi, Sage Publications, 77-102.

Korpi, T. and Levin, H. (2001) Precarious Footing: Temporary Employment as a Stepping Stone out of Unemployment in Sweden, *Work, Employment and Society*, 15, 1, 127-148.

Kowalska, I. and Wróblewska, W. (2001) Transition to adulthood in Poland, in Corijn, M. and Klijzing, E. (eds) *Transitions to Adulthood in Europe*. Dordrecht/ Boston/ London, Kluwer Academic Publishers, 257-277.

Kuijsten, A. (1996) Changing family patterns in Europe: a case of divergence? *European Journal of Population*, 12, 2, 115-143.

Kurz, K. (1998) *Das Erwerbsverhalten von Frauen in der intensiven Familienphase. Ein Vergleich zwischen Müttern in der Bundesrepublik Deutschland und in den USA*. Opladen, Leske und Budrich.

Kurz, K. and Steinhage, N. (2001). Global competition and labor market restructuring: The transition into the labor market in Germany, *GLOBALIFE Working Paper Series*, No. 15, Bielefeld, University of Bielefeld.

Kurz, K., Hillmert, S. and Grunow, D. (2002) Increasing instability in employment careers? Men's job mobility and unemployment in West Germany: A comparison of the birth cohorts 1940, 1955 and 1964, *GLOBALIFE Working Paper Series,* No. 34, Bielefeld, University of Bielefeld.

Kurz, K., Steinhage, N. and Golsch, K. (forthcoming) Case Study Germany: Global Competition, Uncertainty and the Transition to Adulthood, in Blossfeld, H.-P., Klijzing, E., Mills, M. and Kurz, K. (eds) *Globalization, Uncertainty, and Youth in Society*. London/ New York, Routledge.

Ladipo, D. and Wilkinson, F. (2002) More pressure, less protection, in Burchell, B., Ladipo, D. and Wilkinson, F. (eds) *Job Insecurity and Work Intensification*. London/ New York, Routledge, 8-38.

Landman, T. (2000) *Issues and Methods in Comparative Politics. An Introduction.* London/ New York, Routledge.

Latten, J. and de Graaf, A. (1997) Fertility and Family Surveys in Countries of the ECE Region, Standard Country Report The Netherlands, Economic Studies No. 10c, Geneva, United Nations Economic Commission for Europe.

Leisink, P. (1999) *Globalization and Labour Relations*. Cheltenham/ Northampton, Edward Elgar.

Lesthaeghe, R. (1983) A Century of Demographic and Cultural Change in Western Europe: An Exploration of Underlying Dimensions, *Population and Development Review*, 9, 411-435.

Lesthaeghe, R. and Surkyn, J. (1988) Cultural dynamics and economic theories of fertility change, *Population and Development Review*, 14, 1, 1-45.

Lewis, J. and Kiernan, K. (1996) The boundaries between marriage, nonmarriage and parenthood: Changes in behaviour and policy in postwar Britain, *Journal of Family History*, 21, 372-387.

Liefbroer, A. (1991) The choice between a married or unmarried first union by young adults: A competing risks analysis, *European Journal of Population*, 7, 273-298.

Liefbroer, A. (1999) From Youth to Adulthood: Understanding Changing Patterns of Family Formation from a Life Course Perspective, in van Wissen, L. and Dykstra, P. (eds) *Population Issues. An Interdisciplinary Focus*. New York/ Boston/ Dordrecht/ London/ Moscow, Kluwer Academic/ Plenum Publishers, 53-86.

Liefbroer, A. (2000) Changes in Adult Role Attitudes during Young Adulthood: The Impact of Age and Role Changes, paper prepared for the conference 'Value Orientations and Life Course Decisions', Brussels.

Liefbroer, A. and Corijn, M. (1999) Who, what, where, and when? Specifying the impact of educational attainment and labour force participation on family formation, *European Journal of Population*, 15, 45-75.

Liefbroer, A. and de Jong Gierveld, J. (1995) Standardization and individualization: The transition from youth to adulthood among cohorts born between 1903 and 1965, in Van Den Brekel, J. C. and Deven, F. (eds) *Population and Family in the Low Countries 1994*. Dordrecht, Kluwer Academic Publishers.

Likert, R. (1932) A technique for the measurement of attitudes, *Archives of Psychology*, 140, 5-55.

Lindbeck, A. and Snower, D. (1987) Efficiency wages versus insiders and outsiders, *European Economic Review*, 31, 407-416.

Lindbeck, A. and Snower, D. (1989) *The Insider-Outsider Theory of Employment and Unemployment.* Cambridge, MIT Press.

Lindley, R. M. (1996) The School-to-Work Transition in the United Kingdom, *International Labour Review*, 135, 2, 159-180.
Lipsmeier, G. (1999) Standard oder Fehler? Einige Eigenschaften von Schätzverfahren bei komplexen Stichprobenplänen und aktuelle Lösungsansätze, *ZA-Information*, 44, 96-117.
Locke, E. (1976) The Nature and Causes of Job Satisfaction, in Dunnette, M. (ed) *Handbook of industrial and organizational psychology*. Chicago, Rand McNally College Publishing Company, 1297-1349.
Lodewijckx, E. (1999) Fertility and Family Surveys in Countries of the ECE Region, Standard Country Report Belgium, Economic Studies No. 101, Geneva, United Nations Economic Commission for Europe.
Long, S. J. (1999) *Regression Models for Categorical and Limited Dependent Variables. Advanced Quantitative Techniques in the Social Sciences*. Thousand Oaks, Sage Publications.
MacDonald, M. M. and Rindfuss, R. R. (1981) Earnings, relative income, and family formation, *Demography*, 18, 123-136.
Machin, S. (1999) Wage Inequality in the 1970s, 1980s and 1990s, in Gregg, P. and Wadsworth, J. (eds) *The State of Working Britain*. Manchester, Manchester University Press, 185-205.
Machin, S. (2000) Union Decline in Britain, *British Journal of Industrial Relations*, 38, 4, 631-645.
Malthus, T. (1890) *An essay of the principle of population or a view of its past and present effects on human happiness: with an inquiry into our prospects respecting the future removal or mitigation of the evils which its occasions*. London, Ward, Lock & Co.
Manting, D. (1994) *Dynamics in marriage and cohabitation. An inter-temporal, life course analysis of first union formation and dissolution*. Amsterdam, Thesis Publisers.
Manting, D. (1996) The changing meaning of cohabitation and marriage, *European Sociological Review*, 12, 1, 53-65.
Marini, M. (1985) Determinants of the Timing of Adult Role Entry, *Social Science Research*, 14, 309-350.
Marsden, D. (1995) Deregulation or cooperation? The future of Europe's labour markets, *Labour*, IIRA, 67-91.
Mayer, K.-U. (1986) Structural Constraints on the life course, *Human Development*, 29, 163-170.
Mayer, K.-U. (1987) Lebenslaufforschung, in Voges, W. (ed) *Methoden der Biographie- und Lebenslaufforschung*. Opladen, Leske und Budrich, 51-73.
Mayer, K.-U. (1997) Notes on the comparative political economy of life courses, *Comparative Social Research*, 16, 203-226.
Mayer, K.-U. and Schoepflin, U. (1989) The state and the life course, *Annual Review of Sociology*, 15, 187-209.
McGinnity, F. (2002) The Labour-force Participation of the Wives of Unemployed Men. Comparing Britain and West Germany Using Longitudinal Data, *European Sociological Review*, 18, 4, 473-488.
McLanahan, S. and Bumpass, L. (1988) Intergenerational consequences of family disruption, *American Journal of Sociology*, 94, 130-152.
McVicar, D. and Rice, P. (2001) Participation in further education in England and Wales: an analysis of post-war trends, *Oxford Economic Papers*, 53, 1, 67-93.
Meyers, M., Gornick, J. and Ross, K. (1999) Public childcare, parental leave, and employment, in Sainsbury, D. (ed) *Gender and Welfare State Regimes*. Oxford, Oxford University Press, 117-146.

Middendorff, E. (2000) Panta rhei oder der mentale Fluss von Tatsachen: Zur Reliabilität retrospektiv erhobener biographisher Ereignisse, *ZA-Information*, 46, 58-71.

Mika, T. (2002) Wer nimmt teil an Panel-Befragungen? Untersuchung über die Bedingungen der erfolgreichen Kontaktierung für Sozialwissenschaftliche Untersuchungen, *ZUMA-Nachrichten*, 51, 26, 38-48.

Mills, M. (2000) *The Transformation of Partnerships. Canada, the Netherlands, and the Russsian Federation in the Age of Modernity*. Amsterdam, Thela Thesis Population Studies.

Mills, M. and Blossfeld, H.-P. (forthcoming) Globalization, Uncertainty and the Early Life Course. A Theoretical framework, in Blossfeld, H.-P., Klijzing, E., Mills, M. and Kurz, K. (eds) *Globalization, Uncertainty, and Youth in Society*. London/ New York, Routledge.

Miret-Gamundi, P. (1997) Nuptiality patterns in Spain in the Eighties, *Genus*, 43, 3-4, 183-198.

Moran, M. P. (1991) Las Mujeres y el Empleo en España 1987-90, *Revista de Economia y Sociologia del Trabajo*, 13-14, 88-103.

Morgan, P., Allington, N. and Heery, E. (2000) Employment insecurity in the public services, in Heery, E. and Salmon, J. (eds) *The insecure Workforce*. London/ New York, Routledge, 78-111.

Muffels, R. and Fourage, D. (2000) Insecurity, Labour Market Exclusion and Income Poverty. Evidence from Wave 1 and Wave 2 of the ECHP, *Working papers of the European Panel Analysis Group*, Paper 13, Colchester, University of Essex.

Müller, W., Lüttinger, P., König, W. and Karle, W. (1989) Class and Education in Industrial Nations, *International Journal of Sociology*, 19, 3-39.

Müller, W., Steinmann, S. and Ell, R. (1998) Education and Labour-Market Entry in Germany, in Shavit, Y. and Müller W. (eds) *From School to Work. A Comparative Study of Educational Qualifications and Occupational Destinations*. Oxford, Clarendon Press, 143-188.

Namboodiri, K. and Wie, L. (1998) Fertility theories and their implications regarding how low can low fertility be, *GENUS*, LIV, 1-2, 37-55.

Nazio, T. and Blossfeld, H.-P. (2003) The Diffusion of Cohabitation Among Young Women in West Germany, East Germany and Italy, *European Journal of Population*, 19, 1, 47-82.

Nickell, S. (1999) Unemployment in Britain, in Gregg, P. and Wadsworth, J. (eds) *The State of Working Britain*. Manchester, University Press, 7-28.

Nickell, S., Jones, P. and Quintini, G. (2002) A Picture of job insecurity facing British men, *The Economic Journal*, 112 (January), 1-27.

Nikander, T. (1998) Fertility and Family Surveys in Countries of the ECE Region, Standard Country Report Finland, Economic Studies No. 10g, Geneva, United Nations Economic Commission for Europe.

Noack, T. and Østby, L. (1996) Fertility and Family Surveys in Countries of the ECE Region, Standard Country Report Norway, Economic Studies No. 10a, Geneva, United Nations Economic Commission for Europe.

Notestein, F. (1953) Economic Problems of Population Change, Proceedings of the Eight International Conference of Agricultural Economics. London, Oxford University Press, 13-31.

Nowak, S. (1976) *Understanding and Prediction. Essays in the Methodology of Social and Behavioral Theories*. Dordrecht/ Boston, Reidel Publishing Company.

Nowak, S. (1989) Comparative Studies and Social Theory, in Kohn, M. (ed) *Cross-national research in sociology*. American Sociological Assocation Presidential Series, Newbury Park/ London/ New Delhi, Sage Publications, 34-56.

OECD (1996a) *Employment Outlook*. Paris, OECD

OECD (1996b) *Education at a Glance – Analysis*. Paris, OECD.

OECD (1998) *Employment outlook*. Paris, OECD.

OECD (1999a) Thematic Review of the Transition from Initial Education to working Life: Interim Comparative Report. DEELSA/ED(98)11, Paris.

OECD (1999b) *Classifying Educational Programmes. Manual for ISCED-97 Implementation in OCED countries*. Paris, OECD.

OECD (2000a) From Initial Education to Working Life: Making Transitions Work. Paris, OECD.

OECD (2000b) *Employment outlook*. Paris, OECD.

OECD (2001) *Employment outlook*. Paris, OECD.

Offe, C. (1977) *Opfer des Arbeitsmarktes. Zur Theorie der strukturierten Arbeitslosigkeit*. Neuwied und Darmstadt, Luchterhand.

Oppenheim Mason, K. (1997) Explaining Fertility Transitions, *Demography*, 34, 4, 443-454.

Oppenheimer, V. (1988) A theory of marriage timing, *American Journal of Sociology*, 94, 3, 563-591.

Oppenheimer, V. (1994) Women's rising employment and the future of the family in industrial societies, *Population and Development Review*, 20, 293-342.

Oppenheimer, V. and Lew, V. (1995) American Marriage Formation in the 1980s: How important was women's Economic Independence? In Oppenheim Mason, K. and Jensen, A.-M. (eds) Gender and Family in Change in Industrialized Countries, 105-138.

Oppenheimer, V., Kalmijn, M. and Lim, N. (1997) Men's career development and marriage timing during a period of rising inequality, *Demography*, 34, 3, 311-330.

Orloff, A. (1993) Gender and the social rights of citizenship: the comparative analysis of gender relations and welfare states, *American Sociological Review*, 58, 303-328.

Orloff, A. (1996) Gender in the welfare state, *Annual Review of Sociology*, 22, 51-78.

Ostrom, C. (1978) *Time Series Analysis. Regression Techniques*. Second Edition. Newbury Park/ London/ New Dehli, SAGE Publications.

Pannenberg, M. (2000) Documentation of Sample Sizes and Panel Attrition in the German Socio Economic Panel (GSOEP) (1984 until 1998), *DIW Discussion Papers*, 196, Berlin, Deutsches Institut für Wirtschaftsforschung.

Parsons, T. (1949) The social structure of the family, in Anshen, R. (ed) *The Family: Its Function and Destiny*. New York, Harper and Brothers, 173-201.

Pfau-Effinger, B. (1996) Analyse internationaler Differenzen in der Erwerbsbeteiligung von Frauen. Theoretischer Rahmen und empirische Ergebnisse, *Kölner Zeitschrift für Soziologie und Sozialpsychologie*, 48, 3, 462-492.

Pohl, K. (1995) Kinderwunsch und Familienplanung in Ost- und Westdeutschland, *Zeitschrift für Bevölkerungswissenschaft*, 20, 67-100.

Pötter, U. and Blossfeld, H.-P. (2001) Causal Inference from Series of Events, *European Sociological Review*, 17, 1, 21-32.

Preston, S. (1986) Changing values and falling birth rates, in Davies, K., Bernstam, M. and Ricardo-Campbell, R. (eds) *Below Replacement Level Fertility in Developed Countries: Causes, consequences and policies: Supplement to Population and Development Review*, 12, 176-195.

Prieto, C. (1999) Globalización económica, relación de empleo y cohesión social, *Papers*, 58, 13-37.

Raffe, D. (1987) Youth unemployment in the United Kingdom 1979-1984, in Brown, P. and Ashton, D. (eds) *Education, unemployment and labour markets*. London, Falmer Press, 218-247.

Raffe, D., van der Velden, R. and Werquin, P. (eds) (1998) *Education, the labour market and transitions in youth: Cross-national perspectives*, proceedings of the 1998 European Workshop, Edingburgh, Centre for Educational Sociology.
Ragin, C. (1987) *The Comparative Method.* Berkely, University of California Press.
Ragin, C. (1989) New Directions in Comparative Research, in Kohn, M. (ed) *Cross-national research in sociology.* American Sociological Assocation Presidential Series, Newbury Park/ London/ New Delhi, Sage Publications, 57-76.
Recio, A. (1994) Flexibilidad laboral y desempleo en España (reflexiones al filo de la reforma laboral), *Cuadernos de Relaciones Laborales*, 5, 57-74.
Regini, M. (1997) Different Responses to Common Demands: Firms, Institutions, and Training in Europe, *European Sociological Review*, 13, 267-282.
Regini, M. (2000a) The dilemmas of labour market regulation, in Esping-Andersen, G. and Regini, M. (eds) *Why deregulate markets?* Oxford, Oxford University Press, 11-29.
Regini, M. (2000b) Between deregulation and social pacts: the responses of European economies to globalization, *Politics and Society*, 28, 1, 5-33.
Reher, D. (1998) Family Ties in Western Europe: Persistent Contrasts, *Population and Development Review*, 24, 2, 203-234.
Rindfuss, R. R. (1991) The Young Adult Years: Diversity, Structural Change, and Fertility, *Demography*, 28, 4, 493-512.
Róbert, P. and Bukodi, E. (forthcoming) The Effects of the Globalization Process on Transitions to Adulthood in Hungary, in Blossfeld, H.-P., Klijzing, E., Mills, M. and Kurz, K. (eds) *Globalization, Uncertainty, and Youth in Society.* London/ New York, Routledge.
Rogers, E. (1983) *Diffusion of innovations.* New York/ London, The Free Press.
Rosenbaum, J., Kariy, T., Settersten, R. and Maier, T. (1990) Market and network theories of the transition from high school to work: their application to industrialized societies, *Annual Review of Sociology*, 16, 263-299.
Russell, H. and O'Connell, P. (2001) Getting a Job in Europe: The Transition from Unemployment to Work among Young People in Nine European Countries, *Work, Employment & Society,* 15, 1, 1–24.
Ryan, P. and Büchtemann, C. (1997) The school-to-work transition, in Schmid, G., O'Reilly, J. and Schömann, K. (eds) *International handbook of labour market policy and evaluation.* Cheltenham, Elgar, 308-447.
Sackmann, R. (2000) Transformation, Arbeitsmarkt und Lebenslauf, in Sackmann, R., Weymann, A. and Wingens, A. (eds) *Die Generation der Wende. Berufs- und Lebensläufe im sozialen Wandel.* Wiesbaden, Westdeutscher Verlag, 41-56.
Sackmann, R. (2001) Age and Labour-Market Chances in International Comparison, *European Sociological Review*, 17, 4, 373-387.
Sainsbury, D. (1999) *Gender and Welfare State Regimes*. Oxford, Oxford University Press.
Scherer, S. (2001) Early Career Patterns: A Comparison of Great Britain and West Germany, *European Sociological Review*, 17, 2, 119-144.
Schettkat, R. (1995) The marcorperformance of the German Labor Market. A comparision with the U.S. Labor market, in Buttler, F., Franz, W., Schettkat, R. and Soskice, D. (eds) *Institutional Frameworks and Labor Market Performance. Comparative views on the U.S. and German economies.* London/ New York, Routledge, 316-342.
Schömann, K., Blossfeld, H.-P. and Hannan, M. (1995) The segmentation of transitions from school to work in postwar Germany: a dynamic perspective, *Comparative Social Research*, 15, 103-127.

Schömann, K., Rogowski, R. and Kruppe, T. (1998) *Labour Market Efficiency in the European Union. Employment Protection and Fixed-Term Contracts*. London/ New York, Routledge.

Schräpler, J.-P. (2000) Was kann man am Beispiel des SOEP bezüglich Nonresponse lernen? *ZUMA-Nachrichten*, 46, 24, 117-149.

Shackleton, J. R. (1995) *Training for Employment in Western Europe and the United States*. Aldershot/ Brookfield, Edward Elgar.

Shavit, Y. and Müller, W. (eds) (1998) *From School to Work. A Comparative Study of Educational Qualifications and Occupational Destinations*. Oxford, Clarendon Press.

Simó, C., Solsona, M., Houle, R. and Treviño, R. (1999) First Unions Disruption in Spain: Socio-Demographic Determinants, European Population Conference, The Hague, 30 August – 3 September, 1999.

Simó Noguera, C., Castro Martín, T. and Soro Bonmatí, A. (2001) Changing Pathways in the Transition to Adulthood in Spain: Labor Market, Marriage and Fertility Patterns of young People in the last Decades, *GLOBALIFE Working Paper Series,* No. 18, Bielefeld, University of Bielefeld.

Simó Noguera, C., Golsch, K. and Bonmatí, A. (2002a) Globalization and occupational mobility in adult male job careers in Spain, *GLOBALIFE Working Paper Series,* No. 35, Bielefeld, University of Bielefeld.

Simó Noguera, C., Golsch, K. and Steinhage, N. (2002b) Increasing uncertainty in the Spanish labor market and entry into parenthood, *GENUS*, LVIII, 77-119.

Simó Noguera, C., Castro Martín, T. and Soro Bonmatí, A. (forthcoming) The Effects of the Globalization Process on the Transition to Adulthood. The Spanish Case, in Blossfeld, H.-P., Klijzing, E., Mills, M. and Kurz, K. (eds) *Globalization, Uncertainty, and Youth in Society*. London/ New York, Routledge.

Smelser, N. (1976) *Comparative methods in the social sciences*. Englewood Cliffs, New Jersey, Prentice-Hall.

SOEP Group (2001) The German Socio-Economic Panel (SOEP) after more than 15 years – Overview, in Holst, E., Lillard, D. R. and DiPrete, T. A. (eds) Proceedings Of The 2000 Fourth International Conference of German Socio-Economic Panel Study Users (GSOEP2000), Vierteljahrshefte zur Wirtschaftsforschung, 70, 1, 7-14.

Solsona, M., Houle, R. and Simó, C. (2000) Separation and Divorce in Spain, in González, M., Jurado, T. and Naldini, M. (eds) *Gender Inequalities in Southern Europe. Women, Work and Welfare in the 1990s*. London/ Portland, Frank Cass, 195-222.

Sommer, T., Klijzing, E. and Mills, M. (2000) Partnership formation in a globalising world: the impact of uncertainty in East and West Germany, *GLOBALIFE Working Paper Series,* No. 9, Bielefeld, University of Bielefeld.

Sørensen, A. (1983) Processes of Allocation to Open and Closed Positions in Social Structure, *Zeitschrift für Soziologie*, 12, 3, 203-224.

Sørensen, A. and Kalleberg, A. (1981) An Outline of a Theory of the Matching of Persons to Jobs, in Berg, I. (ed) *Sociological Perspectives on Labor Markets*. New York, Academic Press, 49-74.

Sørensen, A. and Trappe, H. (1995) Frauen und Männer: Gleichberechtigung – Gleichstellung – Gleichheit? in Huinink, J., Mayer, K. U., Diewald, M., Solga, H., Sørensen, A. and Trappe, H. (eds) *Kollektiv und Eigensinn. Lebensverläufe in der DDR und danach.* Berlin, Akademie, 189-222.

Sørensen, A. and Tuma, N. (1981) Labor market structures and job mobility, *Research in Social Stratification and Mobility*, 1, 67-94.

Soskice, D. (1990) Reinterpreting Corporatism and Explaining Unemployment: Co-ordinated and Non-co-ordinated Market Economies, in Brunetta, R. and DellÀringa, C. (eds) *Labour Relations and Economic Performance*. Basingstoke, Hampshire, Macmillan Press, 170-214.

Soskice, D. (1991) The institutional infrastructure for international competitiveness: a comparative analysis of the UK and Germany, in Atkinson, A. B. and Brunetta, R. (eds) *The economics of the New Europe*. London, MacMillan, 45-66.

Soskice, D. (1999) Divergent production regimes: Coordinated and uncoordinated market economies in the 1980s and 1990s, in Kitschelt, H., Lange, P., Marks, G. and Stephens, J. (eds), *Continuity and Change in Contemporary Capitalism*. Cambridge, Cambridge University Press, 101-134.

Soskice, D. and Schettkat, R. (1993) West German Labor Market Institutions and East German Transformation, in Ulman, L., Eichengreen, B. and Dickens, W. (eds.), *Labor and an Integrated Europe*. Washington, The Brookings Institution, 102-127.

Sousa-Poza, A. and Sousa-Poza, A. (2000) Well-being at work: a cross-national analysis of the levels and determinants of job satisfaction, *Journal of Socio-Economics*, 29, 517-538.

Standing, G. (1997) Globalization, Labour Flexibility and Insecurity: The Era of Market Regulation, *European Journal of Industrial Relations*, 1, 7-37.

Steinmann, S. (1998/1999) The vocational Education and Training System in England and Wales, *International Journal of Sociology*, 28, 4, 29-56.

Stewart, M. (1999) Low pay in Britain, in Gregg, P. and Wadsworth, J. (eds) *The State of Working Britain.* Manchester and New York, Manchester University Press, 225-248.

Stichweh, R. (2000) *Die Weltgesellschaft*. Frankfurt am Main, Suhrkamp.

Stichweh, R. (2001) *On the Genesis of World Society: Innovations and Mechanisms*. Institut für Weltgesellschaft, Bielefeld, University of Bielefeld.

Stier, H., N. Lewin-Epstein and M. Braun (2001) Welfare Regimes, Family-Supportive Policies, and Women's EMployment along the Life-Course, AJS 106, 6: 1731-60.

Strang, D. (1991) Adding Social Structure to Diffusion Models. An Event History Framework, *Sociological Methods and Research*, 19, 3, 324-353.

Streeck, W. (1992) *Social institutions and economic performance. Studies in industrial relations in advanced capitalist economies*. London, Sage.

Strohmeier, K. P. and Kuijsten, A. (1997) Family life and family policies in Europe: an introduction, in Kaufmann, F.-X., Kuijsten, A., Schulze, H. J. and Strohmeier, K. P. (eds) *Family life and family policies in Europe*. Oxford, Clarendon Press, 1-11.

Strünck, C. (2003) *Mit Sicherheit flexibel? Chancen und Risiken neuer Beschäftigungsverhältnisse*. Bonn, Dietz.

Symeonidou, H. (2002), Fertility and Family Surveys in Countries of the ECE Region, Standard Country Report Greece, Economic Studies No. 10w, Geneva, United Nations Economic Commission for Europe.

Tamames, R. (1995) *La Economía Española, 1975-1995*. Madrid, Ediciones Temas de Hoy, S.A.

Taylor, M. (2000) Work, non-work, jobs and job mobility, in Berthoud, R. and Gershuny, J. (eds) *Seven Years in the Lives of British Families. Evidence on the dynamics of social change from the British Household Panel Survey*. Bristol, Policy Press, 73-106.

Taylor, M. (ed) with Brice, J., Buck, N. and Prentice-Lane, E. (1999) *British Household Panel Survey User Manual Volume A: Introduction, Technical Report and Appendices*. Colchester, University of Essex.

Thomson, E. (1997) Couple Childbearing Desires, Intentions, and Births, *Demography*, 34, 3, 343-354.

Thompson, W. S. (1930) *Population Problems.* New York, McGraw-Hill.
Thornton, A. (1991) Influence of the marital history of parents on the marital and cohabitational experiences of children, *American Journal of Sociology*, 96, 868-894.
Thornton, A., Axinn, W. G. and Hill, D. H. (1992) Reciprocal Effects of Religiousity, Cohabitation and Marriage, *American Journal of Sociology*, 98, 628-651.
Tölke, A. and Diewald, M. (2002) Berufsbiographische Unsicherheiten und der Übergang zur Elternschaft bei Männern. MPIDR working paper, 2002-011, Rostock, Max-Planck-Institut für demografische Forschung.
Toharia, L. and Malo, M. (2000) The Spanish Experiment: Pros and Cons of the Flexibility at the Margin, in Esping-Andersen, G. and Regini, M. (eds) *Why Deregulate Labour Markets?* Oxford, Oxford University Press, 307-335.
Toulemon, L. and de Guibert-Lantoine, C. (1998) Fertility and Family Surveys in Countries of the ECE Region, Standard Country Report France, Economic Studies No. 10e, Geneva, United Nations Economic Commission for Europe.
Towers, B. (1994) Unemployment and Labour Market Policies and Programmes in Britain: Experience and Evaluation, *The Journal of Industrial Relations*, 370-393.
UNESCO (1975) *International Standard Classification of Education.* Abridged edition. Paris, Unesco.
UNESCO (1997) *International Standard Classification of Education. ISCED 1997.* Paris, Unesco.
Van de Kaa, D. J. (1987) Europe's second demographic transition, *Population Bulletin*, 42, 1, 1-57.
Van de Kaa, D. J. (1994) The Second Demographic Transition Revisited: Theories and Expectations, in Beets, G. C. N., Van Den Brekel, J. C., Cliquet, R., Dhooghe, G. and De Jong Gierveld, J. (eds) *Population and Family in the Low Countries 1993: Late Fertility and other current issues.* Lisse, Swets and Zeitlinger.
Van Peer, C. (2002) Desired and achieved fertility, in Klijzing, E. and Corijn, M. (eds) *Dynamics of fertility and partnership in Europe. Insights and lessons from comparative research*, Volume II. New York/ Geneva, United Nations, 117-142.
Vermunt, J. (1997) *Log linear models for event histories.* Thousand Oaks, Sage Publications.
Weiss, Y. (1997) The formation and dissolution of families: why marry? Who marries whom? And what happens upon divorce, in Rosenzweig, M. R. and Stark, O. (eds) *Handbook of Population and Family Economics*, Volume 1A. Amsterdam/ Lausanne/ New York/ Oxford/ Shannon/ Tokyo, Elsevier Science, 81-123.
White, H. (1980) A heteroskedasticity-consistent covariance matrix estimator and a direct test for heteroskedasticity, *Econometrica*, 48, 4, 817-830.
White, H. (1982) Maximum Likelihood estimation of misspecified models, *Econometrica*, 50, 1, 1-25.
Willekens, F. (1999) The Life Course: Models and Analysis, in van Wissen, L. and Dykstra, P. (eds) *Population Issues. An Interdisciplinary Focus.* New York/ Boston/ Dordrecht/ London/ Moscow, Kluwer Academic/ Plenum Publishers, 23-52.
Winkelmann, R. (1996) Employment prospects and skill acquisition of apprenticeship-trained workers in Germany, *Industrial and Labor Relations Review*, 49, 4, 658-672.
Yamaguchi, K. (1991) *Event History Analysis.* Newbury Park/ London/ New Delhi, Sage Publications.

MIX
Papier | Fördert
gute Waldnutzung
FSC® C083411

Kolibri 360 GmbH
Ferdinand-Jühlke-Straße 7
99095 Erfurt, Deutschland
produktsicherheit@kolibri360.de

Druck:
CPI Druckdienstleistungen GmbH
im Auftrag der
Kolibri 360 GmbH
Ferdinand-Jühlke-Str. 7
99095 Erfurt